INSIGHT GUIDES

Mexico

Photographed by Kal Müller
Written by Kal Müller and Guillermo García-Oropeza
Directed by Hans Höfer
Produced by Leonard Lueras
Edited by Sanford Zalburg
Updated by Bernadine Connelly

A P A
PUBLICATIONS

Mexico

Fifth Edition (2nd Reprint)
© 1991 APA PUBLICATIONS (HK) LTD
All Rights Reserved
Printed in Singapore by Höfer Press Pte. Ltd

ABOUT THIS BOOK

When Apa Publications started to stretch its publishing legs outside of Southeast Asia, Mexico was one of its first destinations. The goal was to add to the unique library of Insight Guides by breaking new ground in travel literature. Apa has always aimed its books at the experienced, second generation traveler who is seeking a complete experience from every foreign adventure.

Insight Guide: Mexico fulfills the need of serious travelers who want to understand the history and culture of their destination in addition to the usual tourist information. Insight Guides have won many international awards for their special combination of fine writing, outstanding photographs and frank, clear journalism.

This formula was conceived by Apa founder **Hans Höfer**, a native of West Germany, when he published his book, *Insight Guide: Bali*, in 1970. From the headquarters in Singapore, he has now produced a long list of titles that cover the world.

The Insight editions reflect Höfer's training in the Bahaus tradition of book design, photography and printing. For each book, the best local writers and photographers are sought and put to work under the direction of a single editor who is fully knowledgeable about the subject location. For *Mexico*, the project editor was **Kal Müller** who also did most of the writing and photographing.

Müller, a native of Hungary who moved to the United States in 1951 became interested in Mexico in 1957 when he began making frequent trips to Nogales, an Arizona-Mexico border town. Later, while attending the University of Arizona, Müller ventured deeper into Mexico, usually while on diving expeditions to spots near Guaymas and Mazatlán. In 1962, he stayed in the country for two months visiting Acapulco and traveling to Yucatán. He also lived for two years in Jalisco state with the fascinating Huichol Indians who live in scattered mountainside ranchos. Müller later married a Mexican woman who was working as a nurse with the Indians.

Soon after embarking on this project, Müller enlisted an old friend, Guadalajara architect **Guillermo García-Oropeza** who has published several books about Mexico. An expert in many aspects of Mexican life, Oropeza has also written fiction, taught art, history, literature and architecture at the University of Guadalajara, and has lectured in the United States and Europe. Oropeza wrote 20 percent of *Insight Guide: Mexico*, and also served as a consultant during the final production stages.

José-Antonio Guzman authored the feature story on Mexican music and contributed to the essay on the Totonac Indians. Guzman, a resident of Mexico City, is an eminent musicologist who specializes in pre-Columbian musical instruments.

Patricia Díaz, who has long been active both in Mexico and abroad with the *artesanía* of her country, wrote about the crafts of Mexico.

Juan Lopez, an attorney and official "chronicler" for the city of Guadalajara, penned the Independence story in our history section.

Arjun Sidwell, a San Diego-based journalist, provided a Tijuana-to-Ensenada travel essay that we wove into our Baja California section.

The preliminary manuscripts were guided through final editing and design stages by editor-producer **Leonard Lueras**. Lueras, a

Müller

Oropeza

Guzman

native of New Mexico who has lived in
Hawaii since 1963, helped shape the Insight
Guides into their present form. His first Apa
production, *Hawaii*, became a best-seller
within a few weeks of its release in 1980, and
the next two titles he edited and produced –
Korea and *Hong Kong* – have both received
Awards of Excellence and Professionalism
in Publications from the Pacific Area Travel
Association (PATA), the world's largest
organization of travel industry professionals.

Sanford Zalburg, a veteran Hawaiian
journalist who writes books, edited *Mexico*
into final publishing shape. Zalburg worked
15 years as a reporter and 13 years as the city
editor of the *Honolulu Advertiser* and also
worked for the Reuters news agency (covering the Korean War) and for the *Anchorage,
Alaska Times*, the *Palm Beach Post* (Florida)
the *San Francisco Examiner*, and *Stars &
Stripes*, Pacific edition. He is the author of an
important Hawaii history book entitled *A
Spark Is Struck*: *Jack Hall* and the *ILWU in
Hawaii*.

The "nuts and bolts" section of *Mexico*, our
Travel Tips section, was prepared by **Ellen
Hokanson** in cooperation with Müller, Oro-
peza and **Notra Beatriz Mejia**. Hokanson,
an anthropologist by training, spent some 10
summers of her youth in Mexico living with
her grandparents, longtime residents of
Durango. Glyphs and temple plans in the
Travel Tips section were rendered by **Carol
Uyeda** of Honolulu.

Several other photographers and institutions contributed key shots that added impor-
tant touches to the overall look of *Mexico*. A
very special thanks goes to the Woodfin
Camp and Associates photo agency, Müller's
New York agent, which opened its extensive
photo archive to us and provided photos
taken in recent years by **Thomas Nebbia,
David Harvey** and Müller. Also, a tip of our
sombrero to contributing photographers
**David Stahl, Jan Whiting, Bud Lee, Tom
Servais, Graciela Iturbíde, Guillermo
Aldana E., Jacques Gourguechon** and
Pablo Ortíz Monasterio.

Among the many "literary" persons who
assisted with *Mexico*, Müller would like to
acknowledge the assistance of archeologist-
author **Dr. Jeffrey Wilkinson**, who kindly
reviewed and corrected history and travel
pieces about Veracruz and the Yucatán peninsula; and **Harry Möller**, editor of *México
Desconocido (Unknown Mexico)*, who provided strong doses of original inspiration and
counsel.

In Chiapas, Müller received special assistance from **Frederico Salazar**, who arranged
for local accommodations and transportation, and in Oaxaca he was well cared for by
Gustavo Perez Jiménez, director of tourism
for the state of Oaxaca.

Other institutions and individuals who
contributed to *Mexico* in various ways were
the Consejo Nacional de Turismo; **Lic Mario
Moya Palencia**, the director general of
Fonatur; Turistampa; **Dr. Koitcho Beltchev;
Rosario Urranga** and family; *Surfer* maga-
zine (**Jeff Divine** and **Jim Kempton**); Chi-
huahua rancher **Arturo Castro Vallez; René
Guédic** and **Michel Leroux**, both of the
Alliance Francaise, Mexico City; and **Jose-
Antonio Nava**, as well as **Gabriela** and
Ariel Castellanos, who cared for Müller for
weeks on end in Mexico City. Also, **Mr.** and
**Mrs. José Milmo, Tom Koch, Rene
Kitagawa, Laurel Murphy, John Ander-
son**, and **Linda Carlock**.

–Apa Publications

Díaz *Lueras* *Zalburg*

CONTENTS

MAPS

TRAVEL TIPS

QUE VIVA MÉXICO!

México Eterno. Timeless Mexico. A land of colorful fiestas. A land of swirling contrasts. *México,* the country, is masculine, but the nation, *La Patria,* is feminine. Perplexing, yes, but such male/female dualism has always been the case in Mexico. Even in the divine pantheons of ancient Central Mexico, it was a dualistic god, Ometéotl, who was the principle deity behind all the other gods. Ometéotl, who embodied both male and female principles, was so remote and powerful that only the highest of pre-Columbian priests even knew of His/Her existence.

Even today such sexual dualism affects Mexico's identity. The stereotypical male Mexican image—that of a swarthy, mustachioed *hombre* under a big beige sombrero—dominates the popular international media. But the most profound and *real* of domestic Mexican symbols is a gentle and radiant woman, the much-venerated Virgin of Guadalupe. Indeed, a macho man may win the revolution, but everyone here knows that it was, is or will be La Señora, The Lady, who determines his ultimate success or failure.

Que Viva Mexico! Que Viva! Long Live Mexico! Long Live! her people say when they are pleased, bemused or full of patriotic fire.

Mexico is a land of women with flashing eyes. *"Aquellos ojos verdes..."*—"those green eyes"—a popular old song begins. *Ay,* but so many flashing eyes! She is a nation of 73 million people, and her population is growing at a rate of 2.5 percent a year. India, by comparison, grows by 2.1 percent.

Mexico City—formerly pride of the nation and now a growing source of concern. Cars flick by on the busy Paseo. In one a cabby drives with a taco in one hand and with the other he steers. In another, air-conditioned vehicle, an executive in the back seat reads the financial pages of *Excelsior* and listens to classical music. His chauffeur and bodyguard don't disturb their pin-striped *patrón,* who is oblivious to a group of children kicking a small rubber soccer ball alongside the noisy boulevard. *"Mexico Es Una Ciudad Con Angel."* "Mexico Is A City With Charm" a sign says, full of pride and optimism. From July to November, rain comes in the afternoon and raincoats and umbrellas blossom. The throbbing Reforma becomes a sea of nylon brolleys. Him, Mexico City, the place some *capitalinos* call *El Monstruo,* is now a city of 16 million souls. By the end of this century, it is estimated, The Monster may increase in size to 32 million people—a population that would make Mexico City the biggest megalopolis on earth.

Fiery murals blanket Mexico City's public walls, but smog, *ala Los Angeles,* blankets the sky. Where—*donde está*— el Popocatépetl? The mountain is hidden behind gray flannel, 75 kilometers (46 miles) to the southeast. Alas, no longer is Mexico City a place *Where The Air Is Clear,* as Mexican novelist Carlos Fuentes titled his most popular novel.

Ah, but outside of the wildly growing Distrito Federal, the air is wonderfully clear. Indeed, like other misunderstood places, He/She is an incomplete vision. Like overgrown Mayan temple sites, His/Her bulk is invisible, hidden in a mysterious, prehistoric tangle. Even native Mexicans live as unknowing prisoners in their own awesome geography.

Modern and ancient wonders continue: In Monterrey, Pittsburgh-style factories rise out of the desert. In Tabasco and Chiapas, from a distance, oil rigs look like black exclamation points. And on Pacific and Gulf beaches, some 4 million visitors a year bask under tropical suns, hike up and into ancient Mayan and Aztec pyramids, and then *cha-cha* balmy nights away under moon and torchlight.

Other marvels keep the place yet even more interesting. Some 60 native languages are still spoken here by more than 50 indigenous Indian tribes, and if you are serious about your travel, there are more than 241,000 kilometers (120,000 miles) of roads. It's the most extensive travel network in Latin America.

After the heady days of the oil boom when Mexico had the fastest expanding economy in Latin America, growth dropped to zero. This has begun to improve lately but not nearly enough: the country's exploding population generates a need for some 800,000 new jobs a year.

So, how to explain it all—this fantastic, fabulous, frenetic country?

"One does not explain Mexico," says the philosopher Manuel Zamacona in Carlos Fuentes' aforementioned novel. "One believes in Mexico, with fury, with passion, and in alienation." Like a man. Like a woman. Like timeless Mexico.

Preceding pages, proud survivors of the Revolution pose for a recent reunion portrait; right, a large urban banner honors the Virgin of Guadalupe.

14

17

SMOKING MOUNTAINS AND BLOOMING DESERTS

Mexicans like to tell a joke on themselves. They list the natural resources of their country which God, in a moment of exceptional generosity, bestowed on them: the tremendous treasure of gold, silver and other valuable metals; oil, timber; a lavish coastline with white-sand beaches; waters teeming with fish; mountains full of game. But then, as the story goes, God asked: Why favor one nation so outrageously over all the others? And it was then, so as to balance it off, that He peopled the land with Mexicans.

As is often said, there are many Mexicos. The physical features of the land make for marked divisions. Two great mountain ranges, the Sierra Madre Occidental and the Sierra Madre Oriental, run down from the U.S. border, paralleling the Pacific and the Gulf coasts. The mountains give way to the central highlands, the historic heart of Mexico, an area of about 640 kilometers (400 miles) from east to west and less than 320 kilometers (200 miles) from north to south. This is just one-tenth the size of Mexico, but it contains almost half the population. Mexico City is well on its way to being the biggest city in the world. With its environs it accounts for one out of every five people in Mexico.

Trickles and Floods

Look at the map on page 110. Picture a belt of land 1,280 kilometers (800 miles) long and 160 kilometers wide (100 miles) from Cabo Corrientes in Jalisco on the west to the Tuxtla cities in Veracruz in the east. That mountainous area—known as the New Volcanic Axis—can be said to be the boundary between North America and Central America. South of that line, lesser mountains form the Sierra Madre del Sur, narrowing down at the Isthmus of Tehuantepec to little more than 160 kilometers (100 miles) wide. The mountains rise up again east of the Isthmus and continue into Guatemala, while to the north the Yucatán peninsula has been ironed flat by Nature and consists of a limestone sheet covered by thin soil.

Mountains and highlands portray much of Mexico, but deserts dominate in the north. In Baja California and in the northern states of Sonora, Chihuahua, Coahuila and Durango

Preceding pages, snow-capped Popocatépetl looms above the central plateau's golden cornfields; left, bandillero flowers and maguey cactus.

the desert is the usurper of the geography, and only by means of irrigation can crops be grown. On the Gulf coast too much rain washes the land and farmers have to hack away unwanted growth. At the same time many areas of the north get as little as 10 centimeters (four inches) of rain a year. There are places on the Gulf coast that get as much as six meters (18 feet) of rain a year. In the central highlands where most of the corn and beans are grown, rainfall is erratic. Sometimes a trickle; sometimes a flood.

Many Mexican forests are denuded. Indiscriminate cutting of timber began during colonial times and still goes on. Of course, farmers had to clear land for planting, and in places where large-scale mining went on, the area was stripped of trees. Zacatecas, the silver country, was altered—from woodland to savannah—by tree-cutters. So, large-scale erosion scars the land. The watertable has fallen; even climatic change has come as a result of the destruction of forests. Once, forest areas had a measure of protection; they were hard to get to. That is no longer true. Mexico now has over 241,000 kilometers (120,000 miles) of roads of which about one-third are paved. The country lacks river transportation; there is no Mississippi-Missouri river system. The rivers are few and not navigable.

The road from Mexico City to Veracruz served as the umbilical cord between Mexico and Spain. During the 16th Century land links also were opened to the agriculturally rich Bajío region north of Mexico City and to the mining district of Zacatecas. But when new mines were discovered in what is now southern Chihuahua and an attempt was made to colonize what is now New Mexico, it wouldn't work. It took 1½ years to make the roundtrip with supplies from Zacatecas to New Mexico, a distance of 1,300 kilometers (800 miles). Neither Spain nor Mexico had the money, nor the skill, nor the resources to integrate the great northern reaches of the land, which the Conquistadores so arrogantly had claimed. Unless the land was bound together it could not be held. When the time came, Anglo Americans took over what was then northern Mexico. They had men; they had money; and, most important, they had an overriding determination to overthrow Mexican rights.

During the Díaz dictatorship foreign capital came pouring in and helped build roads and railroads to the north and develop untapped natural resources. It then became economi-

Tarascan girls laughingly tend a flock of sheep in Michoacán; since the conquest, weavings of wool have become an essential part of the state's crafts.

cally worthwhile for American companies to begin bulk ore mining. Foreign capital also financed the exploration for oil. In the aftermath of the 1910 revolution the government expropriated some foreign holdings, but by then a basic communications system was already in place.

There is a trade off: if many areas are still isolated and hard to get to, it has meant that much has been preserved. The nature-lover is bound to applaud. How refreshingly remote are the vast deserts of Baja and the mountains of central Mexico and the jungles bordering the Bahía de Campeche. A marvelous variety of flora and fauna thrives in those places. Some are protected in national parks; some in wildlife refuges. Many of these parks were created by President Lázaro Cárdenas. The government has done well, but not enough. Only a minute portion of Mexico enjoys protective areas. Many of the parks are in the mountains. Popocatépetl and Iztaccíhuatl are the best known mountain peaks. And then Orizaba, the Star Mountain, as it is called. There is a certain sadness about Popo, southeast of Mexico City. You seldom see it anymore from the city; the smog covers all. But on the road as you leave, the white-capped peaks of Popocatépetl and Iztaccíhuatl magically emerge, clearly outlined against a blue sky.

Volcanic Spectacles

In geological terms, cone-shaped Popo (altitude: 5,452 meters or 17,887 feet) is a child. The name means "smoking mountain" in Nahuatl. Now dormant, it once put on spectacular shows. It erupted in 1519 to greet Cortés's arrival, or perhaps to protest. It is said that Moctezuma sent a party of 10 to the top of the mountain to view the eruption. That was a mistake. Only two came back. Iztaccíhuatl (altitude: 5,286 meters, or 17,342 feet) means "sleeping woman." The top is somewhat flattened. A paved road goes to the base of the two mountains.

Pico de Orizaba, or Citlaltépetl (Star Mountain) is 5,700 meters high—18,750 feet. You can't miss it driving along the road between Mexico City and Veracruz. Sailors out to sea are entranced by her. West of Mexico City, the Nevado de Toluca or Xinantécatl (Sacred Bat) stands 4,680 meters, or 15,354 feet, tall. A dirt road, passable most of the year, leads to the crater and the Lake of the Sun and the Lake of the Moon, sacred to the Indians. The lakes are stocked with rainbow

Dawn gently dispels an overnight fog to awaken the village of Tapalpa in southwestern Jalisco; this highland region is famous for its cheese and fruit.

trout. If you land one of them you will have the distinction of having caught a fish in a lake at one of the highest altitudes in the world.

Paricutín is the youngest of Mexico's volcanoes. She was born on February 7, 1943 in a cornfield in Michoacán. Imagine how Dionisio Pulido felt. He saw her emerge from the ground in a tiny sputter. When awestruck Pulido returned with his compadres the next day (can you blame them for being skeptical?), she was a cone six meters, or about 20 feet, high. Then the goddess of the volcano went to work in earnest. Paricutín exploded, hurling great chunks of molten rock a hundred meters up and putting on a fiery-orange lava display. Paricutín continued to be active until 1952 and by that time she had poured out a billion tons of lava. She covered the village of Parangaricutiro, drowned 10 other hamlets, and built a mountain 427 meters (1,400 feet) high. Visitors can reach the site from the village of Angahuan. Enroute they will pass the steeple of the late Parangaricutiro's church, sticking defiantly out of a black lava bed.

Toward the western edge of the volcanic axis, the Nevado y Fuego (Snow and Fire) crater in the state of Colima is not unusually high (3,326 meters, or 10,912 feet), but it is topped by two cones, one of which is snow-covered and the other which periodically emits fumes. The last major explosion occurred in 1913. In 1973 the mountain rumbled and spewed lava and ashes. Some 575 kilometers (about 357 miles) off the West coast of Mexico is the Mexican-owned archipelago called the Revillagigedos. In 1952, the Mariano Barceña mountain there blew its top. The Chichonal volcano in Chiapas exploded in 1982, causing many deaths.

Agricultural Futures

Experts estimate that only about one-third of the land in Mexico has a slope of less than 10 degrees, which is the limit, agronomists say, for efficient agriculture. Of course, many farmers are more concerned with survival than with the most efficient agronomy and so it is not unusual to see a rocky slope, set at an absurd angle, sown with corn. As a result, erosion is inevitable.

The flatland in Mexico is generally located either in the north or in the Yucatán. Much of the northland is desert or semi-desert; much of the Yucatán has only thin soil. From a practical point of view, just about all the land that has agricultural potential is already under cul-

Every Christmas, colorful figures fashioned from hundreds of lightbulbs enliven Mexico City's central square, or zócalo, that fronts the cathedral.

tivation. With proper planning, research and a huge investment, perhaps 1,215,000 hectares (3 million acres) could be added to the 24,295,546 hectares (60 million acres) already under cultivation. Figures are hard to come by. Often government agencies themselves disagree.

The most productive region in Mexico is the northwest. Though it is semi-desert, the narrow fringe between the Sierra Madre Occidental and the sea is blessed with several rivers and with flat land. Under the régimes of President Obregón and Calles, both of whom came from the northwest, a system of dams was built which made the desert bloom. The area is now Mexico's most productive agricultural region. Forty percent of Mexico's irrigated land is in the states of Sonora and Sinaloa and the Río Colorado district of Baja California. Some 20 percent of Mexico's agricultural land is irrigated. Those irrigated lands yield big crops of alfalfa, wheat, safflower, soybeans, cotton and tomatoes.

Other areas of the north raise cattle. A large market has grown for beef in Mexico itself, a clue that a substantial part of the population is moving into middle-class affluence. Much of the rest of Mexico's farm areas concentrate on corn and beans, the eternal staple. The population is growing madly; it had been growing at the rate of 3.5 percent, one of the world's highest, but that has been brought down to 2.5 percent. The cities are big and getting bigger and more unwieldy. Even the rural areas have felt the pressure of more mouths to feed. Subsistence plots grow increasingly smaller and the land becomes less fertile with use. Corn, as is well known, is a soil-exhausting crop.

But for Mexicans, corn is life and it has been the basic staple for hundreds of years and perhaps will always be. The tortilla is Mexico's bread. The average Mexican consumes almost half a kilo a day (over a pound). You can double that figure in much of the rural areas. Indians attach a mystical importance to corn; because it's closely associated with their religions. They grow corn even if government agricultural experts tell them that they ought to introduce other crops as well. To improve the corn yield means spending for irrigation and fertilizer. Unfortunately, corn is less adaptable to research than wheat. At the Rockefeller Center for corn and wheat production outside Mexico City, plant-breeding programs for wheat have been spectacularly

A charro gallops at full speed—just before reining in his horse to stop on a centavo. Impeccable horsemanship is a prerequisite for rancheros.

effective; consider the success of "Green Revolution" wheat hybrids. The center has not had the same good luck with corn.

Silver Horseshoes
And Grey Whales

Coastal Mexico used to have a reputation for being unhealthy. Indeed, it has been only during the last two decades that malaria has been eradicated. Tropical plantations produced most of Mexico's crops of sugar, cocoa beans, henequen and coffee. But Mexico has to compete in these crops with the rest of the world and world prices have been unstable in recent years.

For centuries the export of minerals, and especially silver, dominated the Mexican economy. In colonial times there was so much silver that in some places it was cheaper to shoe a horse with silver horseshoes than with horseshoes made of iron that had to be imported from Spain. Mexico is still *numero uno* in silver production in the world. She also exports lead, zinc, copper, sulphur, antimony and mercury. In 1903, the first high-temperature furnace for refining iron in Latin America was built in Monterrey. Mexico is now self-sufficient in most types of steel, and, in fact, exports steel to Caribbean and Central American countries.

Until 1939, Mexico's exports were made up roughly of 65 percent minerals and 28 percent agricultural products. By 1950, mineral exports had fallen to 33 percent of the total, while agricultural products had climbed to 55 percent. In 1974, when the oil boom began to pick up speed, manufactured products accounted for 54 percent of Mexico's exports, agriculture, 38 percent, and minerals only 7 percent.

Although Mexico is more highly industrialized than most Third World countries, her basic problem is that she has too many people and too little tillable soil. There's really not much more land which could be cleared for cultivation. But if there is not enough prime land for agriculture, there is certainly vast amounts of land in which wild animals can roam. Mexico is a great place for the nature-lover. It has 2,896 species of vertebrates, including 520 mammals, 1,424 species of birds, 685 different kinds of reptiles, and 267 amphibians. Of these, 16 mammals, 13 birds and 9 reptiles are on the endangered list.

The most spectacular of the mammals may be the grey whale, which migrates yearly to

While dragging his stubborn burro up a steep sand dune, a struggling individualist exemplifies northern Mexico's long tradition of rugged self-reliance.

Baja California's Pacific bays to calve and mate. The species, almost extinct a few decades ago, has made a strong comeback. At Scammon's lagoon, their famed breeding ground in Baja, only 250 grey whales were counted in 1937. By 1975 there were 18,000. Scammons lagoon, a huge bay with a narrow mouth, is known in Mexico by its Spanish name, Ojo de Liebre, or The Hare's Eye.

Maritime Machos

Other fantastic abodes are plentiful. At Guadalupe and the San Benito islands off the Baja coast is a refuge for elephant seals. They once disappeared from sight; no one knew what had happened, and then they resurfaced at Guadalupe island. Male elephant seals can reach over six meters (20 feet) in length and weigh almost four tons. The biggest chaps lead a vigorous life; marine biologists estimate that just 4 percent of the males impregnate 85 percent of the females. The offspring is a meter (3.3 feet) long and weighs 36 kilos (about 80 pounds).

These maritime machos have done their duty with gusto. From 1869 to 1892 no human eyes saw any elephant seals in this part of the world. Then a few hard-working males got to work. That they have done their job well can be seen in the latest figures for elephant seal demographics: their population, close to zero at the beginning of this century, leaped upwards to 47,000 on Guadalupe Island alone by 1977.

Tough and hike-loving outdoorsmen can sight great horned sheep in the San Pedro Martir national park in the mountainous interior of Baja. In the Cumbres de Monterrey national park there are black bear, and unconfirmed reports tell tall tales about grizzlies in the wildest reaches of the Sierra Madre Occidental mountains.

Because Mexico is the winter terminus for many migrating species of birds, it is a bird watcher's as well as a hunter's paradise. Most species seem to favor the Pacific coast, reputed to be a duck hunters' nirvana. On the other side of the country, the Rio Lagartos area of northern Yucatán is graced with thousands of pink flamingos. A nearby island, Contoy, is a refuge for even more exotic species. And a year-round fairyland of bright fish and corals is available for skin divers in the Caribbean waters of the Yucatán, especially near the island of Cozumel. But perhaps the most spectacular gift of nature is the Monarch butterfly who brightens eastern Michoacán in winter by the thousands.

Right, a spectacular natural arch at Cabo San Lucas, at the southernmost tip of Baja California; following pages, a flight of pink Yucatecan flamingos.

Mexico's history dates back 21,000 years, measured by the radioactivity of the carbon content of organic material. It all began in Siberia. Ancient peoples came out of Siberia, crossing Bering Strait in quest of meat. Their trek started perhaps 70,000 years ago and they moved down at a pace of, say, 17 miles per generation, well under speed limit, southward, ever southward. From Alaska they went south into Canada and the United States, and eventually reached Mexico. Some hardy sojourners went on through Central America and South America, eventually down to the end of the line, the south of Chile, which they reached some 13,000 years ago.

Certainly it was no movement *en masse*. They came in small groups—two or three or perhaps as many as five families at a time. They had to cooperate with each other in the hunt upon which their food supply depended and they may have even brought with them a rudimentary religion. They had to adapt to weather ranging from the bitter cold of the tundras to tropical forest and jungle and then to arctic conditions at Patagonia.

These ancients were animal and wild-plant eaters. Usually they hunted small or medium-sized animals. Hunt mammoths? It would seem ludicrous with their rude stone tools unless they were bent on self-sacrifice. But they *did* hunt even mammoths. They teamed up in the attack. There was a mammoth killed by men and buried in perpetuity along the shores of Lake Texcoco, which dried up over the centuries and is the site of Mexico City. That mammoth had two legs stuck in the mud. He was, it might be said, working with a handicap and his conquerors took advantage of it.

In the late Cenolithic Age (9,000 to 7,000 B.C.), long after mammoths became extinct, people in what is now Mexico used a crude stone implement to grind grain. This was the forerunner of the *metate*, the slab upon which Mexicans pound corn.

Some dates are unfortunately necessary. They lend spice to a tale of history, even though they are so remote in time that the mind cannot accept them. In about 6,000 B.C., agriculture is believed to have started in Mexico. Fairly tardy, it turns out, since man apparently first grew plants in what is now the Thai-Burma border region around 13,000 B.C., and people in the Middle East grew wheat and barley around 10,000 B.C.

In Mexico the first cultivated species appears to be the avocado pear and the squash.

Sometime around 5,000 B.C. people in Mexico began to grow maize and beans, which forevermore have been the staple of Mexican diet. The first ears of corn were just 3.81 centimeters long (1½ inches). You can see specimens in that most wonderful of institutions, the *Museo de Anthropología*, the Museum of Anthropology in Mexico City. About 3,000 B.C. people began to grow cotton and weave textiles and irrigate the land. In about 2,000 B.C. they learned to fashion pottery. And about 1,500 B.C. they began to fashion gods in their minds.

Olmec Heads Tell a Story

The first and most mysterious of Mexico's great ancients were the Olmecs of the regions now known as Veracruz and Tabasco. They might be called "the Sumerians" of the New World because, like the Sumerians of Mesopotamia, they provided artistic, technical and religious instructions for the civilizations that followed them. They were skilled in agriculture; adept in building canals; artistic in fashioning pottery, jewelry and weapons. Obviously, an uncommon people. However, it took the publication in 1926 of *Tribes and Temples,* a book by Frans Blom and Oliver LaFarge, to call attention to Olmec achievements. Among the book's revelations was that La Venta, an island near Villahermosa in Tabasco, was the site of an Olmec ceremonial center.

Not everybody agreed that the Olmecs were the oldest of Mexico's ancient civilizations. A group of archeologists—the "Mayan Mafia," the irreverent called them—believed the Mayans were the oldest of Mexico's peoples. The Olmecs were merely a Mayan off-shoot, they maintained. That theory was demolished when carbon-14 tests of Olmec artifacts established that the Olmecs were alive and kicking before 1,100 B.C. At that time Mayan culture was not even a gleam in their founders' eye!

A problem arises: How to reconstruct in the mind the nature of the Olmec culture? There are no survivors, of course. We do not even know what language they spoke. Nor are there written records. But there is one indisputable fact, which is written in stone. They

Early settlers of Central Mexico spear a mammoth stuck in mud; centuries passed before the development of agriculture led to complex civilizations.

were great stone carvers. Few other pre-Columbian cultures of the New World achieved their mastery. They did it all. From 30-ton basalt heads and exquisite jadeite miniatures to paper-thin obsidian jewelry. And it is through these carvings that the Olmecs who had no written language speak to us.

The motif that recurs most often in Olmec stone carving is the jaguar, the tawny-coated big cat known in Mexico as *el tigre*, the "tiger," who ruled the jungles. Themes range from a jaguar who allegedly is copulating with a woman to infants with jaguar-like faces. Obviously, the jaguar played a leading role in Olmec religion.

Artist-writer Miguel Covarrubias, known as "the last of the Olmecs" for his analyses of Olmec culture, has shown in a series of draw-

From an overall study of Olmec heads, it seems probable there were two physical types in the Olmec culture; some with negro traits, some without. But where did the negroid features come from? From across Bering Strait evidently. We can discount any migration from Africa. We can tell nothing from skeletal remains. The high humidity and the acidity of the soil have obliterated that proof.

For some strange reason it has been difficult for the world to accept the fact that the aboriginal Mexican could have developed a culture of his own, a unique civilization. Some people believed, amazingly, that someone came and taught these ancient Mexicans. Perhaps people from a lost continent—from Mu or Atlantis. Of course, the idea is an insult. If the ancients of Europe, Asia, and Africa

ings of pre-Columbian sculpture how the jaguar mask gradually was transformed into a rain god. Covarrubias said that some of the faces display "a haunting mixture of human and feline characteristics ... It is often difficult to guess whether a given carving was intended to represent a man disguised as a jaguar or a jaguar in the process of becoming a man."

Those massive Olmec heads seem to have negroid features, but at the same time the eyes are mongoloid. Two of the statues have earned fame and the distinction of acquiring a sobriquet: "The Wrestler" (probably a player in a ceremonial ball game), and "Uncle Sam" (probably named because of the shape of the man's beard).

could develop a complex civilization by themselves, then why not the aboriginal Mexican?

Idiotic stories have been raised about these old-timers. The stories apparently titillated the minds of people of the Western world. Were the aborigines of Mexico *really* human beings? Who taught them? The author Von Däniken *(Chariots of the Gods)* speculated that extra-terrestrial beings dropped in from outer space to help the struggling Mexican Indians. Father Duran, who wrote in the late 16th Century, said that the Mexican Indians were tribes of Israelites because they, too, sacrificed children. All sorts of people were named as the Indians' tutors, ranging, as the author Nigel Davis says in *Voyagers to the New World–Facts and Fantasy,* "from Celts at one end of the Eurasian spectrum to Chinese at the other. . . ."

Revelation came slowly. Sixteen years after Hernán Cortés conquered Mexico in 1521, a Pope of Rome (Paul III) acknowledged in a papal bull that *indeed* the people of Mexico were human beings who must have come originally from the Old World and, happily enough, were descendants of Adam and Eve, even as thou or I.

No one should imply, of course, that the Middle East or Europe or Asia did not influence old Mexico. Perhaps at times a vessel was blown off course or perhaps an impetuous captain of a ship resolved to have a look and as a result a traveler or two landed on the shore. But to maintain that the Mexican Indian developed as a result of such tenuous

contact is foolish. The evidence is simply not there. Those ancient peoples in Mexico developed by themselves, on their own.

Gaps exist in the story-telling. There was little phonetic writing before the Spanish came. True, the Mayans and others wrote with glyphs, and slowly some of the missing pieces are turning up. Those indefatigable diggers of fact—the archeologists—are adding to our knowledge of ancient Mexico.

One of the most remarkable legacies of the Olmecs is the pit at La Venta in Tabasco. More than 7.6 meters (25 feet) deep, the pit was dug out and lined with 480 blocks (weighing more than 907 metric tons) of semi-precious serpentine stone, forming a mosaic. Naturally, it is jaguar-like. The pit was filled

with colored sand and clay and covered, and, thus protected, it remained undisturbed until some 3,000 years later archeologist Matthew Stirling and his crew dug it up. That had to be one of archeology's shining moments, perhaps in its own way as exciting as the discovery of King Tut's tomb near Luxor in 1922 by Howard Carter and the Earl of Carnarvon.

The Olmecs spread their civilization around. In their search for semi-precious stones, they established colonies in central and southern Mexico. When they came in contact with less advanced peoples, they thrust their own culture upon the others. Where Olmecs trod they influenced art forms. They were innovative folk: they introduced the ritual calendar, glyph-writing, their religion, technology, ceremonial centers. All the civilizations that followed in Mexico owe them a debt.

The Olmecs fished; they cultivated the soil. They made the jungle and the lowlands and the mountain sides produce crops. They were good farmers. They had no problem with water; they lived in regions which still have an abundance of rainfall. They dug ditches and channeled the water to the growing crops. They must have known how to use water for transport, else how could they move those immense basalt blocks? There's a lot we can learn from their carvings. First, we know that they were a tightly organized, efficient society. Second, they probably were ruled by a hierarchy of religious leaders who doubled as civilian authorities as well. A memorable people.

It came to an end violently around 400 B.C. The evidence is the mutilation of Olmec stone monuments and sculptures at that time. What happened? Were the lower classes tired of mistreatment? Did they rebel against their rulers? Was there an invasion from outside? We can only guess.

There now ensued some 1,700 years until the time the Aztecs took over the stage of history. During those gap years many cultures developed, flourished, then faded. The best known of these was the Mayan culture, which dominated the Yucatán peninsula and areas south, including what is now the state of Chiapas, and Guatemala. Other cultures grew for a time: the Teotihuacán of central Mexico and the Gulf coast; the Zapotecs and the Mixtec in southwestern Mexico and at Monte Albán, whose tombs yielded a treasure-trove of jewelry and carvings; the mysterious Tarascans of Michoacán, who twice inflicted

Above left, this Olmec altar reflects Mexico's first and most mysterious civilization; right, an Olmec sculpture nicknamed "The Wrestler."

defeat upon haughty Aztecs; the Totonac group of Veracruz, who built the niched pyramid at El Tajin.

The lives of so many of these ancient peoples are shrouded in mystery. Consider, for instance, the Xochicalco ruins in Morelos, southwest of Cuernavaca. There are 1,544 hectares (6 square miles) of interesting ground: a palace, ball courts, a network of caves and passageways, a restored pyramid. On the walls are elaborate carvings—the figures of serpents and of humans. The features seem Mayan. Or are they Toltec? Or perhaps Zapotec? The ethnic identity is still unknown. Mexico is full of these unusual reminders of a long departed era; fascinating, intriguing, mystifying. Timeless Mexico.

Monte Albán, upon which man performed surgery, is the oldest site of post-Olmec culture. The mountain top was leveled, apparently by earlier Indians. It was a monumental task: an area 610 by 245 meters (2,000 by 800 feet) lopped off.

Archeologically speaking, the history of Monte Albán divides into five periods. The first took place between 500 and 550 B.C. The best known sculptures of this period are a series of bas-reliefs known as "The Dancers." The bodies are contorted; they may have been meant to represent medical specimens, jesters or even acrobats. Your guess is as good as anybody else's.

Around 300 B.C., an evolution of the people in the Oaxaca region, touched off phase two of the Monte Albán story. These people built great stone masses and columns. Their tombs are works of art. Perhaps the attention they paid to burial accommodations stemmed from their belief that their ancestors came from the depths of earth and hence must return in proper style.

The Fearsome Zapotecs

The next period—Monte Albán III-A and III-B, in archeological characterization—began at the opening of the Christian era and went on for five centuries. The architecture favored a baroque style. The Zapotecs, who still live in the Valley of Oaxaca, arrived at the start of this period. These early Zapotecs practiced confession as part of the ritual of purification and offered human sacrifices to their gods.

The fourth period of Monte Albán, from 1000 to 1250 A.D., is another chapter in the story of tomb-building. New tombs were laid out; old ones were enlarged. The fifth and final phase of Monte Albán lasted until the Spanish conquest. During this period the Zapotecs were no longer *los principales* in the

hierarchy. Instead a people called the Mixtecs, who came from the Cholula-Puebla area in the north, invaded Monte Alban, mixed with the Zapotecs, and took over Monte Albán as their own necropolis. They were talented people; they turned out fine metal and stone work and carved wood and bone objects.

The Zapotecs built the long, low "palaces" at Mitla. These feature façades, decorated in raised stone mosaic. The geometrical patterns suggest textile designs and resemble the Mayan stone latticework at Uxmal in the Yucatán. The Mixtecs were punctilious; they kept accurate manuscript records of their gods and the geneologies of their nobility. They also took extremely good care of their dead rulers. They preserved the burial chambers of the Zapotecs but first they chucked out the bones of

the occupants and replaced them with the bodies of their own nobles.

The best known of these graves, Tomb 7, was excavated in 1932 by the Mexican archeologist Dr. Alfonso Caso. The grave contained a treasure house of gold. Fortunately, those gold-mad Spaniards never discovered the tomb (graverobbing is said to be the world's second oldest profession). The grave contained more than 500 pieces of exquisite Mixtec art, much of it gold jewelry pieces. Who owned it? A good question. The Federal government and the state of Oaxaca laid claim. Surprisingly, Oaxaca won the right to keep most of these priceless examples of the area's heritage.

El Tajín, in Veracruz, is another cultural site

whose construction began during the latter part of the Olmec era. The first occupants were Huastecs, a branch of the Mayans but separated geographically from their much better known cousins. Through the science of glottochronology (time-analysis of two related dialects), it has been determined that the Mayans and the Huastecs, who once spoke the same language, split into two groups, some 3,200 years ago. That's about when the Olmec culture began.

The Huastecs

The Huastecs developed on their own—nothing nearly as refined a culture as the Mayan, but nevertheless, as the saying goes, their very own. They were valiant—they resisted

El Tajín was destroyed around the year 1100. Evidently no one thought much about the place until a military patrol chanced to pass by in 1785. That kindled a spark of interest. In 1811 the intrepid German traveler-naturalist-writer Alexander von Humboldt visited El Tajín and described it in detail. In 1836 the traveler Carl Nebel published in Europe a series of splendid lithographs of El Tajín. Much later (1934) the Mexican government ordered excavation work on the site, and archeologist García Payón directed it. It is to him that we owe much of what we know about this important cultural center.

Unfortunately, we know even less about the cultures of western Mexico. Those people left us only scant clues, some shaft tombs and pieces of pottery. Colima, Jalisco and Nayarit

Aztec attack. They even shocked the Aztecs. Naked, they faced the invaders. Their teeth were filed and colored; they displayed deformed heads.

The ritual center of El Tajín covers 1,012 hectares (2,500 acres), much of it still not excavated. The Pyramid of the Niches dominates the place. It was probably started by the Huastecs; they, in turn, were pushed out by the Totonacs. The pyramid is obviously an edifice of ritual. The Totonacs completed the central structure, and built other highly decorated stone buildings and a ball court with magnificent bas-relief carving. Evidently the Huastecs exchanged ideas with the inhabitants of that great inland metropolis of Teotihuacán, 30 miles northeast of Mexico City.

never merged into unified kingdoms but remained under chieftains who controlled small areas. Their cultures never coalesced; apparently none fed the other. They built no outstanding pyramids and few religious structures in stone. Our knowledge about them comes from their pottery. But it merely tells us that at one time they came under the influence of the central highlands cultures. We do know from their clay figurines that they believed in life after death. Thus a man was buried with ceramic replicas of his wife, servants and slaves. Obviously, to make life

Above, a Mixtec skull with overlaid turquoise mosaic, from Tomb 7 at Monte Alban; right, a page from the Codex Nuttall of Mixtec warriors on a raft.

enjoyable for him in the after-world.

The clay figures of these people are full of life. They are among the most charming art of Mexico. They depict religious and social scenes: a ritual ball game with a crowd of spectators, women wrestling, lovers embracing, phallic dances, musicians, warriors, and animals, especially dogs.

The Tarascans of Michoacán

Thanks to the Spaniards, we know a good deal about the Tarascan culture of Michoacán. Shortly after the conquest, the first viceroy ordered a Franciscan monk to compile a history of the Tarascans. "Chronicles of Michoacán" (distressingly, some sections are missing) gives us a start in understanding Tarascan culture. The Aztecs claimed that the Tarascans were part of the Chichimeca group of tribes. They and the Tarascans had a common origin, it was said, coming out of seven caves in the north. (This was a romantic idea, unsubstantiated by the art of linguistics. The truth is that the Tarascan language is unrelated to the Aztec or any other Mexican language.)

The discovery of primitive sacrificial stone sculpture called "chac-mol" (also spelled "chac-mool") proves there was some cultural influence from the central highlands. Some may even have drifted up from as far away as South America. For example, think of the Tarascan copper objects, including what may be plowshares. Whence came that metal-

working technique? Perhaps from someone who came by sea from the far south. From South America.

Michoacán means "Place of the Fishermen." The state of Michoacán, of course, borders the sea. However, the ancient religion of the inhabitants was based not on the ocean, but on volcanos. The cult of fire was central to the Tarascan religion. The chief deity, Curicáueri, the "Great Burner," also represented the young Sun. In his honor the people kept fires burning constantly on top of stone ceremonial structures, called "yácatas." The largest is at Tzintzuntzan, consisting of a platform 426.7 meters long and 243.8 meters wide (1,400 feet by 800 feet), with a stairway 91.4 meters broad (300 feet broad).

Except for the yacatas, the Tarascans built

in wood. They left few stone buildings and carvings, but they excelled in pottery, woodwork, copperware, and especially in featherwork. Present day Tarascans still excel at all of these crafts—except featherwork. That art form has been abandoned. The ancient Tarascans knew how to organize for battle; they had well trained military forces. Tariacuari, the first legendary king, welded the rival clans into an alliance. So well-knit was this confederation that they were able twice to defeat the Aztec juggernaut.

The story of the end of the Tarascan kingdom is a sad one. The last of the Tarascan kings, converted to Christianity and went humbly, feather hat in hand, to pay homage and submit to Cortés. Debasing himself, as was the Tarascan custom, he wore soiled and torn clothing, but it did not help. Later Nuño de Guzmán, the most brutal of the Conquistadores, had him burned alive. He said the king had taken part in a conspiracy against Spanish rule, but the real reason was that Caltzontzin was unable to produce enough gold for the Spaniards.

Teotihuacán—For Centuries A Ghost City

We haven't said much so far about the peoples of the central highlands, that part of Mexico which contributed our most detailed knowledge of Mexican history. The last group to dominate the highland plateau were the bold Aztecs, who assimilated the existing civilization they found. It was a complex culture that had existed for centuries. It had developed under the great city-state of Teotihuacán beginning some 200 years before the beginning of the Christian era. By the time the Aztecs arrived, Teotihuacán had long been a ghost town. Still it was so imposing, though in ruins, (it had been burned and abandoned in the 8th Century), that the Aztecs believed the Sun and the Moon were created there. They called the site "The Place of the Gods."

Running down the center of Teotihuacán is "The Street of the Dead." Dominating over all is the Pyramid of the Sun, 65.5 meters high (215 feet). A novice archeologist tried to find out what was inside the pyramid. He was imbued with the urge to dig. So he and his team of workers blasted and removed thousands of tons of stone. But what a keen disappointment! *Nada.* There was nothing inside. And now the rains came and the earth inside the pyramid turned to mud and the amateur archeologist hastily covered up his mistake.

The rain god, Tlaloc, was one of the principal deities of Teotihuacán. That is not surprising. Note how rain gods dominated ancient Mexican culture. Consider the Mayan Chaoc rain god, and Cocijo, the Zapotec rain god. Tláloc was amply rewarded by his followers, both in this world and in the next. There is a well-preserved painting of Tlaloc's paradise which has endured through the centuries. In the painting people are frolicking, singing, and dancing. Birds are singing. The land is lush. All's right with Tlaloc's world.

Let's pick up again at this point the story of Quetzalcóatl, the god of the Toltecs, the deity you will remember as the Plumed Serpent. He was the most important god in Meso-America. His cult developed in Teotihuacán; there

the most important structure is dedicated to him. Quetzalcóatl was a complex god. Laurette Sejourné wrote: "His essential role as the founder of Nahuatl culture was never questioned by any of the historians of the 16th and 17th Centuries. . . . " Quetzalcóatl was king of the legendary city of Tollan. He was a ruler of quality: he strove to enforce the highest code of ethics; he pursued his love for the sciences and the arts. But how unfortunate was the outcome. Jealous enemies (were they divine or were they humans?) schemed for his destruction. A non-drinker, he and his beautiful sister were given *pulque.* Their inhibitions had faded; nature took its course. They made love. Quetzalcóatl woke up next morning with a hangover the size of the Pyramid of the Sun and a feeling of deep shame. He said goodbye, went off to the coast, built a funeral pyre, and threw himself in. His body was destroyed but his heart turned into the planet Venus and there it shines in the heavens.

There are a number of variants on the story of Quetzalcóatl's exit from this life. According to one version, he was supposed to have had white skin and a beard. Instead of casting himself into the flame, he built a raft (some say, of snakes) and left for the east, promising to return someday. When Cortés came to Mexico, the Indians believed that he was an envoy Quetzalcóatl, returning as he had promised.

More myths about Quetzalcóatl: that he descended into the Land of the Dead, found some bones, sprinkled them with his blood, and thus created the human race. He stole maize from the ants and thus introduced food to mankind. He taught man astronomy. He invented the calendar. He taught man how to cut and polish jade; how to weave and how to make mosaic painting with bird feathers. A lively god indeed. The Quetzalcóatl cult emphasized peace, and peaceful living. There were no war gods in his cult. The people of Teotihuacán were governed by priest-kings, who seemed interested primarily in commerce, not in conquest.

Teotihuacán grew in an orderly fashion. At one time the urban area had a population of 100,000, and even included a ghetto of "foreigners." What caused the destruction of this peaceful city? Was it rebellion or an invasion? Again we simply do not know. It appears that some Teotihuacán people resettled at Azcapotzalco, now a suburb of Mexico City. The cult of Quetzalcoatl was kept alive in the central highlands, but especially at Cholula, near the present city of Puebla.

Was it the Toltecs who destroyed Teotihuacán? According to one story, a group of Chichimecas, nomadic hunters, came to central Mexico under the leadership of their king,

Xolotl. They settled down and founded Tula in 856 and became Toltecs. (The term Toltec means "master craftsmen." There were plenty of these in Tula: masons, stone and jade carvers, weavers, metalsmiths, feather workers.) The Toltecs were good warriors and at one time they controlled much of central Mexico. It is likely they became soft and quarreled among themselves. For whatever reason the time came when they could not resist invasion—by other and tougher Chichimecas. They burned Tula in the year 1168 and the population dispersed into central Mexico.

Tula, like many other places of antiquity, lends itself to stories. One legend tells of a ruler named Topiltzin. He was a priest of Quetzalcoatl, and conforming to custom, he took the god's name as his own. Living with

zin, nor were they able to fight as well as his followers. He bested them. Topiltzin settled in Chichén Itzá about 980. He Maya-ized his title to Kukulkan and built religious structures strikingly similar to those he left behind in Tula. He also introduced the cult of Quetzalcoatl—but with important differences. The true Quetzalcoatl followers offered up tortillas, flowers, incense and butterflies to their deity. The Kukulkan adherents demanded human sacrifice and engaged in exotic practices that shocked the puritanical Mayas.

Mayan culture intrigues the world. Undoubtedly, the Mayas were among America's best architects and artists. There is an aura of mystery about Mayan ruins. Skeptical people attributed their culture to ancient Egyptian or Israelite influence. For centuries after the

the Toltecs in Tula were the Nonoalcas, who worshipped a god of human sacrifice, Tezcatlipoca. The Nonoalcas yearned to overthrow Topiltzin so they resorted to the old formula: get him drunk and force him to make love to his sister. Again it happened according to script. Topiltzin awoke in disgrace, set off for the coast, that place of refuge for the shamed, and embarked on a raft.

He made his way to the Yucatán peninsula where he found that the Mayas had developed an advanced culture. Unfortunately for them, they did not have as good weapons as Topilt-

Above, a sculpture of Quetzalcóatl, the Plumed Serpent and the god of the Toltecs. (the most important deity in Meso-America).

Spanish conquest, people could not believe that simple Mayan farmers in the lowlands of the Yucatan or the highlands of Chiapas or Guatemala were the descendants of the creators of Mayan culture.

The Spanish conquerors of Mexico were not much interested in the Indians' culture, except insofar as it could advance Spanish economic and political ends. A few missionaries did study the indigenous cultures and left valuable information. But they were looked upon with suspicion; their work was stored away or given little distribution. It is said that most of our knowledge of the Mayans comes from Friar Diego de Landa, bishop of Yucatán. However, he burned most of the Mayan codices, so that only three Mayan pre-Columbian codices survive.

The publication in 1831 of Lord Kingsborough's book, *Antiquities of Mexico,* spurred interest in the Mayas and marks the beginning of serious efforts to study Mexico's past. Poor Lord Kingsborough! He landed in debtor's prison because he couldn't pay for the paper and engravings in his last volumes.

An American, John L. Stephens, published the first widely distributed, popular work on Mayan ruins. Accompanied by draftsman Frederick Catherwood, Stephens spent almost two years (1839–1841) seeking out Mayan ruins in Honduras, Guatemala and Mexico. His book, *Incidents of Travel in Central America, Chiapas and Yucatán,* contained Catherwood's accurate drawings. The prose is full of insight and experience. Catherwood

ologists include Sylvanus Morley, J. Eric S. Thompson (no relation to Edward Thompson), and Michael Coe. Specialists divide Mayan history into three time-frames: the Formative, from around 200 B.C. to 300 A.D.; the Classical, from the years 300 to 900; and the Post-Classical, up to the Spanish conquest. Mayan civilization reached its maximum height during the Classical period. In the lowlands of the Yucatán limestone provided the craftsmen with first-rate building and sculpture material. (See Travel Section for details on ceremonial sites.) In general, the buildings are of harmonious proportions, often beautifully decorated with stone carving or stucco. The Mayans excelled in portraiture and detail. The main sites are dominated by pyramids which sometimes contain burial cham-

made his drawings in exactly the right light. He cleared the brush and sat patiently waiting. Partly because of Stephens' work, Mayan studies became an almost complete monopoly of the United States until the recently established Center for Mayan Studies at Mexico's National University.

As the American consul in the Yucatán from 1885 to 1909, Edward Thompson devoted his free time to archeological exploration. He even bought a tract of land, which included the ceremonial center of Chichén Itza. Thompson's discoveries include several old Mayan ruins and the Sacred Cenote (a huge well), which contained the bones of human sacrifice, gold and other precious objects.

The most productive among Mayan arche-

bers. Although the Mayans never discovered the true arch, they invented the corbeled vault of fitted stone, each of which projects slightly farther out than the stone underneath.

The dominant theme of Mayan civilization was the passage of time. No other culture was so obsessed with recording time with such precision as the Mayas. They calculated the solar year at 365.2422 days and the moon's period at 29.5209 days. Both figures are so accurate that it was only in the 20th Century that scientists came up with figures ever so slightly more exact. The Mayans calculated time from a date zero, August 13, 3113 B.C., and believed that the universe would end when the Great Cycle of the Long Count ran out on December 24, 2011.

The Mayans needed a precise calendar because coordination of the heavenly bodies determined everything of importance they did, starting with the agriculture cycle. They knew that since the universe moves in cycles, past movements of stars and planets would be repeated. Thus priests could take appropriate action to forestall disaster. It took centuries of work to coordinate these data and it was not until the year 750 that the eclipses of the sun and the moon, for example, were worked out by astronomers meeting in Copán. There a sculptured monument marks the great event. To work out these accurate predictions, the Mayans made amazing advances in mathematics. Even today some highland survivors of the Mayan culture still guide their lives by elements of the classic Mayan calendar. Natu-

rally, present day astrologers feel at home with the Mayas.

The Mayan pantheon (table of gods) was just as complicated as their calendar. We know of 166 named deities, each with four different representations corresponding to cardinal direction. There are also counterparts for the opposite sex. Moreover, every astronomical god had an underground avatar, or incarnation. The chief of the gods seems to have been Itzamna (Lizard House), often represented as an old man with a Roman nose. He was credited with the invention of writing;

Left, El Castillo (The Castle), the main pyramid at Chichén Itzá; above, a fine stucco head from Palenque with a strong Mayan nose and headdress.

he was patron of arts and sciences. In his embodiment as the Sun, he was the husband of the Moon, Ix Chel, the Rainbow Lady, benefactress of weavers, doctors and women.

The Chacs—rain deities—were among other important Mayan gods. The mounted Spaniards with their firearms became associated with the Chacs. The firearms represented thunder and lightning. Horse and rider were thought to be one creature. Some crippled horses were left behind by the Spaniards and they became cult figures to some Mayans. After Cortés's horse died, the horse's skeleton was worshipped.

For a long time it was believed that the Mayans were peaceful and non-violent worshippers of the gods, but now we know this was not true. Mayans cut themselves and bled for their gods. They sacrificed their children, tearing out the child's heart and offering it to the gods. They cut their own ears; slashed their tongues and arms, used a sting ray's tail on their bodies. And there was the gory practice of self-mutilation. A man would pierce the head of his penis, pass a cord through, and douse the statue of a deity with blood.

Mayans fasted and abstained from sex before and during religious rituals and during the planting and harvesting seasons. They had a ruthless code of morals. Woe betide the immodest maiden! They rubbed her private parts with pepper. They slashed open the stomach of the adulterer and removed his intestines.

Obviously the Mayas had a structured and disciplined society or how else could they have erected all those ceremonial complexes? They were governed by priest-rulers. There never was a central capital; instead they had a series of autonomous city-states who, in general, enjoyed friendly relations with each other. None of the classical Mayan sites was protected by fortifications. Evidently, none was needed. From a study of the gods at the various sites, we know that they held fairly uniform religious concepts.

Between the third and sixth centuries, they had much contact with other parts of Meso-America, especially with Teotihuacán and Monte Albán. The Mayans engaged in trade, much of the time moving products by water, over the rivers, and on the ocean in large seagoing canoes. They exchanged textiles, tools, feathers, pottery, carved precious stones, medicinal herbs, incense, farm products, and especially salt. The Yucatán was the most important salt producer. They used cacao beans to trade with, and in the form of currency.

Sometimes crafty counterfeiters took the skin off the beans and inserted a far less valuable substance inside.

And meanwhile how fared the Toltecs at Chichen Itzá? As time went on they became more and more Mayan in speech and outlook. They retained only their heritage; their boast that they were descendants of the warriors of Tula. Toltec domination over northern Yucatán lasted some 200 years and an intrepid Maya named Hunac Ceel Cauich ended it.

It came about this way: the Mayas at times cast humans into the Sacred Well at Chichen Itzá to see if the rain gods who lived at the bottom of the well had a message to present. Few of these people survived; most were human sacrifices. Hunac was thrown into the well, but he came out with a message from the gods: Throw the rascals out! Inspired by those words, the Mayas crushed the people of Itzá and the descendants of the Toltecs.

them. Their culture was in full bloom when the Spaniards arrived. We have accounts of the conquest which deal with the Aztecs, works by missionaries (Father Sahagun's account stands out), and descriptions by surviving members of the Aztec élite who learned Latin script and wrote both in Nahuatl and Spanish. And, of course, there is the masterpiece on Hernán Cortés and the Conquistadores: Bernal Diaz's *The True History of the Conquest of New Spain*.

The rise of the Aztecs took place in about a century. No group in Mexico so quickly rose from savage to imperial ruler. At its apogee, etiquette at the Aztec court reached the point where it even described the proper method of smelling flowers. It was as ritualistic as present day wine-tasting.

gods: Throw the rascals out! Inspired by those words, the Mayas crushed the people of Itzá and the descendants of the Toltecs.

Hunac set up his capital at Mayapan, near present day Merida. This was a true city, unlike the ceremonial sites which never were inhabited except by priests. Hunac started the Cocom dynasty, which partially restored Mayan culture. But around the middle of the 15th Century, the Tutul Xiu family led a revolt against the Cocoms; Mayapan was destroyed, a budding culture was stricken.

The Rise of the Warrior Aztecs

And now to the Aztecs. A great deal of our knowledge of Meso-America comes from

According to legend, the Aztecs and other Nahuatl-speakers came from the seven caves called Chicomózoc, in the north. The Aztecs claimed to have migrated from Aztlán (hence their name), perhaps a home they settled in temporarily after leaving the seven caves. One of their legendary leaders was named Mexitli. Perhaps this gave rise to the name Mexicas, the other name for the Aztecs, and, of course, the reason why the Spaniards called the country Mexico.

The Aztecs were led by their tribal god, Huitzilopochtli. When they arrived on the shores of Lake Texcoco, present day Mexico City, they were dressed in animal skins; they were rude barbarians. They had no technical skill; they were barren of manners. But they were tough and they had faith in themselves.

On an island in Lake Texcoco, they saw a sign which their priests had prophesied to them would end their peregrinations. It was an eagle, perched on a cactus, devouring a serpent. (The emblem of Mexico.) Here they were to build their city, Tenochtitlán, named for Tenoch, one of their leaders. They were not welcomed. When they asked permission to settle there, the ruler of Azcapotzalco gave them a snake-infested marsh. For 75 years the Aztecs learned from their advanced cousins, but never did they abandon faith in their destiny. They kept their spears sharpened. They hired out as mercenaries, but mercenaries seldom win much love. They were patient. In the beginning they lived off snake meat, fish, ducks, and even mosquito larva. They devel-

coco, which then was ruled by the poet-architect-engineer king, Netzahualcóyotl. Slowly the ambitious Aztecs began to dominate.

Itzcóatl (Obsidian Serpent), the first ruler of the independent Aztecs, governed from 1428 to 1440. Under him the Aztecs began their rise. Typical of dictators, he first set about to revising history by ordering all the codices painted before his reign to be burned. Now his appointed historians could glorify the Aztec past as he wished.

The next Aztec ruler was Moctezuma Ilhuicamina. By now the Aztecs were on the march. They were gifted at drumming up wars; they were adept at provoking insults which they used as excuses for belligerence. They still kept their two allies, the Texcocans and the Tlacopan, but only the former were

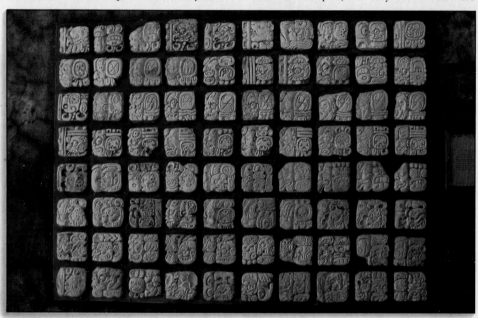

oped an agriculture skill. They build *chinampas,* floating gardens anchored to the shallow lake bottom.

A People Given to War

Everything comes to he who waits. In 1428 Tezotómoc, the tyrannical king of Azcapotzalco, died. Allied with other tribes, the Aztecs defeated Tezotomoc's son, thus winning their independence. They were now on their way. First, though, they formed a triple alliance with the towns of Tlacopan and Tex-

Left, Mayan painting of dignitaries found at Bonampak in the late 1940s; above, date glyphs from Palenque document an astronomical event.

permitted to furnish warriors. The Tlacopan furnished tortillas and porters.

In 1473 the Aztecs established absolute control at home by defeating a faction of their own tribe who controlled the great market at Tlatelolco. In their capital of Tenochtitlán the Aztecs built imposing structures and turned out well-executed sculpture. They were often brutes, but still they had a sense of the artistic. According to some accounts, during the dedication of the temple-pyramid of Huitzilopochtli, they sacrificed 20,000 prisoners of war. They were marshalled, four abreast, in a five-kilometer (three-mile) long file, then driven to the sanctuary on top of the pyramid where priests tore out their hearts. The ritual went on for three days and nights. Then there was a great feast and the Aztecs ate parts of the bodies.

The last and best known of the Aztec emperors, Moctezuma II, began his career as a general, renowned for his courage. However, the warrior-king in time began to mellow; he began to devote more and more time to his priestly duties and less to gory war. He began to question himself, a most regrettable trait in an absolute ruler. This change of character is important; it was responsible, at least in part, for the Aztec defeat by Cortés.

The World According to the Aztecs

Obviously there was a lot more to the Aztecs than blood and guts. Their social system elevated the common citizen; they made him

state theology, separate from a philosophical religion, wherein intellectuals sought answers to man's eternal questions about why he was on earth and for what purpose.

The founder of the universe was called Ometéotl. Under him many gods fought relentlessly among themselves for supremacy which would permit them to rule men's lives and direct the destiny of the world. In Aztec belief, there were five time-spans, or Suns. The First Sun lasted 676 years. This was the god Tezcatlipoca, the Sun of Night and Earth. During his reign, the land was inhabited by giants who lived on acorns. The First Sun was vanquished by Quetzalcóatl who struck him a tremendous blow with a club. He fell into the water and was transformed into a jaguar who ate each and every one of the acorn-fed giants.

feel as though he were playing a vital role. The government was free of corruption. Administrators were excellent. The Aztecs provided a system of education never before seen in Meso-America. They encouraged the arts and artisans responded. But what is most striking about the Aztecs is their capacity for abstract thought—their philosophy, their view of the world.

The Aztecs differentiated between concepts based on observation and experience, on the one hand, and magic, combined with superstitution, on the other. They had a popular religion, worshipping a symbolic reference to natural phenomena in the form of more than 2,000 gods. All of them, it seems, had unpronounceable names. Also there was an official

The Second Sun, Quetzalcóatl, God of the Wind, lasted 364 years. The people ate watercorn. The era ended when the aforementioned jaguar clawed Quetzalcóatl and overthrew him. A great wind arose and everyone perished except for a few monkeys.

The Third Sun was Tlaloc, the Rain of Fire, and his domination lasted 312 years. The people ate corn-like seed. The era ended when Quetzalcóatl (obviously he was still around) conjured up a day-long rain of fire which killed everyone except a few who survived as birds, chiefly turkeys.

Above, Frederick Catherwood's drawing of a Mayan corbelled arch at Labna.

The Fourth Sun, Chalchiuhtlicue, controlled the world for 676 years. Men ate a grain almost like corn. The end came when Tlaloc sent a great flood where all drowned except for a few, who became fish.

The Fifth Sun, the Sun of Movement, is the contemporary ruler. His era started at Teotihuacán, where the gods assembled and decided that he who was brave enough to cast himself into the fire would be the next Sun. No one wanted to, until an unassuming deity called Nanahuatzin, the "One With Pimples," leaped into the flame.

There is an odd similarity in some of this to Greek thought. Each of the first four Suns symbolized one of the basic elements: earth, air, fire, water, much in the same way as in the ancient Greek philosophy defined by Empedocles and transmitted by Aristotle. In the legend of the Suns, the Aztecs accepted the prevailing mythology they found when they arrived at the Valley of Mexico, but the next step was entirely their own myth-making.

You may have wondered why each Sun reigned for a period of time defined right down to an exact number of years. That was deliberate. Note that each Sun's era can be divided by 52, which was a sacred number. The Aztecs came up with the idea of interposing themselves in the struggle of the gods so that the world would not come to catastrophic end at the close of any 52-year cycle. How to prevent this happening? Well, by fortifying the Fifth Sun. How to do that? By giving him the most sacred and life-giving of food; namely, living human hearts. That explains the brutal custom.

Less than 100 years before the Spanish came, there lived a nobleman among the Aztecs named Tlacaelel. He could have become emperor but he preferred to remain the power behind the throne. It was he who was responsible for the destruction of the ancient codices. That permitted the Aztecs to lay claim to close relationship with the Toltec nobility whom they admired. The new chronicles also depicted their tribal god, Huitzilopochtli, as a major god associated with the Sun, a god who lead Aztecs to greatness.

The official state doctrine decreed that the noblest form of death was childbirth for women (the making of warriors), and for men death on the battlefield or as human sacrifice. The souls of such dead persons would bask in glory, according to state doctrine. They would accompany the Sun on his daily journey.

But there were those who were not satisfied with such doctrine. They felt that the mystery of man's existence perhaps never could be understood. They believed that answers could not be sought rationally, but rather through intuition, through poetic inspiration. They called this mood "flower and song." They wrote short poems which set forth their feelings. These poems were tolerated because they did not challenge state theology. Some samples:

Truly do we live on earth?
Not forever on earth, only a little
    while here
We merely dream, all is like a dream
Is anything stable and lasting?

It is true, can it be true that we live
    on earth?
Not for ever here, only for a
    moment on earth
For the hard jade splinters
The bright gold loses its luster
The shiny quetzal feather rips
Not forever here, only a moment on earth.

Where are we going? Where are we going?
In the Beyond will we find Death or Life?
Is there anything which lasts?
On earth only
The sweet song, the beautiful flower.

"Beauty is truth," they are saying, as John Keats said. These poets concluded that beauty is perhaps the only reality. How different than the state doctrine telling male Aztec children that they are here on earth as warriors whose duty it is to die in combat.

It is plain that the military dominated Aztec culture. Soldiers who won fame were given grants of land and positions of wealth and influence. Even when there were no major campaigns underway, the Aztecs carried on "wars of flowers" with their own allies, capturing soldiers whom they put to death. They considered soldiers the best of all sacrifices to strengthen the time-span, or Sun.

Aztec wars of conquest brought them huge gain. It included tribute in the form of agricultural products, cloth, luxury items. Indeed, the people of Tenochtitlán, (the population was estimated variously at between 75,000 and 300,000), lived largely off the tribute paid by subjected peoples. The Aztecs were not interested in occupying the lands of the vanquished—they had too few warriors to spare for armies of occupation. They left the conquered people with their own leaders and government, but demanded heavy payment. Their arrogant tax collectors could always summon the military to punish those who did not produce on time and in large enough quantity. Such a people as the Aztecs were bound to incite a monumental hatred. Which explains why some of the subject tribes so willingly helped the Spanish invaders.

LOS CONQUISTADORES: 'SWORD STROKES AND DEATH'

The Spanish conquest of Mexico is one of the most exciting adventure stories of mankind. Four and a half centuries have gone by and still there is the great question: How could a tiny army led by a law-school dropout conquer the mightiest tribal nation of Mexico's military culture?

Against the tens of thousands of Aztec warriors and allied tribes, Hernán Cortés, the Spanish leader, had fewer than 400 Spanish soldiers in the beginning (including 33 crossbowmen and 17 arquebusiers), plus 7,000 Tlaxcalan enemies of the Aztecs. The Spanish also had 16 horses—"fearsome beasts," they were called—and 10 heavy guns, 4 lighter pieces and plenty of ammunition. The sound and fury of those artillery pieces terrified the Aztecs.

Cortés arrived in Hispaniola in 1504 at age 19. He was strong and smart and ambitious and though he soon became a wealthy landowner, he was restless and craved adventure. Under Velasquez, the governor of Cuba, he organized an expedition to Mexico, sailing in 11 ships. After a battle in Tabasco, he landed at Veracruz, 312 kilometers (195 miles) east of Tenochtitlán, the Aztec capital and showplace, on April 22, 1519.

Cortés Orders His Ships Burned

The first thing Cortés did was to order all but one of his ships destroyed. It was a daring thing to do: cut himself off from the line of retreat. But it was a smart move, militarily speaking. His men now knew beyond doubt that they were on their own: they had to conquer or die.

They began the march inland. The Aztecs should have soon learned that the Spanish could be savage. At Cholula they invited the nobles to a religious ceremony. An old woman informed the Spanish that the nobles were plotting against them. Suddenly without warning, the Spanish attacked with "knife strokes and sword strokes and death." Everyone in sight was slaughtered.

The march went on. Finally, the Spanish reached the outskirts of Teotihuacán. It was a wonderful city: a wide main street, temples, terraces, gardens, and in the distance the blue mountains reaching up. Throngs of the curious beheld the Spanish and their armor and their cannon and their horses. The Spaniards looked at the people, at the canals, the bridges over the canals, and the boats gliding in the water, carrying produce to market. They saw the huge causeways, miles long, wide enough for 10 horses to ride abreast.

Bernal Díaz, a soldier in Cortés' army, described the wonder he felt as he and his comrades first saw the shining Aztec capital. The city "seemed like an enchanted version from the tale of Amadis," he wrote. "Indeed some of our soldiers asked whether it was not all a dream." They saw the great market of Tlatelolco, patronized by some 70,000 people a day; with row upon row of every kind of merchandise laid out for sale.

Moctezuma came out to meet Cortés. The king was about 40, tall, trim, with a wispy beard. His face was lighter in color than the faces of his copper-hued subjects. He greeted Cortés courteously; he thought Cortés was a a divine envoy of the god Quetzalcóatl. He gave Cortés gifts and arranged for the Spanish to quarter in a palace built by Moctezuma's father. They spoke through the interpretation of a woman named Marina, a Mexican Indian. That night the Spanish fired off their cannon. The Aztecs shuddered.

The Spanish Kidnap the King

There followed a week or so of palaver between Moctezuma and Cortés, but nothing much was accomplished. The king remained always polite; Cortés became increasingly bold. By then the Spanish were growing restive and so Cortés decided on a daring stroke. He and his cohorts took Moctezuma captive. They claimed he was merely a hostage, but in fact they had kidnapped the king and were holding him prisoner. Moctezuma could have ordered his people to resist; he chose not to.

Another inverval. Now Governor Velasquez back in Cuba had heard the reports. He feared and hated Cortés and felt he was too ambitious. Velasquez sent an expedition from Cuba to arrest Cortés. Ever the strategist, Cortés sallied forth to meet his countrymen, defeated them, and incorporated them into his army.

While he was away an ugly incident occurred back at the palace at Tenochtitlán. The Spanish troops under Capitán Alvarado who were guarding Moctezuma gave permission to the Aztecs to hold a religious festival, during which the participants were slaughtered. That massacre shook even Cortés and he rebuked Alvarado and told him he "did not do well." The word of the killings spread; the Aztecs arose in rebellion and attacked the Spanish. Cortés pressed Moctezuma to go out and cool his warriors down. The king tried but the Aztecs reviled him, calling him a coward and a woman, and wounded him. The king's spirit was crushed; he refused to talk, he refused to eat. Later he died. Of his wounds? Or did the Spanish kill him? It has never been definitely established.

Cortés was now in a bind. The Aztecs blockaded the palace, destroyed the bridges over the canals, and cut off the Spaniards. They had to get out of town. After midnight on July 1, 1520, the Spaniards slipped out of the palace. They carried a portable bridge to span the canals but at the first crossing so many horses and men marched across that the bridge was wedged so firmly they couldn't

Aztecs also thrust with their copper-tipped long spears.

Spaniards Run for Their Lives

The Spanish were running for their lives. The Aztecs no longer feared the white invaders. All along the road of retreat the Aztecs harassed their foes. Many Spaniards died from greed: carrying too much gold, they could not move nor fight efficiently.

Bernal Díaz wrote that the Spanish lost more than half of their army, all their artillery and munitions, and 57 of their 80 horses. Eight hundred Spaniards died. "We fought very well but they were so strong and had so many bands which relieved one another by turns, that if we had been ten thousand

move it. Also, they were weighed down with Aztec gold.

The Aztecs were sleeping, but a wild running battle ensued as the Aztec battle whistle sounded in the night and gathered in the warriors. The Aztecs threw stones, hurled darts, and fired volleys of arrows. They were experts with the sling. The Spanish wielded their trusty swords; the Aztecs used the *maquahuitl*, a paddle-shaped club inset with razorlike pieces of obsidian. It was said that on occasion a brawny Aztec warrior decapitated a Spaniard's horse with a single stroke. The

Matchbox art: a human sacrifice by the Aztecs, left; and a meeting between Cortés and Moctezuma, right.

Trojan Hectors and so many Rolands, even then we should not have been able to break through."

"Neither cannon, muskets, nor crossbows were of any avail, nor hand-to-hand combat, nor the slaughter of thirty or forty of them every time we charged. They still fought on bravely and with more vigor than before . . . "

When the surviving Spaniards finally escaped, they ran out of food and had to live on wild berries and the few ears of corn they could glean from the fields. If a horse was slain or died, it became the *piéce de résistance* for dinner.

The Aztecs should have followed up their

victory and crushed the Spaniards but they let the remnants get away. Thus, Cortés was able to reach Tlaxcala, and there he received reinforcements of men and arms for the final assault on Tenochtitlán. Again he devised a superior strategy; he ordered 13 war sloops built and armed with cannon. They were hauled to Lake Texcoco, allowing him to control passage on the water and thus cutting off Aztec supplies. He also ordered the cutting of the fresh water pipelines to Tenochtitlán.

On their final assault the Spaniards had 86 horsemen, 700 foot soldiers and 118 crossbowmen and musketeers. The footmen discarded their metal armor and wore the quilted cotton protection of the Aztecs. Again the Spaniards had thousands of Indian allies.

The Spanish Victory

A reinforced Spanish army laid siege for almost three months to Tenochtitlán in 1521. They conquered the causeways first, then the city, street by street. Besides Spanish arms, the Aztec defeat was caused by widespread smallpox brought in by a black slave from Cuba; many also died from a lack of fresh water as the lake around them was brackish. And the Spanish naval siege of the Aztec capital proved to be very successful, cutting off food and other supplies. The Aztec

Above left, Moctezuma taken prisoner; above right, Cortés during the night of his defeat; and right, Cortés with La Malinche.

resistance ended when the Spaniards captured the new emperor, Cuauhtémoc, who tried to flee Tenochtitlán in a canoe.

A Flaming Ear of Corn

Consider the story of the conquest of Mexico from the Aztec point of view, as described by the Mexican scholar Miguel León-Portilla in the book *The Broken Spears*. For years before the Spanish came a miasma of doom hung in the air. A series of omens portended disaster. One night, the sages said, a huge, flaming ear of corn appeared in the sky, dripping blood. Comets flared, trailing tails of fire. A man with two heads was reported walking the streets. On a windless day, the waters of Lake Texcoco rose and flooded the city. A

strange bird was captured who had a mirror set in his head. The bird reportedly was brought to Moctezuma. He looked in the mirror and though it was daytime he saw the night sky and stars reflected. Clearly something was wrong. He took another look and saw a strange army advancing on his capital. The soldiers were mounted on animals that looked like deer.

It was about this time that reports came of the Spanish landings on the coast. The king's fortune tellers prophesied that these strangers would rule the land. Aroused, the king ordered the bearers of these ill tidings to be strangled—but the memory of the tale haunted him. And, of course, Moctezuma knew that legend foretold Quetzalcoatl's return. The description of Spanish fitted the story of the legend. They, too, were white of skin and black of beard.

So the invaders arrived and Moctezuma tried to win them with gold. How the Spaniards loved gold! León-Portilla said they "picked up the gold and fingered it like monkeys. . . . they hungered like pigs for that gold."

The Path of Broken Spears

The destruction of Tenochtitlán was dreadful, the author said. "The cries of the helpless women and children were heart-rending. The Tlaxcaltecas and the other enemies of the Aztecs revenged themselves pitilessly for old offenses and robbed (the people) of everything they could find. . . . The anguish and bewilderment was pitiful to see. The warriors gathered on the rooftops and stared at the ruins of their city in a dazed silence and the women and children and old men were all weeping."

How did the Spanish win with so few combatants? León-Portilla says it is true their arms were superior; the noise and flash of their artillery frightened the Aztecs. But after a while the Indians got used to the noise and they soon discovered that even the fearsome horse was mortal. It was the Spaniards' bravery and expert military tactics that proved as important as their armor or weapons. They were strongly disciplined; their strategy improved with battle experience. They had a brave and skillful leader: Cortés. He had brave and skillful captains. They were great and fearless fighters. At the same time, Aztec battle tactics often were poor. They wanted to capture prisoners, who would be sacrificed to the gods later. The Spaniards knew that if they were taken prisoner their heart would be torn out. It was not easy to capture a well-armed man who knew that.

Cortés' most valuable aide was his Indian mistress and interpreter, Doña Marina, known as "La Malinche." She was presented to Cortés after his first battle in Tabasco. The daughter of a Mexican nobleman, she spoke both Maya and Nahuatl, the language of the Aztecs. How did she learn Spanish? The Spaniard Jerónimo de Aguilar had been shipwrecked off the Yucatán coast and learned the Mayan language. It was he who taught La Malinche Spanish. She was far more than an interpreter, however. She gave Cortés advice on strategy and on the psychology of the Aztecs. Cortés was shrewd in the ways of diplomacy and in the handling of people. He often took La Malinche's advice. (Mexicans consider her the arch traitor.)

'The Guidance of God'

Why didn't Moctezuma, a military man with a record of courage in battle, fight the Spanish, right from the start? Well, there were the omens; there was his belief that Cortés was Quetzalcoatl's envoy. Also, Moctezuma believed that by fighting he would lay his city in ruins. What motivated the Spanish? True, they lusted for gold, but they also had a sense of divine mission. They wanted to win land for their monarch; they wanted to aggrandize his realm. Also they wanted to convert the Indians to Catholicism; to evangelize in behalf of their church. God was on their side, they believed.

Bernal Diaz said the Spanish triumph was achieved "not of our volition, but by the guidance of God. For what soldiers in the world, numbering only four hundred—and we were even fewer— would have dared to enter a city as strong as Mexico, which is larger than Venice and more than 4,500 miles away from our own Castile?"

The Spaniards fought valiantly, but not only for ambitious reasons. Indeed, they were sincerely shocked by human sacrificial and other such barbaric rituals practiced by the Aztecs. It was in marked contrast to the above social situation that Mexico's colonial period began. It was a time that was good or bad, depending on a historian's point of view.

COLONIALISM ... AND INDEPENDENCE

For three centuries Spain ruled Mexico—hardly an enlightened rule, and often harsh colonialism at its worst. Rebellion flared from time to time, but the rebels, including in 1562 Hernán Cortés' son, Martin, and a group of his allies, were always swiftly crushed. Spain ruled with an iron hand.

After they defeated the Aztecs, the Spaniards consolidated their power, subjugated the Indian tribes, and everlastingly reached out for new riches. At the beginning of the 16th Century Spain was one of the most dynamic countries in the world. It was united;

bravely came away with little more than their wounds. "We ought to call ourselves, not the victors of New Spain, but the victims of Hernán Cortés," Bernal Díaz said bitterly.

Encomiendas and Haciendas

The land-grant system had worked this way: the holder of the grant—called an *encomienda*—also received a number of Indians to work for him. It was his duty to protect them and to make good Christians out of them. Most of the encomiendas were too

finally, it had driven off the Moors. It was now ready for new adventures. But trouble stood in the wings, ready to take the stage. At home the Church reigned supreme in influence, while small groups of nobles held staunch political power. A rigid hierarchy prevailed; not a breath of democracy was permitted.

Spain quickly recognized the importance of Mexico, or "New Spain," as it was called. The Conquistadores—those hairy men of daring—were neglected. Spain would not permit the rule of a semi-autonomy overseas. In fact, the Spanish crown eventually took away many of the land-grants which Cortés had given his stalwarts and Spain sent a nobleman from home to rule New Spain as the viceroy. The common soldiers who had fought so

small to be economically viable. The holders of a mere 18—less than 2 percent—could make a living out of them. The others had to find other jobs to keep themselves alive. As agriculture developed, the encomiendas gave rise to *haciendas*, bigger pieces of land bought from the Crown.

Nobody was much troubled by the master-servant relationship that existed between Spaniard and Indian. It was the system of the times. All men were not created equal in the old Spanish world. The Church heartily supported that philosophy. Each person, the

Above, a painting by Casimiro Castro of the National Palace; right, water carriers with clay jars and gourds typify the lower classes of the colonial era.

Church believed, had his assigned station in life; only by humbly accepting his designation could a person reap his reward in the next life.

It took decades to Christianize the Indians. Are they really human? the authorities pondered. Indeed, do they possess a soul which can be saved? Finally, it was decided that, yes, the Indian was a human being.

The Spanish missionaries concentrated their proselyting efforts on teaching the children of the native aristocracy. In 1528, the College of Santa Cruz de Tlatelolco was founded for this purpose. Many of the students aspired to the priesthood but a decree in 1555 prohibited the ordaining of Indians, mestizos or *negros*. Nevertheless, these young men led the fight against the old time

up their child as a slave in his own land.

Silver, Cattle and Land

Nor did the Spanish find the great riches they hungered for. Exploration following the defeat of the Aztecs produced no El Dorados. Only the discovery of silver at Zacatecas, Pachuca and Guanajuato stirred fresh hope. By 1548, Zacatecas had become the second largest city in New Spain and in the vicinity more than 50 silver mines were in operation. Many Indians were forcibly recruited to work in the mines, but still there was not enough labor so black slaves were imported. By 1800 Mexico was producing 66 percent of the world's silver.

Spurred by the shining metal of Zacatecas,

religions of the Indians. Often brilliant, their prestige was enhanced by the prerogatives they were permitted; namely, that they could ride horses, dress in Spanish style, and carry arms.

But of what good religion when the native population was being wiped out, chiefly through disease? Some 80 to 90 percent disappeared in the decades after the conquest. They had no immunity against the white man's diseases, and especially against the smallpox. Moreover, some of the proud Indians refused to accept Spanish rule and there were even instances when whole groups of disenchanted people committed suicide. Others refused to produce children. They did not want to bring

adventurers pushed into the far north, looking for buried riches. These independent men developed an open society of the north, several months' journey from Mexico City and thus well out of the reach and the edicts of the ruling hierarchy. These men were usually *criollos* (Mexican-born Spaniards) or mestizos (of Spanish and Indian blood). They were brazen as brass cymbals, self-reliant and full of hell, much like the pioneers of the American West. Some of them wandered into the Southwest and settled in what is now Texas, Arizona, New Mexico and California, long before the first white man landed on America's North Atlantic shores. Santa Fe, in New Mexico, was founded by some of these chaps in about 1609. These lands were wide open, semi-desert, useful for cattle-raising but not much else.

Cattle-grazing also was important in the rest of Mexico. Large tracts were taken over for grazing. There was now a new hunger—for land. Obviously accumulation of land led to power. So ruthless men seized Indian farmland, often by illegal means. There followed endless disputes about land and water rights, and sometimes the bitterness led to fighting and even killing. The Indians inevitably came out losers. They were kept in servitude because of the debts they accumulated; so, for practical purposes, an Indian family often was compelled to remain on the same hacienda for generations. It could never catch up with its debt. And thus while slavery was officially abolished in the New World in 1548, many

gustinians. Other orders followed, including Jesuits, all bent on saving souls. Each order had its own style of evangelizing. Each was assigned to a different area but at times there was acute rivalry among them.

The Church had another problem: Church vs. Viceroy. Such a rivalry was bound to happen. The Viceroy, representing the King of Spain, had absolute authority in the colony. The Church, of course, looked out after its own interests. A clash was inevitable. Thomas Gage, an English Jesuit in Mexico, left an account of one such confrontation: the story of a Viceroy who with a business associate speculated in grain, which resulted in driving prices up. It almost sounds like a tale of modern Wall Street. The Archbishop tried to intervene but the Viceroy had him arrested. Ex-

Indians remained in bondage anyway. They became among the most exploited people in the world. The Church sought to protect them. There were priests of conscience, such as Fray Bartolome de Las Casas in Chiapas and Bishop Quiroga in Michoacán who set up organizations to help the Indian. But many were neglected.

Church Versus Viceroy

The Church itself had its own problems: intra-church politics, which is always in bloom, and conflict with civil authorities. Several religious orders sent disciples to convert the Indians and by 1559 there were 380 Franciscan monks, 210 Dominicans and 212 Au-

communication of the Viceroy followed; all church services were suspended in Mexico City.

That the Church was wealthy no one could deny. It received a 10 percent tithe from agriculture, from commerce, and from the wealth of the mines, as well as its cut from the native economy, such as it was. The Church owned sugar mills and well-run haciendas. It loaned out money. But on the other hand, the Church stood resolutely for moral authority and somehow succeeded in maintaining the peace in this jambalaya of peoples. Thus the Church accomplished a task that no military could have possibly accomplished.

What mattered most of all to the Spanish Crown was how well New Spain was paying off. The Crown always needed money. Hence it *t'l* d things to help it make money off the For example, the planting of grape e trees was forbidden in Mexico in protect Spain's export monopoly in olive oil. Also, inter-colony trade d since it would compete with im- Spain. From 1730 on, Mexico ort textiles to Peru; again, com- Spain. In fact, Mexico could not with any European country except Spain, though, naturally, contraband trade flourished and a good part of Mexico's silver was smuggled out. Each year ships sailed under heavy guard from Seville in Spain to Veracruz in Mexico, bearing food and merchandise, and taking home mostly silver as well as cotton cloth, vanilla, sugar, leather, indigo

also many poor Spaniards—artisans, small-scale farmers, ranchers. By the 1570s there were some 60,000 Spanish settlers in New Spain. (There were about half a million two centuries later.) Only Spanish people (and for a time Portuguese) were allowed to settle in the colony. A medley of new peoples was being born. There were the *gachupines,* or Spanish-born Mexicans, the creoles, the mestizos, and the *castas* of varying degrees of Spanish, Indian, black and Oriental blood. The authorities kept bureaucratic note of these mixtures, and had a name for each particular mix. By the 18th Century the mestizos and creoles accounted for half the population, but it was the creoles who chafed the most under Spanish rule.

The French revolution, which began in

and *cochinilla,* a red dye. From Acapulco on the west coast a galleon departed about once every year or two, laden with silver and usually bound for Manila.

Sugar cane did well in Mexico but as early as 1599 a decree was passed restricting the planting of cane in favor of corn and wheat. In the states of Tlaxcala and Hidalgo, haciendas produced *pulque,* an alcoholic drink made from the fermented juice of the century plant, a species of cactus called the *maguey.* The Yucatán peninsula specialized in the production of cotton and indigo; Oaxaca produced cochineal; other places raised vanilla, cacao and tobacco.

It is not hard to figure out who did the sweat labor: the Indians, of course. Still there were

1789, led the beleaguered people of New Spain to dream of independence; events in war torn Europe helped nourish the dream.

It went like this: Napoleon looked at Spain and decided Spain could serve as a springboard for an attack on England, and so he invaded. Charles IV abdicated in favor of Ferdinand VII, who gave way to Napoleon. Bonaparte himself was too busy to fool around with Spain so he placed his brother, Joseph Napoleon, better known as "Pepe the Bottle," (he liked his liquor) on the throne of Spain.

Left, the lobby of a Campeche colonial building that was converted into a hotel; above, a luxuriously furnished colonial bedroom in Morelia.

Spain rose against the invader. Far off in Mexico City the élite of the ruling class met to decide what to do—the bishop, the viceroy, the magistrates, the high officials of civic government. Up rose Francisco Primo de Verdad, a lawyer, and as his name implies, he spoke truth. He said that the king of Spain had been overthrown, that a usurper had taken over, and that the sovereignty of the people of New Spain should be returned to its rightful heir, the people themselves, as represented by the town magistrates.

The assembly exploded. Primo de Verdad was called a "heretic," and what is even worse, "a Lutheran." Off to prison he must go and there he died. A suicide? Poisoned?

In 1808, a group of committed men met in Valladolid (today's Morelia in Michoacán) to start talking about independence. They were creoles, men of the middle-class; in other words, people who had the most to gain by a change in the establishment. The Archbishop of Mexico, who was then the viceroy, too, discovered the plot and quelled it.

But a spark was struck. A group of people with the same thought in mind had been meeting in Querétaro, the neighboring state, in the house of Miguel Domínguez, the magistrate, and his wife, Josefa. Always present was the quiet Father Miguel Hidalgo y Costilla, parish priest of the town of Dolores. Also present was Captain Ignacio Allende. Father Hidalgo's thesis was simple and plain: he said New Spain should be free. The friends planned an uprising. They thought they might begin in San Juan de los Lagos in Jalisco toward the end of 1810. They could take advantage of the crowds who would come to the fair and to the religious ceremony honoring the Virgin Mary.

The 'Grito De Dolores'

But word leaked out. Somebody squealed. Doña Josefa heard of the planned treachery and warned the conspirators. Captain Allende speedily rode to Dolores to warn Father Hidalgo. Hidalgo seemed unperturbed. He had a nice chocolate drink and decided to call the people to arms. On the morning of September 16, 1810, he issued his famous *Grito de Dolores,* the Shout of Dolores, the most famous outcry in Mexican history.

Hidalgo had arrived at dawn at his church to say mass. It was Sunday with a lot of parishioners on hand. Hidalgo spoke of insurrection: of killing *gapuchines,* the term of contempt for those born in Spain, the elite, the rulers of Mexico, and the only ones who were legally permitted to hold the highest offices.

Hidalgo asked for equality among men and land for the landless. It was, in fact, the battle-cry of the ages. The revolution had begun. From Dolores a band under Hidalgo marched to Atotonilco. Father Hidalgo brought along a brown-skinned image of the Virgin of Guadalupe, dressed in native garb. The image served as the flag of the rebels, who were armed with spears and sticks. Hidalgo's rabble marched from town to town and wherever they went more men joined. From a few hundred they became thousands and more thousands. Freedom was on the move. They took the mining center of Guanajuato, but sad to relate, they also committed atrocities. They moved triumphantly through the countryside.

The government commissioned a tough army man, General Félix Maria Calleja, to stop the rebels. He was a capable leader and he set out implacably to do the job. And now the horror began. Both sides committed atrocities; both sides shot prisoners, both sides pillaged. It is a pattern often repeated in the bloody history of Mexico.

Hidalgo arrived with his men in Morelia where he had been rector of the seminary. By now he had changed completely: he was no longer the subservient priest, the humble man. He was now a fierce and bold leader of men in combat. He had forgotten the biblical adage: "Thou shalt not kill." From Morelia he went to Guadalajara. After singing a *te deum* in the cathedral of the capital, he went to the palace to receive the obeisance of the local people. Here he formed his first administration. To this day Tapatios (the people of Jalisco) rejoice in the knowledge that the first seat of an independent government of Mexico was set up in their state.

Power corrupts, as Lord Acton said. In Guadalajara Hidalgo either ordered, or at least tolerated, the assassination of hundreds of Spaniards. Captain Allende, his chief lieutenant was revolted and thought about doing away with Hidalgo. Hidalgo issued an edict which abolished slavery. He sent his cohorts on missions all over Mexico to whip up revolutionary fervor; his plans had taken fire. But in the meantime, General Calleja, the methodical, had arrived with an army and laid siege to Guadalajara. There was the usual byplay as each contemplated the other. Then in the second week of January, 1811, the rebels came out to do battle at Puerte de Calderón, some 40 kilometers east of Guadalajara, and were shatteringly defeated. Hidalgo and his chieftains fled north, hoping to reach the U.S. But they were betrayed and captured. Hidalgo was imprisoned in far-off Chihuahua to await his fate. On July 30, 1811, he was shot by a firing squad. He faced death with dignity and impassiveness. The crowning insult came when the Church repudiated him. But he did not die in spirit. Father Hidalgo lives on in the hearts of Mexicans. He was the father of the nation and is so honored to this day.

Nor did the movement die. New leaders sprang up. Among the surviving revolutionary leaders was Ignacio López Rayón, who recruited rebels in the north. A master of strategy, he toyed with the royalist forces, moving with impunity over vast stretches of territory. In Zitacuaro, Michoacán, he sought to form a representative government to rule, incongruously, in the name of that far-off prisoner, Ferdinand VII.

The armed revolutionaries enlisted intellectuals and even rich ranchers. In Mexico City, a secret society sprang up, called the "Guada-

royalist forces. Occasionally, Morelos even threatened Mexico City.

Morelos seized Acapulco. Wherever he went he installed a government and collected taxes. He was a revolutionary but he had a gift for the pragmatic. Revolutions take money. He sponsored the Congress of Chilpancingo which wrote a constitution with a bill of rights, which is the base of Mexico's legal code.

But Morelos' idealism helped undo him. It caused hard feelings; soon he and the Congress were quarreling, and they succeeded in deposing Morelos. Morelos fought a battle, lost it, and was taken prisoner. He was executed. The revolution was now practically leaderless, except for one man and he was on the royalist side: the rich and able Agustín de Iturbide, a creole who hungered for power.

lupes," a name adopted from the name of Mexico's patroness, the Lady of Guadalupe. José Maria Morelos y Pavón, a rural priest and onetime student of Hidalgo, was one of the rebel leaders. He started with just 20 men but because he was savvy and knew men and the terrain, he impressed a number of natural leaders who in time led revolts in Morelos, Puebla, Michoacán, Guerrero and Oaxaca. His best known lieutenants were the priest Mariano Matamoros and three ranchers. They laid siege to cities and often defeated

Above, a painting by Juan O'Gorman depicts the independence struggle. Father Hidalgo leads Creoles, Mestizos and Indians against Spain.

He was a tough fighter and a man with great ambitions.

Down south there was one rebel left who amounted to anything: Vicente Guerrero. Iturbide tried to capture him but Guerrero was too shrewd a combatant to be caught. So Iturbide asked Guerrero to join him, and it came to pass. The royalist Iturbide and the rebel Guerrero embraced, and parleyed, thus marking the end of a 10-year struggle. They came up with the Plan of Iguala, which demanded independence. The newly arrived Viceroy, Juan O'Donoju, signed the Treaty of Córdoba which officially converted New Spain into Mexico on September 27, 1821. Independence had been achieved for a price paid in blood.

NEW FACES: SANTA ANNA, JUÁREZ, MAXIMILIAN

The first half of the 19th Century was a time of bloodshed in Mexico. *Revolución!* The word echoes and re-echoes down the corridors of Mexican history. Those years of turmoil left the country exhausted and drained; commerce was ruined, the land was devastated. Many people lost their lives. From the time the creole priest Hidalgo y Costilla shouted his *Grito de Dolores* (Cry of Dolores) on September 10, 1810 until the triumph of the liberals under the leadership of Benito Juárez, Mexico's greatest hero, it was a time of toil and trouble. Hidalgo cried out for racial equality and for distribution of the land to the peasants. Revolution broke out. The liberals were finally beaten. Hidalgo was taken captive, shot, and his head was put on display.

Mexico's 'Perpetual Dictator'

The charismatic Mexican general-politician Antonio López de Santa Anna dominated the political scene for three decades, earning him the title of "perpetual dictator." A major problem was the racial makeup of the country. Of roughly six million inhabitants at the beginning of the century, 60 percent were Indians, 22 percent were of mixed race, and 18 percent were white. Small but powerful selfish interest groups dominated. The economy was chiefly in the hands of the whites. The great majority lived in poverty and were apathetic about politics. Who was there to trust? Mexico was a disunited, troubled land. There was the vastness of the country; the lack of roads, railroads, and communications. There was insidious foreign influence, and the eternal problem of state versus Church.

Two political groups struggled for power: the conservatives, allied with the Church hierarchy who wanted a centralist government and the retention of special rights, and the liberals, or Republicans, who opposed Church power and favored a government modeled after America's.

Santa Anna joined the Mexican revolutionist Augustín de Iturbide in a fight that led to Mexican independence in 1821. Santa Anna was an opportunist, a shifty man who loved the trappings of power, but frequently was the only politician who could rally his countrymen in time of crisis. The "Hero of Tampico" (he beat the Spanish there), he was elected president in 1833 and began his long career, in and out of office. He was a dictator. He massacred the Texans at the Alamo, thereby gaining the hatred of Texans in perpetuity. In turn, he was badly beaten by Sam Houston at San Jacinto in 1836 and Texas became a republic. He lost a leg trying to repulse the French at Veracruz in 1838. (The leg was buried with honor and a monument raised on the spot. Later the leg was unearthed during a period of Santa Anna unpopularity and cast out.)

War With the United States

Santa Anna commanded the Mexican forces in the disastrous war with the U.S. (1846–1848), and lost half his country's territory in the process. But like the Indian rubberball, he wouldn't stay down. Back he came again and was elected president. Finally, the Juárez Revolution drove him into exile in 1855 and off the stage.

The 19th Century was a time of troubles and setbacks for Mexico. The country's various struggles were of both an internal and external nature. The inner ones involved fighting between liberals and conservatives. They were long and bitter contests that weakened the country and invited ambitious foreign powers to intervene. Liberals preached for the growth of the state and the weakening of the church. They touted laissez-faire economics and used as their political models both the United States and Republican France. The conservatives, meanwhile, were for a well ordered monarchy that would follow the example of the great European kingdoms. The liberals usually won on the battlefield, but after all the battles had been fought, the conservatives usually ended up in power anyway.

Thanks to popular myths that claimed that there were boundless mineral riches in Mexico, European powers became attracted by those riches and harassed the young and weak Mexican republic. Probably the greatest influence on European thinking at this time was a now classical essay, *Political Essay on the Kingdom of New Spain,* written by the German aristocrat-scientist Alexander von Humboldt.

Mexico during this period also became entrapped in more immediate disputes: The American South, for example, wanted then Mexican Texas to become a slave-keeping enclave, and when Mexico, by constitutional prerogative, said that slavery was forbidden, this political issue caused great consternation among Texas' *gringo* population. Added to these troubles was the ambition of the picturesque and catastrophic rascal Santa Anna.

Santa Anna, a man with enough vices to sink any country, caused his country numerous problems, but his greatest prank was the actual selling of a portion of Mexico, under the conditions of the Gadsden Purchase of 1853, to the United States. This sale of 77,000 square kilometers (about 30,000 square miles) of southern New Mexico and Arizona for $10 million proved to be flamboyant Santa Anna's final undoing.

The war with the U.S. was a classic example of the old saying: Might makes right. The Americans were well organized, tightly disciplined, and had ample logistical support. The Mexicans lacked all three of these ingredients for winning a war. Yet they fought bravely and lost only to superior forces. An American force moved south from New Mexico and

Patient Benito Juárez: Dreamer, Revolutionary, Leader

Benito Juárez was an Indian from Oaxaca, a man of brooding, dark features, often likened to Abraham Lincoln as one of his country's greatest leaders. He was implacable; he could be ruthless. In later years he succumbed to the ailment that strikes most politicians: he became a manipulator of men. But he had great courage; he was honest, strong-willed.

Born in 1806 in a village in the Sierra de Oaxaca, he spoke only Zapotec as a child. Taken in as a boy servant in a creole household, he so impressed his master that he helped the boy get an education and eventually Juárez became a lawyer. He was a man

captured Chihuahua; another came from Texas and captured Monterrey, Coahuila and points south. The bulk of the American forces under General Winfield Scott marched inland and captured Mexico City. In the final stage of the fighting, the cadets who garrisoned the castle in Chapultepec Park fought to the last boy. At the end, Juan Escutia, 16 years of age, wrapped himself in the flag of Mexico and jumped off the highest rampart rather than be taken prisoner. The "boy heroes," they are called on the splendid monument in Chapultepec Park.

Though he was a full-blooded Indian from the southern state of Oaxaca, popular Benito Juarez was acclaimed, above, by Mexicans of all racial mixes.

with a cold but logical legal mind, very orderly in his thinking and reasoning, and incorruptible. He had the patience of the Indian and in his long and strife-torn life he needed it. He also had a dream and he achieved it: to lead the liberal revolution that would shake Mexico to the *estribos*, the stirrups.

Juárez served as governor of Oaxaca from 1847 to 1852. He opposed Santa Anna and was imprisoned, then exiled. (He spent some time in New Orleans.) Back home he became the prime mover in the drafting of the liberals' Plan of Ayutla (named for a mountain village), and in the overthrow of Santa Anna. Under the new regime he became minister of justice and drew up the *Ley Juárez*, the Law of Juárez, which attacked the privileges of the

Catholic Church and the military. Those were the two untouchable bastions of power in Mexico.

The Juárez Law, an outgrowth of the liberal constitution of 1857 which Juárez had drafted, emphasized human rights and agricultural reform. The Lerdo Law, which followed, offered church lands for sale, with preference going to tenants who were working the land. A prospective buyer might have a problem: Should he seek material gain but risk the threat of excommunication? This appeared to be no problem at all for wealthy speculators who snapped up the land at bargain prices.

As is readily understandable, the Juárez venture was a revolution in jurisprudence. These laws were bound to stir up enormous

resentment on the part of the conservatives. It meant their downfall. It meant the transfer of power from the whites to the mestizos and creoles. The conservatives contested the new constitution. Ignacio Comonfort, the liberal president who did not have the stomach for battle, resigned and the man of iron, Juárez, took over as president. The bitter War of Reform (1858–1861) broke out. It was a savage war; civil war, the worst kind of war. Hostages and prisoners were executed; people were massacred. Historians refer to those bloody days as the time of "the brush fire sweeping the land."

Above, Emperor Maximilian of Habsburg in an early photograph; right, a splendid field portrait of an Indian girl of Oaxaca by Desiré Charnay.

The Short Reign of Maximilian

On January 1, 1861, the liberal forces marched in triumph into Mexico City and a few days later Juárez came along from Veracruz in his ramshackle carriage. There was no end of problems ahead, however. Because the treasury was bare, Mexico was compelled to suspend payment of its debts to Spain, Great Britain and France. That gave Napoleon III an excuse to invade; he had long dreamed of adding to France's overseas empire. The French were defeated by the Mexicans under General Zaragoza at Puebla, but they were able to consolidate and take over most of the country. Allied with them were the conservatives who hated Juárez and his reforms much more than they hated the idea of foreign rule. By 1863 Napoleon talked Maximilian, the young archduke of Austria, into becoming emperor of Mexico, under French protection and tutelage, of course. Though repeatedly beaten by the French, Juárez refused to surrender. The Mexican forces turned north, all the way up finally to the U.S. border (the place is now the town of Ciudad Juárez).

Maximilian acted much more like a liberal than a conservative. He restricted working hours and child labor, cancelled all debts over 10 pesos, restored communal property to Indian villages, and forbade corporal punishment. He also broke the monopoly of the hacienda stores and decreed that henceforth peons no longer could be bought and sold for the price of their debt. Thereupon, he lost the support of the conservatives and in time he also lost the support of Napoleon who withdrew his troops—they were needed elsewhere. (He faced a confrontation with England, for one thing.) The U.S., which finally finished its bloody civil war, decided that France had no business being in Mexico and strongly protested. Still, Maximilian hung on and refused to leave and was captured. Maximilian was well-meaning, but had been manipulated and then deserted by his ambitious sponsors, Napoleon III and a group of Mexican conservatives.

Juárez was not a bloodthirsty man but he wanted, above all, that respect be paid to Mexico. It could come only from firmness of purpose. He decided to set an example for the world to see. Mexico was a sovereign state. No one could violate its territory with impunity. Juárez cast his ballot—the deciding ballot—for death for Maximilian. On June 19, 1867, the 35-year-old prince was stood against a wall. A brave man, he gave each of the members of the firing squad a gold coin and as the rifle shots rang out, he shouted: *"Viva Mexico! Viva la Independencia!"*

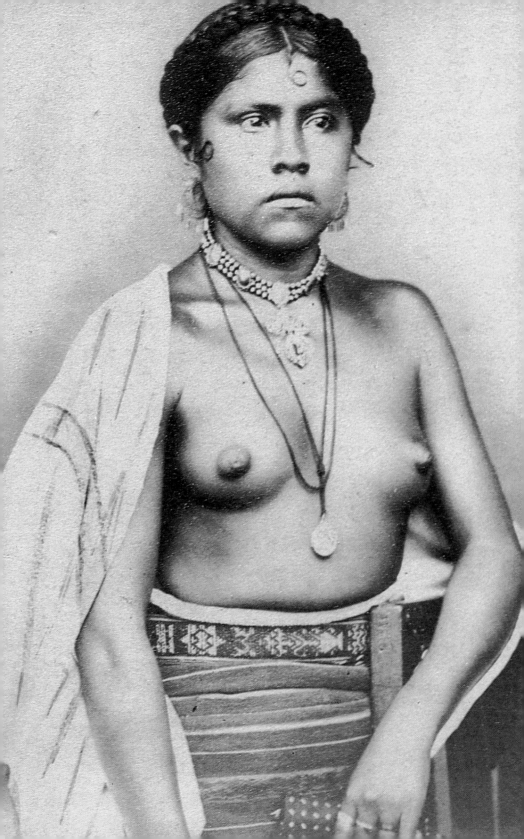

For more than three decades José de la Cruz Porfirio Díaz reigned in Mexico and that long regime has earned a title: the *Porfiriato*. Díaz was ruthless but his rule was effective. Capital poured in from abroad. He snuffed out revolución: he set up the *rurales* and crushed the *bandidos*. He sold three-quarters of the mineral rights of Mexico to foreigners and he doled out blocks of land to his henchmen and supporters, the *hacendados*. He brought peace to the land: roads were built, rail lines were strung. There was progress of a sort, but most of the population lived in abject poverty. Was the modernization of Mexico worth the cost? Who knows?

Díaz was a mestizo who supported Juárez and the reform movement and the fight against Maximilian. Díaz ran for president in 1871 against Juárez and the old man beat him. Díaz charged the election was fraudulent and he led a long revolt against the government. His pitch was this: No one, he said, has the right to keep running for office forever. There ought to be a law against it. How ironic, then, that once he became entrenched, Díaz felt no compunction against running, again and again. His onetime principle of non-reelection went out the window.

Strict Administration

In the beginning of his rule in 1876, Díaz stressed the pacification of his strife-torn country. Pacification extended to both the war-like Apache Indians and the peaceful Yaquis, both of whom resented having their lands taken away by politicians. Once he had things under control, Díaz pressed for modernization of the ancient land of Mexico. Political liberty, he said, would be granted if and when Mexico reached the point where it was compatible with discipline and development. And who would judge when that happy day had come? Well, naturally, Porfirio Díaz. Apparently it never did come during the Porfiriato.

What the country needs, Díaz said, was lots of strict administration and very little politicking. He used his army to enforce his program. He sought out foreign capital on a grand scale. By the end of the Porfiriato (1910), foreign investment amounted to $1.7 billion, mostly American (38 percent), followed by British (29 percent) and French investment (19 percent).

Díaz was a railroad man. The prices paid and the subsidies granted were outrageous for the time, but nevertheless Mexico wound up with a sound railroad system that endures today. Of course, a good network of rail lines meant that Díaz could move his troops hither and yon with alacrity. Naturally, though, the rail system also revolutionized the transportation of goods in a country where there are no inland waterways to do the job properly. Now it became economically feasible to ship cotton by rail from the cotton fields of the north to textile plants in central Mexico. And now steel mills could be built in Monterrey and iron ore railed in from Durango. Railroads also made it possible to develop mining—and not only gold and silver, the old precious standbys—but also coal, lead, antimony and copper. American companies made big investments in mining, and they earned big profits, too.

Wealthy Hacendados

Mining, banking and the oil industry all fell into foreign hands but basic agriculture by the Mexican land-owners was generally neglected; thus in a land where corn is the staple, it had to be imported. During the Porfiriato anyone who did not have legal title to his land—and very few did because of the complicated bureaucratic system—had their land taken away. Most of the productive land was in the hands of some 6,000 hacendados, whose holdings ranged from 2,500 acres to areas the size of a small European country. WIlliam Randolph Hearst, the American publisher, bought 2½ million acres for a song, in return for supporting Díaz in his newspapers. Governor Terraza of Chihuahua controlled 15 million acres, it was said.

The landowners raised cattle and grew exportable cash crops such as mahogany, sugar, coffee, tobacco, rubber and *hennequen*, a cactus fiber used to make rope with. Cotton was grown primarily for domestic use. Foreigners invested in coffee and cotton plantations. Mexico's chief exports during the Porfiriato were gold, silver, copper, oil and agricultural products. A few wealthy Mexicans controlled the economy. Rural dwellers and most people in the cities barely survived.

Díaz was shrewd. He sought a rapprochement with the Church. Though he did not permit the Catholic Church to regain its once formidable holdings (these holdings once included half of settled Mexico), he gave it back some of its lost powers and privileges. He knew that if he appeared to be tolerant towards the Church, he would gain a number of influential adherents. He allowed the Jesuits to return; he offered no objection when the Bishop of Querétaro started the custom of an annual pilgrimmage to the shrine of Our Lady of Guadalupe, Mexico's patroness. He even cleverly managed a marriage so as to benefit his regime. His bride was the daughter of a religious politician who was also a hacendado. So he helped seal the union between army, Church and landed aristocracy. An operator, that man was. All economic interests in the country were beholden to him. He was even a phrase-maker of note, or rather, what seems more likely, a man who recognized a catchy phrase when he heard it, and so bor-

French and the British. He cultivated American politicians and, chiefly through Hearst, he won over American public opinion.

There are horror stories told about the Díaz regime. Some were related by the American writer John Kenneth Turner (*Barbarous Mexico*), who spoke of the plight of the Farm slaves: the beatings, starvation, overwork, the breakup of families. Díaz ruled with an iron hand. His police were effective; their long arm sometimes reached even into the United States. The only real opposition came from radical liberals who fled to the U.S. and under the leadership of Ricardo Flores Magon took to armed rebellion. The U.S. offered a haven to Mexican politicos out of favor. They were crossing the Rio Bravo (the Americans persist in calling it the Rio Grande) long before there

rowed it for his own. Hence to Díaz is attributed probably the best known saying about Mexico:

"Poor Mexico! So far from God and so close to the United States."

Díaz's Talkative End

Díaz, however, managed his American affairs quite well. He catered to his powerful neighbor of the north, but at the same time he gave himself elbow room by dealing with the

Above, a David Siqueiros mural of the aging dictator Porfirio Díza surround by decadent and Europeanized upper classes. The Museum of History.

was any such thing as wetbacks. At one stage Díaz himself jumped the river to find a place of refuge.

Oddly, Díaz's end came because he granted an interview to an American magazine writer. In the interview he declared that Mexico was now ready for real democracy; to wit, an honest election, and that he would welcome real opposition. Francisco I. Madero, a wealthy vineyard hacienda owner of Coahuila, read the story and thought it a good idea. Indeed he wrote a book, *The Presidential Succession of 1910,* in which he, too, called for a genuinely free election. Madero offered himself as a candidate. The book was a success; Díaz arrested Madero, who fled to Texas, disguised as a railroad worker. The chips were down.

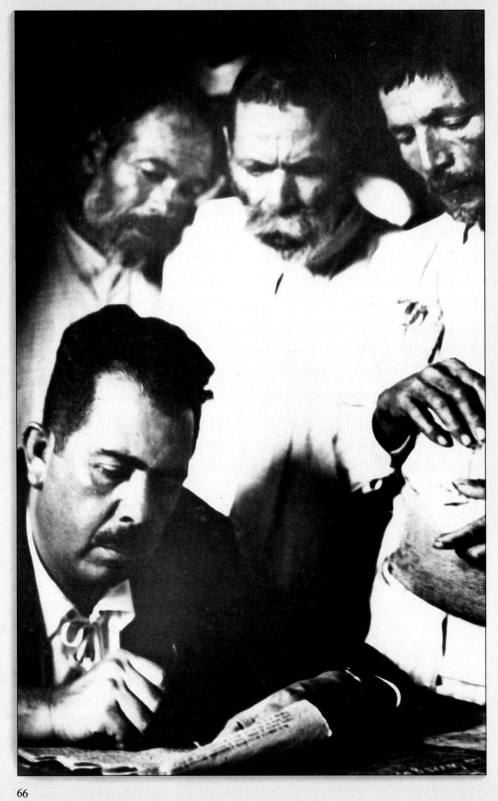

THE REVOLUTION AND ITS TURBULENT AFTERMATH

The years 1911 to 1920 riveted the attention of the world on Mexico. They were hard years, bitter years. There was war, revolution, uprising, revolt, murder. People went hungry; people were tortured, people were shot. As many as a million Mexicans died—one out of every 15 persons. It was not just a short outbreak—it was long-enduring, a revolution which, some historians say, is still going on today.

Consider the dramatis personae: Díaz, Madero, Huerta, Carranza, Obregón, and the two *guerrilleros* who caught the imagination of the world, the flamboyant Pancho Villa in the north, and the silent Indian Emiliano Zapata in the south. For a time Villa (his real name, Doroteo Arango, does not sound half as swashbuckling) even caught the fancy of President Wilson who wanted him to become *presidente* of Mexico.

A popular comic book for Mexican adults asks the question: Who won the Mexican revolution? The answer: The PRI (*Partido Revolucionario Institucional,* or Institutionalized Revolutionary Party). True, other political parties exist in Mexico, but the PRI is the only political party which wins elections.

So, Díaz was ousted. Enter Francisco Madero, a bright little man with the inquisitiveness of a bird, an intellectual but with not much luck. He championed democracy but perhaps Mexico was not ready yet. He had help from Villa and Zapata in throwing Díaz out. Madero wanted an end to social injustice but he lacked the conviction of, say, Emiliano Zapata. Madero was honest but weak, the kind of man given to putting relatives on the government payroll. Instead of making a clean sweep of the Díaz sycophants, he tried to bargain with them. He was naive.

'Tierra y Libertad!'

Madero tried to convince Zapata that he, too, wanted land reform. Zapata had a simple creed to which he remained forever loyal: throw out the landlords and divide the land among the landless. A born leader, Zapata felt the injustice suffered by his people. In 1910 he had taken up arms against the government with the cry of *"Tierra y Libertad,"*—Land and Liberty, and his men began to seize land. If someone got in the way they killed him. Zapata supported Madero until he thought Madero was dragging his feet on land reform and then he dropped him.

Zapata was illiterate but he was very intelligent. He knew exactly what he wanted. He had a schoolteacher write his land reform plan, called the Plan of Ayala. He took over control of most of Morelos and (with Villa) occupied Mexico City. He was the hero of the Mexican agrarian movement and he is a hero still to most Mexicans.

Madero, the quibbler, came to a bitter end. Victoriano Huerta, commander of government troops, bore Madero a grudge and plotted against him. Huerta captured, tortured, then killed Madero's brother, Gustavo, then arrested Madero himself. With the backing of U.S. Ambassador Henry Lane Wilson, Huerta had Madero assassinated.

Huerta formed a government, essentially with the goal of restoring the old Porfiriato of Díaz, which he admired. Huerto, too, emphasized concession to foreign investment. He immediately ran into trouble: the unplacated Zapata of the south, the rambunctious Villa in the north. Venustiano Carranza, the governor of Coahuila who had joined Madero against Díaz, and General Alvaro Obregón, teamed up against Huerta. Huerta got one break: a mistake by President Wilson. Wilson sought to cut off Huerta's supplies and sent American troops to occupy Veracruz. Mexicans had bad memories of the American intervention of 1847. Huerta seized on the incident to try to prop up his sagging popularity. He proclaimed himself defender of the nation's sovereignty. Carranza took his side and he, too, protested the American occupation. Wilson pulled out the American troops but Huerta's troubles just went on and on and he had to resign.

Villa, Carranza and Others Agree to Disagree

Carranza took over but the situation was still grim. Obregón supported him but Zapata and Villa refused to acknowledge Caranza as chief, and more fighting broke out. The north was in chaos; there Villa and his *Dorados,* the Golden Ones, ranged. A *bandido* from Durango, Villa was a horse general in the tradition of the great cavalrymen of history, such as Nathan Bedford Forrest and Jubal Early of the American Civil War. Villa's admirers

Preceding pages, Zapata troopers at a chic Mexico City restaurant; left, President Lazaro Cárdenos signs a land deed for peasants.

looked on him as a Robin Hood. He moved quickly, he struck boldly.

Carranza promised land reform and an end to social injustice. He liked to call himself the "Maximum Leader." (In recent years Fidel Castro has borrowed the term.) Carranza tried to weld together all the factions who had fought Huerta, and for that purpose he called a convention at the town of Aguascalientes, but the delegates agreed only to disagree. According to one account, Villa straightfacedly offered a solution to the impassè; namely, that both he and Carranza be executed. That would solve everything. The offer was not accepted.

In December 1914, while the world's attention was riveted on the war in Europe, Villa and Zapata occupied Mexico City. That must

Obregón pursued Villa and administered a severe beating on him in Celaya in Bajío. Knowing that Villa loved to charge with his horsemen, Obregón had his men dig trenches, lace the ground with barbed-wire, and set up machine guns. The lesson of the war in Europe had not been lost on him. Villa, according to script, led a reckless charge into the teeth of those defenses. It was as heroic and as futile as Pickett's charge at Gettysburg. The Golden Ones were slaughtered. Never again did Villa wield such power.

Carranza tried to consolidate his power and in 1917 he wrote a new constitution. For that era it was a very liberal document and included a number of pro-labor items, such as the right to strike, and eight-hour work day, equal pay for equal work, housing for em-

have been a day to remember. Carranza and his government scrambled to Veracruz. The Zapatistas came in from the mountains. Then came Villa's men in boxcars, with their horses, and their *soldaderas,* or camp-followers, all of them laughing, singing, shouting, firing into the air. A lively day indeed.

So the rebel chieftains were in the capital, but what to do then? They didn't have a clue. They were men of action; they didn't know how to run a government. They had only anarchy to offer. In Veracruz Carranza and Obregón made use of their time to refit. A month later Zapata and Villa left Mexico City and Carranza and the army returned. The two rebels did not hit it off; in Mexico City their men did not mingle.

ployees, and accident insurance. The constitution also aimed at breaking up the haciendas and distributing land to the peasants. The constitution took away the catholic Church's wealth and touched off a wave of anticlericism, even resulting in the slaying of priests. The Catholics were revolted.

Villa was still the gadfly. He tried to involve the U.S. in a war with the Carranza government. Villa's men murdered 16 American engineers in Sonora and raided the New Mexican border town of Columbus, killing some

Above, Pancho Villa sits in the presidential chair; His pal, Zapata, doffed his sombrero for the occasion. Right, an execution during the Cristero Revolt.

people and destroying property. President Wilson ordered General John J. "Black Jack" Pershing to capture Villa, dead or alive, and for 11 months the U.S. Army tried to do it, running up hills and down gullies. Some Americans were killed and wounded; a few guerrilleros were caught. It was all a lesson in futility.

What led to Carranza's downfall was that, like Madero, he lacked a sense of urgency. He didn't spring into action and that was what was needed. Time ran out on him. An election was coming up; he had hand-picked a successor, but when it appeared that the popular Obregón would be the winner, Carranza turned on his old commander and had him arrested. Obregón escaped, disguised as a railroad worker (it had worked for Madero,

came—and was assassinated.

Villa mellowed with age and stopped riding on his raids. He settled down in a hacienda in Parral. One morning in 1923 he set off for town in his Dodge car. He and his bodyguard were ambushed and assassinated.

General Obregón took over an exhausted country, drained by revolution, ravaged by conflict, plagued by foreign debt, and sunk in economic morass. Obregón was clever and resourceful, ambitious and tough. He imposed order and reasserted the power of the central government. The world looked on skeptically. People outside thought of revolution in Mexico as Western-style bolshevism.

Obregón's first job was to make himself secure. Pancho Villa, the terror of the north, was tamed with the gift of a 200,000-acre haci-

why not for him?) Since Carranza was trying to perpetuate his own rule Obregón, as the new president, had to depose him. Carranza boarded the train for Veracruz, the port of the dispossessed, but on his way he heard that government forces were on his trail. He got on a horse and rode north. He was shot and killed as he slept in the village of Tlaxcalantongo.

Zapata and Villa also came to violent ends. In 1919 a colonel in the federal army sent word to Zapata that he and his detachment were anxious to defect to Zapata. He offered in blood proof of his sincerity: he had a bunch of fellow government troops slaughtered. Then the colonel invited Zapata to a parley. The shrewd Indian did not smell a rat. Zapata

enda, and, as we have seen, he departed abruptly in 1923 at the wheel of his 1919 Dodge. Obregón needed foreign capital so he was forced to come to terms with the International Committee of Bankers and he renegotiated his country's 1.5 billion peso debt. Also, in violation of the constitution, he granted rights to the oil companies to continue exploration for oil.

Firing Squads, Land Reform And 'Los Politicos'

For economic reasons he cut down the size of the federal army from 100,000 men to 40,000. That played into the hands of a group of military men with ambitions. They led a revolt and once more the crash of rifle fire resounded in the land. But Obregón obtained arms and ammunition and even a few planes from the U.S. His government forces beat the rebels in Jalisco and Veracruz, and, as the historian Nicholas Cheetham said, "there was plenty of work for the firing squads."

Obregón began land reform and pushed it most enthusiastically in Morelos and the Yucatán, where there were no American landowners, but he was very circumspect in his native northern Mexico. There his personal interests and those of the Americans more or less coincided. Still, he is credited with distributing 2.5 million acres, a fairly modest amount, but still eight times more than Carranza had done.

Obregón was a cynical man and under him corruption thrived. A new class grew up—*los politicos*—men of wealth and position. Perhaps Obregon's most commendable achievement was his appointment of José Vasconcelos as minister of education. A man of profound insight, Vasconcelos built schools all over the country and imbued schoolteachers with a sense of purpose.

During the Obregón regime the civil government's never ending fight with the Catholic Church grew more enflamed. During the Díaz Porfiriato, the Church had regained some of its power and had been hostile to the government all through the years of revolution. By now the military and civil leaders who ran the show were more fanatically anticlerical than ever. They had legal support, as it were: the constitution itself. They harassed the Church; they set obstacles in its course. In 1923, the Vatican's Apostolic nuncio was expelled and so were foreign-born priests. Convents and church schools were closed. In some places sacrilege was perpetrated in churches. In Tabasco priests were forced to marry—or be shot. A running battle went on for three years and extended over into the presidency of Obregón's successor, Plutarco Elías Calles, who became president in 1924. It all reached a climax in Tabasco. There the fiery governor, Tomás Garrido Canabal, tried to destroy Catholicism. His gang of followers, called the "Red Shirts," tore down churches and shot congregation members.

On the other side, Catholic guerrillas—so-called *Cristeros,* whose war cry was *"Viva Cristo Rey,"* Long Live Christ the King—sprang up. They clashed with the *federales* in Jalisco, Michoacán, Guanajuato and Colima. The Cristeros battled for a pro-cleric constitution. At one point in the fanatical struggle the Church was driven underground and priests had to conduct mass in secret in cellars. Eventually a compromise was reached. Religious

services were restored and the government, while not rescinding the decrees considered obnoxious by the Church, agreed to apply them in a conciliatory way.

El "Jefe Máximo"

In 1926, Obregón, hungry for power, convinced the Mexican Congress they should amend the constitution and allow him to run again for president, in contravention of the one-term law. He had his way and was re-elected. On July 17, 1928, he was shot to death by a young man who was allowed to approach him to show him a portfolio of cartoons. The man was a fanatical Catholic and apparently he acted on his own, but many people didn't believe it. They thought they detected the hand of Calles in the act.

Calles became known as the biggest power broker in the history of elected officials in Mexico. He was smarter than Obregón and a much better administrator. Under Calles schools were built, miles of road were carved out, irrigation projects were started. He renegotiated his country's debts; he gave guarantees to private enterprise. He distributed seven million acres. He named the labor leader Luis Morones as his secretary of labor and industry and thus just about eliminated strikes. A shrewd operator.

But under Calles political and moral standards fell. His detractors likened him to a Fascist dictator. He founded a political party, the PNR, or National Revolutionary Party, and through it he controlled his own and subsequent elections (he named his successors: Ortiz Rubio and Abelardo Rodrigues). He brought under the PNR umbrella diverse factions, such as labor, the farmers, the military. The *Callistas* pledged allegiance to him. That was the tight little group of financiers and industrialists and to them he was the *Jefe Máximo,* the top leader. If Obregón was merely ambitious, then Calles lusted for power. If Obregón was at least genial and likeable, then Calles was as loveable as a mud hen. If under Obregón the poison weed of corruption took root, under Calles it grew into full, ugly bloom.

Popular Lázaro Cárdenas

Calles' power ended with the election of General Lázaro Cárdenas in 1934. A mestizo, Cárdenas was a refreshing change: a chief executive who was honest, austere, a bit pawky, as the Scots say, but impeccable. He did more for the common man than any president in the history of modern Mexico. He was, they felt, *número uno.* A Socialist, he was deep in his heart, first of all, a Mexican nationalist, full of pride, full of spirit, gutty.

From 1934 to 1940, 45 million acres were distributed. Perhaps Cárdenas went too fast; some of the biggest, but most efficiently-run haciendas were broken up, which led, naturally, to a fall in agricultural output. The farm cooperatives he sponsored were not efficient enough to make up the loss. Cárdenas had to slow the drive down. The government issued certificates of exemption (from appropriation) to land owners who ran very efficient operations.

Cárdenas encouraged the labor unions. In 1936, Vicente Lombardo Toledano, a Marxist, founded the CTM, the *Confederación de Trabajadores Mexicanos,* or Confederation of Mexican Workers. Cárdenas, who has a

give in. Six months of bickering went on and then the union called a strike. Cárdenas stepped into the strike, appointed a commission, and the commission found for the workers. The companies were ordered to grant a 27 percent wage hike. They appealed to the Mexican Supreme Court. Another six months went by before a ruling was handed down. The court granted the workers' demand and gave the companies a week to pay off. More maneuvering went on. Finally, Cárdenas had enough.

He broadcast on public radio that he was appropriating the oil companies' property and nationalizing the industry. Mexicans cheered. The British were incensed. Mexicans broke off diplomatic relations. President Roosevelt was in office, and of

special fondness for rural people, welded the agrarian movement into one big, government-sponsored group, the CNC, the Confederación Nacional de Campesinos, or National Federation of Farmers. With those two acronym organizations behind him, Cárdenas had a broad political base. Though he listened to Marxists (Lombardo Toledano, for one, was an orator, a writer: persuasive and able), he took orders from no one.

Oil Is Nationalized

Also in 1936, the CTM demanded pay raises and fringe benefits from the foreign oil companies. The companies—American and British—agreed to talk, but were not about to

course, he was the chief advocate of the "Good Neighbor" policy with Latin America. So the U.S. State Department presented what was a comparatively soft note of protest, pointing out that it was Mexico's duty to pay fair compensation. The mills ground very slowly: a settlement with the U.S. oil companies was not concluded until 1942. It amounted to $24 million, plus interest. Payment to the British took even longer. It amounted to $81 million. Tuppence h'apenny, they might have said, when you realize the value of oil these days.

The whole country mobilized to pay for the nationalization of the petroleum industry; here, rural women arrive with chickens as their contribution.

MEXICO SINCE WORLD WAR II

Between World War II and 1982, Mexico's population jumped from 22 million to 72 million—50 million in 40 years. That surging population is an awesome fact that Mexican presidents have to contend with. Mexico, for example, needs 800,000 new jobs every year.

Manuel Ávila Camacho (1940–1946) was president during the years of World War II. A middle-of-the-roader, he stressed economic growth. With the world in flames, it was clear that Mexico had to learn to stand on its own feet so he encouraged the building of light and heavy industry.

Alemán, The Builder

Miguel Alemán (1946–1952) was the first civilian president in Mexico since Madero. A wealthy lawyer, but a champion of labor, he changed the name of Mexico's ruling political party to the Institutionalized Revolutionary Party (PRI). The thinking went like this: that the revolution was permanent—the goal had not yet been reached, but the revolutionaries had planted the seed and it was thriving. Alemán was the former governor of Veracruz and he had resigned that post to run Ávila Camacho's political campaign. He was a mover and a shaker. He campaigned for foreign investment; he improved communications and education and generally raised the standard of living. With an eye on President Roosevelt's "Braintrust," he drafted smart young men into government service. He modernized the railroad system, tied the nation together in a road network, started the vast Papalopan Valley project (modeled obviously after the Tennessee Valley Authority).

However, his biggest achievement was the construction of University City. The National University of Mexico is the oldest university in the New World. It was created by an edict of Charles V of Spain on September 21, 1551. One of the most impressive university campuses in the world, it covers almost 8 square kilometers (three square miles) of buildings adorned with murals by Mexican artists such as Diego Rivera and David Alfaro Siqueiros, among the greatest muralists in the world.

Alemán invited President Truman down for a visit and the man from Missouri came and laid a wreath on the monument to the Niños Heroes, the boy heroes of the century-old war with the U.S. which the Mexicans never have forgotten. It was a thoughtful gesture, and the Mexicans, who are among the most polite people in the world, responded.

The next president, Adolfo Ruiz Cortines (1952–1958), is known to historians as the "Great Consolidator" who tried to consolidate Alemán's gains. He enfranchised women and encouraged foreign investment. American corporate business came down in a hurry to Mexico. Everybody from Nabisco to Sears. But domestic responsibilities continued to grow: by 1958 Mexico had 32 million people; the population had doubled in 24 years.

'Within the Constitution'

Adolfo López Mateos (1958–1964), the next president, was a man of energy, verve, and personality. Under Ruiz Cortines, the revolution had basked in the sun; under López Mateos it came alive again. He realized there was trouble in the land; that the great promises had gone unfulfilled. His forthrightness won the support of the young. He encouraged industry; he sought foreign capital. But he also distributed 30 million acres to the landless, the best record since Cárdenas. He bought out American and Canadian industrial interests (Mexico's movie company, for instance, had been owned by American interests). He stepped up welfare projects, expanded medical care and old age assistance programs, and built public housing.

"I am to the left, but within the constitution," were his famous words. But at the same time he was harsh on *politicos* who were to the *left* of the constitution. He jailed the Communist muralist Siqueiros and kicked out the Communist leadership of the railroad and the teachers' unions. He called out the troops to put down a railroad strike. Yet he also pushed through a law calling for profit-sharing for workers. It was a while in the making but eventually workers covered by the law won yearly five to 10 percent bonuses from their employers.

Fidel Castro came to power in 1959. López Mateos voted against Cuba's expulsion from the Organization of American States and he retained diplomatic relations with Cuba, thereby arousing American annoyance. Yet he condemned Castro in 1962 for permitting the Russians to bring missiles to Cuba. Obviously he was his own man.

Left, you can still rely on the shoe shine man to bring a sheen to your shoes.

Troubled Times

Gustavo Díaz Ordaz (1964–1970), a conservative from Puebla, was president during a time of stress. The PRI didn't realize trouble was brewing and how widespread it would be. It was not long before students were in revolt and campuses were aflame. In 1968 student rioting broke out. The rioters were well organized and aggressive. They could call out half a million people at a rally. In response, the government ordered out troops to maintain order. It was inevitable that clashes would take place and that people would be killed.

There were a number of preliminary skirmishes but the big battle took place on October 2, 1968 in the Plaza of the Three Cultures in the district of Tlatelolco, in central Mexico City. It was just a small demonstration. The police ordered the demonstrators to disband; they refused. Police and army units moved in with clubs and tear gas. What happened then is speculation. Someone fired a shot—whether a soldier or a policeman or a sniper from a nearby apartment building, no one really knows. The police and the soldiers fired small arms and machine guns. The snipers returned the fire. People were caught in the crossfire. Newspaper stories quoted the government as saying 43 persons were killed. Government critics placed the number at from 200 to 400. Two thousand people were jailed.

A man of energy, Luis Echeverría Álvarez (1970–1976) roamed the country before his inauguration as president and visited close to 1,000 communities. He talked to farmers in the fields and workers at their lathes. Echeverría put great stress on helping the rural communities, even, if he had to, at the expense of industrial progress. He was well aware of the volcanoes smoldering; in fact, he had served as secretary of interior during the campus rioting and the bloodshed at Tlatelolco. (He had agreed to hold private discussions with the student leaders, but they had insisted that the talks be broadcast by radio and television and so they broke off.) Because of inflation, Echeverría put a tax on luxury items. Over the radio from Mexico City a sweet-voiced woman plugged Echeverría, calling him a man with a heart, a family man, a man who cares.

During his presidency, red guerrillas operated actively. A few held up tourists on the road; kidnapped and held for ransom barons of industry and foreign diplomats. Gunmen robbed banks and said the money they stole would bankroll "the coming revolution." One of the most flamboyant was a onetime schoolteacher named Lucio Cabañas who raised a guerrilla force in the mountains of Guerrero.

Echeverría brought young people into the government and during his presidency the voting age was lowered to 18. But there were still problems: the population was growing and inflation was roaring along at a 20 percent rate a year. In September 1976, the peso, which was set at 12.5 to the dollar, was devalued for the first time in 22 years, first by 60 percent and soon after by another 40 percent. Toward the end of Echeverría's term, peasants in Sonora seized private lands in the Yaqui Valley. Echeverría declared the seizure legal. His presidency marked a return to Mexico's revolutionary tradition, sometimes at the expense of efficiency and production.

Oil-Rich Mexico

José López Portillo (1976–1982) was far more determined than his predecessor in applying the laws governing foreign investment, but he did not appear so shrill about what he was doing. A law professor, he had served as finance minister under Echeverría. Thus he knew at first hand the financial condition of the country and that's why inflation and unemployment frightened him. He made it clear at his inaugural speech on December 1, 1976, when he said: "Unemployment and the confrontation it brings will weaken our democracy." He knew the government had to show results—for years Mexicans had been losing faith in their government.

Upon entering office López Portillo tried to bring a sense of calm and purpose. He knew the problems—poverty, unemployment, inflation. He tried to give his people heart. He early on set the pattern for his administration.

Suddenly, a bonanza—new and great reserves of oil were discovered. Mexico, the geologists said, was sitting on an ocean of oil. The government admits it has more than 40 billion barrels of proven oil and some experts claim there are up to 250 billion barrels in reserve. They say that by 1985 Mexico could be pumping 4 million or even 5 million barrels a day, twice the 1981 output.

López Portillo was cautious. Forty percent of the oil production is exported; three-fourths goes to the U.S. Mexico does not want to depend on one customer alone, even if that customer is right next door. It wants to use the oil revenues prudently to trigger the growth of other industries. It wants to be able to "digest" the oil revenues, and not permit those revenues to spark runaway inflation and its resulting chaos. Asked if oil would solve all of Mexico's problems, López Portillo said: "No, and to think so would be both naive and simplistic."

The economy grew by almost 8 percent in

1979 and by 7½ percent in 1980. The visitor industry bloomed. New industries sprang up. A new "industrial area" took root along the Mexican-U.S. border. But Mexico is still trying to improve its manufacturing sector. By 1980 the trade deficit had climbed to $3½ billion. It costs more to pay for imports and to service Mexico's growing foreign debt than the country makes from all of its exports, including oil.

The kind of economy Mexico has is neither capitalist nor socialist. Mexico is, sui generis, a developing country with a mixed economy. Given its historic relation to the United States, it is a country whose economic and political projects are tied inextricably to the economic and political directions of the United States. Mexico, however, is an independent country,

milk) were drastically reduced. The result was a horrendous cost increase for subsistence foods and growing hunger among the poor. Inflation, along with this drop in oil prices, has devalued Mexico's peso and prompted the nationalization of private banks to promote financial stability.

Refugees from war-torn Central America pose additional problems for Mexico. Seeking sanctuary from brutal repression in their own nations, refugees flock to Mexico's already over-burdened cities and have added their numbers to Mexico's indigent and homeless. Mexico has urged the United States to avoid a military solution to problems in Central America and maintains friendly relations with Cuba and Nicaragua. Needless to say, this has produced tensions with the

and in their dealings with the United States, Mexican Presidents López Portillo and Miguel de la Madrid, have made this clear.

Throughout the 1980s, Mexico has had to address a turbulent economy—one that continues to be haunted by massive foreign debt and rising inflation. In 1982, for example, an oil glut on the world market cut the demand—and price—of Mexico's chief export. In order to obtain loans from the International Monetary Fund, Mexico had to adopt strict fiscal measures. The peso dropped to 150 per U.S. dollar and government subsidies for essentials (such as tortillas and

Texas border patrolmen look across the Rio Grande for illegal Mexican immigrants.

conservative administrations of Ronald Reagan and George Bush. Drugs, making their way into the United States, have also become a source of Mexico-U.S. conflict—the United States recently issued statements critical of Mexico's inability to combat the production and distribution of illegal drugs.

Although Mexico's financial crisis stabilized somewhat in 1983, a disastrous earthquake on September 19, 1988, shattered all immediate hopes for prosperity and killed thousands. On July 13, 1988, amid opposition charges of election fraud, Carlos Salinas de Cortari was elected President of Mexico. Given current economic strife and evidence of political corruption, Mexico's future seems unpredictable if not a little forboding.

PEOPLE

Nine months after the first Spanish Conquistadores set foot on Mexican soil, the first mestizo—Spanish-Indian—was born. A majority of Mexico's 72 million people are mestizo. There's also a large number of Indians, a comparatively small number of Spanish and other Caucasians, and a sprinkling of blacks and Orientals. And, of course, there are the combinations of all these races.

Central Mexico was the melting pot. The Spanish moved whole communities north—Tlaxcaltecans and Tarascans—to act as a buffer against hostile Indians. Some of the northern Indians fiercely resisted the intruder—and still do. The Tarahumaras, the Mayas and the Yaquis hang onto their old traditions and their tribal lands. In the fastness of the Chiapas highlands the Tzotzils and the Tzeltals retain their old way of life. The Huastec Indians survive in the mountains. However, most of the descendants of the original tribes of central Mexico live in scattered villages around the Valley of Mexico. They include the Nahuas, the Otomi and the Mazahua tribes.

In southern Mexico, in the lands that no one else covets, live many groups—in eroded areas of Guerrero, Oaxaca and Chiapas, and on the thin limestone plateau of the Yucatán peninsula.

How many full-blood Indians are left? According to official census figures, between three and four million. But that is just the core—those who speak their native Indian tongue at home, have retained their racial purity, and their traditions. They live mostly in the marginal lands, the "zones of refuge." They are of infinite variety and of marked cultural differences. Some have been assimilated by Christianity; some have not. Most have learned to exist in tandem with Christianity; a sort of modus vivendi, partly Christian, partly Indian. They worship the saints, to be sure—and their old gods, too.

What has survived might be said to be a primitive religion with overtones of Catholicism and with emphasis on harmonious relationship between the physical and the spiritual world. Perhaps what distinguishes most Indians from mestizos is their orientation toward the community and not toward the individual. The mestizo's attitude is just the opposite; he and his family come first—the community is a distant second. Naturally, the Indians who have kept their culture alive are the ones most isolated from the rest of the country.

We have chosen to discuss in a series of essays a few of the 50 or more tribes who are among the most authentic descendants of the Indians of old. How they live and what motivates them makes them the most fascinating people of Mexico.

MACHISMO OF THE MESTIZOS

The fifty or so Indian groups in Mexico represent a remarkable contrast to their mixed-blood countrymen, the mestizos. There are great differences among the Indians, yet at the same time great similarities. In many parts of Mexico, the mestizo and the Indians often look alike. But the difference is there for the perceptive to see: the difference in language, of course; the difference in clothing, but most of all, the difference in their basic attitudes toward life.

The Indian ideal is to come to terms with life and the universe. The mestizo ideal is to control life. The Indian tends to accept things passively; the mestizo tends to strive to dominate things. The Indian is community-oriented; the mestizo is aggressively individualistic. The Indian willingly subjugates his ego; the mestizo revels in *machismo,* and the vibrant personality.

Mexicans have been inspecting themselves for generations. It was the Mexican intellectual Samuel Ramos who first took a penetrating look at his countrymen's culture. He said they suffered from a sense of inferiority which they responded to with "virile protest." They used their machismo as the "driftwood to salvation." He did not use the word *macho* but that's what he was driving at. He said the European glories in the pursuit of science, the arts and technology. The mestizo, he said, glories in the feeling that he has "a lot of balls."

Ramos blamed the Spanish rule for many of the attitudes still existent. The system of privilege, for instance. People get ahead through a connection with a local boss or a powerful national politician. Ramos believed that this personality cult is "as bloodthirsty as the ancient Aztec ritual; it feeds on human victims."

The poet Octavio Paz presents his insight into the country's culture in the *Labyrinth of Solitude,* a book that is essential to anyone who wants to understand the psychological makeup of Mexico. Paz's thesis is that the conduct of the Mexican male is a mask to conceal his solitude. According to Paz, the Mexican perceives that there are only two attitudes to take in dealing with others. Take advantage of them, or have them take advantage of him. "Screw or be screwed," in the violent language of the street. His honor requires him to face every adversity—even death—with a certain defiance. He must be aggressive and project an image of strength and devil-may-care. He must take the same arrogant attitude toward a business deal, as he does toward a woman. Machismo! To make money is not so important as to declare his maleness and to exploit his associate. A macho must use his power arbitrarily.

Malinchismo

"Sadism begins as a revenge against female hermetism or as a desperate attempt to obtain a response from a body we fear is insensible."

--Octavia Paz

The notion goes back a long time. After all, the country was born from the violent clash of Spanish warriors and Indian tribes. The Conquistadores raped and pillaged. One woman was essential to their conquest—Dona Malinche, the interpreter-instructor-adviser. She is the Great Traitor—nationalist Mexicans revile her; her name has entered the vocabulary. *"Malinchismo"* means roughly the preference of all things foreign to anything Mexican.

The two essential components of the mestizo culture thus can be summed up in the terms machismo and malinchismo.

Above, authority, a pistol and macho mystique; right, an exquisite mestiza typical of that fine Indian and Spanish mixture.

85

HUICHOLS

The ritualistic Huichol Indians of the Sierra Madre Occidental of northern Jalisco are a fascinating window to Mexico's pre-Columbian past. Anthropologists consider them among the people of Mexico least affected by Western cultural influences. Their home in the rugged Sierra Madres shut them off from the Conquistadores. Missionaries arrived belatedly—200 years after Cortés. The Catholic Church was not able to maintain its usual dominant presence because of the remoteness of the place and the cost. In the district of San Andrés Coamiata, for example, the current Catholic missions date back only to the 1950s.

Fire, Growth and the Deer

The Huichols, of course, have adopted Catholic ritual, but with their own embellishment. (For example, some choose to believe that the biblical Joseph won the right to marry the Virgin Mary by winning a violin-playing contest.) The beliefs of the Huichols are their very own and reflect a Meso-American theology that goes back to antiquity. The principal deities are the personalized forces of nature: Tatewari, fire; Nakawe, growth, and Kayaumari, the deer. The Huichols cling tenaciously to their lifestyle and customs. They earn a little money by working on the coastal plantations, through the sale of cattle and by selling their artwork. All contact with others, however, touches them very little: they remain Huichols, and the dynamics of their unique society remains relatively intact.

How did they get there? Where did they come from? There were two possible routes of migration, both from the north, passing along either the eastern side of the Sierra Madres, or on the western side, down the Pacific coast. The Huichols learned agriculture, it must be assumed, through contact with more advanced tribes. They planted corn; they hunted the deer. The old-time settlements were generally far apart, sometimes as much as half a day's journey. There is a myth to the effect that the gods ordered the Huichols to live far apart so that their women wouldn't have a chance to quarrel. But a more logical explanation is that they had to live on slopes where they could plant their corn, beans and squash. And because such fields are scattered, then so are the settlements scattered.

The Huichols hold their most important ceremonies—planting, harvesting, peyote gathering—in a centrally located *tuki* or round temple. The *tzauririka*, or singing shaman, leads the rites. He and the other temple officials are chosen for a five-year term. Almost every Huichol will have held several of these official positions during his lifetime.

Besides being the heart of religious life, the tuki serves as the center of social life. There the Huichol can seek help; there he can exchange ideas. Before a ritual the Huichol often go on a deer hunt. It, too, is an integral part of their lifestyle. There is little socialization between Huichols and mestizos, except during the big fiestas at San Andrés. Mestizos come to the festivals; they sell things, such as pottery, candy, biscuits, oranges and food. They also sell very potent liquor made from sugar cane. Mestizo musicians play—for pay. Mes-

tizo cattle buyers also come to call—as they always do—fiesta, or no fiesta. Huichols sometimes rent land to mestizos who work the land as a tenant farmer, for half shares.

So far there has been no threat to the Huichol way of life—neither from the mestizos nor from the visitors who come out of curiosity. But the mestizos want land for grazing, lumbering and farming and that presents a challenge. To cope with it, the Huichols will need to find competent and strong leaders and they will need to borrow the services of professionals—lawyers, surveyors, bureaucrats,

Preceding pages, a young Huichol signals with a horn to announce the return of peyote pilgrims; left, a shaman is given a sustaining drink; above, an elder is honored traditionally with a gift of food.

and the other accoutrements of modern living. What will happen eventually will depend in large measure on the attitude of the government and the implacable forces of economics. If the price of timber and the price of beef go up sharply, or if minerals are found in the land of the Huichols, then their way of life may be doomed. The sympathetic attitude of the government might fade if there is money to be made in the place they live.

There have been some signs of change. Attitudes have penetrated even the Sierra Madres. Some Huichols have picked up mestizo dress, and the use of the Spanish language. They are starting to learn how to bargain shrewdly and even to behave at times with an adopted arrogance.

their homeland. The soil's not right; the climate's not right. So what do they do? They make an annual pilgrimage northeast to the desert of San Luis Potosi to bring back the sacred cactus, which is so much a part of their life and religion.

A small "dose"—one to four buttons of peyote—takes away hunger, thirst, and even sexual desire. It relieves tiredness. A bigger dose—five or more buttons—results in hallucination. Under its spell the user can readily communicate with the gods.

Before they go pilgrimaging, the Huichol make elaborate preparations that go on for a day and a night. Of course, part of the ritual is making offerings to the gods. A shaman spoke of an experience he underwent during one of his pilgrimages. The memory stays in the

Mexican officials, to be sure, would like to incorporate the Huichols into the mainstream of Mexican life, but they readily understand that to change Huichol lifestyle would mean the end of his culture. And if the land of the Huichols is opened up, surely their culture will disappear in time, and with it a valuable insight into one of Mexico's most fascinating people.

The Sacred Cactus

The Huichols are most popularly known in and out of Mexico for their traditional ritual use of *peyote,* pronounced pā-ō-tē, a species of thornless, spineless cactus well known for its hallucinogenic effects.

Ironically, the Huichols can't raise peyote in

mind. He said he ate 35 peyote plants at a sitting—more than enough to hallucinate on. He looked up and, suddenly, sitting alongside, were two old men whom he didn't know. One of them told him to look into the fire. He did. There he saw a typewriter—the keys clicking away, but nobody was sitting there typing. The machine was going by itself. The strange old man at his side told him to pull paper from the typewriter and read what it said. He did so.

The funny thing about his experience is that ordinarily he can't read. He's illiterate, but now somehow he was able to read the words. No problem at all. All night long the typewriter kept clicking away, unattended, and sheets of paper with typewritten words kept coming out and the man kept "reading" and chanting away. A memorable evening indeed!

Next day his fellow travelers told him about it. They said he had performed the religious rite performed by a singing shaman. It were as though he had been doing it all his life. Obviously, he reasoned, the gods were trying to tell him something; namely, that he was meant to be a shaman.

It's 500 kilometers (312 miles) each way from the Sierra homeland of the Huichols to the sacred peyote grounds near Real de Catorce in San Luis Potosi. It used to be a 20-day walk. Nowadays the Huicho pilgrims walk for a few days from their home *caliguey* (temple), then they take a bus or a truck. They stop off and pay tribute at all the sacred places along the way. Sometimes the bus hurries past a sacred place and does not stop. It's not on the bus-stop schedule. But no problem. The pilgrims throw the offerings out the window as they ride past. The gods will understand.

Peyote Protocol

One thing you must do while on the peyote pilgrimage. You must confess your carnal sins. On the fourth or fifth night of the journey, a Huichol pilgrim ties a series of knots in a string of *ixtle* (cactus fiber)—for every transgression, one knot. Then the confessor stands in front of the fire, speaks of his extra-curricular sexual activity, giving details—names, times, places—and tosses the knotted string into the fire. The gods forgive him his trespasses.

There are other rituals and customs to be performed. The Huichol cannot eat salt during the pilgrimage; they are permitted to drink only a little water; they are forbidden most food. They subsist on plain *tostadas* (dried tortilla made of corn), dried meat, oranges and generous slugs of alcohol. One of the little games they play are the words that are used exclusively on the pilgrimage. Old familiar things get new names. For instance, the sun is called the "satellite," the nose is the "penis," machetes are "registration cards." And once they arrive in the desert, they must go through a series of purification rituals. This is sacred ground. The peyote lives here.

It's not easy to find the elusive plant; only a bit of it peeps up from the ground. The color of the peyote plant neatly matches the color of the earth; a wonderful example of Nature's camouflage. It takes two or three days to gather, let's say, 10 or 15 kilos (22 to 33

pounds) of peyote. They eat a bit right then to communicate with their gods. The rest is dried and taken home. It tastes—well, awful! It's extremely bitter.

Peyote contains more than 25 different kinds of alkaloids, with mescaline the most active ingredient. It has been used in religious rites by Mexican Indians since pre-historic times. What happens when you eat it? Usually you see flashes of color, then things begin to be transformed. For example, a plant or a stone may seem to be a living being. All sorts of fantastic transformations take place.

When they get back, the pilgrims must take part in yet another ritual before they can go home to their families. Everyone eats peyote at the homecoming—even the children. (They wash it down with a chocolate drink.) Peyote

is connected with the ceremonies of planting and harvesting and also with the deer-hunt. It is also connected to the rain god. The shamans take peyote so that they may have the wisdom to diagnose illness. Tribute must be paid all these many gods so that the crops will bloom; so that life will be good. It is a small price to pay for the arduous yet exciting journey into peyote country.

Tourists have begun to turn up in the Huichol country, especially during Easter Week, the only fixed-date festival in the Huichol calendar. Many are young people attracted by stories of the exotic Indians and their peyote. Some of these strangers find the experience among the Huichols fascinating, but many are disappointed.

Left, music for Huichol rituals is typically provided by a miniature guitar and violin; above, strands of peyote set out to dry during a gathering pilgrimage.

CORAS

For 200 years from the time of the fall of the Aztec empire, the fierce Cora Indians of Nayarit kept their loosely organized tribal structure and refused to submit to Spanish arms or to missionary blandishments. Not until 1722 were they defeated. The inhospitable Sierra del Nayar, their homeland, in the western range of the Sierra Madres, kept invaders out and allowed them to keep their independence. As the Jesuit missionary Father Ortega wrote:

"It (the Cora country) is so wild and frightful to behold in its ruggedness, even more than the arrows of its warlike inhabitants, that it

lords. They were used to submitting. Not so the other tribes in western Mexico. Nor could they be defeated merely by killing a few of their leaders.

The Cora Indians became the most implacable of the rebels in this part of Mexico. Their next-door neighbor, the Huichols, hardly figured in this chronicle of resistance, perhaps because they dwelt in an even more inaccessible place and were even less closely organized than the Coras. During the 16th Century much of western Mexico was in a state of frequent rebellion and war. The untamed Indians frequently embarked on their raids. As a counter-measure, the Spanish moved large groups of submissive Indians, including the Christianized Tlaxcalans, into new communities to act as a barrier against

took away the courage of the conquerors, because not only the ridges and the valleys appear inaccessible, but the extended range of towering mountain peaks confused even the eye."

Implacable Mountain Rebels

Nuño de Guzmán, a tough bird, conquered the lowlands of western Mexico, but left the mountain areas untamed and they remained strongholds of Indian rebellion. Except for the Tarascans, there were no tightly organized political entities in western Mexico which could be quickly overcome by the Spaniards' superior arms. Guzmán had the Tarascan king murdered and the Tarascans accepted the Spaniards as their new tribute-greedy over-

the forays of wild tribes. In 1616, the Coras joined in the great Tepehuan rebellion. All through that century they carried out raids on increasing scale.

In came the missionaries who tried to tame the Coras, but in vain. The Indians refused to give up their gods. The Spanish cut off the Cora's salt trade and sent the Jesuit priest Margil de Jesús to make a peace offer. The Spanish delegation was received by a splendid group of musicians, warriors and elders led by Tonati, the sun priest. But though they were polite about it, the Coras refused to bend to Spanish authority.

Later some Cora leaders agreed to pledge allegiance to Spanish rule if they could keep their lands in perpetuity and pay no tribute and have the right to pursue the salt trade without paying taxes. But not all Coras were willing to concede even on those apparently generous terms. Thereupon the Spanish decided that they must resort to force to teach the Coras a lesson. Their first large-scale expedition achieved only partial success. In 1722, the Spaniards, under Captain Juan Flores de la Torre, won a clear-cut victory over the Coras, but the survivors fled into the remote mountains. However, large-scale resistance was over.

The Morning Star: Christianity's Cora Competition

The missionaries who followed the army had the same old problems: how to cope with a recalcitrant people. In addition, at this op-

retained to this day. The missionaries also implanted the ritual of Easter, but the adamant Coras converted it into something uniquely their own.

So, in truth, the missionaries had little success in taming the men of the mountains. When Manuel Lozada led a rebellion that almost captured Guadalajara, the Cora Indians joined in enthusiastically. When the Norwegian explorer Carl Lumholtz visited the Coras at the turn of the century, he found they still practiced their traditional culture to a large degree. He found that the Morning Star was their deity who interceded with the other gods to help Indians in trouble. Lumholtz wrote that the Coras worshipped old stone figures and a large sacred bowl, which was considered to be the patron saint of the community, a

portune moment there was a jurisdictional dispute going on between the Jesuits and the Franciscans over who had the right to save those souls. The Jesuits won—briefly. Some 45 years later, the Jesuits were expelled from New Spain. The Franciscans set up missions in the religious centers, but except during the big fiestas these locations were abandoned by the Indians.

The missionaries did succeed in fostering upon the Indians a Spanish-style civil government of sorts and the titles bestowed for these officers—*gobernador, alcalde, alguacil*—are

mother of the tribe. It could understand only the Cora language.

Even today the Coras (there are only a few thousand of them) live their traditional life, working their subsistence agricultural plots and practicing their own kind of religion. Their money comes from the sale of cattle and of beautifully woven textiles. Like the Huichols, they engage in the ritual use of peyote. The shaman still invokes supernatural beings, and missionaries, who never give up, still try to influence them. The world has crept a little closer on dirt roads and landing strips for small planes, but the Coras still go on being Coras, aloof, proud and independent people of the mountains.

Left, Cora religious and civic centers lie in the few flat areas within the rugged Sierras; above, a group of Coras, painted black, celebrate Easter.

TOTONACS

A man wearing a brilliant suit of color is playing a flute and a small drum at the same time. He is dancing and leaning precariously backwards close to 25 meters (80 feet) up on top of a narrow tree trunk. The trunk sways in the breeze and there is a dramatic moment as the flutist regains his balance.

What is that man doing up that tree? He is the captain of a team and he represents the Sun. He gives a signal and four men who have been sitting at his feet drop backwards. Wait a minute. They do not fall; they are securely tied with a stout rope around their waists. They represent the four essential elements: earth, air, fire and water. They glide gracefully thirteen turns around the pole, moving out farther and farther, until they reach the ground, flip themselves erect, and land feet first. Four men, doing 13 circles each. That adds up to 52 turns, the magic number, and the number of years in the sacred pre-Columbian century.

'Those Who Fly'

The ritual is known as "Voladores de Papantla". It was started by the Totonac Indians and has been adopted by other Indian tribes. The Totonacs, who number perhaps 150,000, have maintained much of their rich cultural tradition. They live in the tropical coastal lands of Veracruz and in the cool highlands of the Sierra Madre of Puebla. The lands have abundant rainfall; irrigation is not needed. But a lot of hard hand labor is.

The Totonacs trace their ancestry back to one of the most distinguished of the ancient pre-Columbian civilizations. In ancient times they excelled at pottery making, stone sculpture and architecture. It was they who built the graceful Pyramid of the Niches at El Tajín. They were subjugated by the Aztecs and had to pay them heavy tribute. The Aztecs also took Totonacs for human sacrifice.

Cortés landed on the coast inhabited by the Totonacs and negotiated an alliance with their leader, who was known amiably by the nickname "Fat Boss." Thus the Totonacs served as porters for Cortés's army, lugging supplies and the heavy cannon over the mountain passes. Because they aided the Spanish they were given a small measure of autonomy during early colonial rule. They kept their communal lands; their leaders were permitted to exercise some power. During colonial times the land of the Totonacs yielded much wealth: they grew sugar cane, tobacco, coffee and va-nilla. But in time the rule of avarice took over. They were forced into labor on the Spanish-owned estates.

Upon them, of course, was impressed the Catholic religion, but they reinterpreted the ritual. "Voladores de Papantla" is an example. It is performed on the anniversary of St. Francis' birth. The rituals of antiquity still adhere. Ancient ways still dictate how the tree is to be chosen; how it is to be cut and transported. But the blessing for the tree and the dancers is performed in church. Often the tree, or pole, is set up in front of the church.

When the pole is erected, usually in front of a church, the Totonacs combine Christian purification ritual with their own magical incantations and the offering of a fowl, food and liquor. These precautions are to ensure that the pole will not take any performers as victims. As a final insurance measure, a live turkey is dropped into the post hole to "receive" the pole. This gobbling fowl is thus ritually crushed as a tree trunk is hoisted into its final position.

The ritual is considered a speciality of the Papantla area of Veracruz. It is a commentary on the times that the dancers have taken steps to organize themselves into a union to protect their own economic interests. (They perform often for visitors). They also want to protect the authenticity of the performance. One must regard skeptically the purity of the dance performed, let us say, in the Acapulco Center.

Outside of Acapulco, your best bet to see a performance of the "voladores" is near Papantla (Veracruz) right in the complex of ruins at El Tajín. A tall, permanent pole has been erected next to the Pyramid of the Niches and teams of Totonacs, usually from Papantla, perform whenever there are enough people to watch. For a reasonable amount of money, you can even arrange to have them stage a private performance.

The Totonacs live a precarious existence, caught up between their traditional lifestyle and the intrusion of the modern world. Oil has been discovered on their land. Large-scale cattle-raising also has pushed them off the land. They live on the basic diet of the Indians of Mexico—corn, beans and chile, supplemented with vegetables, and wild plants. Often wild plants are their only available medicine—as in ancient times. They kill and eat domestic animals usually only during fiesta.

There is a lack of communications; a shortage of schools. The local bosses often are arrogant and arbitrary; the land resources are diminishing. It is not a cheerful outlook.

Voladores ready to fly off the pole.

SERIS

'Those Who Live In the Sand'

The Seris—along with the Lacandones—are among the smallest in number of the Mexican Indian tribes. After centuries of catastrophic contact with the white man's civilization, most of the tribe died off. The survivors have been able to cling to some of their traditions in a part of their homeland on the Gulf of California in western Sonora. In 1600, there were some 5,000 Seris living, but by 1930 only about 175 remained. At present there are approximately 500.

ever saw. It is thought that the Seris battled the Conquistadores in skirmishes, during which they loosened poisoned arrows on the intruders. In 1685, Father Kino visited them on the shore opposite Tiburon island. He liked them; they liked him. But when he asked to be assigned to the Seris for missionary work, he was sent instead to the Upper Pimas. A German Jesuit, Father Gilg, was given the chore of trying to evangelize the Seris and entice them to settle down and stop their wandering. He estimated there were about 3,000 Seris living then. He had problems, it turned out. First, there was little good agricultural land in that semi-desert. Also he was not the *simpático* type. That is clear in this quotation from his writing:

"They (the Seris) live without God, without

The word Seri has been translated as "Those Who Live in the Sand." The Seris were one of six bands who formed an ethnic group. They called themselves *Kunkaahac,* meaning "Our Great Mother Race." They lived in the southern part of the Arizona-Sonora desert, along the Gulf coast, and on Tiburon island in the Gulf. They were hunters and fishermen. They put out to sea in reed boats and killed giant sea turtles with ironwood spears.

Father Marcos de Niza who was searching for the rumored seven rich cities of Cíbola was probably the first white man whom the Seris

A rugged old Seri woman shows the marks and wrinkles of a long life in the hot Sonora desert. Some traditions change, but not their milieu.

faith and without houses, like cattle. Just like they have no religious worship, so too one finds not even the shadow of any idolatry among them, since they have never known or adored either a true or a false deity."

Not quite true, of course. The Seris *did* have a local religion, built around animal deities, headed by the turtle and the pelican. Also, they worshipped the sun and the moon.

Father Gilg denigrated the Indians for their lack of understanding of the Holy Sacrament and the Christian mysteries of faith. However, he praised them for their good qualities. He said they had "none of the vices which have the upper hand amongst almost all heathens: polygamy, lewdness of half-bestial people; there were no rumors of seductions, although the silly thing (since almost everyone goes naked) must mightily excite them to it."

He did not have much success in teaching the Seris to live like good, obedient Spanish subjects and work happily for their white overlords. The Seris are proud; they rebelled. In 1662 there had been an uprising when a band of several hundred Seris fought the Spanish until the last Indian man and woman were killed. Their children were distributed to the mission villages.

Nomadic Wanderers

By 1742, perhaps as many as one-third of the Seris had accepted a settled life in a mission, but the others refused. They were nomadic wanderers; they kept the tradition. They were not tamed. They made forays; they stole cattle. The Spanish built a fort at Pitic in 1748 and tried to induce the Seris to settle on land nearby. They had a measure of success. But when the whites took the land from the Indians, the Seris protested peacefully. Thereupon the Spaniards arrested 80 families and shipped the women off to Guatemala and elsewhere. That was too much to bear. Inflamed, the Seris joined the Pimas and destroyed the mission at Guaymas, then carried out raids on Spanish settlements. But by 1769 a shortage of food weakened their will to fight. Many Seris surrendered and agreed to submit to Christianity and attend daily mass. In 1772, a Seri band destroyed a Franciscan mission near the present settlement of Kino Bay and killed the missionary. They were a resolute people. Their chieftains were the most obdurate. If someone challenged one of them, he had to fight a duel with the chief to determine who would be the big honcho. In 1775, a Seri war chief killed the Spanish governor Mendoza.

After Mexico gained its independence, the government tried to force the Seris to settle near Hermosillo. They herded men and women into Villa de Seris and sent their children to families in various parts of Sonora. But the adults refused to stay put and their children escaped from their foster homes, rejoined their parents and they all continued their nomadic life.

'Queen of the Seris'

In 1854, a Seri raiding party attacked along the Guaymas-Hermosillo road and captured a girl named Dolores Casanova, daughter of a prominent Guaymas family. Lola—her nickname—took up the Indian way of life. She became known as the "Queen of the Seris" and she was the subject of many tales. Even though the shaman, Coyote-Iguana, killed her father, Lola followed him to Tiburon island and had several children by him.

Near the end of the century there were only some 500 Seris left who still carried out raids. The government mounted a campaign against them and rounded up about 150. A rancher named Encinas set up a large cattle range and provided jobs and instructions to the Seris. But, unfortunately, the ranch happened to be a place where the Seris had traditionally hunted deer and rabbit and they felt that now they could "hunt" cattle, too. That was the background of the ten-year Encinas War between cowboys and Seris. It was not opéra bouffe; it was deadly serious. In one raid, 75 Indians were killed. Heavy penalties were set. For every head of cattle the Seris rustled, a Seri was executed.

By 1920, only a few of the Seris left were nomad hunters. Some settled temporarily outside a small Mexican fishing village on Kino Bay and got into fishing. There was a boom in the market for shark livers in the 1930s, so the Seris went shark hunting. They abandoned their reed boats and built sturdy plank boats and some bought outboards. The government organized a fishing cooperative with an ice house and weighing station.

Then came the 1950s and another source of income: wealthy Americans who had discovered the great sports fishing off Kino Bay. It was only natural by then that many organizations would take an interest in the Seris. Anthropologists began to study them; linguists translated the New Testament into the Seri language; Protestant missionaries made nominal Christians out of them. Prohibited to the Seris was their old and gaudy custom of painting their faces—all to the dismay of visitors and anthropologists.

And slowly the Seris appeared to prosper and increase. But those independents of old now have to earn money and spend it, like you or I, on clothes, food, fishing gear, medicine, liquor—yes, even on radios and automobiles. They have to make a living, sad to say. So they sell the fish they've caught; they make baskets, shell necklaces, and beautiful ironwood carvings of animals.

The main group of Seris, some 300, live at Desemboque. They still weave heavy, decorative baskets from a fiber called *torote*. The Seris fashion pottery and ceramic figurines, as well as shell necklaces. They are also good mechanics. It is said that a century ago they could shape a piece of equipment for their Mauser rifles, using only a file for a tool. Their skill is still alive. They now know how to keep their outboard motors in good repair.

LACANDONES

Another tribe that has been able to live its own life is the Lacandones, who up until comparatively recently escaped the ravages of civilization because they dwell in the vast Chiapas jungle. The inhospitality and remoteness of the place kept invaders out. However, that has ended. Over the years, lumbermen, hunters, merchants and researchers have arrived. They trade with the Lacandones, exchanging alcohol, firearms, food and clothing for precious wood, tobacco, and chicle. Tourists come there and think how picturesque the Indians look and pay them to pose for a picture. For the proper fee, the Indians will take off their pants and put on their traditional sacklike robes.

People of the Jungle

The Lacandones live in two- or three-family units. They worship their old gods and eke out a living from the jungle. They are few in number but they are still somewhat protected by the formidable surroundings which kept out the missionary. For what would it profit a missionary to venture into the jungle where he would find only a few souls to save? Better to descend upon a bustling village.

The Lacandones were seldom heard of until the French anthropologist Jacques Soustelle, and his wife, Georgette, visited them in 1933. Soustelle called the place a green hell. It was hard to get in and hard to get out of. Soustelle said no sun penetrated the thick carpeting. The ground was a mass of rotting vegetation; even walking was a struggle. Yet the Lacandones moved about easily. The trees looked tortured, something out of a nightmare. Over all towered the giant mahogany. There were endless immobilized pools of water which never gave off a reflection because the sun rarely penetrated below. There were few animals, except for chattering monkeys, and strangely, very few insects except on river banks.

This is Lacandones country—huge flatlands drained by the great Usumacinta river and by many of its tributaries. A land of lakes and waterfalls and plants and strange things which grow madly. That is their home: the heart of the jungle. Even now it is a feat to get there, especially during the rainy season, which is most of the time.

The Lacandones must rely on themselves alone. They have had to adapt. They know, of course, which plants are beneficial and which are harmful. By the time a boy is 12, he, too, knows how to survive in the jungle.

The word Lacandones comes from *Lacantun,* meaning Great Rock, an island in Lake Miramar and the home of their ancestors, who were a branch of the Itzae Mayas. The island was discovered in 1530 by Captain Alonso Dávila, acting under orders of Francisco Montejo, the conqueror of the Yucatán. That remote settlement on the island was destroyed by Pedro Ramirez de Quiñones in 1559. It was rebuilt by the Indians and then attacked again by Juan Morales Villavicencio in 1586. The Spaniards wanted to drive the Indians out of the jungle so they could use them as laborers. Unwilling to submit, the Lacandones set fire to their huts and fled.

To the Lacandones the most important deity is the Sun God. He is accompanied by the other gods in a complex mythology which father passes on to son. They believe the Sun passes the night in the subterranean world. They perform rituals and give offerings to insure that the Sun will appear promptly next morning. They believe the Sun goes "home" at night to a house of stone and that he eats and drinks like a human being. To the Lacandones the old Mayan ceremonial centers are objects of special veneration. They believe their god Atchakyum lives in the Yaxchilan

Chomping down on a home-made cigar, a Lacandone wearily eyes a visitor; these people are very susceptible to germs carried by curious outsiders.

complex; thus, small groups go there to make offerings of incense and food.

The fabulous Mayan center at Bonampak was unknown until the 1940s when the Indians showed it to an American who had been living with them. Soustelle himself was given VIP treatment there. He was shown a plumed, double-headed serpent of excellent workmanship, probably a Toltec inspiration. The Lacandones also showed him sacred red and black drawings, including hand prints, on a formidable cliff along the shores of Lake Metsaboc. The face of the cliff could be reached only by dangling down from the top, clinging to a strand of vines.

Soustelle found the Lacondones living in small clearings, walled in by the jungle. There they planted cotton, tobacco, chile, corn,

wealthy, for he will have the benefit of the work done by the daughters' husbands.

The Lacandones used to do a lot of hunting with bow and feathered, silex-tipped arrows. Their quarry usually was monkeys, then wild turkeys and wild pigs. The jungle is not the healthiest place in the world to live. The Lacandones suffer from malaria and rheumatism induced by the dampness. They also succumb readily to the white man's diseases. They often die of influenza; they can even die from a common cold. No visitor having a cold is allowed into their country.

Their contact with the white men began in earnest during the later part of the 19th Century when the mahogany industry started and access roads were built. Logs were hauled to

yuccas and bananas. There were never more than a dozen people in a community. They slashed and burned the land, used the clearing for three or four years, and then moved on. By then the soil was exhausted. There were not many children; the Lacandones looked for places in the jungle they thought would be favorable for women's fertility.

Because there is a lack of womenfolk, men sometimes "marry" infant girls. The husband lives in his father-in-law's house and works for him for a number of years. As soon as the child grows up, she cooks for her husband as soon as she is able to. The Lacandones' concept of wedded life is more about eating together than sleeping together. For a man to have a good crop of daughters means he is

the rivers, then floated to the Tenosique. Some Lacandones worked for lumber companies to get money to buy axes, machetes, firearms and liquor.

The few Lacandones who have managed to survive to the present have seen dramatic changes during the last few years. A dirt road (dry-season only) gives them access to Palenque. They also were given legal ejido title to vast tracts of their jungle by former president Luis Echeverría. With money received from lumbering concessions, they have bought trucks, clothing and other joys of civilization.

The French explorer Desiré Charnay took this formal group shot of a group of Ladandones during travels through Chiapas in the mid-19th Century.

TARASCANS

lages have won acclaim for their specialty: Santa Clara for its copperware; Ihuatzio for rush mats; Patamban for green pottery; Paracho for guitars.

Deftly handled by the girl's nimble fingers, the soft clay was quickly taking shape. Soon a jolly demon appeared under her subtle touch. He had horns, of course. What proper demon doesn't? He also had an irresistible grin. Again, par for a demon. You know the chaps. They are bewitched. She added him to her work: four devils having a party. At their feet lay another clay devil. Later she would paint them, harden them by fire in her backyard kiln, and take them to market.

The Tarascan village of Ocumicho specializes in making clay devils in great variety. An

'Chronicles of Michoacán'

Before the arrival of the Spanish, the Tarascans had welded together a militaristic empire strong enough to check the Aztec war machines. Perhaps because the Tarascans were a hardy people, the Aztecs considered them a relation, but, in truth, the Tarascan language is not like other Indian languages. Some people have tried to trace the Tarascans to a Peruvian tribe, but this again seems most unlikely. Consider the linguistic and cultural differences. At this point there's no way to trace

example: the devil riding a motorcycle, shaped like a fish, running over a snake. Tarascans go back a long way to pre-Columbian times. They were renowned artisans even then.

The Tarascan Indians live in the northern part of Michoacán around Lake Pátzcuaro and to the west on the *meseta* or plateau of Tarasca. Census figures differ widely as to their numbers; an educated guess would be around 80,000 who still speak their native language. Many also speak Spanish, too, of course.

Today's Tarascos are best known as fishermen and craftsmen. They make pottery, copperware, lacquered bowls and trays, wool weavings, guitars, leather goods, wood masks, hats, mats and furniture. Many vil-

them. What we do know about them comes largely from "The Chronicles of Michoacán," an illustrated document prepared by a Franciscan monk.

Shortly after the Spanish conquest, the Tarascans found they had a great friend and protector in the person of Don Vasco de Quiroga. A lawyer and personal friend of the Spanish monarch, he was designated a member of Mexico's Royal High Court of Justice. That same body had condemned the odious Nuño de Guzmán for his assassination of the Tarascan king, Tangaxoan. Consecrated as

Lake Pátzcuaro, among the most scenic spots in Mexico, has many Tarascan villages along its shores and on islands within the large lake.

priest and bishop on the same day, Quiroga went to Michoacán to Christianize the Tarascans and protect them against the abuses of Spanish landlords. Father Quiroga organized hospitals in the missions. He changed the capital from Tzintzuntzan to Pátzcuaro. He took some Tarascans to Spain to show people they were human beings and deserved humane treatment. He treated them with kindness and courtesy and they have never forgotten him. They bestowed upon him a nickname of affection—"Tata"—Father. Only one other white man earned that mark of respect and the nickname of Tata: Lázaro Cárdenas, himself from Michoacán.

Tata Quiroga encouraged the Tarascans to pursue their crafts. They fashioned impeccable feather mosaics for him. They modeled the

figures of their deities with a paste made of pulverized cornstalks and orchid extract. So light in weight were these images of the gods that they could carry them into battle. Perhaps it was Father Quiroga who encouraged the Indians to fashion the figure of Christ onto a corn paste and occasionally this art form is still practiced.

During colonial days the Tarascans had to adapt themselves. Caught between Christian strictness and Spanish greed, they had to tiptoe carefully. Trade was controlled by Spanish merchants; there could be no exchanges of goods between Indian villages. All had to pass through markets in white-dominated towns. The Tarascan artisans produced wooden furniture, leather and metal goods for the Span-

ish and pottery, mats and masks for their fellow Indians.

After independence some of their communal lands were turned into private property and purchased, often for a song, by whites. Under the Díaz Porfiriato this venality accelerated.

Making Fine Handicraft

Carl Lumholtz, a Norwegian explorer and chronicler of Indian tribes, came through the Tarasco land at the turn of the century. He saw how the Tarascans had adapted to their new religion. Farmers buried stone replicas of their old deities in the fields to obtain a good harvest. But at the same time they also appealed to San Mateo (Saint Matthew), who was responsible for fruitful harvests. Suppose the weather turned cold before the harvest was in? Then the Tarascans would dump San Mateo's image unceremoniously into cold water.

Lumholtz observed that the Tarascans were not able to live merely by working the land. Many had to devote themselves to making handicraft. Making handicraft was a tiring job. It took such a long time to fashion it and the work brought absurdly low prices. Buying and selling cooperatives did not exist. The artisans had to pay a high price for supplies. Yet the Tarascans persisted, and they still do today. They have continued to make their usually fine products. One reason is to have enough money to fulfill what is called their "cargo." This refers to a post of honor which brings prestige to the holder. However, cargo-holders have the responsibility of arranging and paying for fiestas. So it is not hard to figure out why production usually shoots up just before an important fiesta. They need the money.

In his effort to help the Tarascans, President Cárdenas tried to foster a sense of self-sufficiency in the rural villages. His idea was that villagers could participate in the national economy while at the same time retaining their traditional way of life. It was a dream that for many reasons has not worked out satisfactorily. Many Tarascan men must seek work outside their villages. It is impossible for them to make a living there. Some even make the long trek to the border to seek work in the United States.

If you drive through Michoacán, you will see artisans at work, especially in the smaller communities off the main highways.

On the island of Janitzio in Lake Pátzcuaro; a woman repairs the net used by her husband to catch that highland lake's delicious white fish.

TARAHUMARAS

Chihuahua's mountain fastness is the inhospitable place of refuge of the Tarahumara Indians who refuse to accept the Mexican way of life. Here they take their stand. For the Tarahumaras who wanted to keep their own culture there were only two choices: to fight and die, or retreat into the mountains. There are now probably about 50,000 Tarahumaras living in a 50,000-square-kilometer chunk of the Sierra Madres in northwest Chihuahua.

Fighting the White Man

Aside from a fleeting contact with a few of the Spaniards, the Tarahumaras first learned about the white man from Jesuits who made their way north from Durango at the beginning of the 17th Century. At first there was curiosity and the meetings were peaceful, but in 1631 silver was discovered in southern Chihuahua. The rush was on. The Spaniards needed labor for the mines. They forced the Tarahumaras to do the hard work. That touched off trouble that lasted for decades.

Some of the bloodiest revolts and reprisals in the history of Mexico took place in Tarahumara country. The first rebellion was led by Teporaca in 1648 and the first victims were missionaries. The Jesuits had tried to stop mistreatment of the Indians but they had little success. To the Tarahumaras, however, the enemy was the white man. Missionaries were white. In the intensity of their hatred, the Indians slew the missionaries and mutilated their bodies. That hatred led them even to believe ludicrous rumors about the missions. Such as a fable that church bells spread measles and smallpox.

After years of fighting, the revolt was crushed. But in 1690 another rebellion began and it, too, met defeat. There was always war. Many bands of Indians preferred death to surrender; others retreated into the inaccessible Sierras. Some Indians out of convenience accepted a superficial form of Christianity and were partially assimilated into the white man's culture. Obviously they could only stand on the lowest rung; they held menial jobs, but they stayed alive.

Mexican independence brought no relief to the Tarahumaras. Spanish power was gone but the Mexican government didn't have the funds to help and moreover was preoccupied elsewhere. Thereupon the warlike Apaches began to raid Tarahumara settlements. It didn't matter to the Apaches that the Tarahumaras were fellow Indians. Nor did it matter what religion—if any—they practiced. They were fair game in Apache eyes.

More trouble came. The law of 1825 opened unused land to colonization. Onto the best lands of the Tarahumaras poured an army of landless. The Tarahumaras were shifting agriculturists; they seldom cultivated their land on a permanent basis.

'People With Light Feet'

The Norwegian explorer Carl Lumholtz reported that the missionaries' efforts to induce the Tarahumaras to live in communities was largely unsuccessful. It went against the grain of the Indians. They preferred to move their homesites. Lumholtz said the missionaries exerted only slight influence on the Indians.

Many areas received only an annual visit by a priest. And as with other Indians whose contacts with priests were marginal, the Tarahumara ritual adoption of Christianity retained an aboriginal flavor. Christ and the Virgin Mary simply became another important male and female in the Tarahumara pantheon. The Catholic calendar was added to the aboriginal calendar. During Easter week, the Judases and the Pharisees dance, and Judas is burned in effigy on Holy Saturday.

Similarly, Christian Tarahumaras have their own way of interpreting the universe.

Above, cave dwellings are still used by some Tarahumara as one of several homes; right, as in centuries past, Easter is a cross-cultural holiday.

They believe that if rain fails to fall on time, it is because the devil has bound the Lord, hand and foot, and made him sick, or that the Indians haven't offered enough food to God. These Tarahumaras consider themselves to be the sons of God. (Mexicans, they consider, to be the sons of the devil.)

The Tarahumaras are best known as great runners. They dearly love a foot race. Not sprints, such as the 100 meters, but long-distance running. Long, long distance. Say, 180 kilometers (100 miles). Non-stop! Talk about the Boston Marathon. What's 26 miles in a marathon to a man who can run four times that distance? Lumholtz talks about a Tarahumara Indian who ran 960 kilometers (600 miles) in five days.

Races are held between two teams of up to

Mexico, the Tarahumara still make ritual use of peyote. It is used by shamans for healing procedures and other rituals. Lumholtz was told that when God left the earth to live in heaven, He left peyote as a remedy for his people. Our inquisitive Norwegian also found out that peyote was used as a safeguard against witchcraft and when it was applied externally was a good treatment for snake bite, burns, wounds and rheumatism. The plant was considered sacred and offerings had to be made to it to insure that it would not produce insanity.

At present, most Tarahumaras live in an enclave in the Sierra Madre Occidental. Perhaps 20 percent of them retain their traditional way of life. Their basic difference from other Mexican Indian types is not so much that they

20 runners who, as they move along, kick a wooden ball. They do it day and night. How do they train for such an arduous physical feat? Well, for one thing they abstain from drinking *tesguino*, a corn brew. Magic also plays a role. According to their unusual pharmacopoeia, the best remedy for a debilitating spirit is to smoke a mixture of tobacco, dried turtle and bat blood.

These Indians also are a betting people. Old men may risk their entire meager flock of goats, sheep or cattle on a race. With such an emphasis on running, it's no surprise that the Tarahumaras should call themselves, "Rar'amuri," meaning The People With a Light Foot.

As with other Indian groups in the north of

accept or reject Christianity, but that they desire to isolate themselves from other Mexicans.

There is no native organization that represents all the Indians, but thousands have come to large congresses organized by the government. Some of the local leaders demand legal titles to their land, schools and teachers, better roads, telephones, doctors and medicines, legal help, control over their forestry resources and political self determination on a local level. But other community leaders have no desire to integrate into the nation; they want no schools or roads because they feel these improvements will only lead to exploitation. They demand only the right to lead traditional lives—with no outside interference.

TZOTZILS AND TZELTALS

In the highlands of Chiapas, near San Cristobal de las Casas, live some 200,000 Indians, divided almost evenly between the Tzotzils and the Tzeltals, both of whom speak a Mayan dialect. They have been able to keep aloof from other Mexicans and retain their old way of life because they are stubborn, tough-fibered and committed.

This is marvelous country. A writer speaks of passing through "layers of cold before entering the cool mountain sunshine of the Chiapas highlands." The Tzeltals live on the lower slopes of Chiapas' central mountains

communities are made up of a central village and outlying farms, which are often a steep climb, several hours away. The civil officials reside in the village with their families, while most of the others live in the nearby hills. The village comes noisily alive only for Sunday market and the periodic fiestas, at which heavy drinking and setting off firecrackers seem a major objective to outsiders.

Spirits and Saints, Indians and the Church

Yet there is a key to explain the harmony of life in the mountains. Each individual has status in his community. He lives on good terms with all supernatural beings—the traditional gods, ancestral spirits, and saints

while most of the Tzotzils live in the same area above the 1,500-meter (5,000-foot) line. Both tribes keep their distinctive style of dress and cultural and social traits.

Often, though, there is no love lost on neighboring Indian brothers. It seems to be a tradition carried on through the centuries. When the Chamulas, which are a Tzotzil group, resisted the Conquistadores, the soldier-historian Bernal Díaz allied himself with the Zinacantecan Indians who lived only a few kilometers away.

Since there is no tribal consciousness, identity and sense of belonging are imparted by the community. So each community is separate; there is no tribal amalgamation. The

whom the Spanish introduced. The villagers offer food, incense and flowers to the powerful gods who control their lives. The villagers are comfortable with each other; they are on good terms with all the deities. So it is understandable that if someone leaves the community, they all feel offended. The wayward one is considered a traitor; he failed in his duty, he abandoned his trust. Shame on him.

The Spaniards savagely exploited these Indians. Their lands were seized and they were forced to work on plantations. During colo-

Above, drinking is an essential part of Tzeltal ritual; right, making traditional pottery at the village of Amatenango in Chiapas near Guatemala's border.

nial times, when no good roads existed, the Tzeltals were used as porters—beasts of burden—to carry heavy loads to Veracruz, almost 1,000 kilometers (625 miles) away. Many died. They were used to the bracing mountain air, not the debilitating heat of the lowlands. If they rebelled they were put down ruthlessly.

Relations between the Indians and the Catholic Church often were strained, and even hectic. Few of the early missionaries tried to understand the traditional Indian rites. They simply thrust Christianity down the Indians' throats. The churchmen sought to break up the Indian idols, baptize the heathens, and convince them to accept an inferior status and serve the Spanish. Their reward would come, they said, in the hereafter.

Local Rebellions

These uprisings were always local affairs—Tzotzils and Tzeltals could never get together and wage military action on a large scale. Most of the time they meekly followed the orders of the Church. During the revolution of 1910, the bishop of San Cristóbal talked the Chamulas into serving the conservative cause. An Indian leader, called Pajarito, or Little Bird, led a band who initially won a few skirmishes. But it was only a short-lived spree: Little Bird was defeated and his feathers plucked. He was, in brief, executed. Some of his followers paid a humiliating and painful price: their ears were cut off.

The triumph of the revolution did not put an end to Indian degradation. *Ladinos,* which

Such treatment was bound to spark rebellion. An example was the Chamula uprising in 1869. The Indians were tired of praying to a foreign god. They killed the white priest and on 'Good Friday they crucified a 12-year-old boy. They meant to create their own martyr; their own "Christ." With only a few exceptions, the Church backed the exploitation of the Indians. There was, however, the great benefactor, Father Bartolomé de las Casas who defended the rights of the Indians. But alas, he himself kept black slaves. His beneficence was not all-inclusive. By and large, the missionaries led a life of ease, even of luxury. And sometimes they paid for their indolence. Priests were killed during the bloody rebellions which flared periodically in Chiapas.

literally can mean "cunning" ones, exploited them shamefully. Labor recruiters, called *enganchadores* ("those who hook") would advance the Indians money for necessities or for liquor and then force the debtors to work off their debts in lumber camps or on coffee plantations. It was human exploitation at its most despicable.

In public, the Tzeltals venerate Christ as God, but in their homes they sometimes also worship Chulmetic, goddess of earth. They also believe in Uch, a supernatural being who helps makes the corn grow. There are Tzotzils who believe in Hz'k'al, a phantasm who is black and has a penis one meter long. Both the Tzeltals and the Tzotzils have established a sort of modus vivendi with Christianity, a live-and-let-live philosophy. Often they identify diseases with either the saints or with their own indigenous spirits. If the sickness came with the advent of the Spanish, then the saints are to blame for it. But if it already existed before the Spaniards came, then their own traditional spirits are behind it.

Some Tzotzils believe that the saints and the gods hold periodic meetings at which time they decide whether to punish human beings by visiting upon them an ailment, or by bringing on a bad crop. The Indians believe that the celebration of mass is a community obligation to the saints. Their civil authorities visit the dwelling places of the supernatural beings—the mountains, caverns, springs—and there they pray, play music and offer drinks and food to appease the spirits.

If even after these efforts, a person should become sick, then they deem it to be just punishment for his sins. It is up to the shaman at this time to intercede in behalf of the unfortunate one, who thereupon must recognize his faults and promise to lead a better life.

The gods, of course, play their role in the life of these Indians, closely connected with a man's first and foremost obligation which is to plant and care for his field of corn. In his mind it is his relation with corn which distinguishes man from animals. These Indians consider it a waste of time and energy to try to grow crops other than corn. Of course, this makes them the despair of agronomists who want them to raise a variety of crops. But the Indians believe that a man must provide sustenance for his family—and that comes from his corn crop. He should also have enough left over to be able to contribute some corn for fiestas. For the gods give to man and man must give to the gods.

Traditional, Timeless Beauty

In the Chiapas highlands the visitor will see some of the most gorgeous costumes in Mexico, such as finely embroidered blouses and soft woolen shawls. The Zinacantan men wear red cotton ponchos and straw hats festooned in ribbons. The women go barefoot—rain or shine or cold. They do not like to be photographed. They feel that if they are captured on film, part of their spirit may be imprisoned—unless, of course, you are willing to pay enough to redeem their soul.

Cultural assimilation, obviously, is an acute problem for these people. Sometimes the Indians seek to emulate the culture of the *ladinos,* who once exploited them. Rural-Indian school teachers might serve as an example of this disturbing phenomenon. Often the teacher denies knowledge of his own language and refuses to wear native clothing or to keep the Indian faith. But even though he may be barely literate, a teacher exudes an aura of prestige. To the Indians, reading and writing are magical arts. So the ill-taught teacher is respected, even venerated, and provides a model, albeit a dubious one, for other Indians to emulate.

It is once again a repeat of an old fallacy: whatever comes from the "outside" is better than the indigenous. Still, there are Indians who see for themselves the flaw in this reasoning. They recognize and cherish the value of their traditions and so far the Tzotzil and Tzeltal communities survive and continue to cling to their customs. But for how much longer?

That strange but perceptive author, B. Traven, wrote with great sympathy of the Mexican Indian. He said they still recognize that "certain immaterial matters such as the infinite beauty of wild flowers, or the possession of a little desert-like place, or riding an Indian pony into the rising sun early on a tropical morning, or journeying at night by a creaking carreta with a full moon popping up between the large horns of the bullocks . . . are worth more than certain amounts of money." Unfortunately, the glamour of "outside," consumer-oriented cultures is an attractive devil, but Tzotil and Tzeltal cultures have survived nonetheless.

Above, a Tzeltal official with typical and prominent cheekbones; right, participants in a religious festival outside their church at Tenejapa, Chiapas.

PLACES

For the visitor Mexico is heady stuff. Balmy, palm-studded beaches, spectacular mountain vistas, fascinating-cities, marvelous cultural monuments of antiquity. All-night nightclubs, great dining. Swimming, fishing, snorkeling, boating. And a land where men are macho (sometimes) and women sweetly demure (usually).

Because of very large recent devaluation of the peso, Mexico is considered one of the best vacation bargains in the world for the American and European traveler. The price is right. You can drive along good roads. Gas is cheap. (Make sure, however, that you buy auto insurance *for* Mexico.) You can fly down, or sail down, take a taxi in from San Diego or El Paso, or chug in on a train.

There's no way, though, to see Mexico all on one vacation. The place is too big, too diverse. Consider just a few highlights: the world's most incredible train ride, across the Sierra Madre Occidental, from Chihuahua to the Pacific coast; the 150-foot high dive off a cliff into Acapulco bay; tumultuous Mexico City; the Mayan ruins of the Yucatán.

It's a good idea to pick one region and "do" it. Or explore one theme: say, colonial architecture, handicraft, or market places. Down Mexico way you can't run out of things to see.

There is an old Spanish saying that if you wish to bring back the treasures of the Indies, you must take with you some treasure. In other words, you should be informed before you venture forth. Do your homework. Know the place.

It's a good idea, too, to know some Spanish. You don't have to be a professor. It's indispensable if you want to strike out on your own off the beaten track. Sure, *"Se Habla Inglés"*—they speak English at all the hotels and in the border towns and in Acapulco and Cancún, the meccas. But you need a bit of *español* if you take off on your own. No need to be grammatically perfect. The Mexicans will applaud your effort. They'll smile and think of you as *simpatico*—an *amigo,* or friend. It's one of the nicest words in any language, and, indeed, Mexicans are among the most polite people on earth.

So, *bienvenido,* welcome, to Mexico.

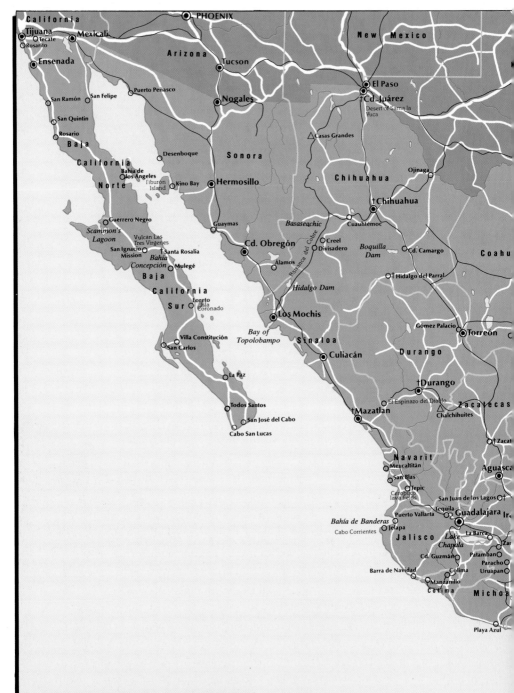

MEXICO: POINTS OF INTEREST

key to the symbols: O general interest site
† religious site
△ ancient site

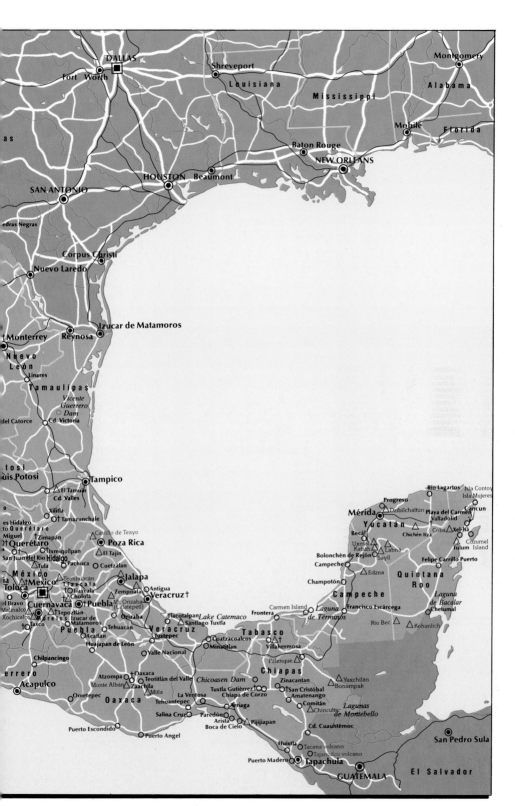

111

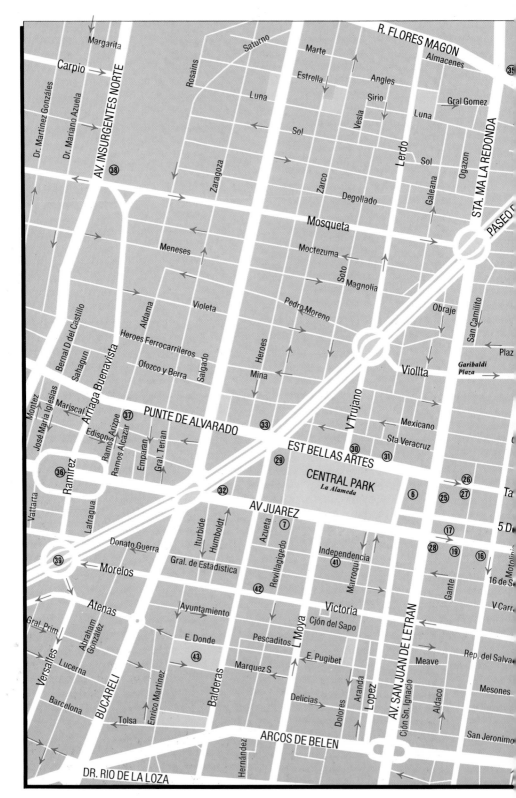

CENTRAL MEXICO CITY

key to the symbols: O general interest site
† religious site
Δ ancient site

1. La Merced (Market) O
2. Cathedral of Mexico †
3. Sagrario †
4. El Templo Mayor Δ
5. National Palace O
6. Palace of Fine Arts (Bellas Artes) O
7. Hotel del Prado O
8. City Hall O
9. El Monte de Piedad O
10. Museum of Mexico City O
11. El Hospital de Jesus †
12. School of Medicine O
13. San Ildefonso
   (Escuela Nacional Preparatoria) O
14. Ministry of Public Education O
15. House of the Marquis of San Mateo
   de Valparaiso O
16. Palacio de Iturbide O
17. La Casa de los Azulejos
   (House of Tiles) O
18. Templo de La Profesa †
19. Templo de San Francisco †
20. Templo de La Ensenanza †
21. Templo de La Santisima †
22. Templo de Loreto †
23. Templo de San Agustin †
24. Templo de Santo Domingo †
25. Correo Mayor (Main Post Office) O
26. El Caballito O
27. Palacio de Mineria
   (School of Mining) O
28. Latin American Tower O
29. Pinacoteca Virreinal O
30. Templo de San Juan de Dios †
31. Templo de La Santa Veracruz †
32. Santo Tomas de Villanueva
   (Hotel Cortes) O
33. Templo de San Hipolito †
34. Church of Santiago †
35. Ministry of Foreign Affairs O
36. Monument to the Revolution O
37. Museo de San Carlos
   (Palace of Buenavista) O
38. Central Railroad Station O
39. Monument to Columbus O
40. Pino Suarez Metro Station O
41. International Telephone Office O
42. Long Distance Telephone Office O
43. Crafts Market O

115

MEXICO CITY

You may hate Mexico City and find it terrifying. You may come to love it and find it fabulous. Hate or love, you cannot ignore it. Mexico City! Crowded, contaminated, chaotic. Mexico City! Compelling, exotic, even beautiful.

Sprawling Ciudad de México has the finest restaurants, the best stores, the most luxurious hotels, the swingiest nightclubs in Mexico. (Acapulco, of course, claims it has the bawdiest night spots.) In Mexico City is concentrated the wealth of the nation. Here is the power structure; the seat of government. Here is the finest in cultural life: music, the arts, dance. Here, too, is the heady breath of freedom. It is a place of opportunity and even the lowliest Mexican, gawking as he ambles along the Paseo de la Reforma, tests the air and dreams of affluence. Yet at the same time Mexico City is very provincial still, preserving many of the ways of life of her colonial and Indian past.

The city is surrounded by Aztec villages where Nahuatl, the old classical language, is still spoken, and on the 12th of December, one of the main fiestas becomes a great Indian celebration in honor of the Brown Madonna, Our Lady of Guadalupe. Apart from its exotic aspect, Mexico City offers a major share of Mexican art, in museums, buildings and murals, ranging from antiquity to contemporary, and all mixed in a surprising way.

The city is not just a huge, modern metropolis full of skyscrapers, freeways and people. The city has much to offer, but you must know where to look. And at the same time you must have patience, a trait which is the national virtue. In Mexico patience smooths the way; in Mexico patience makes the aggravations of life tolerable.

El D. F., La Gran Tenochtitlán

To begin with, something should be said about the name of the city. Although *La Ciudad de México* or *México, Distrito Federal,* are its official names, Mexicans call the city simply México (Méhee-co), or even, more informally, *El D.F.,* because the country is a federal republic. The capital is in a federal district—*Distrito Federal,* in Spanish. Of

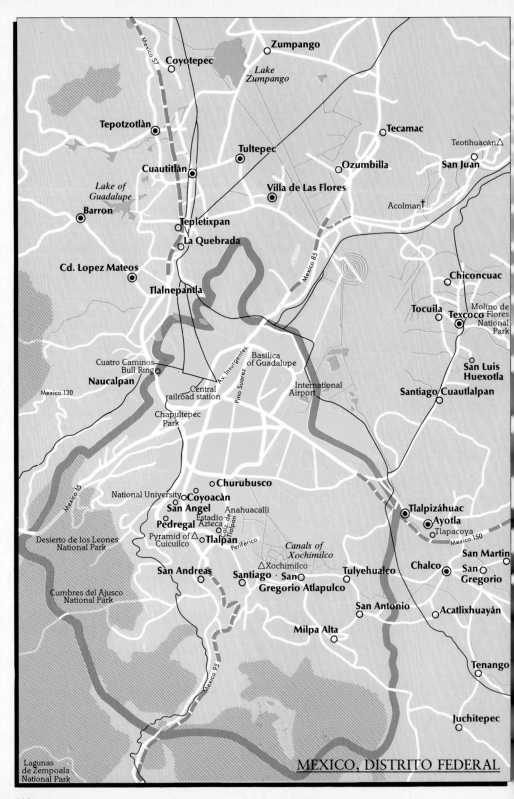

Zumpango

Lake Zumpango

Coyotepec

Mexico 57

Tepotzotlàn

Cuautitlán

Lake of Guadalupe

Barron

Tepletixpan

La Quebrada

Cd. Lopez Mateos

Tlalnepantla

Tultepec

Villa de Las Flores

Tecamac

Teotihuacàn△

Ozumbilla

San Juan

Acolman†

Mexico 85

Chiconcuac

Tocuila

Texcoco

Molino de Flores National Park

Cuatro Caminos Bull Ring

Naucalpan

Mexico 130

Central railroad station

Av. Insurgentes

Pino Suarez

Basilica of Guadalupe

International Airport

San Luis Huexotla

Santiago Cuautlalpan

Chapultepec Park

Churubusco

National University

Coyoacàn

San Angel

Pedregal

Anahuacalli

Estadio Azteca

Pyramid of Cuicuilco △

Tlalpan

Periférico

Mexico 15

Desierto de los Leones National Park

Cumbres del Ajusco National Park

San Andreas

Santiago · San Gregorio Atlapulco

△Xochimilco

Canals of Xochimilco

Tlalpizáhuac

Ayotla

Tlapacoya

Mexico 150

Tulyehualco

Chalco

San Martin

San Gregorio

Acatlixhuayán

San Antonio

Milpa Alta

Mexico 95

Tenango

Juchitepec

Lagunas de Zempoala National Park

MEXICO, DISTRITO FEDERAL

118

course, the city has outgrown the minuscule district and a large part of the metropolitan area is located in the neighboring state, also called—to add to your confusion—*México,* or *Estado de México.*

In grand old pre-Columbian days the city was named Mexico-Tenochtitlán, and Mexicans still like to refer to their capital as the *Gran Tenochtitlán.* But whatever you call it, the city is now an enormous metropolis where some 14 million people live. By the year 2000 the population may be 23 million or 26 million, or some say even 32 million, which will make it the largest city in the world. That prediction touches off a feeling of consternation, and at the same time, pride. Most Mexicans think that the growth of the city has been a miracle. Mexico City had scarcely a million people in the 1930s, though in colonial times it was the biggest city in the Americas.

After a naval siege (Cortés built a fleet on the spot), Tenochtitlán fell to the Spaniards in 1521. The city was burnt and razed by avenging Indians, allies of Cortés, who were delighted to humiliate and degrade their old-time enemies, the Aztecs. That should have been the end of the affair, but Cortés was shrewd. He built his new capital right on top of the old Aztec capital. Even then, sensible people were against the idea but political consideration was more important than expediency and so, in the middle of Texcoco lake, was built "The Most Noble and Loyal City of Mexico," a distant possession of Charles V of Spain, Mexico City.

Though no longer like Venice, the city was, in a sense, a floating city. Solid foundations were necessary in order to support the heavy stone buildings, since the soil was so watery and porous. The result has been that over the years most buildings in town have sunk, or they lean over, like the Tower of Pisa. Moreover, at regular intervals the city was flooded by the surrounding lake. Thus it was necessary to dry the lake up. Some suburbs in the eastern part of the city still are flooded every rainy season.

To compound the problem, Mexico City is also surrounded by volcanic mountains. There is **Popocatépetl,** the majestic, and **Ixtlaccíhuatl,** the beautiful, and a dozen or so minor mountains in the vicinity. This means that Mexico City was built in an area of frequent earthquakes. But don't be frightened. The

Diego Rivera's 'The Great Tenochtitlán,' the National Palace.

temblors of modern times have been mild and only lend spice to the excitement of being there. Only a few buildings have been damaged; modern Mexican architects are famous for their engineering skills. Mexicans will tell you proudly that the 42-story Latin American Tower sways gracefully in a 'quake. But, not to worry. Mexico City overcomes.

Being so big and so confusing, the city is not to be conquered in a day. It takes time. The best way to see it, of course, is on foot. Go walking and savor its charm. Here are some of the routes you can take.

El Centro, or México Viejo

Downtown corresponds roughly to the old Aztec and colonial capital. Small as the old Mexico City is compared to the present day megalopolis, still it is big enough to wear you out if you walk. Basically, it is made up of about 100 city blocks. Its boundaries, roughly speaking, are **República de Peru** to the north; **José María Izazaga Street** to the south; **Circunvalación-La Viga** to the east; and to the west what is now officially known as **Eje Central Lázaro Cárdenas,** but what everybody in town calls by its old names:

San Juan de Letrán and **Niño Perdido.** (You should be informed right away that some streets in Mexico City change names every few blocks. But, not to worry.)

The **Centro** goes from sordid to majestic. It is Spanish, Indian, French romantic, and modern. It is a business district, a market place, a colonial slum and a fancy shopping area. It is all very confusing but delightfully Mexican, and once you get the hang of it, it is by far the most interesting part of Mexico City. It tends to be overcrowded during the work week, but on weekends it has an exotic and even relaxed charm.

The Centro's center is the **Zócalo,** the popular name for **Constitution Square.** It was the main Aztec ceremonial center, with open spaces, pyramids and palaces. The Zócalo has been transformed many times. Up to a few years ago it was a provincial square: palm trees and a tram terminal. Now it is a huge flat surface, a convenient place for political rallies. It is imposing, too. There is nothing to impede the view of the magnificent buildings surrounding it.

The Zócalo is also the core of Mexican history. Walk around it and you will get a comprehensive course in Mexican art.

Rivera wit: a muraled Cantinflas takes from the rich to give to the poor.

120

Start with the north side. Here are two vast churches—the **Cathedral of Mexico** and the **Sagrario**. The cathedral, supposedly the largest religious building on the continent, is an encyclopedia of Mexican colonial art. Construction took three centuries. It was begun in the Spanish Renaissance style and finished in French neo-classical style of the early 19th Century.

The cathedral is huge and impressive and a rich repository of decorative art. Even in a quick visit you can enjoy its somber but magnificent interior, softly illuminated through contemporary stained-glass windows that give off a mellow, golden light. Like all cathedrals of its time, the Cathedral of Mexico is a complicated building, 100 meters (328 feet) long and 46 meters (151 feet) wide. It is organized in five naves, the central one being reserved to house the choir and the main altars. The main altars are *El Altar del Perdón* (The Altar of Forgiveness), which is used for the most important ceremonies; and at the end of the nave, the magnificent *Altar de los Reyes* (Altar of the Kings).

The **Altar de los Reyes** is one of the masterpieces of Mexican colonial art. It belongs to the late baroque style, called *Churrigueresco*. It was built and carved by **Jerónimo de Balbas** and finished in 1737. It is like a giant and overdecorated niche, in which two paintings, one representing the Assumption of the Virgin and the other the Adoration of the Magi, are flanked by golden columns, sculptures, moldings, angels, flowers and all those fantastic shapes of baroque imagination. This is the great Mexican *retablo*, all movement and color and madness. It was reserved for the expected visit of the king of Spain (who never came). The **Altar del Perdón** is located near the entry and it was so named because of the special benefits which it was said to confer to those who prayed and performed acts of devotion. It, too, is the work of Jeronimo de Balbas and again there is a huge retablo, crowned by a festive arch that frames a beautiful painting of St. Sebastian. The altar is flanked by a majestic organ. Apart from these altars, the cathedral has 14 chapels along the eastern and western walls. They are unusually dark and slightly secretive but some contain rare treasures.

The exterior of the cathedral is impressive and elegant. The main façade was

The Zócalo's illuminated cathedral.

finished by the famous sculptor and architect, **Manuel Tolsá**, but the towers are the work of another artist, **José Damián Ortiz de Castro**, who crowned the massive towers with two original bell-shaped structures.

Preserved by Faith

The **Sagrario** is the cathedral's neighboring church. Built in the 18th Century in baroque style, it is a graceful building with a highly decorated stone façade and a fanciful shape. Unfortunately, the constructor, the Andalusian architect **Lorenzo Rodríguez**, forgot to furnish the Sagrario with a robust foundation. The result is impressive cracks in the walls and an obvious tendency to lean a bit, as though the building were weary. But in Mexico City, inclined or even half-sunken buildings do not necessarily collapse. Faith, perhaps, keeps them standing.

The beauty of the Sagrario is the way it harmonizes with the cathedral, though the two buildings are totally different in style and shape. The best view is from the center of the Zócalo. It's worth walking around the cathedral, especially toward the east where you will find a picturesque square with a fountain and a monument honoring one of Mexico's heroes—**Fray Bartolomé de las Casas.** He was a Spanish bishop who dedicated his life to defending the Indians. He suggested, in good faith, that blacks be brought from Africa to do much of the hard labor, and that contributed to the infamous slave trade.

'El Templo Mayor'
And Diego Rivera Murals

Up to a few years ago, across the street from Fray Bartolomé's square there were a few seemingly unimportant Indian ruins. Those ruins, it turned out, are now the ambitious archeological project called "**El Templo Mayor.**" It's an attempt to explore the area where the main Tenochtitlán pyramid once was located. These diggings have already yielded rich treasure, the main piece being a great stone slab representing the **Coyolxauhqui,** goddess of the moon.

Toward the east end of the Zócalo is the **National Palace** of Mexico. This is the official seat of the presidency, though not the president's home. He lives at Los Pinos near Chapultepec park. However,

the **National Palace** is the seat of power in Mexico. In pre-Columbian times the Aztec emperor built a palace on the site. The National Palace is a complex building. Up until recently it housed the archeological museum, complete with a School of Anthropology. Now it contains two ministries: Treasury and Presidential Planning. There is also a rather somber and dull museum honoring Benito Juárez, Mexico's liberal hero. But for the visitor the Palace offers two main attractions. One is the building itself with its nobly proportioned patios, and the other is the murals on the main staircase and first floor corridors painted by **Diego Rivera,** Mexico's great muralist.

Though the murals are very good, they are like all of Rivera's murals—confusing and ambitious. The one on the staircase walls attempts to portray the entire history of Mexico—Indians, Spaniards, mestizos, *et al.* The result is somewhat like a huge group photograph of Who's Who in Mexico, from the creation of the world up to a future Marxist revolution. A note: the inflamed Marxist imagery in Mexican murals does not reflect the official ideology in practice, which is a middle-of-the-road political philosophy.

Detail, the cathedral's facade.

Rivera's mural on the staircase is a personal, naive, and charming vision of Mexican history by a man in love with the Indian past. Rivera hated the Spaniards to a ridiculous degree. He was a practicing Marxist, though he was a millionaire. (Indeed, he was even expelled from the Communist party.) But the mural, as a painting, is beautiful. Full of soft and glowing colors, and it reminds you of the late baroque retablos. Instead of saints and angels, however, Rivera painted all the heroes of Mexico that only a patriotic schoolboy has taken the trouble to know.

Along the corridors Rivera painted scenes that painstakingly represent pre-Columbian life. Utopian as they are, they reveal his great knowledge of Indian culture. The best of his works are in Mexico City. In the downtown area are two important murals, one in the **Palace of Fine Arts,** and the other, perhaps the better of the two, in the lobby of the **Hotel del Prado,** across from Alameda park. But if you like Rivera, you should go to two other places. One is the Chapingo Agricultural School, in the city of Texcoco, some 48 kilometers (30 miles) from Mexico City. The other place is **Anahuacalli,** the exotic Aztec pyramid-palace Rivera built in the south part of Mexico City in which to house his collection of Indian art.

El Grito Presidencial: 'Viva la Independencia!'

The National Palace is the scene of one of Mexico's most popular festivities, *El Grito,* or The Shout. This event takes place during the night of September 16, when the president of Mexico appears on the main balcony of the *Palacio* to ring the very same bell with which Father Hidalgo summoned the people of his congregation in Dolores and started the War of Independence. El Grito is a short but emotional ceremony. The president proclaims once again the independence of Mexico and the crowd in the Zócalo shouts lustily: *"Viva Mexico. Viva la independencia!"*

The other buildings around the Zócalo are of minor nature. The one at the south end is the **City Hall.** On the west side are private buildings of even lesser import, with the exception of the one that houses that vital Mexican institution, **El Monte de Piedad.** That means "The Mount of

A fanciful curbside shoeshine.

Mercy," which is simply an enormous pawnshop. It was founded by **Don Pedro Romero de Terreros,** a millionaire miner of colonial days. He understood that nothing is more bothersome than being short of cash and in need of a friendly loan. Since friendly loans were hard to come by in 1775, he opened the institution to help his needy countrymen, and made a friend or two in the bargain. And the Monte has become an important part of the life of the city, especially before holidays. Long lines form; people drop off a cherished family possession—a clock, a musical instrument. They need some *dinero,* maybe for a few days' fun in Acapulco.

With the Zócalo as a main point of reference, you can organize a visit to the Centro. Go east and you will find a slum where colonial palaces doze and crumble in the sun. Round about is a popular Indian commercial area, the heart of which was once the great La Merced market. This was the central market of Mexico City, arranged around an old monastery of which only a beautifully arcaded patio remains. The area is full of character. Near the San Lázaro Metro station is the huge **Legislative Palace,** built in a pre-tentious and boring style. By all means, skip it.

South of the Zócalo, the neighborhood is slightly better and there are two buildings worth a visit. One is the **Museum of Mexico City** (20, Pino Suarez Street), housed in the former palace of the **Counts of Santiago de Calimaya.** The palace is a good example of a colonial townhouse with a fountained patio, corridors and an endless number of rooms. Across the street from the museum is the chapel of the oldest hospital built in the New World—**El Hospital de Jesus,** established by Hernán Cortes. It is located in the very place where he met Moctezuma for the first time. The church has an impressive mural by **Jose Clemente Orozco.** All around are decaying colonial buildings. Among the celebrities is the house of **Don Juan Manuel** (90 Uruguay Street). It is famous because of its original owner, the outrageous Count Don Juan Manuel Solórzano. He had a most disquieting habit. He would walk in front of his house after dark and inquire of passersby what time it was. If they knew and were foolish enough to tell him, he thereupon set upon them and killed them on the spot. First, though, he offered them his

An urban 'gospel writer.'

congratulations because they knew exactly the hour of their death.

Gospel Writers and Cantinas

North of the Zócalo is the former university area of Mexico City. The new campus is in the southern part of the city. The other is the old campus. Two former schools are worth visiting: first, the **School of Medicine** (Brasil and Venezuela Streets), and the **Escuela Nacional Preparatoria**, also known as **San Ildefonso**. The School of Medicine faces the Plaza de Santo Domingo. In the portals people employing ancient typewriters write letters for illiterates. They are called the *evangelistas* or gospel writers, and they belong to an old and honorable Mexican profession. The preparatory school was a Jesuit school in colonial times. It played an important role in Mexican culture. The old walls are covered with classic Orozco murals, and murals by **Fernando Leal** and **Jean Charlot**.

Near San Ildefonso is the **Ministry of Public Education**, an uninteresting building that exhibits exciting murals by Diego Rivera. They were the first murals commissioned by the government after the revolution.

Downtown, crosstown traffic.

In the area (Honduras and Lazaro Cardenas) is another attraction: the **Plaza Garibaldi.** Garibaldi, as it is known, used to be notorious. It had taverns, street musicians, popular restaurants and assorted pleasures, including a redlight district. Nowadays it has become dignified. It is no longer its old self. It has been given a complete face lift.

Let's go walking in the Centro on the way back to the Zócalo. The two main streets are **Madero** and **5 de Mayo.** The atmosphere is mostly 19th Century but there are a few colonial buildings around; this is the business and financial district. There are nice restaurants, such as **Prendes** or **El Danubio,** old clubs and traditional hotels. There you will also find some of the best *cantinas* (taverns) in town, watering spots such as **La Opera, Bar Alfonso** and **La Luz.** They used to be male sanctuaries but a recent law has opened them to the ladies.

Colonial Casas

In colonial times this was a residential area and many *palacios* were built there covered with the red volcanic stone *(tezontle)* of Mexico City. Among those which survive three are worth visiting. One is the former house of the **Marquis of San Mateo de Valparaiso** (Venustiano Carranza and Isabel la Católica) and now the central bureau of the **Banco Nacional de México.** Another, and more attractive, is the so-called **Palacio de Iturbide** (17 Madero Street), which was a colonial palace. It served as the only good hotel in town during much of the 19th Century and now is the home of a financial company. It has been beautifully restored and decorated. Also, you should see **La Casa de los Azulejos,** the House of Tiles (Madero and Condesa), which once belonged to a colonial count and now houses a Sanborn's combination restaurant, drugstore and bookshop. The place is well preserved and it's a nice place to drink *un cafecito* and talk in the covered patio.

You can find almost anything in El Centro. One should not forget to mention the great colonial churches in the area: **La Profesa, San Francisco, La Enseñanza, La Santísima, Loreto, San Agustín, Santo Domingo,** but they are there especially for those who can appreciate their flavour.

Opened during colonial times, La Ala-

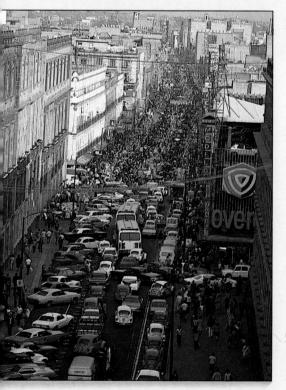

meda (literally Promenade of the Poplars) was the outgrowth of the city the Spaniards had built on top of Tenochtitlán. In the beginning the Alameda had many purposes: it was a park, a market, a site for the burning of heretics, one of the few entertainments provided during colonial days. But in the 19th Century the Alameda was transformed into a romantic park full of fountains, sculpture, and the inevitable music kiosk. Every Mexican town has a central square with trees, flowers, a kiosk, and at least one monument to a solemn hero. There are paths to walk along and benches on which to while away the time. The square is the heart of provincial life. So, too, the Alameda, which, in the middle of a noisy and chaotic city, is a fragment of laid-back provincial Mexico.

In the Alameda there is even a monument to Beethoven. Among the works of art in the square is the **Hemiciclo**, an operatic tribute in white Italian marble to Juárez, and two charming, though erotic girls, also in marble, named in French, **"Malgré Tout"** (In Spite of Everything), and **"Désespoir"** (Despair). One of the pleasures of La Alameda is to sit in a chair while a young man shines your shoes and you read a newspaper or gawk at the passersby.

The opulent cantina 'La Opera,' left; and below, the Casino Español.

Aztec Art Deco
At the Bellas Artes

La Alameda has important neighbors. First, **Bellas Artes**, the Palace of Fine Arts. This is Mexico's most important theater. It was begun in 1904 by an Italian architect, **Adamo Boari**, but was not finished until 1934 by the Mexican architect **Federico Mariscal**. That explains the double personality of the building. The exterior is pure *art nouveau*—full of flying sculpture and floral decoration, all in white Italian marble. The interior, however, might be defined as *Aztec art deco*—dark and reddish Mexican marble, looking monumental but with a touch of the sinister.

Bellas Artes is a combination of theater and exhibition hall. It houses a permanent show of modern Mexican painting and some murals desperately seeking more space in the narrow corridors. The Rufino Tamayo murals are full of cosmic poetry; the Orozco's full of violence. The Rivera mural was commissioned by John D. Rockefeller in 1934 for Radio City, New York, but Rivera tauntingly painted a militant Marxist allegory which hardly suited that center of capitalist endeavor. So it didn't last long there. The Bellas Artes collection also has some good David Siqueiros murals.

One of the theater's well publicized attractions is the stained-glass curtain, made by Tiffany of New York, and showing the volcanoes, Popocatépetl and Iztlaccíhuatl. It is a masterpiece of high-class kitsch. On stage the well-known **Ballet Folklorico** of **Amalia Hernández** performs. It's a colorful spectacle and fascinating, if not exactly a genuine panorama of Mexican folklore dancing. Visitors generally are thrilled by it; most find the folkdancing charming and well worth seeing.

Across Lazaro Cardenas Street from Bellas Artes is the **Renaissance Venetian** building of the postoffice (**Correo Mayor**). A few steps from the Correo, hard by Tacuba Street, is a touching new arrangement of Mexico's most beloved monument: **El Caballito**, or the Tiny Horse. The name is a Mexican understatement. The sculpture is huge and formal. It depicts the Spanish king Charles IV, who was highly unimportant; indeed, he was a nonentity. Napoleon forced him to abdicate in favor of Napoleon's brother, Joseph Napoleon. But Charles IV had the good luck of being immortalized by great artists. Goya painted a magnificent portrait of Charles IV's family; **Manuel Tolsá** sculpted the Mexican Caballito.

Tiny Horse has been galloping all over Mexico City looking for a permanent stable. Once he adorned the Zócalo; then the University's patio, and for many years he stood gallantly at the crossing of the Paseo de la Reforma, at Avenida Juárez and Bucareli Street. But as traffic grew El Caballito became a nuisance; he was in the way and had to be moved. Now he resides at his present location and appears to be satisfied there. There's plenty of space; he can be viewed at leisure. There are nice buildings for neighbors, such as the magnificent **Palacio de Minería** (School of Mining), also a work of Tolsá and one of the best neoclassical buildings in the country.

Among the neighbors of La Alameda is the skyscraper at Lázaro Cárdenas and Madero-Juárez, known as the **Latin American Tower**, 176.5 meters tall (580 feet). La Alameda is flanked by two important streets—**Avenida Juárez** and **Avenida Hidalgo.** Juárez is the most fashionable of the two, but perhaps that distinction is wearing off. It is lined with hotels, restaurants and stores that cater to the visitor. At the western end of La Alameda is a museum housing colonial painting, the **Pinacoteca Virreinal**. It's in a former church, **San Diego,** and boasts paintings from many of the colonial masters, such as **Echave, Juárez, Cabrera, López de Herrera,** *et al.*

Mexican colonial painting is not everyone's cup of chocolate. Of course, it is derivative from Spanish and Italian models. Always religious in subject, it tends to look somber. But it is consistent in quality and once you get the hang of it, it can be fetching.

The Alameda portion of Avenida Hidalgo has a completely different atmosphere from the cosmopolitan look of Avenida Juárez. Hidalgo is modest, more genuine. Two small colonial churches (**San Juan de Dios** and **Santa Veracruz**) face a tiny square and preserve some flavor of the old days. Nearby is the **Hotel Cortés.** This was not Hernán Cortés's residence at all, but an inn, **Santo Tomás de Villanueva,** built by the Augustinian fathers in the 18th Century.

Walking west, at Avenida Hidalgo and Paseo de la Reforma, there is another colonial church, **San Hipólito,** built at the spot where the Spaniards were defeated by the Aztecs on the *Noche Triste,* the Sad Night, August 13, 1521, when they tried to skip out of town. This small church is the only landmark commemorating the Spanish conquest that Mexico is so keen to forget.

Paseo de la Reforma, The City's Great Way

West of La Alameda, through Hidalgo or Juárez Streets, you come to the **Paseo de la Reforma,** Mexico City's most famous boulevard. It could be in Paris; it could be in Buenos Aires. It is one of the great white ways of the world.

Tall buildings line this grand avenue. The traffic is fierce. There is an air of excitement about the Paseo. To the northeast the Paseo is less exciting and less fashionable. You still see the traffic circles that are often clogged, undistinguished monuments and a huge housing development called **Nonoalco-Tlatelolco.** Nonoalco-Tlatelolco is not beautiful nor impressive but is worth a visit because of the Square of Three Cultures (**Plaza de las Tres Culturas**). The square is an archeological site representing pre-Columbian culture. There is the interesting and bold **Church of Santiago,** which represents colonial culture and the pretentious, and the rather bland **Ministry of Foreign Affairs** building. In 1968 the square was the site of a national disaster. Police and army troops shot and killed a number of students and others protesting police brutality and a lack of democracy in the country.

Stand for a moment at the hectic crossing place of the Reforma, Juárez and Bucareli. There stands the tall, dark tower, the **New National Lottery Building,** across from the **Old National Lottery Building.** Today a new tower looms against the skyline, the **Pemex Building,** or national petroleum building, which carries with it the promise of wealth and prosperity. From the crossroads the Reforma marches grandly along. Bucareli is Mexico City's Fleet Street, the street of newspapers, and Avenida Juárez becomes **Ejido,** at the end of which is the bulky monument to the revolution. It is perhaps the biggest art deco building in the world. In the beginning, the **Monu-**

ment to the Revolution was the huge central dome of the never-completed legislative palace. It was part of Porfirio Díaz's plan to transform Mexico City into a sort of brown-skinned Paris. But the revolution interrupted that grand scheme and the gigantic, empty iron structure was left to rust for years until an enterprising architect transformed it into the not-too-beautiful but nevertheless imposing monument to the revolutionary movement. There they are buried together— all those revolutionary leaders who in life couldn't stand each other.

Just across the street from the Monumento is the **Frontón México,** that sports cathedral to jai-alai, a Basque ricochet ball game that is one of Mexico City's great passions. A few blocks to the north of the Monumento is the **Museo de San Carlos,** housing a collection of fine European painting. There is some interesting 19th Century Spanish painting. The graceful neoclassical building, the former **Palace of Buenavista,** is worth a visit.

Farther north is the **central railroad station.** Mexican railroads are ubiquitous, marvels of railway engineering, and utterly unpredictable.

A Seine In Cement

During the Díaz regime the Paseo was a grand promenade, full of shade trees and every few blocks offering a monument. The grand finale, of course, was Chapultepec park, crowned by the romantic castle, El Castillo. Octavio Paz, the best known of Mexico's contemporary poets, said the Paseo was Mexico City's river, a sort of Seine in cement, majestically crossing the best part of town. It was the part of town that either looked like Paris or tried to look like Paris. But, alas, the Paseo's success was also its undoing. The French-looking mansions were torn down and in their place up went skyscrapers, big and little. Polluted air ruined the trees and plantings. Along came the automobile: *adios* horses and carriages. But even vulgar and proletarian that it is today, the Paseo is still a robust street; some even say a beautiful street. And so are its monuments. Going southwest toward Chapultepec is a monument dedicated to **Columbus.** A few blocks farther along at the crossing of the Reforma and Insurgentes is a monument to the last Aztec emperor and first Mexican hero, **Cuauhtémoc.** He ruled during the siege

The city's busy stock exchange, at right; and left, the domed Bellas Artes.

of the city by Cortés. Cuauhtémoc became the perfect romantic hero, valiant and doomed, and this monument to him is, appropriately, a fine blend of romantic sculpture and Indian art, as interpreted by an academic artist. It seems like something out of opera; Cuauhtémoc looks like a Roman senator wearing a feather hat. There he stands, the uncontested ruler of chaotic traffic at one of Mexico City's busiest crossroads.

The next monument on our monumental trek is perhaps the most beautiful on the Reforma: **El Angel.** She stands gracefully on top of a tall and elegant column, commemorating the country's independence. All around are towers and expensive buildings, such as the **María Isabel Sheraton Hotel** and the **American Embassy.**

The Curious Zona Rosa

South of Reforma and between Cuauhtémoc and the Angel is a district formerly known as the **Colonia Juárez.** Rather fashionable in the old days, it was gradually transformed into **La Zona Rosa,** or the Pink Zone, an elegant neighborhood crowded with fancy boutiques, expensive restaurants, hotels and stores which cater to visitors. Deep down, La Zona Rosa also aspires to a sort of snobbishness. She seeks to be considered perhaps European, perhaps international, a cosmopolite in the heart of Mexico City. Hence such street names as Hamburgo, Niza and Copenhague.

The result is rather humorous. This is not Belgravia, or the Faubourg Saint-Honoré. It is not even Los Angeles's Rodeo Drive. Yet it is colorful and chaotic— in short, Mexican. There are some good restaurants, such as **Bellinghausen, Estoril** and **Passy,** some nice boutiques and a lot of nightclubs. There is even a gay center. Indeed, cosmopolitans will find La Zona naïve and provincial, but lively.

One of Zona Rosa's curiosities is the huge circle where the **Insurgentes Metro Station** is located. In other cities a subway station is just a subway station; no more, no less. Here it is a pretext for exhibiting urban space on a grand scale. (By the way, don't visit the Mexico City Metro during rush hours. The reason is obvious. Go during off-hours.) The Metro is clean and some of its stations are fascinating. One called **Pino Suarez** boasts an Aztec pyramid, the real thing.

Cruising the Paseo de la Reforma, circa 1910.

It's no trouble getting around on the Metro: wall maps are clear and easy to follow. (Note: A detailed Metro line map is reproduced in the Guide In Brief section.)

Chapultepec Park's Romantic Ghosts

Chapultepec park is not only the largest wooded area in Mexico City but one of the few places for open-air relaxation in the capital. It is also a place of great historical importance. In pre-Columbian times, the city's drinking water came from Chapultepec because the lake that surrounded Mexico-Tenochtitlán was salty. From times of old, Chapultepec attracted Mexico's rulers who lived there. It is believed that the famous Indian king **Netzahualcóyotl** had a palace here. **Viceroy Matías de Gálvez** built a summer home there which, in time, became Mexico's military academy. During the Mexican War the invading Americans attacked the military school, known as **El Castillo.** Some teenaged Chapultepec cadets died defending the school and became great national heroes, "Los Niños Héroes, the Child Heroes."

If the Mexican War provided Mexico with the perfect heroes, it also provided the country with the perfect villain, **Antonio López de Santa Anna.** He managed simultaneously to affront both Mexicans and Americans. In reality, though, he was the ultimate *picaro,* or rogue, one of those colorful dictators so plentiful in Latin American history.

Chapultepec Castle also is inhabited by the ghosts of **Maximilian** of Austria and his empress, **Charlotte.** Their story reads like a 19th Century popular novel. Maximilian was the prince who became the tragic, short-lived emperor of Mexico, under auspices of France. When the French army left for home, the forces of Benito Juárez defeated Maximilian; he was captured and shot. Charlotte went insane and died years later, forever dreaming of the adventure in Mexico that went wrong.

Esthetically speaking, Chapultepec Castle is a monument to all those romantic follies. It now houses a **Museum of Mexican History** and is worth a visit. The Castle also is a good place from which to see Mexico City in all its grandeur. Also, if you like Mexican murals, at Chapultepec are some of the most impor-

acapoaxtlas, easant-clad oldiers, in dependence ay parade.

tant, including the Siqueiros hall painted with themes of the revolution. Chapultepec park, which originally was a place for simple relaxation, has a zoo, botanical gardens and a lake. There are museums and theaters. Visit the Museum of Modern Art, the Tamayo Museum, and, of course, the world famous National Museum of Anthropology, one of the outstanding buildings in the world.

Bravo, Velasco, Tamayo
And the Goddess Coatlicue

The **Museum of Modern Art** has a good collection of modern Mexican painting and interesting exhibitions, but to some the most authentic attractions are two small but beautiful permanent exhibits. One is dedicated to the great Mexican photographer, **Manuel Alvarez Bravo;** the other is a collection of landscape painting by **José María Velasco.** The Velasco collection is a nostalgic testimonial to the Mexico of old. Though not as famous as the muralists, Velasco was indeed a great painter.

The **Tamayo Museum** is housed in an expensive and clever building conceived by designers **Zabludosky** and **González**

de Léon. The musem has a rather nondescript collection of contemporary art which is not worth a visit, but it does have some beautiful Tamayos, including a grand and warm portrait of Tamayo's wife, Olga.

The *Antropología,* or **Museum of Anthropology,** is a classic building. Designed by **Pedro Ramírez Vásquez,** it offers a pleasant and spectacular arena with a patio half covered by an immense sculptured umbrella. It is one of the great museums of the world; *London Times* calls it the greatest. It is extremely large and takes time to savor. But even if you move around with dispatch, at least take in the marvelous **Sala Mexica,** the Mexican hall, dedicated to Aztec art and history. It is the jewel of the museum; it has atmosphere, it is enticing. There is, for instance, the famous **Aztec Calendar,** and the heroic sculpture of the Goddess of Earth and Death, **Coatlicue,** as well as a most entertaining group of models of life in pre-Columbian times.

Each visitor will find his own preferred hall. The museum is organized as follows: Introduction to Anthropology, Meso-América, Origins, Preclassical, Teotihuacán, Toltecs, Mexicas, Oaxaca,

On Reforma Boulevard, at right; and below, the Angel and a natty Zona Rosa jeweler.

Gulf Cultures, Maya and Cultures of North and West.

Once you have seen all these halls on the patio level, remember there is another museum on the second floor. This is the **ethnology museum,** describing the life of contemporary Indians. The museum is decorated with contemporary murals. Some are illustrations for the exhibits; some are there because they fulfill the national mania not to let any wall go unadorned. Outside the museum is the Paseo de la Reforma again which goes west to enter residential areas occupied by well-to-do Mexicans, neighborhoods such as **Lomas de Chapultepec, Bosques de las Lomas** and **Polanco.**

Follow Busy Insurgentes
To the Brown Madonna

Insurgentes is the great north-south avenue of Mexico City. It is not as beautiful nor as aristocratic as the Reforma, but it is a thoroughfare of convenience. It makes the city easier to get around. From the Cuauhtémoc Monument, crossing Reforma and going north you will reach **Buenavista,** the train station. A few blocks farther on is the western end of the Nonoalco-Tlatelolco housing development and the tall, triangular-shaped **Banobras,** a bank building. Farther on you will enter the wild traffic circle built around an operatic pyramid, the **Monument to the Race.** Like all people in search of an identity, Mexicans are obsessed with race. In theory, at least, they are proud to belong to *la Raza de Bronce*—the bronze race. Though that concept is glorified in murals, sculpture, and in the speeches of officialdom, many Mexicans, in truth, prefer to look as little bronze-like as possible.

A few miles north is the **Basílica of Guadalupe,** a major attraction. The church, whom some people irreverently call a *monstruosidad,* recently replaced an old colonial building and contains *the* image of **Our Lady of Guadalupe,** the **Brown Madonna,** which is a great national religious symbol. According to history, in 1531 an Indian named Juan Diego saw the Virgin on top of a hill near the present day Basílica. Miraculously, she left her image in his *tilma,* a sort of fibrous cape worn by Indians. This image became the symbol that is found in most Mexican homes, stores and places of work. Even buses, trucks and taxicabs

The fountain of Diana, off Reforma

carry a small altar, usually over the dashboard, a tribute to powerful Guadalupe. She is not only the Madonna, but the Mexican Madonna, the Indian Virgin. Mexicans have adopted her as their fighting flag and even hard-bitten politicians who are known as anti-clerics tread softly when speaking of the Brown Madonna.

On December 12th thousands of penitents make the pilgrimage to Guadalupe on the anniversary of her 16th Century apparition. It is a national holiday; hundreds of thousands crowd around the Basílica to serenade the *Virgencita*.

Permit us to retrace our steps at this time to the south half of Insurgentes. It is a commercial street, lined with tall buildings as it progresses toward the nicer part of town, **El Sur,** where even the air is slightly better. Among landmarks there are the huge **Hotel de México,** one of the city's largest buildings. It's worth a visit for two reasons: one is the revolving restaurant on the top floor from which you can view Mexico City spread out below; the second attraction is the **Siqueiros Poliforum,** a sort of chapel of the arts daringly painted by **Siqueiros,** top and bottom, and even on the ceiling.

A few blocks south is an uncompleted project for what was intended to be the **City of Sports.** Among the finished structures one is important—the **Plaza Mexico,** the world's largest bullfight ring. (On the south side of Mexico City on the Calzada de Tlalpan is another enormous sporting arena, the **Estadio Azteca,** one of the biggest soccer stadiums in the world.)

Chic San Angel

Farther south, Insurgentes takes in the fashionable village of **San Angel.** Once it seemed to be quite some distance from Mexico City but the city's sprawl now encompasses it. Somehow, though, it has managed to retain some of its own atmosphere and charm. It has crooked, cobblestoned streets and secretive mansions, many hidden behind high walls and fabled gardens.

Among buildings here worth a visit is the **El Carmen** church, which has tile-covered domes and a serene cloister. Every Saturday a handicraft market, known as the **"Saturday Bazaar,"** is open in **San Jacinto square,** a sort of upper-middle-class Indian market place. Also in

Entry area, the Tamayo Museum.

San Angel is a place full of aristocratic appeal, the **San Angel Inn,** a fine restaurant well worth the tab to eat there. A former hacienda, San Angel Inn is nicely decorated and serves good food. Wealthy Mexicans go there; they are folks who are nostalgic for the charms of a departed era.

There are other nice old villages in Mexico City's southland, such as **Coyoacán, Tlalpan** and **Churubusco.** In all of them are grand old houses that retain their colonial elegance. In Coyoacán don't miss the **Frida Kahlo Museum,** if you love Mexican art. This was the home of Diego Rivera and his last wife, Frida, a surrealist painter. In it is the memorabilia of Diego and Frida, including their love letters and Frida's colorful Indian dresses.

At Coyoacán is a drab and mournful museum-memorial to that first great heretic of the Communist faith, **Leon Trotsky.** It was in his home in Coyoacán in August, 1940, that Trotsky was assassinated by a Spanish Communist who apparently was sent on the mission by Josef Stalin. The assassin used an alpenstock.

The National University And Flowery Xochimilco

Insurgentes Sur, south of San Angel, crosses the big campus of Mexico's **National University** (UNAM). Constructed in the 1950s, it was for a long time an architectural wonder, breathtaking, dazzling in its bold use of color, murals and sculpture. Nowadays its prestige has waned; moreover, students have splashed away on the walls and statues with their own uninhibited brand of graffiti. Still, the campus is worth a visit. Of special interest is the central library where **Juan O'Gorman** covered the four huge walls with stone mosaic, and the stadium which is decorated with a brutal stone mosaic by **Diego Rivera.**

The campus was built on top of a lava field. The **Pedregal** part is one of Mexico City's posh residential areas. Here you see the expensive and elaborate houses with strange gardens sprouting out of dark lava soil. At the end of the campus, Insurgentes crosses the **Periférico,** a freeway decorated with modern sculpture. In keeping with the theme of modernity, a huge shopping center, called **Perisur,** seeks to resemble those lavish shopping centers which have swallowed up the suburbs of many an American town.

Near Perisur is another but different attraction: the oldest structure in the valley. It's the round pyramid of **Cuicuilco,** built perhaps as long as a thousand years before the Christian era. It's not handsome by any means; there it stands, remote as time, indifferent as stone, implacable, surrounded by the strange suburbs of Mexico City and glittering Perisur. Mexico City, the incongruous.

And not far from Cuicuilco is **Xochimilco,** a name that trips along on the tongue, the only remnant of the old lake city of Tenochtitlán. Xochimilco and floating gardens: the two are synonymous. Xochimilco is a floating village; its farm land is a sort of raft *(chinampas),* and instead of streets, there are canals bordered by tall cypress trees. On the canals barges adorned with flowers ride splendidly.

In the old days Xochimilco was the favorite promenade of the *capitalinos* (the residents of Mexico City). There they went to eat and drink and ride in the flowery boats. They always kept a photograph for a souvenir and there must be many a cherished, yellowing photo tucked away in an album.

Monument to Mexico's Constitution of 1917, at right; and below, the fascinating towers of Satelite.

136

MEXICO CITY
DAY TRIPS

East, north and west of Mexico City is the state of Mexico; to the south is Morelos. Just a weekend trip away are Hidalgo to the north; Puebla and Tlaxcala to the east. This is historic Mexico. With Mexico City as its core, this region is the heart of the country. It forms a mosaic of peoples and of geography that ranges from cold but stately pine forests to hot and humid valleys bursting with plant life.

Let's follow five routes out of Mexico City and try to make as few detours as possible. But, remember, please, that the really important things in Mexico frequently are those that are hard to get to.

---

1   North to Tepotzotlán
On Querétaro Road

Querétaro Road, an extension of a busy freeway in Mexico City known as the Periférico, starts in the northwest part of the city near the bullring known as **Cuatro Caminos Bull Ring** and crosses industrial and middle-class suburbs of the sprawling *norte* of the city. Along the

Gilded interior, Tepotzotlán.

way are the **Satélite Towers,** five tall, slender and brightly colored structures, designed by Luis Barragán and Mathias Goeritz. They are among the world's most attractive water towers.

Farther north, about 26 kilometers (16 miles), right at the toll gates is **Tepotzotlán,** famous for its magnificent church and monastery, which have been called one of the jewels of colonial art. Indeed, it was *the* place chosen to house the national museum of the art of the Viceroyalty. In the 16th Century the monastery was designed to serve as a school for Indians. Later it became a seminary for the Jesuits. A few years later it was converted into a museum and cultural center.

Rich Baroque Catholicism

Tepotzotlán is one of the masterpieces of Mexican baroque and late baroque style. It is different from European baroque; it is not just a transplant from overseas but a genuine, native product. Baroque goes well with Mexican sensitivity. In its lavish use of color and movement, in its excesses and in its unbounded imagination, are the soul of Mexican art. Perhaps Mexicans at heart are a baroque

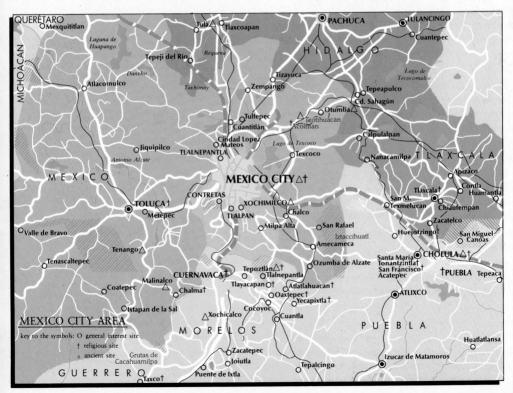

people, helplessly in love with color, with murals, with ornament. In them lives a fantasy that often verges on the surreal. So there is Tepotzotlán, noted for its fine baroque and *churrigueresque,* which is the name given to late baroque in Spanish-speaking countries.

The main church of Tepotzotlán, which was completed in 1762, has a rich but not excessive façade, carved in light-colored stone. It is typical of Mexican colonial churches: flanking the door and central window are four richly decorated columns which serve to frame the niches with sculptures of saints. Tepotzotlán has a single but graceful belfry, also deliciously carved. In the interior of the church, Mexican baroque architecture combines highly textured surfaces with clean, plain surfaces. All of which makes for a healthy and pleasant contrast. The interior of the church is a medley of golden *retablos.* The retablo, a gilded wood structure, grows and multiplies itself like an exotic tropical plant, covering the walls and transforming them into a mysterious, glittering surface. This results in an inspired way to frame paintings and sculpture. Inspect the charming retablo of Our Lady of Guadalupe, which boasts of paintings by one of the masters of the colonial era, Miguel Cabrera.

The retablos framing the main altar may be compared to the best in Mexico, such as those of the **Altar de los Reyes** in Mexico City cathedral. In good churrigueresque retablo, the identifiable element (column, arch, niche, molding) is twisted and decorated beyond recognition. It becomes part of a great unit, something on the order of an oversized piece of Oriental jewelry. Moreover, each retablo tells a religious story. Each saint, each image, has been put there for a reason—never by whim. In a way, it might be said that the organization of the religious images of a retablo is as precise as the seating arrangements for guests at a banquet.

In order to *read* a retablo obviously you must know who those saints are, and how they are related. Those in Tepotzotlán, of course, are all related to the Jesuits and their history. The church itself is dedicated to **St. Francis Xavier,** the great friend and follower of St. Ignatius of Loyola, founder of the Jesuits. The church is flanked by chapels. The chapel dedicated to **Our Lady of Loreto** is one of the curiosities of Tepotzotlán. It contains a replica of the house in Nazareth where the Virgin is supposed to have lived.

The chapel of Loreto has an eccentric neighbor: the **Camerino.** In the Camerino—literally, a dressing room in a theater—the clothes of the Virgin's images were changed. Here at Tepotzotlán the Camerino's retablos are carved in honor of St. Peter and St. Paul and the Immaculate Conception. The roof is decorated with angels, flowers, shells and paintings. You could not ask for a more charming dressing room.

The monastery at Tepotzotlán houses the **Museum of the Viceroyalty.** Among the favorite halls is number 15, which has a colorful carving of St. James (Santiago), patron saint of Spain, impersonating Matamoros, who led the war of liberation against the Moors. Santiago is among the most popular saints in Mexican colonial art. In hall 19 is a wondrous painting of the Virgin of Bethlehem, attributed to the Spanish master Murillo. In hall 20 is the "Wedding of the Virgin," by one of the best colonial painters, Juan Rodriguez Juárez; in halls 32 to 41 is a rich collection of ornaments, jewelry and other *objets d'art* used in the cult of baroque Catholicism.

Extracting pulque.

Tula's Atlantes

About 50 kilometers (31 miles) north of Tepotzotlán is **Tula,** an archeological center which played a major role in the pre-Columbian life of central Mexico. Tula was founded around the beginning of the 10th Century when Teotihuacán already had been destroyed and Mexico-Tenochtitlán was still in the future. Thus Tula is another link in the chain of cultured settlements that preserved the spirit of civilization in the Mexican highlands. Tula was founded by King Ce Acatl Topiltzín (Our Lord One-Reed), who was a member of one of the nomadic tribes known as Chichimecas. Tula became the capital of the Toltecs, a people of culture. Ten Toltec kings ruled Tula for 312 years—until Tula was destroyed by Chichimec come-latelies. Though there is no written history, myths spun about Tula are abundant. They thrive on the air of central Mexico.

The most important building in Tula is the **Temple of the Morning Star;** Tlahuizcalpantecuhtli's temple, that is. It is formed by a lower gallery, covered in pre-Columbian days by a roof supported by columns. Behind the gallery is a pyramid,

Atlantes, at Tula.

some nine meters (30 feet) high, supporting *atlantes,* or columns. Atlantes are Tula's most important contribution to Mexican art. They represent Quetzalcóatl as the morning star. He is dressed in warrior garb, wearing a pectoral in the form of a butterfly. On his back he carries a round shield in the form of the setting sun and in the center of the shield is a human face.

Atlantes are among the masterpieces of Mexican architectural sculpture. The bodies of the warriors, their clothing and their ornaments all conform to strict architectural form, yet they make a powerful statement.

Other structures in Tula have survived the centuries. Perhaps the most fascinating is the **Coatepantli,** or Wall of Serpents, raised along the north and west sides of the pyramid. Almost 2 meters (6½ feet) tall, it is crowned and decorated with that universal motif of ancient Mexican art—the serpent in motion. In what is known as the **Burnt Palace,** near the pyramid, is the *Chac Mool,* another typically Mexican art form. The Chac Mool is the reclining figure of a priest. On his chest is a receptacle in which were placed offerings to the gods.

2   Sacred Teotihuacán, Along the Road to Pachuca

This northbound road is the continuation of Insurgentes Norte out of Mexico City and leads to the exit of Teotihuacán and Acolman. **Teotihuacán,** of course, is a very important place, one of the holy places, such as Jerusalem or Mecca. It Meso-America, the City of Quetzalcóatl, and the city chosen by the gods as the place from which to create the universe. In more humble terms, Teotihuacán is a major archeological center, one of the best preserved and most beautiful in Mexico. But be aware: Teotihuacán is not spectacular in the sense that the Mayan cities, lost in tropical green, are spectacular. Its charms cannot be enjoyed by the frivolous; its beauty is subdued, even sober. It is the true beauty of the senses, the classic beauty. Even the landscape is simple and serene; not too dry, not too fertile. The hills are softly contoured and the valley is high and typically ample and Mexican.

The ceremonial center is formed by a wide causeway—more accurately, a very long series of plazas and esplanades, lined with platforms and structures and leading to a group of pyramids built in front of the great **Pyramid of the Moon.** The Spaniards named the causeway *"Calzada de los Muertos,"* the **Causeway of the Dead.** It begins at an enclosed square, called the Citadel and contains the **Temple of Quetzalcóatl.** Halfway between the Citadel and the Pyramid of the Moon stands the most impressive building of ancient America—the **Pyramid of the Sun,** the magic heart of all of this precise urban design.

Start at the Causeway of the Dead. You may get a bit of a shock at this moment for, irreverent as it may seem, here are located a shopping center and a minor museum. Leave them until the end of your visit. Save your energy for the long walk ahead. The Citadel is a huge square, each side measuring some 366 meters (1,200 feet), surrounded by four platforms crowned with small pyramids. The name is a misnomer. That military title—Citadel, which the Spanish called it—is totally alien to its purpose.

At the southeast end of the Citadel is a pyramid, the back of which was demolished and uncovered another pyramid, the beautiful Temple of Quetzalcóatl.

Nahua girls, Cuetzalan.

This temple is filled with exquisite sculptural decoration, based on the theme of the serpent in motion, and with masks of the gods Quetzalcóatl and Tlaloc, the god of rain.

Why did the builders of Teotihuacán hide such a marvel under the cover of a new pyramid? It is incomprehensible. But such was the custom in ancient Mexican architecture; all pyramids hide earlier buildings. The Pyramid of the Sun measures 220 meters by 225 meters at its base and 63 meters in height (721 by 738 feet and 206 feet high), not in the same league, of course, with the Great Pyramid of Cheops in Egypt, which mounted on the same base, reaches a height of almost 144 meters (472 feet).

Why compare the two? There is logic in it. Both were designed apparently as astronomical structures. True, each had a different *raison d'être*. The Mexican pyramid was not primarily a place of burial, but rather a sort of exalted platform on top of which a tiny temple and an astronomical observatory were placed. Admittedly, the Egyptian pyramid is much superior technically to the rather primitive Mexican pyramid. But human beings like analogies and comparisons and as a result there's no way to stop people from comparing the two pyramids, especially those who think that all ancient civilizations came from outer space and that places such as Teotihuacán, Stonehenge and the Egyptian pyramids are the result of earthly contact with Unearthly Visitors.

If you prefer another explanation, Teotihuacán and its Pyramid of the Sun are simply an expression of the importance given by an agricultural society to astronomy and the measurement of time. Considered in this light, Teotihuacán is a remarkable, but human, scientific achievement. Apart from its scientific value, the pyramid has an undeniable beauty attained by geometric simplicity and by endless repetition of the same theme. Curiously it is a repetition that does not strictly avoid the monotonous, but somehow produces a feeling of the sublime and the transcendental at the same time.

It is only proper at this point to speak of the improper. Teotihuacán could do without those inconsiderate people who merely come to trample over these sacred stones and who feel nothing for the place. But that is the way of all famous places on

Pyramid of
he Sun at
eotihuacán.

earth. Unfeeling souls come to gawk, not to feel. If you want to capture the essence of the place, come early. Or maybe you should make it a point to go there when the weather is bad and the crowds are sparse. Or come at opening time or near closing time. Or come in midweek.

Ah, but what magic there is in visiting the place at just the right time! Say, when the sun is setting and illuminates the buildings with a soft and eerie light. It is then that Teotihuacán seems transformed. You may feel sad or exalted but certainly you will be moved by a feeling of awe and reverence. This is hallowed ground.

Augustinian Acolman

Near Teotihuacán is another religious monument of a different faith. It is Acolman, a monastery built by Augustinian monks in the 16th Century. **San Agustin de Acolman** is a lovely example of a typically Mexican genre: the 16th Century fortress-church. Such churches, with accompanying monastery, were built just after the conquest when pacification was not yet complete. It was a time of fervent Christianity. At the same time, Spain was a country still flirting with the Middle Ages, but which also had been seduced by the Italian renaissance. All of these strangely unrelated factors are present in the fortress-church of the 16th Century and in San Agustin de Acolman. The church is located in an ample atrium; large atriums were necessary to accommodate the great number of converts who went there for instructions but who could not yet be received inside the church. In the middle of the atrium is a remarkable mission cross, carved by an anonymous Indian sculptor who interpreted the symbols of Christ's passion in an Aztec style. The façade of the church is simple, with two distinct areas: a blank and strong "fortress" wall, crowned with a castle-like parapet, and a delicately carved inner façade done in Spanish renaissance style, the *Plateresco;* that is, the art of the silversmith.

You will see the same façade elements that you saw in Tepotzotlán: the door, the central window, but here they are totally different. Whereas in Tepotzotlán there was baroque folly, here at Acolman there is youthful and gracious elegance. The church interior, too, is a happy, though unlikely mix: the massive fortress walls support a delicately laced Gothic roof, while a simple but beautiful retablo covers the apse wall. The cloister in Acolman is a mixture of Middle Ages and Renaissance but the spirit is medieval, even Romanesque, with strong arches and columns. There are many 16th Century churches and monasteries all over Mexico, but few like Acolman that can be visited so easily. In no other place are a major archeological center and a beautiful colonial monument to be found, side by side.

Don't fail to explore the surrounding countryside. Nearby is **Otumba,** where the Aztecs were defeated by Hernán Cortés in one of the decisive battles of the Spanish Conquest. Farther to the northeast is **Ciudad Sahagún,** one of Mexico's industrial experiments. The region is typical of central Mexico; desert plains and hills in which the main product is the cactus plant from which *pulque* is extracted. It is the national beverage: peculiar tasting, frothy, beerish, loaded with vitamins. It is said to be very nourishing—the best excuse in the world for a favorite drink. During colonial times and in the 19th Century, big pulque plantations were developed. In a barbaric way the manor houses of such plantations were magnificent. Some survive—such as **Xala,** near Ciudad Sahagún, which has been transformed into a hotel and preserves something of its early grandeur.

---

3   Heading East to Puebla, A Colonial Gem

The road to Puebla is a continuation of the great avenue called **Calzada Ignacio Zaragoza** that begins near the airport in the unattractive eastern part of Mexico City. A slum area built in the Texcoco Lake basin, Calzada Ignacio Zaragoza is the backbone of proletarian Mexico City. At its outer city reaches this traffic artery runs by a sprawling community called **Netzahualcóyotl,** a bedroom suburb with a working class population of two million-plus. It is oftentimes called "Mexico's third largest city." Once the calzada leaves the urban area behind, the road to Puebla enters a beautiful but cold and rainy mountain area. And once it crosses the mountains, it descends into the ample valley of **Puebla,** a city founded during colonial times and now a growing industrial center. Puebla is the capital of the state with the same name. It has preserved some of its old character and possesses some of the most important colonial works of art in Mexico. One such gem is Puebla's elegant and majestic cathedral. Some call the cathedral the finest in Mexico.

It was built from 1588 to 1649 in the most refined architectural style of the Spanish renaissance, the *Herreriano*. Named for Juan de Herrera, the architect of the Escorial (the classic monastery and palace in New Castile, near Madrid), the style is severe and elegant and pays its respects to Roman architecture. It lasted for years before surrendering to the baroque. The main altar is the work of the famous neoclassical artist, Manuel Tolsá.

If you exclude the cathedral, you might say that the architecture of Puebla is a sweet Mexican version of Spanish baroque, interpreted through a great profusion of tiles and plaster decoration. Best example is perhaps the **Casa del Alfeñique** that houses the regional museum. In it are good examples of ceramics produced in the state, along with memorabilia from that great event in Puebla history, the Battle of the 5th of May, 1862. That was when a Mexican army, led by General Ignacio Zaragoza and including battalions of Indians, defeated a French army. The victory of the 5th of May boosted Mexican morale and they later brought French intervention to an end. That event's anniversary is celebrated annually throughout Mexico on every Cinco de Mayo in many spirited ways.

Puebla is a city with remarkable colonial architecture: magnificent palaces such as the one containing the great **Palafox Library,** lavish churches such as the **Iglesias de la Compañía,** and mysterious convents such as **Santa Monica,** which operated secretly until 1934. Inspect the **Chapel of the Rosary** *(Capilla del Rosario),* an adjunct to the **Church of Santo Domingo.** This is Pueblan architecture at its best. The Rosary Chapel is a caprice of late Mexican baroque architecture. Dedicated to the Virgin, it has feminine charm and displays naïve and contagious joy. The Capilla del Rosario proves that Mexico's baroque is totally different from the baroque of Europe; it is less serious and self-conscious.

Visit the 19th Century market downtown. Puebla's market is one of the last of these colorful grand old markets built by Porfirio Díaz who sought to transform Mexico into a carbon copy of France. The iron structure of Puebla, like the one

eotihuacán's venue of e Dead and e Pyramid f the Moon.

in Guanajuato, shows how strong the culture of Mexico really is and how difficult it is to domesticate Mexico. Mexico remains *siempre* Mexico.

Sample Puebla's Camotes, Mole, Rompope and China Poblana

Puebla is associated in Mexican minds with colonial grandeur, with General Zaragoza, with the start of the Revolution of 1910, and also with four minor but all-important things: *camotes, mole, rompope* and *China Poblana*.

Camotes are sweet potatoes which Puebla women prepare with fruit and sugar and it makes a very popular sweet. Mexicans have a sweet tooth. Mole is a sauce—a taste treat of Pueblan cuisine. It was invented by a nun during colonial times who wanted to please her gourmet bishop. Mole is made with chile, spices and chocolate, and God knows what else, and is poured over turkey or chicken. Like any great dish, good mole requires a lot of work. It might be called the national dish, though it has a number of competitors for that honor. Mexico has one of the richest cuisines in the world, but not many of the truly exotic dishes are served in restaurants patronized by visitors.

From Puebla, too, comes rompope, a sort of eggnog, and the favorite drink of nice old Mexican ladies. It is said to be the children's introduction to alcohol. China Poblana is a legendary girl of colonial days whose attire has become a candidate for the national dress.

Cholula is a Puebla suburb. In Pre-Columbian times it was a major center of religious cult. During the conquest, Cortés, fearing an ambush at Cholula, set up an effective counter-blow which resulted in the killing of some 3,000 people. Later, a plague decimated the town and so Cholula, once a city of great importance, became an impoverished village.

Perhaps somehow to restore the departed glory of the place, the authorities decided to cover Cholula with churches. It is said that Cholula has 365 churches or chapels, one for every day of the year. Some are remarkable, such as the **Convento de San Gabriel** with its beautiful 16th Century temple and vast chapel, and the **Capilla Real,** which was inspired by the mosque of Córdoba. However, the main attraction in Cholula is the **Santuario de los Remedios**, a tiny church

San Francisco Acatepec, at right; and below is Cholula, circa 1920.

placed on top of what looks like a hill, but in reality is a pyramid. It is the largest pyramid of Mexico, one of the most ambitious construction jobs ever undertaken. In recent years archeologists began trying to probe its mysteries.

In **Huejotzingo**, a short ways from Puebla, is a Franciscan monastery of the 16th Century. Though primitive and pleasant, it preserves one of those curiosities of Mexican art—the **Capillas Posas**—literally, inn-chapels. They were built in the corners of an atrium, a place to take your ease during long and tiresome religious processions. Those at Huejotzingo are among the best in Mexico. The town is also famous for woolens, sweaters and *sarapes*, or blankets. The truth is that these days the wool is mixed with synthetic fibers, but, alas, that's the blended way of the world.

San Francisco Acatepec and **Santa María Tonantzintla** are two villages on the road to Oaxaca with remarkable churches. Both churches belong to the popular Mexican baroque style. The interior of the church at Tonantzintla is covered with playful plaster decorations which show how deeply baroque forms penetrated Mexican sensibility. It's a splendid example of how Indian artisans adopted Spanish techniques and iconography.

Historical Tlaxcala

Tlaxcala is a tiny state, the neighbor of Puebla. The capital is also named **Tlaxcala** and it has another beautiful baroque church in the village of **Ocotlán.** Perched atop a hill, the church seems as lightly spun as sugar candy that could dissolve in the first hard rain. But there it has been sitting since the 18th Century. In Tlaxcala is another famous religious building: the **Convento de San Francisco.** That church has a wooden roof in the Moorish style *(mudéjar).* Imagine how exotic that looks in an Indian town.

Tlaxcala also is famous historically because the Tlaxcalans helped Cortés conquer Mexico. Brave soldiers, they served gladly in the Spanish forces because they hated their old enemy, the Aztecs. A mural in the **Palacio de Gobierno,** painted by **Desiderio Hernández Xochitiotzin,** tells the story of these Indians. Other historical landmarks are the pulque haciendas that prospered up to the time of the revo-

tricate
terior
church,
onantzíntla,
ft; and
elow, some
oughing in
e highlands.

lution. Among the best are **San Barto-lomé del Monte, Ixtafiayuca, San Cristobal Zacacalco** and **San Blas.**

4   South to Cuernavaca

Out of Mexico City, Insurgentes Sur becomes the highway to **Cuernavaca,** probably the busiest thoroughfare in Mexico because Cuernavaca is *the* weekend resort for the capital. That's where the *capitalinos* look for pure air, nice weather, privacy and the bliss of silence. It is an escape from the cacophony of Mexico City. That, of course, is the promise: fulfillment is another thing. A fortunate few can take refuge in a mansion, encompassed by high walls and protected from the hot sun by huge shade trees, *laureles,* or laurels from India. Cuernavaca has always attracted the élite. Aztec emperors built palaces in Cuernavaca. Cortés built a pleasure dome there. But for the visitor Cuernavaca can be disappointing. Aside from mansions and good hotels, the city has little to offer. Two public places are recommended—the **Palacio de Cortés** and the cathedral.

The Palacio de Cortés is now a mu-seum. A Spanish castle in the middle of a tropical city, it exhibits one of the best murals in Mexico, painted by **Diego Rivera.** The mural depicts the history of Mexico and Morelos state. There is a beautiful portrait of Emiliano Zapata, the revolutionary. It was a gift to the Mexican government from Dwight Morrow, the American ambassador in the late 1920s and father-in-law of Charles Lindbergh.

The cathedral is very old, imposingly fortress-like, and built within a garden. The interior has been redecorated in a modern style of great simplicity and cleanliness.

If Cuernavaca is somewhat disappointing, the state of Morelos, though one of the smallest in Mexico, is beautiful and full of surprises. One is **Xochicalco,** an archeological site of which little is known. In contrast to grim Tula, or solemn Teotihuacán, Xochicalco (Place of the House of Flowers) is pleasant and surrounded by green landscape. Moreover, its architecture is more playful. The main structure, the remarkably well-preserved **Pyramid of the Feathered Serpent,** is a decoration full of writhing life.

Sunday ma
selling clay
comales an
water
containers.

One subterranean thought: If you like caves, the most famous, **Grutas de Cacahuamilpa,** is in Morelos. They are enormous, intriguing and frightening to the claustrophobic.

Taxco, Mexico's famous silver-working town, is near Xochicalco, some 72 kilometers (45 miles) south of Cuernavaca and about a third of the way between Mexico City and Acapulco. It is one of few Mexican towns to have been declared a national monument, meaning that residences and developers are forbidden to build in any non-local style or to change the character of the town in any way. And for good reason. Taxco is about as picturesque a place as you will find anywhere: narrow, cobblestone streets twist up and down hills, all eventually leading to the zocalo in front of a gem of a colonial church, the **Santa Prisca.** The town proper has more than 10,000 residents and about five times that number live in scattered communities on nearby hills. Houses are of stucco-covered adobe, roofed in red tile, and have plants overflowing their balconies. If driving around is nerve-wracking, walking is a pleasure. Take it easy on the steep, uphill stretches—you may puff a bit but the views are rewarding.

Taxco, of course, is synonymous with silver. There was a short-lived boom there, starting in 1529, but it soon played out. The real pay-off came to a French chap, Joseph de la Borda, at the beginning of the 18th Century. Untold millions poured out of Taxco-area mines, making Borda one of the richest men in Mexico. He changed his name to José de la Borda and between 1751 and 1758 built one of the most fantastic churches in Mexico: Santa Prisca. To explain the millions he spent on the church, Borda was fond of saying: "God gives to Borda and Borda gives to God." Of course, he never mentioned the thousands of Indians who died in his mines for both Borda and God. Fortunately for both the Indians and God, the mines played out shortly after Borda's death.

Having had an exciting moment of glory, Taxco reverted to its former sleepy self for a couple of centuries—or until another foreigner found his way to town. William Spratling was a professor at Tulane University when he first came to Taxco and found that the locals still scraped a bit of ore from the played-out mines and then smelted the metal in back-yard furnaces. Spratling—or Don Guillermo as he became known—gave up teaching and created a line of silver jewelry in a Taxco workshop which he opened in 1932. He hired local youth, taught them silversmithing skills, and integrated pre-Columbian designs into the jewelry. So good and unusual were his pieces that fancy clients such as Neiman-Marcus and Bonwit Teller competed to buy Spratling's output. Eventually, many of his former student-craftsmen set up their own shops. Today there are more than 300 of them in business in Taxco today.

A word of caution: there are no great bargains as the prices quoted are about the same as in Mexico City. The advantage here is that you can see a tremendous variety of silverwork and also watch the artisans hand-craft their exquisite products. Most of the best silver outlets are near the zocalo, which sits on one of the only level and relatively spacious places in this hilly town. The church of Santa Prisca is also on the zocalo, as it should be. Santa Prisca's exterior, dominated by twin baroque, 40 meter (130 foot) towers, has been undergoing extensive renovation. It's timely carved stone facade is more than matched by its gilded interior. Both teem with saints and decorations. Take special notice of the organ and the excellent carvings on the wooden pulpit. Before leaving town, take a peek at the **Museum of Don Guillermo Spratling** which, aside from many early silver objects, houses its founder's fine pre-Columbian collection.

After a few hours in Taxco you will understand why there are many retired expatriates here. Indeed, English is heard more often than Spanish on the zocalo. A Mexican comic once drew many laughs when he mentioned refusing an invitation to visit Taxco because he didn't speak English. There are plenty of inexpensive accommodations and decent restaurants in town. During Easter, when there are processions, penitents and a recreation of Christ's last hours, you need way-ahead confirmed reservations. The rest of the time, Taxco makes for a good overnight stay on your way to or from Acapulco. It is also a good place to take a break from your explorations around Mexico City, and it's only a hop away from the state of Morelos.

Morelos is the sugar bowl of Mexico. Cortés brought sugar cane there, along with black slaves. The slaves were rebellious and perhaps instead of sugar planted the seed for the agrarian movement in Morelos. Zapata was the great leader and his battle cry, *"Tierra y Libertad,"* has echoed throughout the land. There is his portrait in every village in his native Morelos: the huge bristling mustache, the *charro* (rancher) attire, the sombrero, the deep, sad look in the eyes.

Morelos is rich in old monasteries, most of them built in the 16th Century in a fortress style. Time has dealt gracefully with them. After years of exposure to tropical rain and wind, they now look like old and peaceful castles.

You get to **Tepoztlán** (do not confuse it with Tepotzotlán) along a modern road north of Cuernavaca. There is the customary 16th Century convent, primitive and charming, surrounded by a landscape of beauty which may remind you of Chinese brushwork. An odd-looking group of hills make up the **Sierra**. The most important is the so-called **Tepozteco**, which serves as the base for a temple dedicated to the god Tepoztécal, god of crops and drunkenness.

East of Tepoztlán are **Oaxtepec** and **Cocoyoc,** Indian villages and vacation towns. Oaxtepec has a big hotel; Cocoyoc an expensive hotel. There are mon-asteries in Oaxtepec and in the neighboring villages of **Tlayacapan** and **Atlatlahuacan.** Perhaps the best is in **Yecapixtla,** a short distance east. It resembles a proud and military Moorish castle.

To get to the vicinity of those snow-capped wonders, **Popocatépetl** and **Iztac-cíhuatl,** take the Amecameca road through a pastoral land that contrasts with the tropical countryside you left behind in Morelos.

---

5   Westward to Toluca

Several roads connect Mexico City with **Toluca,** capital of the state of Mexico. A direct road leaves from Chapultepec park via the Avenida Constituyentes. Once it leaves Mexico City behind, the road goes through a surprising countryside: tall pine forests that remind you of Germany. But once you cross the mountain range and go into the **Toluca Valley,** you are truly in Mexico again: dry, golden fields, cacti, adobe houses. Toluca is a typical provincial city with some Victorian-style buildings, colonial churches, a large central square, narrow streets and the inevitable *portales,* or ar-

Snow-capped Nevado de Toluca.

cades. They are the heart of town. At dusk everybody seems to be there, idly walking along, just like the Italian *passeggiata*, flirting, gossiping, window-shopping. This is what makes dusk the best time of the day.

Toluca has its own food and drink specialties. The drinks are called *moscos* and are sold at the portales. They come in bottles with long spouts. Moscos are famous because, like all street liquor, they are *"muy traidores,"* as the Mexicans say. "Very Treacherous," Toluca is also famous for its fruit jam, very good candy, and spicy *chorizos*, or Spanish chili sausage, all sold at the portales. Meanwhile, Toluca cathedral is an unmitigated horror. Don't miss it.

Out of Toluca you have two options: go on south to **Ixtapan de la Sal,** or west to **Valle de Bravo.** The road to Valle de Bravo crosses a flat valley of Toluca. To the left of the high Nevado is a snow-capped volcano that reigns over the area. The landscape changes constantly, from European-like forests to Mexican valleys. Valle de Bravo is definitely of mountain heritage; on a pleasant lake white sails drift. In town thatched roofs overhang the streets. There are houses with white walls and stone chimneys. Mexico City people love the Valle.

At Ixtapan de la Sal, America's 'Shangri-la'

The road to Ixtapan de la Sal crosses the same sort of landscape but the place is full of history. This is a land of Indian tradition, blended with colonial. A good example are the ceramics produced in **Metepec,** a village near Toluca. The pottery shows imagination, especially those wrought in the *Arbol de la Vida*, or Tree of Life, theme. This is a simple interpretation of the tree in the Garden of Eden. All of the dramatis personae of that great tale—Adam, Eve, the serpent, the angels—are described in toy-like fantasy.

Farther south in **Tenango** is an interesting archeological center that includes the remnants of a palatial temple which was once the dwelling of the rullers of the valley.

Ixtapan de la Sal is a bathing station, semi-tropical and flowery. The main hotel, the **Hotel Ixtapan,** is worth visiting. It is described as the "Shangri-la of America," and its waters are said to be rejuvenating. The hotel is indeed a delight because of its fantastic bad taste. However, the bathing area is in classical style: Greek and Roman goddesses officiating over the private hall. You can take a pleasant dip; the food is good, the service is good. The main building produces a certain sense of nostalgia in visitors from the U.S. and Canada because apparently it reminds them of the 40s, the time the place was built.

Near Ixtapan de la Sal is the village of **Malinalco.** Built in a ravine, Malinalco was a resort in Aztec times and is the site of an impressive mountain temple. The main structure, the **Cuauhcalli,** or House of the Eagle, is carved out of the rock. There is a circular chamber with an eagle marking the center of the floor.

Near Malinalco is the **Church of Chalma,** a place of pilgrimage. During the first five days of the year **Chalma** village is crowded with thousands of pilgrims, who worship a miraculous Black Christ. Once the worshipping is over, the penitents dance and drink and many get drunk. From Chalma, you can return directly to Mexico City, reluctantly back to the 20th Century.

Sailing, at Valle del Bravo.

GUADALAJARA, JALISCO, A MEXICAN'S MEXICO

Jalisco, west of Mexico City, is a fascinating state, one of the most important in the country. It has agriculture, and booming industry, and a coastline that beckons to the visitor. Its capital is Guadalajara, second biggest city in Mexico with a population of 3.2 million. All of this and Jalisco is the home of *mariachi* music, too. Those bubbly musicians, so symbolic of Mexico, have been given a little square of their own in Guadalajara, the *Plaza de los Mariachis,* near the Libertad Market. And well do they deserve it.

'Spanish' Guadalajara, 'La Perla del Occidente'

Let's start our visit in **Guadalajara.** A splendid city, perched like Denver on a "mile-high" plain (actually, 1,524 meters high), it is a sophisticated city which in this era of hustle-bustle still has managed to retain a good deal of the charm of a departed era. Guadalajara has the best climate in North America. Clear, dry and mild, it is in the 70s and 80s all year round. Ah, those lucky *tapatiós, as they* are called. (That name derives from an old Indian expression that means "three times as worthy." It's a boastful nickname that's quite descriptive of Guadalajara's proud character.)

Guadalajara is a city of parks and monuments and flowered lanes and nice old plazas and gracious old buildings and urban districts and supermarkets that are as fancy and bountiful as any in norteamérica and art galleries and bookstores and gourmet restaurants and luxury hotels and lovely parks with fountains and quaint *trolebuses,* all red and white, that glide along on rubber tires, and the best murals in the country (Orozco's). Si, Guadalajara! Indeed you are *"La Perla del Occidente"* (Pearl of the West). No wonder visitors want to overstay their reservations.

Guadalajara was founded in 1542 and was meant to be the capital of the kingdom of New Galicia, independent from New Spain. That was the dream of Nuño Beltrán de Guzmán, the conquistador who took the place. A man of soaring ambition and savage disposition, Guzmán never attained his dream. Still, Guadalajara managed to remain independent of Mexico City and Guadalajara's archbishopric was as rich and powerful as Mexico City's. Guadalajara, in fact, always retained some political and judicial autonomy. Early on, the city also created its own university, and students came from as far away as southern Texas, then, of course, part of New Spain.

From the beginning, Guadalajara enjoyed a regional importance, becoming, so to speak, the capital of the vast Mexican west. The city is located near one of the few passages through the mountains leading to the fertile Pacific coast. Though Guadalajara is a big city, most of its points of interest are downtown.

The Cathedral. A huge religious building, it is the symbol of Guadalajara. Its two Gothic-style towers (impure Gothic, that is) are the city's central landmark. They are covered with unbelievably-yellow tile. The cathedral is surrounded by plazas that form a cross. It is pleasant to stroll there in the open ground, which is an oasis amidst the bustle of a big city.

The square in front of the cathedral is named **Plaza de los Laureles.** There is a fountain commemorating the founding of Guadalajara. To the north the square shows off a Greek-looking columned en-

Preceding pages, quiet Tapalpa town below, Cuervo is the oldest Tequila distillery.

closure, the **Rotonda,** which is the burial place of Jalisco's famous men. Some have their own monument placed along the path of the **Plaza de los Hombres Ilustres.**

The Square of Two Cups
And Orozco's Masterpieces

To the south is **Plaza de Armas,** originally Guadalajara's main square, marketplace, training grounds and the place where executions took place. But that was long ago. Now it is a pleasant square with a bandstand adorned with attractive sculpture in a happy style, brought in from Paris. The most unusual of plazas is the one to the east, **Plaza de la Liberación,** but known by everyone in Guadalajara as the **Plaza del 2 de Copas.** Square of the 2 of Cups? How did it get its name? Well, cups were one of the suits used in Spanish-style playing cards. The Dos de Copas is one of Mexico's most beautiful squares. Designed by Ignacio Díaz Morales, Guadalajara's great contemporary architect, the square blends in a dignified manner with the colonial buildings surrounding the plaza; it also frames the back of the cathedral and the façade of the **Degollado Theater,** which is one of the best 19th Century theaters in Mexico.

A handsome late baroque building in *gold-hued stone, the* **Palacio** de Gobierno (Place of Government) faces the Plaza de Armas. Its façade is in a festive military style; its central patio is enclosed by classical arcades. But the chief attraction is a magnificent mural painted by the late **José Clemente Orozco,** Jalisco's foremost modern painter. The mural is a homage to Father Miguel Hidalgo, the revolutionary priest who touched off the Revolution. It is perhaps the most passionate statement made by any Mexican mural. One side of the huge triptych is known as "The Clowns"—a savage satire about ideologies that exploit people.

Facing the Hombres Ilustres plaza is a former seminary, a charming baroque building with lush garden surrounded by Roman arches. It houses the **State Museum,** a combination of art and history museum. The recently restored 19th Century Degollado Theater, built in romantic style, offers some wonderful murals, which decorate the ceiling. Behind the theater is a huge, new square, or rather, a series of squares known as the **Plaza Tapatía.** *Tapatío* is the name given Guadalajara residents, which we already have

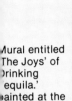

Mural entitled The Joys' of Drinking Tequila.' Painted at the Tequila Sauza factory.

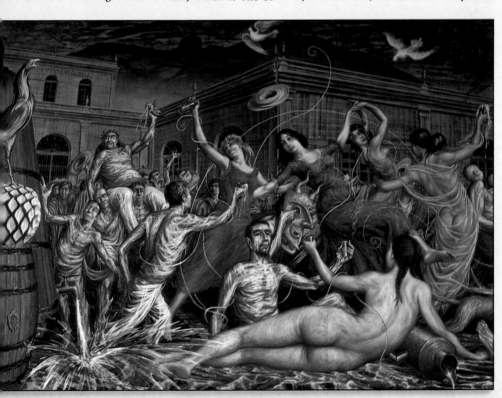

encountered. Plaza Tapatía is built in an affected style; contrived looking, really. Unfortunately economic considerations overruled the plaza's original stylistic lines, but it leads to one of Mexico's most important colonial buildings—the **Hospicio Cabañas.** Founded by one of Guadalajara's great benefactors, Bishop Juan Ruiz de Cabañas y Crespo, this former orphanage is now a cultural center. Ruiz de Cabañas was a man of piety who financed the huge building which is built around a series of patios. At its center is a magnificent chapel. The chapel was decorated in the late 1930s by Orozco with murals depicting the ties between Spain and Mexico. He could not resist also painting a series of political satires.

Orozco's murals at the Hospicio are generally regarded as among the masterpieces of modern art. They are the crown of Mexican mural painting. Four giant male figures decorate the dome. No one is certain what they mean. Orozco, a harsh and silent man, never offered an explanation. Figure it out for yourself, he seems to be saying. The dome paintings are supposed to represent the four elements: earth, water, wind and fire, which, in symbolic manner, are also the stages of spiritual development. Manuel Tolsá, Mexico's best known colonial architect, designed the Hospicio.

Who doesn't like the color and the bustle (and the bargains) at the huge central markets of Mexico? **Mercado Libertad** is the Guadalajara version. It is a neighbor of the Hospicio's. Close to the market is **San Juan de Dios Church** which is the core of the city's traditional center. Here the music and the drinking never stops. The noise is concentrated in the **Plaza of the Mariachis,** which we already have discussed, and there the musicians play their *corridos* (street ballads).

The street on which the Mercado Libertad, the church and the Plaza de los Mariachis are located, the Calzada Independencia, is the backbone of popular Guadalajara. It used to be, until a few years ago, the river that made Guadalajara possible. It is not by any aesthetic standards a beautiful street, but it's bustling and full of life. Due north of the Calzada you will find a huge soccer stadium, the **Estadio Jalisco,** a shrine to the most popular sport in Mexico. Guadalajara is a "futbol" fanatic's dream city. It used to have *five* Major League "futbol" teams (there are still four). All Mexican

Dancing the Jarabe a la Tapatio.

kids worship the players, many of them imported from South America's two soccer powers, Brazil and Argentina; workers here spend much of their meagre salaries on tickets for the two or three games that take place weekly during the seemingly endless futbol season. They also gamble on regular soccer sweepstakes called *pronosticos.*

Unfortunately, Mexico's passion for futbol is an unrequited love. No matter how many times Mexico has attempted it, she has never won that coveted World Cup which every four years is the Planet's major bone of contention.

A few miles further north along the Calzada, Guadalajara offers a nice bonus: the majestic **Barranca de Oblatos.** This is a canyon at the bottom of which the **Rio Santiago** slides into the tropics and the distant Pacific. The Barranca has strong, sculptural stone walls softened by luscious, green vegetation. During the rainy season, there is an impressive, temporary waterfall.

San Francisco and **Aranzazú** are two remarkable colonial churches in the southern part of the downtown area which are remnants of a magnificent group of churches and monasteries built by the Franciscans. The churches served as the center of the Franciscans ambitious effort to extend their missionary work from central Mexico all the way to the Californias. San Francisco and Aranzazú face two pleasant *jardines* (public gardens) and were the heart of one of the city's best neighborhoods. It has been transformed into a financial district. Aranzazú is the more artistic of the two churches. Tiny and feminine, Aranzazú has some diminutive but elegant golden retablos, the only ones left in town. Terrorists in the 1930s burned the retablos in San Francisco church.

Santa Mónica and **San Felipe Neri** are two churches on the west part of downtown which are the best in Guadalajara. Santa Mónica is a nuns' church. The facade is enhanced by a prodigious carving done in the late baroque style. In a corner in a niche is a giant sculpture of St. Christopher, primitive and toy-like. The women of Guadalajara still pray and chant a song to St. Christopher to help them find a man (or to help them get rid of the one they had).

San Felipe is a very grand church. It may well be the most accomplished example of Guadalajara's religious archi-

Cathedral and modern shopping center in Guadalajara.

tecture with its exotic-looking belfry and well-proportioned dome.

The **University of Guadalajara's** central building is a comparatively recent addition, dating from the 1920s. Here again are splendid Orozco murals. One mural in particular draws a great deal of attention: a big fresco showing rogues leading the gullible masses on the road to hell. It is Orozco in his most biting and bitter mood.

Behind the university is a big Gothic church which is fashioned after the cathedral of Orvieto in Italy, and known as the **Expiatorio.** The locals are much enamored of it. They are pleased that this European-looking expatriate dwells in their semi-tropical city.

Walk around. The city is enchanting. View the *portales*, or arcades. The most important street to visit is Avenida Vallarta, west of the university.

Serene Lake Chapala

Southeast of Guadalajara is **Lake Chapala,** Mexico's biggest lake. The *Laguna,* as it is known, has a serene beauty. Along the north shore are the weekend homes of wealthy *Tapatios* and retired *norte-americanos.*

Consider before leaving Jalisco three small villages which are famous in their own fashion. Two are suburbs of Guadalajara—**San Pedro Tlaquepaque** and **Zapopan,** and the third is the village of **Tequila,** a few kilometers north of Guadalajara. We knew you would recognize the name.

San Pedro Tlaquepaque is nationally famous for its ceramics. In the good old days, ceramics produced here had a remarkable quality and simple elegance. But then commercial success came, and tourism and much of Tlaquepaque's pottery fell to abysmal aesthetic depths and shattered artistic sensibilities. A great deal of San Pedro's current production is sheer horror, but very nice traditional pieces are still made here. They are of colorful, geometric designs typical of the region. The town guards its best ceramic works, however, in its local regional museum.

Recently, too, modern ceramics forms have been introduced by artists such as the renowned Jorge Wilmot.

San Pedro Tlaquepaque also is good to visit because it will give you an idea of how Mexican villages looked in the past.

Fishermen, Lake Chapal

160

Its cobblestoned streets, spacious and secretive houses, and noisy central square, the **Parián,** have an old time charm about them. The Parian has long been a place favored by tapatíos who flock here to listen to mariachis, drink beer, eat a notorious kid-goat barbecue dish called *birria,* and watch passersby. The town has many magnificent houses that were built here during the 19th Century by wealthy Guadalajara citizens who, for some absurdly paranoid reason, considered San Pedro to be safer than Guadalajara in the event of an earthquake. San Pedro's best restaurant, **Sin Nombre** (Without A Name), is located in one of these mansions.

Zapopan is another of the famous pilgrimage centers of Mexico. Every rainy season the town takes an image of the Virgin to Guadalajara to protect the town against floods and then takes the image back home again on October 12th. It must be one of the best attended pilgrimages in the world. Zapopan's **Basilica** belongs to that strong baroque style found in many places in rural Mexico.

Then there is Tequila, famous, naturally, for its drink which is extracted from

Potter, Tonalá.

a blueish-green cactus plant, a variety of *maguey.* Similar to vodka in color and stronger, tequila grows yellow, or golden, as its proud producers claim, with age. It is an aperitif and knowledgeable tequila drinkers never suffer it to be mixed. That is sacrilegious. What is the proper way to drink it? Well, taken before a heavy Mexican midday meal (around 2 p.m., that is), you should drink it with a little salt, some strong lemon and *sangrita,* a liquid made with oranges and hot peppers. Indeed, the ritual movements one must make in order to "properly" drink tequila go from the placing of some grains of salt on the top of your fist, licking them, then, after sucking some drops of lemon, having a drink from a *fajo* or *caballito* of tequila. A sip of sangrita will end the operation. All this complication has, of course, a logic all its own. The idea is to establish a precise and satisfying balance of strong flavors in which tequila's pure, sweet fire is complemented by the hotness of sangrita, the acidity of lemon, and the relief given by those grains of salt.

Good tequila drinkers use the liquor in moderation; they have a healthy respect for it. A friend talks of his grandfather who never missed his daily *fajo* (the cup in which you drink tequila) until his departure from this world at age 92.

Though every Mexican touts his own special brand of really good tequila, frequent nominees for *the best* commercial tequila would be **Herradura,** both in its normal and well aged varieties (añejo), and the tequila brands **Tequileño, Centinela, Cuervo** and **Orendain.**

Jalisco is a state with strong rural traditions and a rich folklore. In this fascinating part of the country, the charros and mariachis thrived. Jalisco's traditional music, the *son jaliscience,* is among the great expressions of Mexican folklore. The song, "Guadalajara," is almost a second national anthem. Jalisco is the traditional home of Mexican *machismo.* Think of the mustachioed charro, riding his horse, singing a Jorge Negrete song, and shooting from the hip. He never misses. At least that's how Mexican movies portray him. Jalisco is a Mexican's Mexico. Perhaps it is also a place where myths are born and take wing. Of a Mexican life that is always free as the air; clean as the water in a mountain stream, courageous and care-free as the charro, in film, on his horse. Did it ever exist? Or was it a macho romantic's dream?

Six Other States of Central Mexico

A big block of central Mexico—almost as big as France—takes in six states which offer much for the traveler who has the time, patience and curiosity to explore. We're talking about **Zacatecas, San Luis Potosí, Aguascalientes, Guanajuato, Querétaro** and **Michoacán**.

Let's start in the center with the state of Guanajuato and work our way around. There are many roads to follow. **Guanajuato** city is the capital of the state and one of Mexico's most famous tourist spots. During colonial times the city was the center of a rich mining area, one of the greatest producers of silver in the world. During the wars for independence, the mines were flooded; during the Porfirio Díaz regime they were opened again and brought new prosperity. Then came the Revolution and once more the mines were abandoned. They have been reopened in recent years when the price of silver escalated.

Periods of prosperity produce great buildings and longer periods of poverty help preserve them. Guanajuato, like many cities that once were prosperous and then stagnated, is remarkably well preserved. It is now a national monument.

Crazy-Quilt Guanajuato

Guanajuato is a crazy town. Built in a ravine and upon a river that from time to time flooded the town, the city does not have a single street that runs along in a straight line. They all go their crooked ways, up hill and down dale, or fall flush into an abyss. In some houses you enter through the roof. It is quaint and charming and romantic.

The old river that ravaged the town has been covered and is now Guanajuato's scenic freeway, called **Padre Belauzarán** street. A mix of tunnels, streets, and crosstown roads, Padre Belauzarán meanders along the basements of the town's old buildings, from time to time offering an exit into some shady square or busy street. How can you not be touched by a street like that?

What to see? Begin with **Jardín de la Unión**, the square in the center of Guanajuato. It's a nice, fresh provincial *jardin*,

where you can sit and rest. It has two remarkable neighbors, **San Diego** church and the **Teatro Juárez**. San Diego is delightfully *churrigueresque*, a good example of the subtle and feminine way Guanajuato dealt with the baroque. The interior is mediocre. Don't go in. Teatro Juárez is the embodiment of 19th Century architecture at its most delirious. A tiny theater built during Guanajuato's second stage of prosperity, the Juarez took the form of a "French-Moorish" style. Notwithstanding, it manages to blend in somehow with the colonial surroundings. A critic said he would call it a Gilbert and Sullivan style, or Jacques Offenbach style. Sui generis, that is. Unique.

Two blocks west from Jardín de la Unión is a narrow square known as **Plaza de la Paz.** More than a square, really, it is a monument imprisoned between two busy streets. It represents a lady playing the role of peace-maker. Roundabout, the buildings are remarkable. One is the **Basilica of Our Lady of Guanajuato,** whose image is worshipped in a chapel in the church. King Philip II of Spain offered the image of the Virgin to Guanajuato. Like Guanajuato itself, the image has a base of local silver. Another fashionable building in neoclassical style is the **Casa de Rul y Valenciana,** designed by **Eduardo de Tresguerras,** a great 18th Century Mexican designer and architect.

The University building is hardly colonial. It is, in fact, an outstanding example of unmitigated fake baroque. Huge, white and unavoidable, Guanajuato nevertheless is proud of it. People pay it the best of compliments; they come to see it. **La Universidad** has a noble neighbor, however—the **Church of the Company,** the grandest church in town. Its dome is beautiful; the interior truly impressive, though not ornate. Near the University building is the house in which **Diego Rivera** was born.

Plaza de San Roque is a typical Guanajuato church that has become famous since it became the stage for the production of *"Entremeses Cervantinos,"* the famous farces of **Miguel de Cervantes,** the great Spanish writer. The Entremeses, which are light and funny, have become a tradition in Guanajuato. Because of official support, they have been expanded into an international cultural festival.

La Alhóndiga is an impressive building, originally a grain storage. During the War of Independence, it was converted into a fortress by its Spanish defenders. A piece of Mexican history follows: Protected by a slab of stone which he carried on his back, a miner, called the **Pípila,** rushed the door of Alhóndiga, set it on fire, and the rebels poured in. Today the place is a museum with murals by **Chávez Morado** and a collection of paintings by the 19th Century artist of Guanajuato, **Hermenegildo Bustos.**

Brave Pípila's Monument And 'Moon,' 'Backbone' and 'Kiss'

Guanajuato's market is huge and noisy and full of good and bad smells—like any big central market should be. The French iron structure looks out of place, but at the same time manages to blend nicely with Guanajuato's mixed-up scene. **The Pípila,** honoring the fellow who rushed the door, is a huge, operatic-looking monument on a ridge overlooking the city. Not much as a work of art, it does look nice with Guanajuato as a backdrop.

Los Callejónes (alleys or lanes) are more like some sort of urban canyon than ordinary streets. They succeed in supplying a sort of circulatory system through which flows the life of the city. In

Statue of Don Quixote and Sancho Panza, at Guanajuato.

166

Guanajuato people circulate, or engage in *"callejonear."* That is, they walk around with no particular goal in mind. They go up and down the crooked alleys in search of a friendly door, a flowery balcony, or an inviting girl. The *callejónes* have enticing names: "Shell," "Moon," "Bronze," "Lion," "Backbone," "Grave," "Mandate," "Angels," "Holy Child," even "Hell." Perhaps the most famous is the "Kiss" *(Callejón del Beso),* an alley so narrow that it has led to a story of two ill-fated lovers (a Mexican Romeo and Juliet) who were kept apart but were able to kiss each other while sitting in their windows on *opposite* sides of the callejon.

Outside Guanajuato is **La Valenciana,** another rich baroque church, perched on top of a mine. The church has a golden retablo of highest quality. From the church you can get a nice panoramic view of Guanajuato.

'Artistic' Allende

San Miguel de Allende, northeast of Guanajuato city, is well known these days because it has attracted artists and writers. Visitors have since been lured there to see what an artists' colony looks like. For many years the town was small and seedy, but now it is a success. Allende's chief attraction is the parochial 19th Century church, built in a fantastic and impure Gothic style. The *parroquia* (parish church) stands white and enormous in the center of town. It can be seen from all the streets that descend from the surrounding hills. In front of the church is the inevitable square where visitors from all over take their ease at budget prices. **Plaza de Allende** is surrounded by 17th and 18th Century houses. The most important belonged to the Allende family and to the **Counts of la Canal.**

Don Miguel Allende was a young officer who conspired with Father Hidalgo in the fight for independence. Allende became one of the most important military leaders for independence. The Counts of La Canal are the "Medici" of San Miguel. Rich and devout, they furnished the money to build **La Santa Casa de Loreto,** one of San Miguels' outstanding churches. You can admire the lavish and whimsical *Camerino,* or dressing chapel. The Palace of the Counts, hard by Allende square, is among the most aristocratic in Mexico. Near it is the church

Throwing a bull by his tail.

and convent of **la Concepción.** The huge dome is inspired by the dome of Les Invalides in Paris. The church is the property of the clergy, but the convent belongs to the government and has been transformed into a cultural center.

What about the art turned out by the young painters of San Miguel, many of whom came down from the U.S.? It may or may not please you. Meantime, San Miguel, taken by surprise by its fame, goes on with its serious work, tending crops, raising a few pigs and cows.

Near San Miguel is the village of **Atotonilco,** which has a baroque curiosity called the **Santuario.** It is decorated with frescoes, painted by the colonial artist **Miguel Antonio Martínez de Pocasangre.**

Dolores Hidalgo, Home of the 'Grito'

Dolores Hidalgo, in northcentral Guanajuato, is the cradle of Mexican independence. It was here that **Father Miguel Hidalgo,** the parochial priest, proclaimed his *Grito de Dolores,* the Shout for independence from the Spanish rule. It happened in the early hours of September 16, 1810, and those who heard it were his sleepy congregation who had gathered for mass. Hidalgo was a smoldering creole, a man of learning, an activist. He became the moral and political leader of the independence movement. He had no military training but at one stage his forces—peasants out of the villages and the hills—controlled a large part of western central Mexico. In the end he was defeated, imprisoned, and shot.

Dolores lovingly preserves the beautiful **Parroquia** where Hidalgo uttered his Grito. It is always politically expedient for Mexican presidents to go back there and repeat Hidalgo's inspiring proclamation. Dolores is a typical Mexican town, undiscovered by artists or writers. The houses are solid and secretive, with shady patios. There are lovely, peasant churches; there is the rough but luminous landscape.

Celaya, Salamanca, Irapuato and **Leon** are four Guanajuato cities located in central Mexico's largest valley, the **Bajío.** A prosperous agricultural area, the Bajío is called the "Breadbasket of Mexico." The four cities were founded during colonial times and are growing madly. None is

Tough old rancheros, Atotonilco.

favored by visitors, though they may have something to offer. **Celaya** has some elegant buildings, a memorandum of late colonial times. The **Church of el Carmen** is another of Tresguerra's works marking the triumph of the new neoclassical style brought from France.

Salamanca was once a sleepy and boring agricultural town. In recent years PEMEX, the national petroleum company, chose the place as the site in which to build a huge refinery. Now Salamanca is prosperous and chaotic and the air is polluted. One of its redeeming qualities is the church of **San Agustın**, which possesses some of the richest retablos in Mexico.

South of Salamanca is **Yuriria,** a farming village with a 16th Century convent. Artistically speaking, **Irapuato** is not worth mentioning. **León** on the other hand, though also poor in art, is a lively city. It's Mexico's shoemaking capital and there are thus a number of cobblers here who have struck it rich and built elaborate houses with gardens big as a stadium. Money is not God, as the Mexicans say, but it can perform miracles. Such a miracle was performed in converting the dilapidated old central

Plaza de Leon into a pleasant square.

León has nice hotels, and good places to eat and to get plastered, such as the **Cırculo Leones,** a half block from the Plaza, and the fantastic **Panteón Taurino,** decorated with the paraphernalia of bullfighting. Leon's regional dish is meat, in the Argentine style. That has come about because the city has two professional soccer teams and a number of soccer players from the Argentine belonged to the teams and now have retired and opened restaurants. Near Leon is a mountain that marks the geographical center of Mexico. It is called the **Cubilete** (the Dicebox). On top is a monument of Christ, with open arms blessing the valley.

Colonial Queretaro

Alongside Guanajuato is the state of Queretaro. Its capital, the city of **Querétaro,** attracts people who like colonial art. Though Queretaro has become industrialized, history is engraved upon it. You can walk the streets of the capital and see it. Queretaro city is both a city of religion and history; in every block is a convent or a church. Querétaro has been a stage for some of the greatest episodes

Neighborhood toy seller.

in Mexican history. There events took place that accelerated the proclamation of Independence. Querétaro was witness to the downfall of Maximilian, the pretender king. Here the Constitution was signed. There is clerical and monastic Querétaro and there is also secular and political Querétaro. Both are intertwined, giving the city a unique character and flavor not found in any other colonial city. Understand Querétaro and you know something about the history of Mexico.

Heroic Doña Josefa

Let's deal first with history. The chief monuments are the **City Hall**, the **Theater of the Republic** and the **Cerro de las Campanas** (Hill of Bells). Each represents a period of Mexican history. The City Hall or **Casa de la Corregidora** is a proud building facing Querétaro's most charming square. During colonial times, it was the residence of the local governor, or *corregidor*.

In 1810 the governor's wife, **Josefa Ortiz de Dominguez**, was involved in a plot to proclaim the independence of Mexico from Spain. The plot was discovered but

Doña Josefa alerted the other conspirators. That enabled Father Hidalgo to get on with starting the movement for independence. At City Hall is a plaque commemorating the event, but, curiously enough, the atmosphere of the Casa de la Corregidora (and the square fronting it) does not speak of independence and fervid revolution, but instead is thoroughly colonial in demeanor. This monument in the square is not dedicated to Father Hidalgo but rather to a consumate aristocrat, **Don Juan Antonio Urrutia y Aranda,** Marquis of the Villa del Villar del Aguilla. Talk about a stately name and title! He may not be the hero of independence, but it was he who built the magnificent aqueduct that brought water to Querétaro.

The **Teatro de la República** was the place where passionate discussion went on concerning the writing of the Constitution of 1917. The theater is tiny, an unlikely stage for historical drama. The **Cerro de las Campanas,** a low, barren hill outside town, was the place where Maximilian was executed. A witness to the deed was Edouard Manet, who painted a picture of the execution. The place, naturally, is grim. There is a huge and not very

Golden Mexican grapes, Aguascalientes.

attractive sculpture of Benito Juárez, who confirmed the findings of the court-martial which condemned Maximilian to death. There is a humble chapel dedicated to Maximilian.

'Ave Maria' Gargoyles

Religious Querétaro is represented by a collection of churches and convents all over town. The best are as follows: The former monastery of **San Francisco**, which houses the **State Museum**. A local variety of the baroque, the building is a serene and happy structure with wide-open patio, corridors, flowery arches and elegant stairways. The **Federal Palace**, which used to be an Augustinian monastery, is one of the most beautiful structures in Mexico. It belongs to the late baroque style, with fantastically carved columns and arches. The Gargoyles leering from the walls are supposed to be uttering the "Ave Maria" in sign language.

Santa Clara is one of the many churches belonging to nuns' congregations. In Querétaro these churches are usually more charming and delicate than their counterparts. Santa Clara, though

simple on the outside, has a marvelous interior. The walls are covered by overflowing retablos. The grill separating the choir from the congregation is a masterpiece of feminine baroque. Outside is a fountain dedicated to Neptune, another work of the famous artist, **Tresguerras.** **Santa Rosa de Viterbo** is another nuns' church. Its buttresses look more Chinese than European; the interior offers grand retablos and an admirable organ. The **Convento de la Cruz** is simple and devout, a bit eerie, perhaps, since it is said to be inhabited by the ghost of Maximilian who was imprisoned there until the day he was shot.

Querétaro likes a bullfight. It has a good bullring and its *feria* attracts famous *toreros* and enthusiastic fans. Outside Querétaro city is **San Juan del Río,** a white village with narrow streets and solid provincial houses. It is not as aristocratic as Querétaro, but offers the true atmosphere of rural Mexico. San Juan del Río has some interesting crafts, especially stone cutting and basket weaving. Near there is the village of **Tequisquiapan,** famous as a resort. Here are thermal baths and handicraft on display.

At dusk, Morelia.

The place is a growing center of wine production.

Mexican Wine Country

Let's discuss the grape. Although Mexico has a long tradition in wine-making, (after all, it was the first country in the Americas to plant vineyards), wine has not been popular until now. The upper classes import their wine from Europe. But in recent years the demand for wine has grown; production has risen spectacularly.

Mexican wine is unpredictable. A vintage may be excellent one year and inferior the next. A popular game is to discover which wine *"Esta saliendo bueno,"* "Is coming out well," and then everybody tries to buy all he can of it. However, the wines of Tequisquiapan, and especially the whites, are among the most dependable in Mexico. As a rule, in Mexico, the whites are good, the reds are a mystery, and the sherries, *oportos* and brandies are always suspect.

Near San Juan del Río is an old hacienda that has been transformed into a hotel. Known as the **Mansión Galindo,** it is one of the most beautiful hotels in Mexico. Like the wine, Mexican hotels and restaurants can be somewhat unpredictable. Mansión Galindo boasts a strong architecture: decoration arouses nostalgia, the gardens are superbly kept. The hotel usually is full of guests. And yes, it is expensive.

The capital of the state of Aguascalientes (Hot Water) is **Aguascalientes** city. Here again we are in grape country. The town calls itself the "Grape Capital of Mexico." For centuries Aguascalientes city remained blessedly obscure, but now winemaking has blown its cover. Most of the grapes wind up as Mexican brandy, unfortunately only slightly related to Spanish brandy or to French cognac. But it has become *the* drink of Mexico's emerging lower middle-class. (Upper class Mexicans never touch the stuff. The less affluent and the poor drink pulque, tequila or mezcal.)

Aguascalientes is a pleasant town. A major point of interest is **San Marcos park,** described as a *"Jardín Romántico,"* a provincial garden from the 19th Century. Starting on April 25th, San Marcos is host to the famous feria—bullfighting, of course, and dancing and singing and brandy drinking. Many a bottle

Fishermen, on Lake Pátzcuaro.

172

is emptied. Many a peso is wagered. Though gambling is illegal in Mexico, it goes on all the time. Those who can't make it to Las Vegas go to the **Feria de San Marcos** in the romantic garden of Aguascalientes.

Marvelous Michoacán

Everyone has his favorite state in Mexico. For some it is Veracruz. For some Chiapas, or even the desert reaches of Baja Sur, or the shrill mountains of Chihuahua. Or the beaches of Guerrero. For many it is Michoacán. So Mexican, they say. Certainly it is one of the most beautiful states. Mountains, lakes, rivers, Indian villages, volcanoes, colonial cities. A feast. Michoacan is a sort of scale model of Mexico.

Morelia in northeast Michoacán (formerly known as Valladolid) is the capital of the state. The road from Mexico City is marvelously scenic. Known as the **Mil Cumbres (A Thousand Peaks)**; it goes by pine-covered mountains, past cool waterfalls, and around breathtaking curves. If you're doing the driving, keep your eye on the road. If you're looking, keep on looking at the scenery.

Morelia is a colonial town: the walls are built of soft-colored stone. The climate is mild. Life moves in slow tempo. Inevitably there is the cathedral, a grand building in pure Mexican baroque style with tall towers. At its side by the **Zócalo**, the central square, is the baroque **Palace of Government**. Inside is a colorful mural by **Alfredo Zalce** that describes the beauties of this state and outstanding events in its history.

The cathedral and the palace of government are on **Madero Street**. The facades of the buildings are the advertisement for a placid and elegant colonial city. (The word "colonial," by the way, is not a perjorative, with disdainful meaning. It means simply an association with the old days when things were nice and even beautiful. Some people sigh for those "good, old days," and there is even a literature that has sprung up, nostalgic for those departed times.) Morelia has a good regional museum that is located in a former Franciscan monastery. Each room is devoted to handicraft from a different village. The result proves the infinity of Michoacán village craftsmanship. Thus the state has preserved some of its richest Indian tradition.

The **Palacio Clavijero**, a former Jesuit seminary, is one of the most distinguished buildings in Mexico. It now houses bureaus of the state government. The superb court follows the example of Castillian tradition. Founded in 1660, it was named in honor of **Francisco Xavier Clavijero**, a Jesuit who taught here. Colegio de San Nicolás, one of the oldest universities in the Americas, is in Morelia and occupies a well-preserved baroque building downtown. Even more attractive is the old convent of **Santa Rosa** which housed the first school of music in the Americas. It faces a soothing plaza, which has a romantic monument to Cervantes, the Spanish writer. Morelia offers good hotels, either in colonial buildings such as the **Virrey de Mendoza** or the **Posada de la Soledad**, or in mountain-village style structures, such as the **Villa Montaña**, straddling a hill overlooking Morelia.

Butterfly Nets of Pátzcuaro

West of Morelia is **Pátzcuaro lake**, surrounded by Indian villages. The fishermen use butterly-like fishing nets. The fish don't seem to mind. In the middle of the lake is **Janitzio island**, on which is implaced a giant sculpture of **Father José María Morelos**, whose name abounds in Morelia. Along with Father Hidalgo, Morelos was one of the most important men of the independence struggle. Morelos was, as the historian Nicholas Cheetham described him, "a stocky, bulldog of a man . . . an astute, tenacious mestizo." Cheetham said he made a splendid partisan. On November 2nd, the Day of the Dead, the cemeteries on Janitzio are decorated with flowers; candles are lit, food is offered to the departed. People cry and sing and talk and get drunk and speak often of the names and deeds of their loved ones, the *"muertitos,"* whom a good Mexican never, never forgets.

Pátzcuaro is a town on the south side of the lake that is pure Indian. Some might say it has a beauty of its own: whitewashed adobe houses, overhanging wooden roofs, cobblestoned streets. There are remarkable buildings, such as the **Colegiata de Nuestra Señora de la Salud** (Our Lady of Health), the church of **St. Agustín**, which is decorated with murals by **Juan O'Gorman**, the House of the Eleven Patios, a tourist bureau and crafts center, and the House of the Giant, the former residence of the **Counts of Menocal.** Pátzcuaro may itself be a work of art. **Lake Pátzcuaro** has its fans. The French tour guide, *Guide Bleu,* calls it "one of the most beautiful (lakes) in the world, or at least one of the most photogenic."

You cannot travel in Michoacán without hearing about **Tata Vasco,** a greatly venerated man though he has been gone well over four centuries. He was a Spanish bishop who dedicated his life to preserving the Indian customs and their way of life. Don Vasco de Quiroga is much beloved by the Tarascan Indians, since he worked for years to give them a fair shake in life.

Place of the Hummingbirds

Near Pátzcuaro is a village with the rare name, **Tzintzuntzan.** Tzintzuntzan (Place of the Hummingbirds), one of the chief archeological sites in the state, was the ancient capital of the Tarascans, Michoacán's most important tribe. Tarascan is a musical language, no kin at all to Nahuatl. The Tarascans were never conquered by any other tribe until the Spanish arrived with their armor plate and cannons. To this day the Tarascans keep their traditions, their language and their way of life. It is especially alive in the mountain redoubts. They also preserve some of their *yacatas,* or ancient temples. You might call the yacata a small-fry platform that was used as a burial place.

Uruapan is not a fancy place but here is the beginning of another Michoacán— the *Tierra Caliente,* or tropical lands. Uruapan is the center of a rich agricultural area, located at the exact border between the mountains and the hills. The surrounding countryside is remarkable. For instance, **Tzaráracua,** a tropical park with lovely waterfalls.

Near Uruapan is **Paricutín,** the volcano that first erupted in 1943. It is sleeping now, or perhaps just taking a siesta. All around is evidence of its power: the fields covered with black-sand ashes which are slowly producing green life again, as lava does. The area is dotted with Indian villages known for their handicraft, their cooking, or the beauty of their surroundings. Here's a list: **Paracho, Santa Clara, Charán, Cotija, Zirahuén.** Like all of Mexico, Michoacán is full of surprises, full of contrast. Consider the **Ciudad Lázaro Cárdenas,** once a distant coastal village and now the

Then active Paricutín volcano, circa 1944.

site of one of Latin America's biggest steel mills. Steel in Michoacán? Yes. The old life changeth.

Zacatecas' Chalchihuites

Let's jump north to **Zacatecas**, which is the point of contact between Mexico's central-western region and the far north of Mexico. Those two areas are as different as if they were in different countries. Central Mexico is green and densely populated. The place has great historical significance and is rich in archeological treasure. In contrast, the north is huge, barren and empty. Life there always has been hard; its inhabitants never have enjoyed the refinements found in the central highlands. Even the cooking is simple and elementary.

In pre-Columbian times Zacatecas was an important cultural area, the site of at least one major archeological find— **Lake Quemada.** Protected by fortifications, the place, in the western part of Zacatecas, flourished from the year 900 to 1200. Much ceramic treasure has been unearthed there. The style gives evidence of contact between the Mexican art style of the highlands and the simpler geo-

Indian with his peyote.

metric art style of the American West.

Though geographically part of the north, Zacatecas became, culturally speaking, part of the highlands because it was rich in mines which attracted settlers and produced wealth. So it came to be that **Zacatecas city,** surrounded by dry and forbidding mountains, boasts some of the best colonial architecture in Mexico. The façade of its cathedral is probably the most ornate in the country, delicately, but at the same time, forcefully carved. Do not be surprised by the treasures of Zacatecas city. For many an *aficionado* it is one of their favorite places in Mexico. It has a curious atmosphere, a combination of the vigor and roughness of a border town, softened by surprising refinement. The houses, which can only be described as aristocratic, are graceful, with their forged balconies and window grills. The hard, gray stone of Zacatecas is sculpted with sober elegance.

In **Guadalupe,** a suburb of Zacatecas, is a remarkable convent which has been transformed into a museum.

Victorian San Luis Potosí

Similar to Zacatecas is the western part of the neighboring state of San Luis Potosí. There is the same grandiose but harsh vista of rocks and mountains; the same lunar landscape, empty of human presence. And then, suddenly, as in Zacatecas, out of nowhere springs a thoroughly civilized city: **San Luis Potosí,** capital of the state with the same name. The state itself is large and multi-faced. The east *(Huasteca Potosina)* is hot and tropical; the center, full of dry plains, and the west, mountainous and difficult.

San Luis Potosí city is a Victorian city. There's an air and a feel of Europe. You see it in the main square. You see it in the buildings. Note, for example, the **House of Culture,** once the residence of a wealthy British mining family named Meade. But the jewel of San Luis Potosí is the church of **El Carmen,** adorned with shells and multi-colored tiles, and with a retablo of highest quality. The **Teatro de la Paz** is undistinguished but pleasant and is surrounded by a square.

Like any old mining town, nearby **Real del Catorce** is full of ghosts and lost grandeur. It is located in desert land that produces another source of visions and euphoria—*peyotl,* the hallucinogenic cactus that still plays such an important role in the lives of many Indian tribes.

Mexico's North, 'El Norte'

To most Americans who venture across the border, Tijuana and Mexicali and Nogales and Ciudad Juárez and Laredo and Matamoros—that's Mexico. And that's all of Mexico they ever see.

Mexico's Northland is vast, sparsely-settled, semi-desert or mountain, and you must go many a weary mile before you get to the population centers. For 3,200 kilometers (2,000 miles), the U.S. and Mexico share a common border. To the average American the Mexican is a stereotype: he's a wetback; or he's a lazy man drowsing under a sombrero; or he's a slick mustachio lusting for blondes; or he's a fat and corrupt petty bureaucrat. Similarly, the Mexican paints in his mind the stereotype of the *yanqui,* the gringo. He's a pink-skinned tourist in checkered bermuda shorts, loud and arrogant, or too naive, who assumes that the whole world speaks English. People, it is unfortunate, live by stereotype.

The visitor to Mexico who is *simpá-tico* can indeed enjoy the borderland. If

you have taste you can pick up many excellent pieces of handicraft, both decorative and utilitarian. Of course, there is plenty of useless *kitsch* for sale—if that's what you want and apparently many visitors do. That's why it's for sale. If your palate is discriminating, you can also find good food, and not a vapid imitation of Mexican-style cooking. If you want action, well, the border towns can supply that, too: jai alai, *charreada* (rodeo), bullfights, dog races, horse races. And if you want to visit the redlight districts, you can. It may even be instructive, but hang on to your wallet, please, and keep your sense of humor. *Caveat emptor,* the old Romans used to say and it's still good advice. Let the buyer beware.

The Mexican northland contrasts markedly with the rest of the country. It looks different; its history is different, it *is* different. You should have a bit of its history tucked away in your mind before you go visiting. It will enhance your enjoyment of the place.

Cities of Gold

Most of the area south of the border—the states of Sinaloa, Sonora, Chihuahua, Durango, Coahuila, Nuevo Leon, and most of Tamaulipas—were once the domain of the Chichimeca Indians. They lived mainly by hunting and gathering. When some of them got together under a leader, they went out raiding. It was a way of life.

Take a big leap now and span the hundreds of miles between the outposts of Meso-America in Durango and Zacatecas to the site of **Casas Grandes** in northern Chihuahua. There archeologists have found proof of a bright people, who knew how to irrigate the land, and build five-story-high adobe communal houses and water tanks. Casas Grandes combines elements of the Pueblo Indian civilization of the southwestern United States and the influences of Meso-America. Then around the year 1300 the place was abandoned. Why? Who can say.

For centuries Casas Grandes was deserted and then a strange group of four persons came wandering by. It was the fantastic explorer Cabeza de Vaca, two Spanish companions and a Moorish slave. They were on a little jaunt that took them seven years, a walk in the sun through the southwestern part of the United States and northern Mexico from

Preceding pages, a Chihuahua cavescape; and left, a dapper Pancho Villa the Gulf of Mexico to the Pacific Ocean. The four voyagers lived by their wits. They showed the Indians how to cure ailments; that made them supernatural in the Indians' eyes. Cabeza de Vaca spread the word to the Spanish. He spoke of the fabulous wealth of Cíbola, told to him by his Indian friends. The Spanish took the bait and began a series of expeditions to the north, which eventually opened northwestern Mexico to colonization.

Another fabulous explorer, Francisco Coronado, debunked the de Vaca myth. He and his party set out from Compostela, walked across Sinaloa and southeastern Arizona and reached Cíbola country—the land of the Zuñi Indians of New Mexico. But there was no gold in the Seven Cities of Cíbola. Coronado sent some of his lieutenants farther along on the quest and one of his lieutenants even reached what is now Kansas. But there was no gold, no silver. The north of Mexico was forgotten. It was too poor to colonize.

Mining finally was the lure. It began with the silver mines at Zacatecas, then Durango, then the rich silver lode of Santa Bárbara in southern Chihuahua. It

was a 17-year-old nobleman, Francisco de Ibarra, who led the expedition which opened up silver-rich Chihuahua. In 1554 he set out with his party from Zacatecas. They twice crossed the rugged Sierra Madre and found extensive silver deposits. Ibarra showed tact beyond his years in dealing diplomatically with hostile Indians; pacifying them by words, rather than by weapons. His explorations led to the founding of New Spain's largest province, which included the present states of Durango, Sinaloa and Sonora. It was called New Vizcaya in honor of de Ibarra's home in Spain.

The last major exploration to the north set out from Santa Bárbara at the end of the 16th Century and was led by Juan de Oñate. They went up Chihuahua, across the Rio Grande and into New Mexico. There they laid out a town, built a church and houses and began to till the land. They forced the Indians to work for them; an uprising resulted; many colonists were killed and the others forced to flee. The Spanish crown decided to hold off on any more adventures into the north.

Rebellious Indians:
Tepehuanes, Tarahumaras, Apaches

Settlers did drift in—but in small numbers. Saltillo and Monterrey were founded. Still, the enormous north Mexico was practically empty. Indians were christianized and exploited. It was not hard to dominate them in the Mexican northeast, but it was a different story in the west. There the Indians rose in bloody revolt. The first uprising was the Tepehuan rebellion of 1616. Hundreds of Spaniards were killed; thousands of Indians were put to death in revenge. Then came the fierce rebellions of the Tarahumara Indians.

Why the brutality? Simple. The Spaniards needed workers. As Cortés once said, "If I wanted to be a farmer, I would have stayed in Spain." The Spaniards forced the Indians to work the land and to sweat in the mines. Indian settlements around the missions provided a concentration of manpower. The role of the missionary is ambiguous. True, they often defended the Indians and protested their mistreatment. But it was obvious they liked the idea of keeping the Indians in large communities where they could be easily controlled. It is no wonder that the Indians hated the whites—any white, in-

Geronimo's Apache cousins were the scourge of Chihuahua. The Apache chief poses, circa 1885.

83726

cluding missionaries. When they couldn't find local Indians, the Spaniards imported "tame" Indians from central Mexico, usually Tlaxcaltecans or Tarascans. The Tlaxcaltecans came north in large numbers to work in the mines and on the land. In Saltillo, for example, 400 Tlaxcalans were imported to set up an agricultural community and build the cathedral.

The Spanish could not control the Apaches. For 150 years the Apaches chose warfare as a way of life. They captured horses from the Spaniards, mounted raids, and conducted guerrilla warfare, hit and run style. They became experts at it. They wisely refused pitched battle. They had no bases which could be destroyed and they operated in bands. The Spaniards built a chain of *presidios* (forts) across northern Chihuahua to try to contain the raids but the Indians easily slipped past. Spanish settlers had to abandon their ranches; it was too dangerous to stay there.

Finally, the Spanish found the solution: indulgence. They first persuaded the Apaches to settle down near the presidios. There was a lure: they gave the Indians a food ration, liquor and even some firearms. That quelled the Apache fighting spirit, at least temporarily, and the rebels rode on their raids no more.

Northern Mexico was not part of the war theater for much of the Mexican War of Independence. True, Father Hidalgo was executed in Chihuahua but most of the fighting took place in central Mexico. Now, once again, the Apaches hit the campaign trail. There was no longer sufficient funds to keep them in the style to which they had become accustomed. They renewed their raids. North Mexico panicked. The Mexicans offered a bounty for Apache scalps; some renegade Americans took up the offer.

Wars of Intervention

By now American settlers had begun to occupy Texas, then New Mexico and Arizona. It was not long before more than 20,000 Anglos, as the whites were called, were living in Texas, as against some 3,000 or 4,000 Mexicans. Numbers *do* tell. That was the beginning of the end of Mexican Texas. The Mexican War (1846–1848) began. Mexicans call it the War of Intervention, which it was. The Americans, for grievances both real and imagined, invaded all the key points of

north Mexico: Guaymas, Chihuahua, Saltillo, Monterrey. Mexico was stripped of its territory north of the Rio Grande, half of the country.

In 1864–1865 the Mexicans dealt with another invader—the French army which supported the Emperor Maximilian who was imposed on the Mexican people. President Benito Juárez fled to the north with his government, and remained practically in exile across the Rio Grande in Mexico from El Paso. The U.S. government was pro-Juárez, but there wasn't much it could do about helping him. It had bigger matters on its mind; namely, the Civil War. For northeast Mexico the American war was a blessing. Cotton, produced in the American South, could be shipped only through Mexican ports. The South was blockaded. When the war ended, the U.S. government brought diplomatic pressure on France to get out of Mexico. The French did; the troops were recalled, but Maximilian continued his futile fight to stay on the throne. He was captured and shot.

Porfirio Díaz brought relative peace and modernization to northern Mexico. The Apache problem finally was resolved. The U.S. government herded

Porfirio Díaz in his youth.

them into reservations and, in Chihuahua, a Mexican armed force under Colonel Joaquín Terrazas defeated the last important band of Apaches, under Victorio.

Revolutionary Northerners

If the War of Independence was largely a central Mexican episode, then the Revolution of 1910 was mostly a northern Mexican affair. With the exception of Emiliano Zapata in Morelos, all the major figures of the revolution came from the north: Francisco Madero and Venustiano Carranza from Coahuila, Alvaro Obregón from Sonora and Pancho Villa from Chihuahua.

One can speak of the northern Mexican's character which is distinct from the people of the rest of Mexico. There paternalism is the norm. On the contrary, the northerner is known for his individualism, his self-reliance. He comes quickly to the point; he doesn't equivocate, he doesn't beat around the bush as his southern countryman does. Remote and without much help from the central government, the northern Mexican fought the Indians and developed the land and made do on his own. The northern Mexican often looks on the federal government with suspicion. He believes the higher-ups in Mexico City are interested mainly in meddling. Northern Mexico has close ties with the United States. Many Mexicans of the north admire the Americans, do much of their buying across the border, and even wear Texas-style boots, stetsons and Western clothes.

Northwest Mexico was neglected until the missionaries began to work among the tribes in the 17th Century. The Jesuits were most successful with the Pimas and the Opatas; they achieved results with the Mayos and the Yaquis, but they made little headway with the headstrong Seri Indians. The priests introduced domestic animals, showed the Indians new crops, taught them better ways to farm and to build. Many Indians quickly took up the new life.

The problems grew when Spanish colonists arrived and tried to take the most fertile lands and force the Indians into hard labor. Naturally, they resisted. Split into many tribes, spread out over great distances, the northern Indians could not be conquered at one blow. So rebellion flared, on and off, over the decades. As more Spaniards moved in, the bitterness hardened.

The gallant Villa leads his brave Dorados.

Expulsion of the Jesuits, Persecution of the Indians

When the Jesuits were expelled from Mexico in 1767, the missions they had founded disintegrated and the northwest Indians lost their only protector and spokesman. They were ground under heel. Whites brazenly encroached on tribal lands. The Yaquis, a fighting race, reacted angrily and the Spanish dealt with them harshly. So did the Mexicans, after the country gained its independence. There is one ghastly incident on record: A group of Yaquis sued for peace. In response to their protests, the Yaquis were herded into a church, artillery guns were trained on the church and 120 were slain. Finally, the authorities decided that the only way to resolve the problem was to deport the Yaquis *en masse*. They were rounded up and sold into peonage for 60 pesos a head to work on the henequen plantations of the Yucatán and the tobacco plantations of the Valle Nacional in Oaxaca. Some of the Yaquis broke out of confinement, took the hills and continued to fight.

During the revolution of 1910, Yaquis joined General Obregón's forces and made the best of soldiers. They wanted their tribal lands back but that was not convenient for the government. In 1917, Lázaro Cárdenas forced them into submission. But when Cárdenas became president in the 1930s, he ordered a dam built on the upper Yaqui river for irrigation, and set aside one million acres for the Yaquis. It included the whole north bank of the river and part of the south. Much of the south bank still was held by the whites, but the Yaquis realized this was the best possible deal they could get. They set up a reservation, took over their own tribal lands, and they control the land to this day.

Other Northwest Indians did not fare as well. The Seri Indians were either killed or died of disease. The tribe was reduced in number from 5,000 to less than 200. The Opatas, on the other hand, assimilated readily. They learned Spanish and intermarried. They cooperated in the battles against the Apaches.

The tribes of the Northwest were way off by themselves for years in a rugged, remote corner of Mexico. They took little part in the life of the nation. They were marginal, for example, to the independence movement of the 1810s. The

A Pershing American Army scouting party.

182

region was isolated, weak, unprotected. It practically invited invasion. The French, led by Gaston Raousset de Bourbon, captured Hermosillo in Sonora in 1852. Another adventure, led by Henry Crabb, an American from California, was aimed at capturing northern Sonora in 1857. In both instances, the Mexicans reacted vigorously, defeated the invaders and executed the leaders.

Northern Rulers

In time the Northwest developed muscle and conscience. When the 1910 revolution broke out, the Northwest took part wholeheartedly, providing troops and the general (Álvaro Obregon) who emerged victorious after the inevitable internal power struggle. For a decade, Mexico was ruled directly or indirectly by the "Northwest Mafia," first Obregón, then General Plutarco Elías Calles.

Land reform was implemented slowly in the Northwest. Large tracts were not taken over until President Cardenas's program. By law, private land holdings are limited in size, but there's a way to get around it. Titles are registered under the names of a number of relatives and thus large sections are controlled by a single person. He has the capital and presumably the know-how to make the most efficient use of the land. The question naturally arises: Should these tracts, acquired by amalgamation, be divided up among the land-hungry who have neither the technical skill nor the capital to run a productive operation? It is a question that is never satisfactorily answered. At the moment the "small" property owner is holding his own, but what of the future?

The Northwest is highly productive. Sonora leads the nation in cotton, wheat and soybean production. Sinaloa tops the other states in tomatoes, most of which go to the U.S. Sinaloa also raises a hefty crop of wheat, cotton, sugar cane and chickpeas, which are exported chiefly to Spain and Cuba. Although the silver mines of the Northwest are practically exhausted, the mines of Cananea in northern Sonora make that state the leading producer of copper in Mexico, while Chihuahua heads the nation in mining revenues.

Revolutionary action 'round an adobe barricade.

BUSY MONTERREY
AND VICINITY

Most Americans who drive into Mexico from Texas shed their inhibitions in the streets of Laredo before crossing the Rio Grande. The same thing happens at Eagle Pass and Brownsville. Across the river and into Mexico come millions of visitors: the margarita lovers, the cultural buffs, but mainly those who want to see something different. The border towns may have a slightly tarnished charm but that is enough. In their own way they are beguiling. But do not, dear visitor, be fooled into thinking that this is all there is to Mexico. The border towns have one overriding mission: to part you from your dollar as painlessly as possible. Bordertown Mexicans speak English, naturally, and often prefer dollars to pesos.

If you are looking for the real Mexico, you must go on, sometimes for miles and miles. Indeed, the attractions of northeast Mexico are those of the outdoors: scenery, hunting and fishing.

That robust city of muscular industrial activity, Monterrey, dominates this section of Mexico. Dynamic Monterrey is the center of private enterprise and lives sometimes in uneasy relationship with the paternalistic federal government of Mexico City. The men who run Monterrey's industry tend to have closer cultural ties with the United States than with the rest of Mexico. They admire American knowhow, American marketing procedures, and American business methods. This does not mean they are not patriotic Mexicans and proud of their achievements, but it does mean that they often speak of government interference. In fact, they sound like American businessmen. Many Monterrey well-to-do send their children to the U.S. for schooling. One of the best known industrialists founded the Monterrey Institute of Technology, patterned after the Massachusetts Institute of Technology. It is probably Mexico's outstanding university. Monterrey youth even play American-style football.

The 'Pittsburgh of Mexico'

Some people call Monterrey the "Pittsburgh of Mexico." It is full of interesting sights. The center of the town, the **Plaza Zaragoza,** is a large, pleasant square bordered by a colonial cathedral that is worth visiting. Nearby is a large free-form sculpture by Rufino Tamayo, Mexico's best known living artist. The church of **La Purísima Concepción** is a good example of modern, prize-winning architecture. In the church is a statue, which, it is said, once miraculously stopped the Santa Catarina river from flooding the city. The finest example of colonial architecture is the **Obispado**—the **Bishop's Palace**—which is located on a hill and affords an excellent overview of the city, with an impressive mountain backdrop called **Cerro de la Silla** (Saddle Peak). There are bullet holes and shellfire scars on the former church of the Obispado, which is now a museum; they are souvenirs of the American invasion of 1846.

There's a nice way to start or finish a tour of Monterrey, especially if you are thirsty. Make a tour of the **Cuauhtémoc Brewery.** It produces fine pilsner-type beer—a beer which aficionados claim is as good as the best beer brewed anywhere. The brewery is Mexico's biggest and oldest (Carta Blanca and Bohemia brands) and has led the way in providing good wages and benefits to its workers. Wage-earners of Monterrey are among

García Cave, Monterrey area, left; and below, local industry.

the envied of the country. Often they get free medical care, subsidized housing, 40 percent off their home-delivered groceries, and even free piano lessons.

Credit for Monterrey's industrial development is often attributed to the Garza-Sada family, free-enterprisers who emigrated to Mexico from Spain in the 19th Century. Monterrey produces 25 percent of Mexico's manufactured goods, including half of the country's manufactured exports. The Alfa Group of Monterrey is Latin America's largest privately owned company and the first in Mexico to be listed in Fortune magazine's 500 of the largest non-United States corporations.

If capitalism appears to be thriving in Monterrey, then so does radicalism. There is still present the Mexican dilemma: too many people, too few good jobs. A decade ago a student-led Communist group took over some public lands and set up what has become a going community called *Tierra y Libertad*— the old revolutionary slogan of that bold revolutionary, Emiliano Zapata. This community has its own schools, hospitals and, most important, its own vigilant police force.

Calcified Caves, Sarapes And a Movie-Making Town

It's worth exploring the area around Monterrey. About 35 kilometers away is **García Cave,** a well-lighted marvel of calcified shapes. You reach the cave via cog cablecar. **Horsetail Falls** is a short drive away. You can picnic and look at the triple cascade called the **Three Graces.** En route you pass **La Boca dam,** where there is good fishing and water sports. For a spectacular view of the city, try **Chipinique Mesa,** where the well-to-do of Monterrey have homes. If you want to see spectacular rock formations, then drive out to **Huasteca Canyon,** and just walk and gawk.

A divided superhighway runs from Monterrey to **Saltillo,** capital of the neighboring state of Coahuila. The **Santiago Cathedral** in Saltillo is an excellent example of baroque colonial architecture. Shops offer a good selection of leather and silverware but the town's speciality is the production of colorful sarapes, many of them woven at the **El Saltillero Mill.** Try Saltillo's *pan de pulque,* a pulque bread.

If you like a long spell of driving, you

Coahuila vineyards.

can head for Mazatlán on the Pacific coast, some 700 kilometers away. On the way, by making a short detour, you can visit **Parras**, the home of Mexico's wine industry and, incidentally, the home of Francisco Madero, leader of the 1910 revolution. Farther on, the road goes by **Torreón** and the **La Laguna** cotton district. Push on and you reach **Durango**, a city that has a fine Mexican flavor but is not distinguished. It is a cattle center and a lumbering center. Round about town you will see permanent movie sets, and indeed the place is a movie-making center. From Durango prepare yourself for what is probably the most spectacular drive in Mexico. From **El Espinazo del Diablo** (The Devil's Spine), the road winds like a top and drops down to **Mazatlán,** a city of beaches, seafood and sometimes very good surfing conditions.

There are all sorts of places of interest in northeast Mexico. From Matamoros or from Monterrey, you can head for **Ciudad Victoria.** There's good fishing at the **Vicente Guerrero dam.** You may catch a black bass weighing three kilos (7 pounds) or more, but that's nothing. In the **Soto Mariana river,** you might hook up with a tarpon weighing 17 kilos (35 pounds). That's exciting!

Spicy Tampico

"Tampico, Tampico. On the Gulf of Méjico . . ." You know the song. Now that's a lively place. Overcrowded, yes, but full of color and full of spice. Not very charming, to be sure. In a land of spectacular scenery **Tampico** is flat-chested. But it is full of vitality; full of juice. Take a walk downtown. See the gawdy riverfront district. Sample some of the best seafood in the country.

If you are devoted to archeology, you will probably want to make a trip to the Huastecan ceremonial center of **El Tamuín,** some 32 kilometers (20 miles) away. It is not too easy a side trip and involves a ferry crossing east of **Ciudad de Valles.** The site is on a bluff high above the **Tamuín river.**

Of course, you can reach central Mexico by the road which shoots down from Monterrey through **San Luis Potosí.** For diversion, try a short sidetrip to the ghost mining town of **Real del Catorce.** It will make a nice break.

Ciudad Valles is in the region called **Huasteca,** named for the Maya's distant cousins who settled there. From Ciudad Valles, you go through jungles of bamboo palm and banana trees. Just before you reach **Tamazunchale** (to remember the name think of it as Thomas 'n' Charlie), you can make a side-trip on a paved road to the Huastecan village of **Xilitla.** In Tamazunchale, which is in the southeast tip of San Luis Potosí, is a fine 16th Century church. On Sunday the marketplace is crowded with Indians come to do their weekly shopping. If you are an ornithologist, the place to do your bird-watching is in the vicinity of Thomas 'n'. This is also a paradise for the lepidopterist. In fact, you can buy well-mounted butterfly specimens in many of the town's shops.

From Tamazunchale there's a rough but scenic 320-kilometer (200 mile) drive to **Pachuca** in the state of **Hidalgo,** not far from Mexico City. Look out for stray animals on the road; be careful of hairpin turns. You will see lovely valleys; people at work in the fields. **Zimapán** has an unusual Moorish-looking church with a massive tower and many tiles. **Ixmiquilpán** is an important Otomi Indian center with interesting colonial architecture. Stop off in the market where the best buys are wool weavings, pottery and silver jewelry.

Baccus drinks in Coahuila winefest.

Rugged Chihuahua, The Central North

For the land traveler in northern Mexico the terrain dominates all: those precipitous mountains, the deserts and the vast distances. If you grow weary behind the wheel, think of a Spaniard named Cabeza de Vaca. Early in the 16th Century this explorer and three friends walked from Texas to the Pacific, through northern Mexico. It took him seven years. Of course, he did not have to be back on the job at a certain date; nor did he have kids in the backseat, demanding a stop every half hour for relief or refueling.

The Sierra Madres

Let's discuss the route from Texas, south. (The route from Arizona is covered in the Pacific Coast section and the route from California in the Baja chapter.) There are two great mountain ranges confronting you: the **Sierra Madre Occidental** in the west and the **Sierra Madre Oriental** in the east. The Sierra Madre Occidental is by far the more rugged; the

Sierra Madre Oriental does not present such an imposing obstacle. Between the border crossing at El Paso-Ciudad Juárez and Guadalajara, in central-west Mexico, a 1,600-kilometer (1,000 miles) stretch, there are only two ways to cross the mountains to the Pacific, unless you want to hike it like Cabeza de Vaca: the railroad from Chihuahua City to Los Mochis on the Pacific coast, or the road from Durango to Mazatlán. Going south from Chihuahua City, it's another 800 kilometers (500 miles) to Torreon, where you can head east to the coast. Or if you continue south it's another 320 kilometers (200 miles) to Zacatecas where you can turn east. Not until you reach the central Mexican highlands do you have a wider choice of roads to pick from. The north is road-sparse.

Northern Mexico, a vast area, is different from the rest of the country. The fiestas are less colorful; there's not nearly as much production of hand-made crafts; little colonial architecture remains. The pre-Columbian ceremonial centers are not great drawing cards; only the Tarahumara Indians have retained an appreciable measure of their traditional way of life. But on the other hand, what a place

Chihuahua ranchero.

for the hunter or the fisherman! What a spectacular country!

The Mexican wilderness ends with the states of Durango, Zacatecas and San Luis Potosí. There are two logical north-south axes: one from El Paso to Zacatecas and the other from Laredo on the border to San Luis Potosí. There are many side trips you can take and unless you are hell-bent to reach a sun-baked beach or Mexico City, there are two places you should stop and see: Chihuahua City and Monterrey. You can use either town as an overnighter only, or as a base for exploring the areas.

Honky-Tonk Juárez, Mormons and Mennonites

Ciudad Juárez, just across the border from El Paso, is Chihuahua's biggest town and caters to millions of American tourists. Many see the city, go no farther, and tell people they've seen Mexico. It's an interesting town. You can go to the bullfights, or to the greyhound races or the horse races and lose or win a packet. You can even go to the dentist (a surprisingly lot of Americans do) because you pay a lot less than in the U.S. for dental work.

Drive straight down highway 45 to Chihuahua City, or take detours and see a number of points of interest before reaching the capital city. Out of Ciudad Juárez, you swing right for **Casas Grandes,** home of several thousand Mormons whose ancestors refused to give up polygamy. The Mormons have converted 5,000 Mexicans to their religion.

Near Casas Grandes are the ruins of a culture that is part Pueblo Indian and part Meso-American. South of Casas Grandes is **Babicora,** where William Randolph Hearst once owned a 354,000-hectare estate (875,000 acres), which was expropriated by the government in the early 1950s. Soon you come to **Mennonite country,** where some 15,000 German-speaking farmers work their land. It is they who deserve credit for making the state a leading producer of oats, cheese and meats. Mennonites, the Mexicans say, do not mix much; few speak Spanish and they do not inter-marry. As it is Mennonite custom to shun luxury and modernization, they still drive around in horse-drawn carts which will remind you of a departed era. However, you may see a pickup truck or two—not everyone respects the old order. Yet TV is taboo in

Mennonite family gathering, west of Chihuahua.

the homes, and ten-children families are not uncommon. They are a strange but fascinating people.

The town of **Cuauhtemoc,** about 95 kilometers (60 miles) west-southeast of Chihuahua City, is the Mennonite center for commercial activity, though no Mennonites live there. They come to town to do their shopping and their gawking. During the day you will see them—overall-clad men, married women dressed in black, and maidens in bright dresses.

From Cuauhtemoc you drive over a partly-paved, partly dirt road to the waterfalls of **Basaseáchic.** Do inquire about road conditions beforehand, especially during the rainy season. There are a few cabins near the falls, but play it safe and plan either to make the roundtrip in one day, or take along a sleeping bag. The falls plunge over 300 meters (more than 1,000 feet). It's an easy walk up the end of the road to the top of the waterfalls. Or, if you are in good shape, walk down *la ventana* (the window) about half-way down for a spectacular view. It's best to hire a local guide as the path is not clearly marked.

'Ay, Chihuahua! Cuanto Apache!'

Chihuahua City, founded in 1709, is a dynamic town, full of places of interest. It's also a good base for exploring the area. It is not unusual in the city to see Tarahumara Indians in traditional dress, taking in the town. Mostly they are window-shopping. You can buy the famous hairless Chihuahua dogs, but take care! Make sure you know what you are getting: that cuddly pup may grow up to be a mongrel monster, not an amiable Chihuahua. Be sure, that is, that you get the real McCoy. The Chihuahuas once upon a time were used by the Aztecs as bed warmers, and occasionally for a midnight snack.

The baroque cathedral on the main plaza in town is one of the few outstanding architectural gems from the colonial period found in the north of Mexico. The project was financed by voluntary contributions of the miners working in the nearby silver mines. An aqueduct and the **Church of San Francisco** also remain from colonial times. The **state capitol** is lined inside with paintings depicting the history of Chihuahua. In the inner courtyard there is a monument to the memory of Father Miguel Hidalgo, whose *grito*

aroused his countrymen to revolution. Father Hidalgo was executed here. **Quinta Gameros,** a Victorian manor house which dates back to the turn of the century, houses a regional museum.

And there is a museum dedicated to Pancho Villa, the old ruffian-Robin Hood. The place was the home of Luz Corral de Villa, one of his wives, who died in 1981. Movie fans might be interested in seeing a house in town that is a copy of Tara, the stately mansion in "Gone With the Wind."

If you want to go hunting, make arrangements through the hotels or travel agencies. The best known hunting lodges are the luxurious "La Estancia" in Mennonite country and "El Halcon." You can go horseback riding, play tennis, go swimming, or laze away in a sauna. Just out of town is the old **Hacienda de Quinta Carolina.** You can see what it contains for a modest fee. It will give you an idea of what splendor money could buy at the end of the 19th Century.

A good paved road leads northeast toward **Ojinaga.** About 9 kilometers (5 miles) before you reach the town of **Aldama,** you will see the mission church of **Santa Anna de Chinarras,** one of the few

Basaseachic Falls.

Jesuit-built churches outside the Sierras. Farther along, you pass **Pueblitos** where some of Pancho Villa's fighting men (the Golden Ones) were placated with 20 acres apiece of irrigated farmland. They also got their farm tools and a year's grubstake. The government was hoping that would keep them from shooting things up.

Coyame, northeast of Aldama, makes rope, a spirited drink and wax—all from various species of the cactus plant. This gives you an idea of what the countryside hereabouts looks like. It was in 1880 in the desert country north of Coyame at **Tres Castillos** that Colonel Terrazas finally defeated and broke the back of the Apaches. That marked the beginning of the end of the Apache raids in Chihuahua.

A few kilometers east of Coyame a dirt road goes to **Cuchillo Parado** (Standing Knife), a strange rock formation near the Rio Conchos. Once the rock formation was *in* the river, but the rivers of Mexico (see the Rio Bravo, or Rio Grande, as the *norteamericanos* call it, as an example) sometimes change course. About 18 kilometers (10 miles) beyond the Cuchillo Parado turnoff, the road begins to climb

until you come to a lookout at the **Peguis barranca** overlooking the **Rio Conchos** far below. You might as well picnic here before returning to Chihuahua since there's not much to see on the road to Ojinaga.

On the World's 'Most Scenic Railroad'

If you can take the train from Chihuahua to the Pacific, do it. It's a most exciting train trip along the "World's Most Scenic Railroad." That's not hyperbole; it is fact. Self-powered Fiat coaches run everyday from Chihuahua to Los Mochis and Topolobampo on the Pacific. If there's nothing holding the train up, then you make the trip during daylight hours and you can see the magnificent scenery of the Sierra Madres.

The construction of the splendid railroad was originally the dream of a man named Albert K. Owen, but it took many years, and many attempts, to push the railroad through. It was completed finally in 1961 by Mexican engineers. The track was begun in 1898 out of Chihuahua and reached Creel in 1912. Then came all the obstacles: revolution, lack of

money, and incredible engineering problems. The last 160 kilometers (100 miles) were the toughest. That stretch was begun in 1952 and it took nine years to put through. You do not have to be an engineering expert to appreciate how formidable was the task. In that last stretch are 39 bridges and 86 tunnels. There are places where the track switches back and forth as it descends a particularly steep grade. Lean back, relax, and enjoy it.

If you like to, you can get off at **Creel** and spend a few days in the mountains. It's way up—2,500 meters (about 8,200 feet) altitude. In the vicinity there are colonial mission churches, waterfalls, mines, and even a couple of decent hotels. From Creel a road of sorts leads to **La Bufa** and the once fabulous mining town of **Batopilas**. There's still some mining done in the area, a non-luxury hotel in town, and dollops of marvelous wilderness. There is also a partially paved road from Creel to the Basaseáchic Falls.

In many places, especially around Creel, you will see Tarahumara Indians dressed either in Western-style garb, or in the traditional white cotton and red headband. Some may dress in a combination of both styles. There are 50,000 Tarahumaras, one of the largest Indian groups left in Mexico. They are rugged fellows. The men take part in races, some of which go on for three days and nights, non-stop, and cover hundreds of miles. Seeing how stalwart these chaps are, the authorities tried to persuade them to enter marathon races. Ah, but it turned out that the marathon distance—just over 41 kilometers, or 26 miles—is too short a distance for them. They're just getting warmed up. These durable men can run a deer down and kill the animal with a knife.

There's a 20-minute stop at **El Divisadero** and from here you can admire the **Barranca del Cobre,** which is deeper than the Grand Canyon of the Colorado. If that's enough time for you, you can stay on the train and go on. If you want to stay longer, you can, of course. There's an excellent hotel perched on the edge of the Barranca del Cobre.

If you wish to get off the train and make a stop, you have to make sure you tell the man when you buy your ticket. You can ship your car by train (not on the rail coach, of course), but be sure to make arrangements well ahead of time.

Copper Canyon, the Sierra Madre.

192

Parral's Thunderbolt Virgin

Driving south from Chihuahua City you will see the state's richest agricultural regions. It is here they grow the famous chile peppers. From the city of **Camargo**, 157 kilometers (98 miles) southwest of Chihuahua, you can zip over to **Boquilla Dam**, which is stocked with black bass from Canada. That is why the body of water is called **Lake Toronto.**

Hidalgo del Parral is a thriving town with an active mine, called **La Prieta**, 149 kilometers (93 miles) farther on. Once silver was the main support of the economy but now there is also lumbering and commerce. There is a fine old colonial church, dedicated to the **Virgen del Rayo,** the Thunderbolt Virgin. It is said that the church was paid for in gold ingots by an Indian miner. He refused to reveal the location of the mine, even though he was tortured. Another church, **Nuestra Señora de Fátima,** is constructed of ore-bearing rock: gold, silver, copper, lead, zinc. Even the pews are made of rock. Obviously, the idea was to seek divine guidance and protection for the miners.

Parral is famous because it's the place where Pancho Villa, driving his Dodge sedan, was assassinated in 1923. There's a museum in town which contains old photos and a number of Villa mementoes. It is said that Villa was hit by 16 bullets but that he was still able to draw his pistol and dispatch one of the nine assassins before he succumbed.

The man who is supposed to have led the assassination team went free after spending only eight months in jail. All sorts of tales have grown out of the event. One was that Pancho Villa's head was dug up and sold for $10,000. All that can be said for sure is that when the government decided Pancho Villa was an authentic revolutionary hero and his body was dug up for reburial in the Monument to the Revolution in Mexico City, the diggers couldn't find Pancho's skull.

The central government's belated decision to elevate Villa to the ranks of the country's other distinguished revolutionary heroes is evidence of the controversy that surrounded—and still surrounds—this most colorful of tough hombres. Many conservatives still consider Villa an ordinary bandit, but popular songs and stories have made him the best known of Mexico's legendary and larger-than-life historical characters.

Desert
cave wall
paintings,
Chihuahua.

195

BAJA CALIFORNIA,
THE 'HOT OVEN'

Until the 1,700-kilometer long (1,050 mile) highway was completed in 1973 from Tijuana to the southern tip of Baja California, most of the peninsula was explored only by those with private planes, or boats, or those with lots of money. Now you can drive down a paved road or take a bus to any of the major points in Baja. The highway is only a narrow ribbon. Of course, you can get off the road and explore—by horseback, in the seat of a four-wheel-drive vehicle, or by boat. Or you can walk. Baja translates into "lower," but the beauty of the place is on a high plane.

Fish Stories and Amazons

For many Americans, Baja is the best fish story ever written. Author Zane Grey fished the Gulf around the turn of the century and ever since both writing and non-writing fishermen have found it a place where fish stories come true. There are at least 650 species of fish in the waters off Baja.

The best work on Baja is *The Forgotten Peninsula*, published in 1961 and written by Joseph Wood Krutch. In 1940, John Steinbeck and his friend and cohort, the marine biologist Ed Ricketts, wrote *Sea of Cortés*, a story about Baja. Steinbeck's novella, *The Pearl*, was a story the author heard in La Paz, capital of Baja. Earle Stanley Gardner wrote eight books on Baja. Robert Louis Stevenson wrote part of *Treasure Island* while relaxing in the port of Ensenada.

The peninsula was opened, Christianized and depopulated by the Spaniards. An early Jesuit missionary wrote of idle Indians, each supported by a number of complacent wives. However, the good life for them didn't last long. The Church gathered them in. Smallpox and syphilis wiped them out. Of the 40,000 indigenous inhabitants of Baja, there are less than 500 left. Those few survivors live in the north.

In the south all that is left of the Indians' ancestors are some cave paintings to show they existed. There are some 400 known cave sites, which are 500 to 1,000 years old. Erle Stanley Gardner, that prolific author of detective books, did some detective work himself and discovered some of the caves.

Cortés heard that some of the Aztec gold came from the north and he was given a charter to do a bit of exploring. He sent out ships under Diego de Becerra in 1533. Everything went wrong. De Becerra was assassinated by the ship's pilot, who, in turn, with 22 other crew members, was slain by Indians when they landed at what is now La Paz. The survivors came back with some pearls and a lot of harrowing tales, including the story of maidens clad only in strands of pearls. That must have titillated Cortés. He himself set sail for Baja and landed at La Paz. He found some pearls and named the place Santa Cruz and set up a colony which failed. But he did not find the maidens dressed in pearls.

A few years later, Francisco de Ulloa sailed up Mexico's west coast, discovered the mouth of the Colorado River and sailed around Baja to the Pacific side, as far as Magdalena Bay. Thereupon, for years, the Spaniards forgot about Baja. Pirates started operating out of Baja, and raided Spanish shipping. Many a buccaneer sharpened his skills off the stringbean-shaped peninsula. In 1587 Thomas Cavendish captured a treasure-laden Manila galleon off Cabo San Lucas.

The Saving of Souls

In the 17th Century Father Kino, a Jesuit mission-builder, sailed to Baja, journeyed across the peninsula and had a good look. He concluded that if there was no wealth in Baja, aside from pearling, then at least there were a lot of Indian souls to be saved. Father Salvatierra, a Jesuit, founded the first mission at Loreto in 1697. For 70 years, the Jesuits built churches and taught the Indians. When the Jesuits were expelled from Mexico in 1767, the Franciscans were given the monopoly on soul-saving. Six years later the Dominicans took over. Some 30 missions, in all, were founded in Baja, but they were abandoned by the 1850s. There simply weren't enough Indians left to make it worthwhile. According to one report, there were 50,000 Indians in Baja in the 17th Century, 20,000 in the mid-18th Century, and only 3,700 in 1842.

Loreto, the site of the first mission, served for 130 years as the capital of both Baja and Alta California. It remained the leading town in Baja until a storm leveled it in 1828. The capital was then moved to the pearling center at La Paz. During the

Mexican War, the U.S. Navy invaded the main ports of Baja and fought a battle at Mulegé. For a time it seemed as though Baja was going to be attached to the U.S. as war booty, but it was not. Some Americans, though, tried to annex the peninsula. William Walker sacked La Paz in 1853. He wanted to incorporate Baja into the Union as a slave state. In 1911, amazingly, some Mexican revolutionaries teamed up with some American anarchists and a group of land developers to try to take Baja over. The Mexican government sent in troops to quell their ambitions. Yankees quickly realized the potential of the irrigated regions of northern Baja. For example, the Colorado River Land Company which farmed near Mexicali. In 1946 the Mexican government bought the land company out.

Baja never had enough precious metal to make mining worthwhile. There was a little silver mining in colonial times and a mini-gold rush in the late 19th Century. In 1887 the French operated a copper mine, called El Boleo, in Santa Rosalía. In 1953 it was taken over by the Mexican government. The island of San Marcos produces gypsum; in Guerrero Negro saltworkers gather some five million tons of salt annually at a saltworks there that is often called the world's largest of its kind.

Baja's population and its economy both are concentrated in the north. Bumper crops are produced in the irrigated lands around Mexicali: cotton, alfalfa, wheat, tomatoes, grapes. Workers in northern Baja get the highest minimum wage in Mexico.

Baja is twice as long, but much skinnier than Florida, and longer than Italy, even with its "boot" on. Baja broke off from mainland Mexico millions of years ago. Once upon a time the tip of Baja, now Cabo San Lucas, was located between Mazatlán and Puerto Vallarta. A great crack in the San Andreas fault created the Gulf of California; the Pacific Ocean rushed in. The water is 1,800 fathoms deep off La Paz. The Gulf narrows as it moves north; the tides are powerful and tricky, the wind is strong. That means it's hard to handle a small boat and it can be very dangerous. If you are not an experienced boatman, you should rent a boat with an experienced local crew. One of the islands in the Gulf is named **Salsipuedes,** which translates roughly into "Get out of here if you can."

The Bahía Concepción

Good-Time Tijuana:
Mexico's Fastest-Growing City

Tijuana (Tee-Wanna) is perhaps the most mispronounced, ill-talked-about, problem-ridden border city in the world. It is also the most frequently visited, so it must be doing something right. Over 40 million tourists a year couldn't be wrong.

"T. J." began as a sparsely-settled international border crossing in 1848. Now, in 1982, it is the fastest growing city in Mexico, with a population estimated at a million people. That's a twenty-fold increase from its 1950 population of 50,000.

During Prohibition days, and up through the years of World War II, Tijuana was known as one of the earth's foremost "Cities of Sin." Although it has never quite lived down its early scarlet and Blue Foxed reputation, Tijuana has in latter years become better known for many other, more mentionable attributes.

● **A Shopper's Paradise:** Tijuana is a bonanza of bargains for every item made in Mexico, plus almost every product manufactured anywhere else in the world. Everything from Russian caviar to Spanish leather to French perfume to Italian fashions to Japanese silk to Cuban cigars. It's all there, and it's all cheap. The main reason for this is Tijuana's status as a Free Zone, meaning all imported goods can be surprisingly low-priced, since they are duty free.

Some good shopping places are **Sara**, for fashion and crystal; **Casa de Mexico, Tolan** and its **Annex,** and the **Government Store,** for authentic Mexican handicrafts. All these are on **Avenida Revolución**, the main downtown drag that has recently undergone $10 million worth of renovation without losing its basic charm. Other fine browsing and bargaining areas are the **Tia Juana River Basin Development,** complete with a new **Cultural Center; Boulevard Agua Caliente** and the race track vicinity; and the **Fronton Palacio** complex.

In addition to inexpensive merchandise, a wide variety of services can also be very reasonably obtained. Automobile repair, upholstering and painting; shoemaking; hair-care; watch repair and clothing alterations.

● **An Eater's Heaven:** There are many excellent, moderately-priced restaurants in Tijuana. Some have tree-shaded, tiled terraces. Some have plant-laden patios.

San Francisco Mission, Central Baja.

Some have some other sort of equally interesting atmosphere. Some have little to look at but lots to eat. All have the diner deliciously in mind. For example, sample the heaping, sweet fruit plates at **Frutería Aguilar;** the steaming, savory soups at **Tortas Freddy;** the crisp, piquant Caesar salad at the quaint **Hotel Caesar** where it originated; the large and tempting lunch buffet at **Victor's Coffee Shop;** the thick, choice steaks at **d'Lino's;** the firm, fresh-from-the-boat fish at **Reno's;** the succulent lobster and other sensational seafood at **La Costa;** the tender, tasty quail at **Coda Taco;** the mouth-watering, zestily-authentic Mexican menu at **Gran Teocalli.**

• **An Adult Playground:** Few places can sport what Tijuana offers in the way of grown-up pleasures. **Agua Caliente Race Track** with the greyhounds and the horses (and some huge 5–10 payoffs). A handsome **Jai Alai Palace** with a very popular restaurant and bar, **Tia Juana Tilly's,** adjoining it. In Tilly's, you can keep one eye on the betting action, via closed-circuit TV, while you use the other to stay abreast of the frenzied action on the dance floor. Two **bullrings** where dashing matadors dodge big, bad bulls for six corridas each Sunday from May through September. The bullfights are true spectacles with all the trimmings. The spectators who can keep the longest, strongest streams of bota-bag wine squirting into their mouths win the plaudits of the surrounding crowd—and generally lose consciousness before the final fight and have to be dragged out like the poor toros.

The once-legendary **Long Bar** on Avenida Revolucion is no longer what it once was (at 160 meters, or 500 feet, it was the lengthiest in the world), but there are still enough standard-sized bars, with super-sized margaritas, to hang you head-over-heels for the rest of your life. Also, there are enough discos to beat the band; enough mariachi bands to beat your ears to a rhythmic pulp; and enough naughty, naked night clubs to beat you out of your bottom dollar.

On the Toll Road to Ensenada

From Tijuana you can go east 55 kilometers (34 miles) to **Tecate,** known for its brewery (that creates Tecate and Carta Blanca beers) and **Rancho La Puerta,** the famous fitness resort. Then move on an-

Hussong's gregarious cantina, Ensenada.

other 145 kilometers (90 miles) to **Mexicali** (across the border from **Calexico**), the thriving, agriculturally-inclined capital of Baja California and the point of departure into the Mexican mainland—or you can do as most do and head south from Tijuana toward Ensenada and the beautiful land of lower Baja.

Take the Ensenada Cuota (toll road) Highway out of Tijuana. (Note: If you are driving your own car, it is very important to purchase Mexican auto insurance before even sticking your front bumper across the border. U.S. insurance is not valid in Mexico, and uninsured accidents are seriously frowned upon by the policía. A night in the infamous Tijuana jail would not be a noteworthy addition to your itinerary.) Soon you will pass the majestic **Plaza Monumental** (the Bullring by the Sea). Once you have gone 32 kilometers (20 miles) south of Tijuana you will come to **Rosarito Beach.** Stop for a while and enjoy this town's charm. Stay overnight in the **Rosarito Beach Hotel** if you can. It's superb. In fact, you may wish to stay there forever if you have a penchant for wining, dining, dancing, sunbathing, beach-combing, and riding horseback along the silver sand next to the emerald Pacific.

A little farther down from Rosarito Beach you'll come to a tiny restaurant called **Nuevo Puerto.** Only stop here if you're hungry and want outrageous lobster at a conservative price.

The 80-kilometer (50 mile) drive from Rosarito Beach to Ensenada is at times spectacular, remindful of Big Sur in Northern California. Here and there you'll be hundreds of feet above untouched coastline. Pull over at one of the many lookout points, tiptoe to the high, rocky edge and digest the panorama. See the waves crash. See the sea birds soar. See the mighty Pacific flow into the far horizon.

Along the way you'll find excellent surfing spots (K-38½, K-39 and K-42 are favorites) and comfortable places to camp. If you've packed your hang-glider, by all means fling yourself off one of the convenient cliffs.

Ensenada is a city of 150,000 people that has grown up around beautiful **Todos Santos (All Saints) Bay.** Ensenada's culture and atmosphere are more genuinely Mexican than Tijuana's, making it a favorite place for tourists due to its more relaxed, less commercial nature. En-

Surfing at K-39.

senada is also a duty-free zone, so the shopping here is a principal draw. Prices are perhaps even lower than in Tijuana. Bargain-hunters usually beat a path up, down, and all around **Avenida Lopez Mateos.** Stores especially worthy of interest are **Asin, Dorian's Fonart** (the Government Store), **Originales de Mexico,** and **Bazar Moctezuma Miscelaneas.**

The World's 'Yellowtail Capital'

Ensenada is definitely a haven for those who love water sports. Fishing reigns supreme. This city bills itself as the "Yellowtail Capital of the World" and with good reason. Besides yellowtail, there are barracuda, bonito, albacore, white sea bass and a bevy of other hard-fighting, great-tasting fish to be sought in the surrounding waters. Charter boats are reasonable and first-rate. They will take you out for half a day, a whole day, or for a week-long trip to the tip of Baja Peninsula and around into the Sea of Cortez for some of the finest fishing to be had anywhere in the world.

Whale-watching charters are also very popular. They even cast you off in inflatable boats so you can actually pet the huge, but friendly creatures. Some say you haven't lived until you've patted the velvety side of a gray whale that's big enough to migrate off with a condominium on its back.

If you think they don't catch fish around Ensenada, just visit the open-air **Fish Mercado.** You'll be amazed at the number, variety and size of these big-eyed specimens from the deep. You'll be equally amazed (and amused) at the cacophony of bargaining and kibitzing going on. Don't be shy—buy a lobster to broil, or an 18-kilo (40 pound), meter-long yellowtail to strap to the hood of your car.

Two other things of particular interest in Ensenada are the historic winery at **Bodegas de Santo Tomas** and **La Bufadora,** an impressive blowhole that makes like Old Faithful out on **Punta Banda.**

If you like the whine and howl of powerful engines, you may want to visit Ensenada in June when the famous Baja Internacional Off Road Race kicks up clouds of dust from its starting point here. All manner of wheeled vehicles with daredevils driving them roar off to challenge the hazards of the Baja Peninsula. Only the strong survive—and even they have their livers turned into chocolate

shakes by the time they cross the finish line.

When it's time for dinner, you're in luck. There's out-of-this-world, from under-the-sea abalone at **The Tiger's Cave Restaurant.** There's some fabulous Mexican fare at **La Ermita Restaurant** in **Hotel Mision Santa Isabel.** (Try the special Mexican coffee.) And there's **El Rey Sol,** a French/Mexican restaurant that is widely considered as the best in Baja.

Visit **Hussong's Cantina.** This wicked water-hole has been in operation for 90 years—ever since the gold rush days at nearby Real de Castillo—and has come to enjoy a level of college crowd popularity exceeded only by its decibel-level of noise and its upper-register Richter scale-rating of raucousness. Play assured, there's a nitery for everyone's nuance in Ensenada.

Near Ensenada are lodges catering to hunters and horseback riders. There are also many celebrated surfing spots such as the glassy and fast right slide off the San Miguel jetty. South of Ensenada you are in authentic Baja country: mountains, desert. A road cuts across the peninsula to San Felipe, or you can follow the transpeninsular highway which parallels the Pacific. Below Ensenada the **San Pedro Mártir range** dominates the landscape. The tallest peak has three names: **La Providencia** (Providence), **El Picacho del Diablo** (Devil's Peak), and **Encantada** (Bewitching). Take your pick. It is 3,095 meters high (10,154 feet).

Bewhiskered Boojum Trees

San Quintín, 200 kilometers (125 miles) south of Ensenada, is the first place with amenities on the Pacific coast. At **San Ramon** is a modern hotel. You can go clamming and surf-casting. South of San Quintin you will begin to see the strange *cirio* trees *(Idria columnaris).* Aficionados call them boojum, a word invented by a botanist with imagination who had read about fanciful desert creatures in Lewis Carroll's *The Hunting of the Snark.* The boojum tree is found only in a belt across Baja, and nowhere else. The young trees have pencil-thin branches which sprout from the tree trunks like whiskers.

Near the south end of the boojum area, a paved sideroad leads to **Bahía de Los Angeles** on the Gulf's calm waters, protected by the aptly named **Isla del Angel de la Guardia** (Guardian Angel Island).

The facilities are few (small motel, trailer park and small store, which has gas, most of the time). On the other hand, the fishing and shelling are great and the view is splendid. A tiny island, **Isla la Raza,** is a wildlife refuge.

Back on the main road, going south, you reach the **28th Parallel,** where a concrete eagle marks the boundary between Baja California Norte and Baja California Sur. Just south of this border, **Guerrero Negro** offers hotels, restaurants, stores and gas. It's just an overnight stop, unless you want to visit the salt works.

The whaling season is on between early January and mid-March. Ask at your hotel about visiting calving grounds in the nearby lagoon. As many as 6,000 whales turn up. Mama whale gives birth to a half-ton offspring, who drinks 190 liters (50 gallons) of his mother's milk a day and puts on almost half a kilo (one pound) of weight an hour. The calving grounds are called **Scammon's lagoon,** after an American sea captain who discovered the whales here and wrote a book about whaling. Scammon had a dry sense of humor. He described being chased by an enraged mother whale: "I sung out to the men to pull for the shore if

The Eiffel Church and a Boojun tree, below.

they loved their lives; and when the boat struck the beach we scattered. I'll admit I never stopped to look round; but when the boat steerer yelled out: 'Cap'n, the old whale is after us still,' I told all hands to climb trees."

From Guerrero Negro, the highway cuts across the peninsula to the Gulf. About two-thirds of the way, you should stop at **San Ignacio.** The mission church, recently restored, is the most charming of what is left of colonial architecture in Baja. Located on a quiet plaza with laurel trees, the church is a perfect example of symmetry and baroque façade. It was built by Indians under the orders of a Jesuit priest, Father Piccolo, who founded the mission in 1716. It is built of rock, not of adobe (dried mudbrick), and thus has survived the centuries. Father Piccolo also planted date palms. There are now 80,000 and they are the basis of the town's economy.

The Eiffel Church

Out of San Ignacio, the **Volcán Las Tres Virgenes** (Three Virgins Volcano) is dead ahead. Fat-trunk elephant trees *(Pachycormus discolor)* sprout from the

lava beds. Water is stored in the thick trunks; thus the trees can survive rainless years. After some hairy curves, you drop to sea level at **Santa Rosalía** on the Gulf. The town is hot most of the time and accommodations are not good. Don't stay overnight but before you move on take a look at the old ore-processing company, which is still working. And don't miss the **Eiffel Church.** Yes, it was built by the same French engineer who erected the Eiffel Tower. The church originally was designed to be built in Africa. As a prefabricated structure, it won second prize at the 1889 Universal Exposition in Paris. It was then taken apart and packed in crates, preparatory for shipment to Africa. But then, for some reason, it just stayed in port (Brussels), still in the crates. Finally, someone from the El Boleo company bought the pre-fab for a church in Santa Rosalía. And it was shipped to Baja and put together.

From Santa Rosalía, an overnight ferry goes to **Guaymas** on the Sonora coast. The road south from Rosalía follows the dry Gulf coast to **Mulegé** at the opening of **Bahía Concepción.** In July and August the town is stifling hot, but usually for the most part the palm trees and plant-ings along the Santa Rosalía river make Mulegé a pleasant oasis. There's an old mission church on the outskirts of town, comfortable hotels and good fishing.

South of Mulegé, the highway runs along Concepción bay. To the west is the desert, with a beauty of its own. There you can see the world's tallest cacti, the giant cardon *(Pachycereus pringlei)*, shooting up 20 to 25 meters (65 to 80 feet). **Loreto** is about 136 kilometers (85 miles) from Mulegé, on the Gulf. In 1829 a hurricane wiped the town out. However, the original church, the **"Mother Mission,"** has been reconstructed and is worth a visit. There are good hotels and excellent sport fishing. You can take a boat to nearby **Isla Coronado,** and be entertained by sea lions.

From Loreto the road follows the coast and winds up in the **Sierra de la Giganta** (Lady Giant) as it cuts inland, then goes straight south through a fertile region, **Villa Constitución.** You wonder why the desert is fertile. It's the ground water. Constitución has 20,000 people, big for Baja. From there you can reach the Pacific port of **San Carlos,** or continue on the main road to La Paz.

La Paz means peace, but it has seen lots

Saltworks, Guerrero Negro.

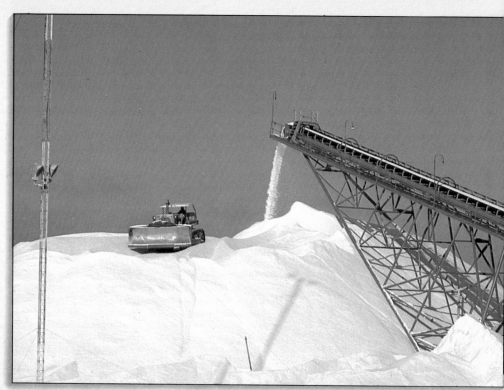

of violence. You remember Diego de Beccerra who came to an untimely end in 1533 on the first expedition to the place? Several succeeding attempts at settlement failed, due to lack of supplies, epidemics and Indian rebellions. Why would *anybody* want to settle there? Pearls, that's why. White pearls, pink pearls, black pearls. The oysters which fashioned those lovely pearls thrived until 1940 when suddenly a mysterious disease wiped them out.

Sports fishermen have discovered La Paz. Now there are good hotels and fine shopping. One of the chief attractions is coral jewelry. Ferries run to Mazatlán and Los Mochis. The highway continues on down to the tip of Baja at **Cabo San Lucas**, a former supply station for the Manila galleon that is now an exclusive tourist center, air conditioned by ocean breezes.

San José del Cabo is some 180 kilometers (109 miles) south of La Paz. It is the most important town on the southern tip of the peninsula, serving as a commercial center that supports nearby agriculture and cattle raising. The town is pleasant and on its outskirts there is a growing tourism project with beach accommodations, restaurants, roads and electricity.

Spectacular Land's End

Less than 32 kilometers (20 miles) further, you reach land's end at Cabo San Lucas, a place where the Pacific meets the Gulf in a spectacular series of rock formations dominated by a natural arch. If you want a closer look at the arch, there are many small boats you can rent for that purpose. Along the way, sea birds soar and sea lions relax or frolic. Fishing is unsurpassed and there are several luxurious if expensive resort hotels that formerly could be reached only by private plane. Three of these deluxe hotels have landing strips; most maintain excellent tennis courts and all have superb dining.

From Cabo San Lucas you can swing back to La Paz along the west coast on a good but partially unpaved road which follows the Pacific and deserted beaches before reaching **Todos Santos** and cutting back across the peninsula. Or, from a new dock at Cabo San Lucas, you can ferry yourself, family, car, trailer and Baja memories to Puerto Vallarta on the mainland.

A ferry steaming through the Sea of Cortez.

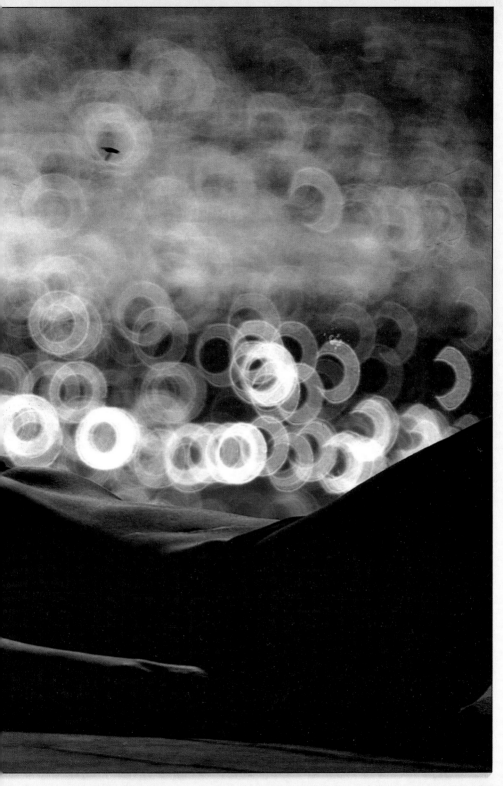

207

THE PACIFIC COAST,
A SUNSEEKER'S TRAIL

From Sonora to Chiapas

The beaches of Mexico's west coast are for sun-worshippers. Soon you will be able to drive all the way down the coast along a paved highway, from the Colorado river in Sonora to Puerto Madero in Chiapas. Road construction was going on full speed in early 1982. But even when the road is finished, do not expect to see the ocean all the way down. Tropical vegetation often blocks your view and sometimes the highway makes its way a few miles inland, parallel to the coast. The last stretches to be paved are south of Manzanillo to Playa Azul and from Puerto Angel to Salina Cruz. During the rainy season it is best to inquire what road conditions are like.

At night along the coast of Sonora it can get chilly during the winter. The good old Aztec sun will be out in the daytime to warm you up, but the water will be too cold for a swim. Thanks to ocean breezes, the Pacific coast seldom gets muggy like the Gulf coast. It can get hot, though, making an air-conditioned car a joy to ride in. The ocean can get rough; there may be big waves and an undertow, except in protected bays. So be careful if you go swimming.

The coast does offer you the benevolent sun, great beaches, good fishing, and delicious seafood. But there is almost no colonial architecture; nor interesting archeological sites. And most of the handmade craft for sale is produced elsewhere in the country. You might take in a bullfight in some of the bigger towns, but that's about all of the big excitement there is — aside from hooking a fish, enjoying a melodramatic sunset, or relaxing on a lovely beach. And aside from Mazatlán's colorful carnival, none of the fiestas are *fantásticas*. Still, you can always head inland to traditional Mexico if sea and sun and beaches and fishing are not your thing.

The tourist season from mid-December through Easter week brings the biggest crowds. During the Christmas and Easter seasons you must have confirmed reservations at the hotels, unless you plan to camp under a palm tree or sleep on the beach. Usually the rest of the year you

Preceding pages, a Pacific Coast sunworshipper; left, the very posh Princess Hotel outside Acapulco; and below, a side road not far from Puerto Vallarta.

can drift into a resort town and find accommodations.

Flights connect frequently with all the popular resorts, either directly from the U.S. or from Mexican centers. There are also first-class buses. But most American visitors drive. That's the way of independence; that's the cosy way to go. Resort towns have all kinds of accommodations—from luxury to cabin class. Don't sleep on the beach; it may not be healthy, and you can get ripped off. You can always find modest accommodations where you and your belongings will be safe. Don't leave cash or valuables lying around. It's just not good sense. Many of the resorts, particularly in the north, offer trailer facilities, with water and power hookups.

Fish, Lemon and Beer

Restaurants abound. Like the Greeks, the Mexicans open restaurants. Prices range from the sublime to the ridiculous. It's not hard to find decent *comida* at very reasonable prices. Because there is such a great demand for shrimp in the U.S., most native shrimp go north by cold trucks and are sold in the American market. The few that remain at home tend to bring a premium price. So don't eat shrimp if you've got budget on your mind. Stick to fish, which is often prepared in mouth-watering ways. You can buy baked or fried fish on the beach, perhaps prepared by the wife of the man who caught the fish. Lemon will be thrown in free and there's usually good, cold Mexican beer to wash it down.

Restaurants on the beach or in beach hotels usually have the best-quality seafood, and, of course, it's the most expensive. The old adage holds true: the farther you are from the beach, the lower the prices. A good idea: Eat where the average José eats. Generally, the place is inexpensive and the food plentiful. Do not, however, be taken in by what you may see happen on a Sunday afternoon. Mexican families sometimes splurge on seafood on Sunday, and hang the expense.

Yes, you can catch your own, but don't expect to save money doing it yourself. The resort towns have boats for rent, complete with tackle, crew and cold beer. Prices vary greatly. Ask around. If you go out don't forget to wear a hat and bring suntan lotion. The sun can be your undoing.

Yankee yachts, San Carlos Bay.

It's a good idea to discuss your plans at your hotel or at the local tourism bureau. They are a great help. The better hotels often have a tourist agency in the lobby. They speak English. They can tell you about deep-sea fishing, hunting, excursions, and everything you can do of interest. Chic boutiques in the hotels are expensive, naturally. Still, they may have items you won't be able to resist, ranging from elegant, made-for-the-tropics clothing to exquisite craft. Except in the most posh of the boutiques, it does not hurt to try to bargain. And do bargain with the street or beach vendor. It's a way of life.

All right. Wear a skimpy bathing suit on the beach. The Mexicans living in the beach resorts have grown accustomed to it by now. But don't go *au naturel*. That's a no-no. And don't go around in bathing suit or beachwear too far *off* the beach.

Tricky Tides, Seri Indians And Beans That Jump

From north to south down the Pacific coast, the place is alive with resort areas, one after another. All offer different types of accommodations, restaurants, fishing, and often hunting. Let's start with **Puerto Peñasco,** or **Rocky Point,** in the northwest corner of Sonora, a bit over an hour's drive from Lukeville, New Mexico. It's a fishermen's small town turned resort. If you take a boat out, be extra careful: tides are tricky and winds are strong in the shallow waters at the head of the Gulf of California, or Sea of Cortés, its alternate name.

A few years ago no one went to **Kino Bay,** except perhaps to see the occasional band of Seri Indians. There were a few Mexican fishing families who minded their own business and were not interested in anyone else. But the beach was attractive; Phoenix and Tucson are not far away and it was only natural that visitors would start coming. Now there is a newly paved road, zipping down from Nogales to Hermosillo, the state capital. **Hermosillo** offers good food and accommodations. Visitors can stroll around the central square and examine the cathedral but the beaches and the ocean are the big lure and they seldom tarry.

The Seri Indians at Kino Bay retain some of their traditional lifestyle; the few who are left, that is. You can photograph them—for a small fee. You can purchase some of their fine ironwood animal carv-

Fishing dock at sunrise, Guaymas.

ings. Off Kino Bay is **Tiburon (Shark) Island,** a wildlife and game preserve. You can rent a boat. You need a permit but there's no hassle about getting it.

Guaymas, along with **San Carlos** and **Bacochibampo Bays,** are beach resorts which emphasize sport fishing. From Guaymas a daily ferry runs to **Santa Rosalía** in Baja California. The two bays northwest of town, across the Sea of Cortés, are tourist preserves. San Carlos offers a large, well-protected marina, jam-packed with boats. Condominiums, hotels and beach homes are strung along the beach. Twenty-five years ago this was "out in the sticks," a place to go to skin-dive.

South of Guaymas is a Yaqui reservation. They are an admirable people; no other Indian tribe in Mexico fought for so long and so hard for their liberty and their tribal lands. Soon you pass through **Ciudad Obregón,** an agricultural center and a base for deer and duck hunters. **Navojoa,** south of Ciudad Obregón, is the center of a major cotton-producing area and the home of the Mayo Indians. A detour from Navojoa takes you to **Álamos** in the foothills of the Sierras. Once a rich mining town of the 18th Century,

Álamos still boasts some of the best examples of colonial architecture on the Pacific coast. By the beginning of the 20th Century, Álamos was practically a ghost town. After World War II, however, some wealthy Americans discovered the town and rebuilt many of the fine colonial homes. The best of these has been converted into a hotel which overlooks the main plaza. The baroque façade of the church of **Nuestra Señora de la Concepción** (1784) faces a bandstand *(kiosko),* which is unusual because of the paintings on the ceiling. On a different level, Álamos is also the home of the Mexican jumping bean, whose internal battery, which is not rechargeable, is a hyperactive larva.

Tomatoes and Opium

From Álamos-Navojoa, the main highway goes to **Los Mochis.** Thanks to irrigation, Los Mochis has become a boomtown, producing rice, cotton, winter vegetables, sugar cane, and marigolds. Marigolds are pretty but smell funny. What you may not know is that when marigolds are fed to chickens, it makes the yolks of the eggs a brighter yellow.

The Plaza, Alamos.

From Los Mochis you can go yourself or ship your car aboard the train to Chihuahua; it's the most spectacular mountain ride in Mexico. From Mochis, too, it's only a short hop to **Topolobampo** and the **Animas beach.** There are fighting gamefish in the ocean; goose and duck-hunting on the land. The rocky island of **Farallon** (sometimes called Animas Island) is a breeding ground for sea lions and attracts flocks of seabirds. The underwater marine life around the island is colorful.

From Mochis, you can take a sidetrip to **El Fuerte,** through rich, irrigated farmland. You can fish for catfish and carp in the artificial lake in back of **Hidalgo dam** or hunt for gamebirds in the hills. From Mochis to Mazatlán, the highway cuts through **Culiacán,** capital of the state of Sinaloa. Out of this state comes an incredible amount of tomatoes and a lot of opium, both destined for the U.S. (The opium is legally exported; it is used for medicinal purposes.) Once marijuana was grown in the hills but that led to controversy and then open warfare but all that, it is said, has ceased, thanks to Operation Condor, a U.S.-supported program carried out ruthlessly by Mexican

soldiers and police. Culiacán is a modern city. The nearby beaches are bypassed by visitors, but not by the local residents.

Mazatlán: 'Place of the Deer'

Tourists head straight for **Mazatlán,** the Mecca of vacationers, hunters and fishermen. Accommodations are plentiful and inexpensive. (Prices double during Carnival Week, be warned.) For a panoramic view of town and ocean, climb the hill to the lighthouse at **El Faro.** The central plaza is typically Mexican. It is not unusual in the plaza to see herbal medicine neatly laid out for sale. The cathedral, a mosaic of styles, is graced by a fine and unusual façade with intricate carving of volcanic rock. Shoppers should try the **Mazatlán Arts and Crafts Center** and the **Indio Gift Shop.** There are pleasant boat trips around the harbor. A stiff drink of tequila will heighten your appreciation of Mazatlán's spectacular sunsets.

The city itself is fascinating. In pre-Spanish times, the Indians of the area produced fine polychrome pottery. During colonial times pirates were a menace. A lookout was built on what is now

Mazatlán,
the West
Coast's
biggest
shipping
port.

called **Cerro de Nevería** (Icebox Hill) to look out for sea marauders. The port became important after docks and harbor works were constructed and communications were opened with the rest of the country by road and railroad. Mazatlán (the name means "Place of the Deer") is now the most important port on Mexico's west coast and is the home base for the country's largest shrimp fleet. Is it necessary to say that the billfish fishing is great? Fishermen take something like 9,000 marlin and sailfish a year off Mazatlán.

The next resort along the main highway south is **San Blas.** On the way, a slight detour will take you to **Mexcaltitán,** an island with pretensions. It likes to be called the "Venice of Mexico." Venice it is not; however, during heavy rains the streets are flooded and you have to pole your way around in a canoe. The seafood is splendid here, but don't look for luxury hotels. The town is a bit rundown; still there are hotels and restaurants handy.

Driving can be hazardous. Be careful of the big trucks grinding their way uphill just before the San Blas turnoff. Keep cool and don't be a hot-dog driver. After the turnoff, you can relax as you descend into a tropical canyon: dense vegetation, palm trees, banana trees, avocado, mango, papaya trees, and that salt-water-loving hardy specimen, the mangrove. Make sure you have insect repellent on hand: San Blas has ferocious gnats, known as *jejenes.*

A popular way to spend some time is to take the jungle boatride up the **San Cristóbal estuary** to **La Tovara springs.** The water is clear as crystal. You ride through a green tunnel of vegetation; you can swim at the springs, picnic, or eat at the food stands. You can also take a boat trip to offshore islands and even to **Islas Marias,** where convicts are held.

Also in San Blas you can visit the old fort and customs house, which hark back to the port's importance in colonial times. It was once a ship-building center, and the point of departure for exploring the Pacific Northwest. Father Junipero Serra's ship *La Concepción* was built here and the Good Father made his missionary trips in it to California. Ships were built here for the Philippines' trade and once warships hid out in **Matanchén bay,** on the lookout for pirates.

The 'Venice of Mexico,' Mexcaltitlan.

From San Blas you have to backtrack and go past **Tepic** before reaching the resort town of Puerto Vallarta. Tepic's a nice place. There's a pleasant zócalo, flanked by a cathedral with Gothic towers. You can visit the fine regional museum, which houses pre-Columbian ceramics. You can buy Huichol handicraft, far cheaper than in the resort boutiques. Outside Tepic, before reaching the Vallarta turnoff, you go through the **Cerobuco lava fields,** which stretch out on both sides of the highway and make you think of a moonscape.

Two Puerto Vallartas: 'Old Town' and 'Gringo Gulch'

Puerto Vallarta owes its name to Hollywood. It leaped into fame as a result of the filming of "Night of the Iguana" on **Mismaloya beach** just outside town. The jungle itself nourished the steamy romance of Richard Burton and Elizabeth Taylor. They spread the word about the town and they bought a home in what is now called **"Gringo Gulch."**

Vallarta is located on the spacious **Bahía de Banderas.** There are two different Vallartas, separate and unequal. The old town, astride the **Cuale river,** has tile roofs, donkey traffic, and a church topped by an imposing crown, shaped like the Virgin of Guadalupe's. Old town retains at least some of the flavor of a Mexican town. The other Vallarta is a tourists-only, hotel-lined stretch of beach and sea. It is more antiseptic-looking than the old town but hardly authentic Mexican. However, both sides of town offer para-sailing, an easy and spectacular parachute ride behind a speedboat. There are excursions you can take by boat or catamaran. You can go off to idyllic **Jelapa,** a bay which is accessible only by boat. There you can rent a bungalow-type *palapa,* or stay in a small hotel, if there is room. You can go horseback riding, or ride a burro up an airy mountain to a waterfall and dunk your toes in the icy water. You can go out for eight hours on a catamaran. You can fish for sailfish, marlin, dorado, tuna. You can eat fresh fish.

From Puerto Vallarta the road goes 272 long kilometers (170 miles) to the next resort, **Barra de Navidad.** Near Vallarta, the road snakes in and out of a jungle-covered canyon, lined with waterfalls. Above a waterfall is **Chico's Paradise,** a restaurant. The highway goes past fishing villages which are slumbering in the sun and perhaps will awaken only when someone gets an idea to put up yet another hotel. About 140 kilometers from Vallarta you pass **Playa Blanca,** a Club Med facility. **Pueblo Nuevo,** farther along, is a budding American-style resort community. Then comes Barra de Navidad, a sleepy beach. The weather is hot, the water is clear, accommodations are inexpensive. The place is geared mainly for vacationers from Guadalajara. Barra de Navidad was once a piece of history. In 1564, Miguel López Legazpi sailed off from here to conquer the Philippines. In April or May, the Green Roller comes to call. He is not a dice-player. He is a monster of a wave, almost tidal-wave-size (10 meters in height!), which periodically comes rumbling in at **Cuyutlán.**

The World's 'Sailfish Capital'

Manzanillo, in Colima state, is but a hop away now. It's a busy railhead and port, with traffic-choked, narrow streets. There are a few good hotels, in and out of town, and for the affluent there is the top-of-the-line **Las Hadas** complex. Built

Offshore parasailing.

215

by the Patiño Bolivian tin-magnate family, Las Hadas (The Fairies) is a pseudo Moorish-Mediterranean Disney-World-like development. Now owned and managed by Monterrey's Alfa Group, the rococo complex offers the best there is in comfort.

Manzanillo used to be Guadalajara's port to the Orient. It is still a thriving harbor town, which now claims the title of "Sailfish Capital of the World." Not far inland is the capital city of **Colima,** a short ride through the lemon groves. Colima is dominated by the **Nevado de Colima,** an often snow-capped and still slightly rumbly volcano. At the **Museum of Western Mexican Cultures** are exquisite pre-Columbian pottery, including samples of the famous dogs who were meant to be served as a snack. Another museum houses 350 antique cars.

Highway 200 was being built (early in 1982) running parallel to the coast. Ask about road conditions, especially during the rainy season. **Playa Azul,** at the moment Michoacán's only resort, is a modest, inexpensive black-sand beach resort which is shunned by the jet-setters. Following down the coast, you bypass the new and dynamic town of **Lázaro Cárdenas.**

Ixtapa-Zihuatanejo

Along the road is Ixtapa-Zihuatanejo. A few years ago **Zihuatanejo** was a small, insignificant fishing village, and **Ixtapa,** next door, was a place of equal importance. Then the planners in Mexico City who had discovered Cancún determined that this was an ideal resort site.

Amazingly, the computer said Ixtapa. And thus it all began; first, what builders call the "infrastructure": roads, water lines, sewers, communication lines. Soon luxury hotels, swimming pools, a golf course and parking lots emerged from the jungle. Naturally, Zihuatanejo next door had to be spruced up, too. The weather's great; the beach is splendid. In come the visitors. All the action is centered around the hotels. Zihuatenejo has three separate hotel areas, with prices well below Ixtapa's. Another fairy tale come true.

Another 224 kilometers along the road past a number of fishing villages and you come to Acapulco, Mexico's oldest and best known beach resort, and one of the leading visitors destinations in the world. And that's a story in itself.

A lively mask from Guerrero, right; and below, sand-carrying mules.

216

ACAPULCO

Acapulco is one of a kind. There's nothing like it in Mexico—or anywhere else. It claims to be the greatest pleasure resort in the world and it well may be. Acapulco has something for everyone: opulence for the jet-set hedonist; fun and games for the budget-minded. Perfect weather. Food ranging from American bland to *pâté de fois gras*. From *huevos rancheros* to hot ol' Mexican food that sears its way down your throat. (Watch those small green chilis. They burn like lava.) Acapulco has all kinds of accommodations, at all kinds of prices, and everything is set against a background of mountains meeting the sea. Is any place on earth more spectacular? Entertainment? *Ay Chihuahua!* You can even boogie at a roller-skate disco.

The action in this *balneario* (bathing resort) goes on 24 hours a day. The night was meant for living it up, but there also are the physical fitness buffs who rise with the sun and jog around in the cool of the morning. That's also the best time to buy the freshest fruits in the town market and enjoy freshly-squeezed orange juice, Mexican-style eggs and a heap of refried beans in the inexpensive restaurants that cater to the locals. It's a good time, too, to practice your Spanish. Mexicans like to hear visitors try out their Spanish, stumbling though it may be. And morning, too, is the time to get down to the tennis court, or tee off at a golf course, or go water-skiing, before the crowd arrives. Or go out deep-sea fishing.

In Old Acapulco:
Treasures From the East

First, a bit of history: Soon after the Spaniards conquered the Aztec capital in 1521, they picked Acapulco to be their main port on the Pacific coast for the exploration of the South Seas. In 1564, Miguel López de Legazpi, a Basque sailor, led an expedition from Acapulco. He reached the Philippines, re-took them in the name of Spain, and founded Manila. For 250 years, galleons sailed to and out of Acapulco, the Mexican terminus of the Asian Connection. Something like 200 million pesos worth of silver was shipped out of Acapulco to exchange for

High-diving heroics at La Quebrada, left.

Bahía de Acapulco

El Veladero

Playa Hornos
Morro Rock
Playa la Condesa
Playa Azteca
Farallón del Obispo
Golf Course
Cici Park
Playa Icacos

Malecón
Zócalo
La Quebrada
Playa Manzanillo
Playa Honda
Playa Larga

Playa Caleta
Playa la Roqueta
La Roqueta Island

ACAPULCO

1. Fort San Diego
2. Centro Acapulco
3. Las Brisas (hotel)
4. Condesa del Mar (hotel)
5. El Mirador (hotel)
6. Posada del Sol (hotel)
7. Arts & Crafts Market
8. Boliches (bowling alley)
9. Ritz Hotel
10. Colisea Arena
11. Bull ring
12. Jai-alai courts
13. Soccer stadium
14. Baseball stadium
15. Cathedras
16. Sport fishing docks
17. Tourism office
18. Mirador observation point

the silk, porcelain, spices and ivory of the Orient.

Naturally, that rich shipment spurred the pirates and freebooters, and the English enemies of Spain. British men-o-war fell upon Spanish shipping. A special target was the Manila galleon, plodding along to Acapulco. Sir Francis Drake captured the ship *Nuestra Señora de la Concepción,* sailing out of Acapulco with cargo transferred off a Manila galleon. The English geographer, Richard Hakluyt, wrote that "we found a ship with a cargo of linen and plates of fine white earth (bone china) and a great quantity of silks, all of which we took, (along with) a gold falcon and a great emerald."

Acapulco armed itself to resist. **Fort San Diego** was built in 1616 and powerful cannon were mounted. The pirates were too smart to venture too close to shore. In 1776 an earthquake leveled Fort San Diego, but it was rebuilt.

In colonial times Acapulco was a sleepy town that came alive only when a Manila galleon approached. On its way south along the Mexican coast, the ship stopped briefly at La Navidad on the Jalisco coast and a messenger rode hell-for-leather to Mexico City with the news. In the capital, church bells pealed and a special mass was celebrated. The merchants made up mule trains and set out for Acapulco to be there when the treasure ship tied up to an old *ceiba* tree. Bags of gold and silver were set out on the beach and the merchants implored the bureaucrats to finish their work quickly. The reward came when the ship unloaded: it carried fine porcelain from China and Japan—figurines, carved ivory pieces, made-to-order drapes and hangings for churches, furniture, fine silks and metal work.

The Mexican War of Independence brought an end to the galleon trade. Father Morelos, the priest-warrior, captured Fort San Diego from its Spanish defenders. Thereafter the town was forgotten for a long time until a few wealthy Mexicans and some Americans discovered it.

Tan Is Beautiful

In Acapulco, tan is beautiful. The pallid new arrival enviously eyes the golden-brown beachboys. So, first things first, the Pale One thinks, and he sets out immediately to acquire a status tan so that

17th Century
Dutch view
of Acapulco.

he won't be mistaken for a new arrival. The price he often pays is a burn; he looks like a broiled lobster. In Acapulco, it is well to remember, the sun's rays are more direct and penetrating than up north.

There are plenty of things to do. Most shops and boutiques open at 10 o'clock, when most jet-setters are still asleep. Hotels cater to late-risers. You can get out of bed at noon and still not miss breakfast. After noon, you can meander along the beach, take a ride along the 11-kilometer (seven miles)-plus **Costera Miguel Alemán** boulevard which hugs the bay. It gets warm at mid-day but there are special sidewalks designed, not only for barefoot *condesas,* but also for plebeians. The sidewalks absorb the heat and make barefoot walking bearable. Check out the **Centro Acapulco** complex of shops and get your bearings from there—most likely you'll return for other attractions. There are also plenty of shopping areas along the Costera. You can't go hungry; it's impossible. Everywhere there are places to eat.

Evenings are for great dining and entertainment. Watch a spectacular show or go discoing. During the "in" season, the disco scene is as stroboscopic as anywhere. Naturally, everything livens up after midnight. You don't have to worry about getting home. You can always find a taxi to deposit you at your hotel.

By now you will begin to understand what brings some three million visitors to Acapulco every year. It's the action. It's the excitement. It's the weather. Acapulco offers a lot of sunshine. Even in the rainy season, from June until October, it's still sunny. (The rainy season, in fact, means showers during the afternoon; they're a great accompaniment to a siesta.) The rest of the day the sun can turn you into a tostada. Year-round daytime temperatures range between 80 and 90 degrees, dropping off about 10 degrees during the night.

Prices vary with the season. Mid-December through Easter is the "in" time: the best weather, the highest prices. You need to make reservations well ahead of time, especially for Christmas and Easter seasons. It is then that affluent Mexicans stream in. The jet-set favors February. Smart money people come in November and early December, which is when the weather is ideal but prices haven't popped yet.

Panorama, Acapulco Bay.

'Pre-Columbian' Hotels?

Let's discuss the hotels. Twenty years ago it was possible to sleep on the beach, though there was the risk of having your shoes stolen from under your backpack. Beaches, however, are not hotel rooms, the authorities have decided. So don't try to camp out there. You have a lot of choices. There are 16 daily, 45-minute long flights to Acapulco International Airport from Mexico City. The airport is 24 kilometers (15 miles) from downtown Acapulco. About 9½ kilometers (6 miles) toward town you will spot the **Acapulco Princess** and the **Pierre Marqués** next door, a fabulous two-hotel complex which is like a small self-contained city. Built to resemble a pre-Columbian pyramid, the Princess is, architecturally, the classier of the two. All rooms have terraces awash with tropical flowers. The posh Pierre Marqués was built by the late zillionaire J. Paul Getty and is under the same management as the Princess. Aside from their isolated splendor, the attraction of the two hotels lies in their available extras: two golf courses; at last count, 20 outdoor tennis courts and two air-conditioned indoor courts; plus swimming pools, restaurants, nightclubs, bars. Anything the most finicky guest may desire. And no town bustle to disturb you.

Next step toward town is the **Puerto Marqués,** on a bay separated from Acapulco Bay by a high hill. There's just one hotel, the **Torreblanco,** but plenty of water sports and lots of open-air restaurants along the only street. From Puerto Marqués, the scenic highway climbs up until, reaching the crest of the hill, the panorama of Acapulco Bay unfolds below you. It's a grand sight. Dropping down just a bit, you can't miss the pink **Las Brisas,** considered by some to be the finest resort hotel in the world. It is made up chiefly of small luxury bungalows carved into the hillside. Each has a superb view and a private swimming pool. There are also two large swimming pools for guests, along with beach, tennis, dining and—the hotel's trademark—pink-and-white jeeps for the use of Las Brisas guests.

Going down the highway to sea level you reach the Costera Miguel Alemán boulevard. At the east end of this boulevard are high-rise condos, then tall, deluxe hotels. You wonder if perhaps there aren't too many, but you must realize

Laser-hopping; Acapulco by nightlights.

they are packed when the winter rush is on. Three of the foremost are the giant El Presidente, the Condesa del Mar, and the Plaza International Regency Hyatt, which is the most elegant of the trio.

The great strip of the Costera continues to the west side of the bay and into downtown Acapulco. Here are the inexpensive hotels, unlisted in the brochures, but even their rates vary according to the season. You can also find family-style hotels, patronized chiefly by budget-conscious Mexicans.

Tourism began in Acapulco back in the 1930s along the Peninsula de las Playas, the word for beaches. The first resort was built there in 1934. Excellent accommodations can still be found but naturally they are not ostentatious and do not shine like the superstar hotels. The prices of course are lower in this area. There are two special places on the peninsula: the hotels clustered around Caleta beach on the south shore, with a view of Roqueta Island, and the Mirador Hotel overlooking the cliffs of La Quebrada. That's where Acapulco's famed high divers perform their spectacular leaps—like diving out of a 15-story window.

All the better hotels have their own

dining rooms. They offer American, Continental, Mexican, and quasi-exotic cuisines. For a change, make an occasional foray out of your hotel and try something different. There are dozens and dozens of restaurants to choose from, ranging from a café the size of a sidewalk stall to gourmet restaurants.

Folklorico Ballet, Laser Discos And the Divers of La Quebrada

Acapulco can challenge the world in its after-dark entertainment. There's something for everyone—from teeny-bopper to octogenarian. Serious action at the discos seldom starts till after midnight. The early-to-bed can find entertainment after 7 p.m., so no need to despair. Usually, the classier the hotel, the better its entertainment. If you want the best of local shows that cater to the visitor, try the Pierre Marqués, the Caleta and Holiday Inn. They feature frequent "Mexican fiesta" nights. The same goes for the Centro Acapulco's Plaza Mexicana and Los Mariachis.

Centro Acapulco offers some of the best all-around entertainment in town, though old hands who are satisfied only with the authentic may scoff. The Netzahuacóyotl Theater regularly presents Mexican Folkloric Ballet. In the same complex, the Juan Ruiz de Alarcón Theater offers fine-arts events, usually imported from Mexico City. The Centro's El Internacional features Vegas-style revues. The Disco Laser features mirrors and lightbeams. Both cater to the funlover who could care less about culture.

Unless you have the time to see them in a native festival in Veracruz or Puebla, make it a point to view the Voladores, the Flying Indians or Birdmen. They glide gracefully down from on top of a high pole at the Plaza Azteca, next door to the Plaza International Regency Hyatt. For more high-flying action go to the El Mirador's La Perla nightclub terrace. There is where the torch-bearing young men dive 45 meters (150 feet) off the cliff at La Quebrada into the Pacific. They risk life and limb. The dive has to be timed just right—as each wave comes in—otherwise the diver will dash himself onto the jagged rocks. You have to be there when the dive is scheduled: at 9:15 p.m., 10:15 p.m., 11:30 p.m., and 12:30 a.m. daily.

If you want to do some jumping around yourself, you have lots of opportunity. You could go to a different disco spot every night of the month and still have another baker's dozen to check out. Some are frenzied. Among the better known are **Armando's Le Club**, Acapulco's first and still *numero uno* disco; **The 9**, a gay spot; the **Gallery**, with female impersonators; the **Baby-O**, where the beat throbs until dawn; the **UBQ** (Ultimate in Beauty and Quality), with a view of the bay; **Le Jardin**, a jet-set glitter place; and **Charlie's Chili Bar and Dance Hall**, a place *Playboy* magazine said "is as close to a hellzapoppin' disco scene as the Mexican Pacific has to offer."

A word about disco ladies. Mexican girls may flirt under the right circumstances, but *usually* that's as far as it goes. Prostitution is tolerated in Acapulco's **Zona Roja**. Lady visitors should be aware that latino gigolos can be lots of fun but they expect payment for performance. Some of the joints can be titillating, a few even dangerous. Others are bland enough to be included in nightclub tours.

What do the over-50s do for fun? Well, the more energetic go discoing, just like the young in limb. Some middle-aged couples seem to prefer a show and a nice dance place. Some of the best supper clubs are **Tiffany's** at the Acapulco Princess; **La Perla**, overlooking where the high divers perform; **El Fuerte,** which has splendid flamenco; **El Numero Uno** of the Plaza International Regency Hyatt, which has gypsy-romantic ambience; the same for **El Techo del Mar** at the Condesa del Mar, and the **Windjammer** at the Paraiso Marriott.

Shopping and Sporting

If you like to shop, speak loudly and carry a big bag. All the big hotels have shops where you can get sportswear, and accoutrements. Shops line long stretches of the Costera Miguel Alemán. It is almost impossible to bargain in any of these shops, but bargaining is de rigueur with street and beach vendors. The Centro Acapulco offers quality handicraft which is expensive. In some of the shops you can watch the craftsmen at work. Across the street, **Fonart** is a government-operated crafts' museum with selected items for sale at reasonable prices. Near the Continental Hotel, the **El Patio**

shopping center offers top-grade clothing, leather goods and sandals. For silverware try **Platería San Francisco** on the Costera, and **Taxco el Viejo**, near La Quebrada. Be aware: prices are stiff. For more reasonably priced handicraft go downtown and look around the Zócalo, especially in the **Arts and Crafts Market.**

Acapulco is a sportsland. There are three golf courses: a nine-hole, public course just off the Costera toward the east end of the bay, and the two aforementioned 18-hole courses, almost back-to-back at the Acapulco Princess and the Pierre Marqués. Arrangements can be made for non-guests to play. There are pros available. Green fees are reasonable.

At last count there were more than 80 excellent tennis courts, some with lighting and air-conditioning. They are not inexpensive. The best include the courts at the Acapulco Princess, the Pierre Marqués, the Hyatt Regency, Las Brisas, and Armando's Taj Mahal. All courts have pros. They charge hourly rates.

You can bowl at the **Boliches,** across the Costera Alemán from the **Ritz Hotel.** You can go big-game fishing—sailfish, marlin, tuna. The best months are November to May. You can go small-game fishing—dolphin, barracuda, yellowtail, bonito, pompano, red snapper. Boats can be chartered through your hotel or directly at the downtown **Malecon,** for up to $200 a day. (Less in the off-season.) You have to make an early start: rise and shine at 6 a.m. for 7 a.m. departures.

Surfing is prohibited in Acapulco but the bay is not good for it anyway. Water-skiing is the major water sport. The best place to learn (and the calmest water) is at Caleta beach and near the downtown area. The best diving is at the underwater shrine of the Virgin of Guadalupe in shallow waters off **Roqueta Island.** Sailboats of all sizes can be rented on many of the beaches. Para-sailing is easier than it looks and worth the short (five-minute) jaunt. Take your camera and a wide-angle lens. You start from the hotel-front beaches.

Spectator sports include lightweight boxing and heavyweight wrestling. Both are at the **Coliseo Arena.** Check your hotel desk for Sunday afternoon bullfights at the ring near Caleta beach. Near the bullring on the peninsula jai-alai games are held nightly, except Mondays. Soccer and *beis-bol* (baseball) can be enjoyed. Mexicans are avid ball fans. Have you forgotten where Fernando Valenzuela comes from?

Other Diversions

Tours by land and sea are the best and cheapest way to get your bearings and make certain you don't miss any Acapulco attraction. The city tour lasts about 3½ hours and covers everything, from the Princess Hotel to the La Quebrada divers. The tour leaves your hotel about 10 a.m. and 4 p.m. A typical night tour starts at 9 p.m. and also takes 3½ hours. You may see the flamenco show at the El Fuerte, the Voladores' flying dance and the Cocoloco nightclub show at the Acapulco Princess. A drink is given you at each place.

You can tour the bay by water on the **Bonanza,** the **Fiesta** and the **Sea Cloud.** That will let you see some of the most luxurious private homes in Acapulco, facing the bay. You'll go out to La Quebrada and Puerto Marqués for a swim. These boats also offer a late afternoon sunset cruise and a nightly moonlight cruise, with drinks, music and dancing.

A tour bus leaves at 10 a.m. for the small village of **Coyuca,** and goes on to

Folk-dancing at the busy Centro Acapulco.

La Barra where a boat meets the bus. It makes a cruise around the lagoon to show you a tropical setting, including the birds for whom the place is a refuge. You return about 5 p.m.

The Centro Acapulco is Latin America's largest convention center. It offers shopping, the flying pole dance, food and drink, international art films, art exhibits, theaters, nightclubs, mariachi, and the **Ballet Folklorico,** under the direction of Amalia Hernández.

There's not much in the way of historic buildings—just the **Fort San Diego,** which you may remember 'was built to guard against pirate attacks. The old cannon are still in place. There's no admission charge.

The **Zócalo** is the heart of town and there you can feel you are in Mexico, and not in a resortland. There are parks and benches and shade and a cathedral built in the 1930s, with a mosque-like dome. There are open-air cafes, inexpensive restaurants, shopping. A skip away across the Costera are the docks where the boats moor that go deep-sea fishing.

Beaches? The town's full of beaches, each with a different character. First the spacious **Revolcadero,** open to the ocean.

Anyone can go there, not merely the guests of the adjoining pair of hotels, the Princess and the Pierre Marqués. Mexican beaches are government property; no one can keep you off them. You can rent a horse and have a brisk gallop down the sands. You can go body-surfing.

Puerto Marqués is a village on a bay adjacent to Acapulco. There's just one hotel but a lot of seafood restaurants. The water generally is calm; there are paddle boats and small sailing craft for rent. A nice place to go water-skiing.

Acapulco Bay is divided into beach sections. **Icacos** is the first you see out of the airport. The water is calm. **La Condesa** beach, between the Continental and Presidente Hotels, offers the best surf. Locals and foreign gays frequent the beach. **Los Hornos** beach (Acapulco's once-fashionable Afternoon Beach) begins where La Condesa ends and goes on as far as the customs dock. **Manzanilla, Larga** and **Honda** beaches, just past the downtown area, are frequented mainly by budgeters who put up in the low-priced hotels nearby. **Caleta** beach (Acapulco's once-fashionable Morning Beach) is around the south side of the peninsula, facing Roqueta Island and the entrance to the

A local craftsman's rococo and baroqueish beetle.

bay. The water is calm but the beach isn't the same old elegant stretch it used to be. Beaches, too, seem to wear out their welcome. From Caleta you can take a small ferry to the uninhabited island of Roqueta.

Eight kilometers (five miles) west of town is **Pie de la Cuesta**, a fishing village with a lot of open beachfront and many restaurants. *Si*, visitors are welcome. It is the best place to watch a gorgeous sunset but a rough place to swim because there's a vicious undertow. Beyond is **Coyuca lagoon**, which is much calmer. Coyuca abounds in catfish, snook and mullet. You can rent a small fishing boat there. It's a tropical paradise—water hyacynth, herons, egrets.

Victorian-Style Transport

In getting around you should be aware that taxis do not have meters. Naturally, there's the temptation to rip you off. Make sure you and the cabbie agree on the price you are to pay *before* you take off. Check at your hotel to find out how much a ride should cost. Fares are reasonable, if you can bargain a little, especially in Spanish. There are also plenty of car rentals. Prices vary according to make and model. You have to have a credit card. Be sure you buy Mexican insurance. During the winter season it's best to reserve a car well ahead of time, especially if you want, say, automatic transmission. You can also go places in Victorian style—take a ride in a horse-drawn carriage.

As in other port towns, the biggest fiesta is **Carnaval**—Mardi Gras—held just before Ash Wednesday. Also, the **Festival of the Virgin of Guadalupe** (December 12) is marked by fun and fervor.

What do you do for information once you've arrived? In Acapulco there are two sources to keep you up to date. First, the tourism office on Costera Miguel Alemán boulevard, No. 187 (phone 22170, 26009, or 26016). They speak English, of course. They can tell you all about special events, such as bullfights, baseball games, or fiestas. You can tell them about any gripe you have. Second, your hotel front desk can give you all kinds of information on tours, costs, phone numbers, and how to get reservations.

A word to the wise: you may have heard of **Acapulco Gold**. It is not panned in a tomrocker on a nearby stream. Also, it's against the law to deal in, buy or use marijuana, and it could land you in a very unpleasant jail. It also can be dangerous; it may have been sprayed with paraquat. *Caveat emptor.* It's still good advice: let the buyer beware.

Acapulco is a town with growing pains. It expanded too fast when all that the developers could think of was building more hotels. The place started to lose its charm; visitors were turned off, tourism began to drop. There was the insanity of the traffic, slums and pollution. The population surged to well over half a million as unemployed people from all over Mexico came looking for jobs. Many settled in the hillside slum of **El Veladero**. On the next hill were the homes of the rich; they looked at each other: the opulent wealthy and the dingy poor.

As part of the sprucing up plan the Costera Miguel Alemán has been widened to six lanes; the connecting spur to the main highway to Mexico City is being widened to 12 lanes. Bypasses help relieve the congested inner-city routes. The town is also paying attention to such details as the heat-absorbing sidewalks, which we mentioned earlier, and new pedestrian crosswalks that glow in the dark. Restrooms have been cleaned up; there are new lifeguard stations and more trash containers on the streets. Attractive sales kiosks dot the beaches.

The progress plan also lays great stress on improving the parks. Centro Acapulco has been expanded. A children's park has been proposed to be built above an underpass on the Costera. It will offer a sealife park, with accent on water sports. It will accommodate 5,000 visitors at a time. The new **Papagayo park** in central Acapulco will someday feature a museum built in the form of a Manila galleon. A new fountain, which will shoot a 65-meter-high (200-foot) jet of water, is planned for **Morro Rock** off the shoreline.

All these efforts have been appreciated, it is plain to see. Visitors are flocking in. There are plans for new hotel rooms. The Acapulco Princess is adding more than 300 rooms. The Continental Hyatt and Las Brisas are undergoing renovation. A second Holiday Inn and a second Hyatt are being built. The gaps along Acapulco Bay's long and gentle shoreline are filling in.

Acapulco is a tribute to the spirit and determination of man to make something fantastic in "the place of thick reeds."

VERACRUZ & YUCATÁN, SUNSPLASHED ANTIQUITY

Mexico, bordering the Gulf, is shaped like a fishhook and the Yucatán peninsula is the bait which has lured many a voyager. The latest are the tourists who are charmed by a land of antiquity with a place in the sun.

Spanish Chronicles

In 1511 the first Spaniards to land in the Yucatán were a sad lot of shipwrecked sailors. The Mayans carved them up for sacrificial offering—all except two. One was Gonzalo Guerrero who married a local princess and fathered the first mestizo. Later he helped direct armed resistance against the Spaniards. The other was Jerónimo de Aguilar, who later was chosen by Hernán Cortés to serve as an interpreter.

In 1513, Ponce de León landed briefly in the Yucatán. He went on, of course, eventually to Florida in search of eternal youth. In 1517, Francisco Hernández de Córdoba landed in the northern Yucatán. He followed the coast to present-day Campeche where he fought a battle and was defeated by the Indians. He survived and mistakenly spread the word that Yucatán was an island. In 1518, Juan de Grijalva landed on Cozumel island, then sailed around the Yucatán peninsula and discovered the estuary of the great river in Tabasco which now bears his name.

Several of Cortés's soldiers, including Pedro de Alvarado, and Bernal Díaz del Castillo, both saw Mexico for the first time during Grijalva's expedition. From out at sea they gazed in wonder at snow-capped Orizaba, Mexico's highest peak. In 1519, Cortés set out from Cuba on his historic conquest. In the Yucatán he found Jeronimó de Aguilar, who by then spoke fluent Mayan, and he followed Grijalva's route around Yucatán. He landed in Tabasco and after winning a battle near the Grijalva river, he was presented with a gift of twenty maidens by the defeated Mayas as a token of supplication. One was La Malinche, who became Cortés's mistress, interpreter and trusted advisor. She helped him forge an alliance with the Totonacs and they helped the Spanish against the Aztecs, their ancient foe. La Malinche quickly

Preceding pages, a Mayan fort at Tulum; below, a Rivera mural detail shows what El Tajín may have looked like.

learned Spanish and she taught Cortés how to get along with the Indians. She bore him a son, before he gave her away to one of his captains.

The bitter struggle between conqueror and conquered had begun. In northern Veracruz Nuño Beltran de Guzmán crushed the Huastec Indians and sent them into slavery to the Caribbean. Francisco de Montejo subdued the Yucatán in a 15-year-old ordeal. Gonzalo Guerrero, our shipwrecked friend, turned turncoat and led the Mayans against the Spanish. But it was not Spanish arms alone that did the Indians in; it was the internal strife among them. They never united in a common front against the Spanish; they bickered, they fought with each other. The Spanish consolidated their victory with the founding of the city of Mérida in 1542, on the site of the Mayan city of Ichcansiho.

For 300 years Mexico was a colony. The central part of the country was exploited; it yielded mineral treasure. The hot and malarial Gulf coast was neglected, except for the port of Veracruz. The authorities in Mexico City seemed totally uninterested in the Yucatán peninsula. The Yucatán, moreover, was enmeshed in a web of legal entanglement. Politically, it was under the viceroy of New Spain; judicially, it was under the royal high court for Mexico; and militarily, it was the direct responsibility of the king of Spain. All of these power-wielders were far off and not too vitally interested.

Not-So-Splendid Isolation

If one word could serve to sum up the colonial history of the Yucatán, that word would be "strife." There were constant wars with the Mayas, attacks by pirates, friction among the Franciscan monks, the civil authorities and the clergy. Often drought struck and hunger ravaged the land. It was ironic: not enough water in one place (northern Yucatán); too much in another (Tabasco). Some areas in Tabasco got more than 5 meters (17 feet) of rain a year. Sixty percent of the state is made up of lagoons, swamps and rivers. During the rainy season the watertable rises over the level of the ground.

Campeche, too, had its problems. (The word in Mayan means snakes and ticks.) Since Campeche yielded neither gold nor

The conquest of Yucatán as seen in an early engraving.

silver, the first colonists were ready to abandon it and seek their fortune elsewhere. A royal order forbade this, so the Spaniards settled down in their *encomiendas* to exploit the Indians. The port town of Campeche acquired some importance and even worked up a rivalry with Mérida, the capital of the province. As a result of this competition, Campeche broke away and formed its own separate state.

Throughout the colonial period, Mérida was by far the most important city in the province. It was the seat of civil and religious authority; it boasted a fine cathedral, a monastery and civic buildings. The Spaniards lived in the center of town, while the Indians and mestizos lived in the segregated outer parts. Valladolid became the only other town worth mentioning. In fact, it was a most aristocratic of towns, proud of its pure Spanish blood. It tolerated on the scene only the most essential of Indian servants.

Certainly the colony of Yucatán was not a pot of gold. Its economy was tenuous: the export of hides and beef to Cuba, beeswax, cotton cloth, salt and handicrafts to the rest of the country, and logwood (*palo de tinte, palo de Cam-*

peche) to Spain. The province was self-sufficient in food, but it lived in not-so-splendid isolation.

Pirates, Epidemics and Wars

It must be admitted that if the high authorities paid little attention to the Yucatán, pirates surely did. The pirate business thrived in those days. Spain's rivals—France and England— often aided the freebooters. The ship in which Cortés dispatched some of Moctezuma's treasure to Spain was captured by a French privateer and most of the loot ended up in the French king's treasury.

At sea, men like Hawkins and Drake roamed freely. No Spanish convoy was safe. After the defeat of the Spanish Armada in 1588, the Dutch joined the sweepstakes. In the Caribbean, in the Gulf of Mexico, the Spanish no longer ruled the waves. Spanish strength was spread thin. In the Yucatán peninsula pirates hid out in the Laguna de Términos in Campeche and in Belize. England officially took over Belize, making it a crown colony, and what could Spain do? It was fun and games being a pirate. You might risk losing your head but you gambled on

The Pastry War saved French pride

making a fortune. Pirates often attacked the Yucatán coast towns. In 1683, a gang of more than 2,000 men who sailed under the Black Flag swooped down on Veracruz, captured the town, and hauled away millions of pesos worth of loot, along with hostages who brought a nice ransom.

Epidemics and harsh treatment reduced the number of Indians and so black slaves were brought in. The Church apparently did not disapprove. Bishop Bartholme de las Casas, for example, advocated massive employment of black slaves (he owned a few himself), in order to free the Indians. Some of the blacks were not willing to accept their fate passively; they ran away and hid out in the mountains of Veracruz. They raided farms and outposts until a military force was sent to subdue them. Some of the survivors settled in San Lorenzo de los Negros.

During the 10-year struggle for Mexican independence, the Yucatán and Veracruz played only a small role. The Yucatán was far off; only the port of Veracruz, astride the country's main line of communication, saw a little action. At the beginning, there was a short-lived conspiracy in Veracruz, led by a 17-year-old boy, Evaristo Molino. He was quickly captured and shot. The Spanish clung to the Fort of San Juan de Ulua until 1825; four years after Mexican independence had been won.

Veracruz became increasingly newsworthy. In 1838 the French blockaded Veracruz in what history chucklingly calls "the Pastry War." During one of Santa Anna's military campaigns, his troops took some pastries from a French-owned store. There were other grievances, to be sure, and the French put it all together and proclaimed they had been wronged by the Mexicans. They called for help and the French government employed gunboat diplomacy. When a blockade of Veracruz port didn't bring quick results, the French landed troops. To the rescue galloped Santa Anna. He was wounded in the leg; the leg was amputated and buried with full military honors.

In March, 1847, Americans landed troops in Veracruz and marched inland during the Mexican War. Again, Santa Anna was summoned. He led a futile attempt to stem the invaders. The U.S. Navy took the coast town of Frontera in

Tabasco and bombarded the capital, San Juan de Tabasco, now Villahermosa.

In 1864 Maximilian landed at Veracruz and under protection of French troops imposed himself on Mexico as emperor. Again, enter Santa Anna. He returned from exile, landed at Veracruz and issued an ineffective proclamation against Maximilian's rule. Eventually, the French had to leave (through Veracruz, of course). In 1914 U.S. troops occupied Veracruz for two months. Indeed, the port town has witnessed over the years the curtain opening and the curtain dropping on memorable highlights of Mexican history.

'We Don't Understand You'

The Yucatán peninsula also had its brief moments of excitement, though on a subdued level. The Yucatán always preferred to handle its own problems; for that reason it favored the form of federal government which governed least. When the centralists won the power struggle in Mexico, the Yucatán reacted by declaring its independence. During the contretemps with the central government, Santiago Iman, a local patriot, armed the Mayas and induced them to fight the federal troops. Thousands of Indians volunteered. They overran Valladolid and expelled federal troops from Campeche. The Yucatán was ready to erupt. Who would have thought that the docile Mayas could become so aroused? That was the start of the Caste War.

The reason was obvious. In Montejo House in Mérida, one of the oldest Spanish-built houses in Mexico, there is a large sculpture and on its façade there is depicted a Spaniard with his foot on the head of an Indian. It's a lamentable fact: the two races never got along with each other. Indeed, the name for the Yucatán peninsula may have come from the Mayan words, *"ciu-than,"* meaning "We don't understand you."

Consider a bill of particulars. The Mayans had been treated shamefully. In truth, they were exploited. During colonial times the Indians were forced to work for the whites and to pay tribute. Their lands were taken away. They were humiliated; ground down, despised. As a result of mistreatment and epidemics, the population sharply declined. The Spanish took even uncultivated land that was deliberately allowed to lie fallow so that it could regain strength. The soil is poor; a crop can be grown only for two or three years, then the land must be laid to rest. All of this the Spaniards ignored. They wanted land for sugar and tobacco and they took it.

All of these things explain why the outrage of the Indians grew and it broke with a volcanic force. The fury was directed against every white person; the Indians meant to exterminate the whites. Some Mayas were armed with rifles, but most preferred to do their work with a machete. The Indians killed even the priests because they had lost much of their respect for priests. Clergymen often earned as much as 14,000 pesos a year through parish fees; an Indian laborer made 12 to 36 pesos.

The Mayas' wrath yielded a gruesome harvest. When they overran Valladolid, the Indians raped the girls from the best families. They captured and slew white men on the spot. The survivors fled to Mérida and Campeche, the only two towns not captured. The whites appealed to Spain, to France, to the United States—or to anyone who would help them defeat the Indians. No one took up the offer even though the settlers offered the country itself as a reward for military aid.

What did the Indians in was the appearance of winged ants. The ants presaged the arrival of the rainy season. The Indians were farmers, not soldiers. They could have run the whites into the sea, but instead they returned home to plant corn for they knew that unless the seeds were in the ground before the rains came, the corn would not grow and they would starve. So the whites owed their salvation to an early arrival of flying ants.

When the Mayas left, the whites recuperated. From Cuba came rifles, artillery and gunpowder. The federal government in Mexico City sent troops and supplies. A thousand volunteers came from the U.S. to fight as mercenaries, for pay and the promise of land. The Mexicans reorganized their forces and they set out to teach the Mayas a lesson. Their vengeance was merciless. They killed the Indians wherever they found them—in their homes, in the fields. Some Mayas were taken prisoner and sold as slaves to Cuba. Some escaped to the backwoods

Yucatán's
Caste War
decimated
whites and
Mayas alik[e]

234

and went on fighting a guerrilla war, attacking isolated haciendas.

The land suffered. From 1846 to 1850, the population of the Yucatán fell from 500,000 to 300,000. The district of Valladolid lost three-fourths of its inhabitants; Tekax was reduced from 134,000 to 35,000. Close to a third of the population was wiped out.

Taking Orders From The Talking Cross

To regain their nerve and bolster their spirits, the Mayas revived the image of the Talking Cross. The cross had been a pre-Columbian symbol, representing the gods ·of the four cardinal directions: north, east, south and west. In Mayan belief when one of the crosses "spoke," you listened. Faith welded the Mayas together. They set up a community, named Chan Santa Cruz (Small Holy Cross), laid out like a mestizo town. Only priests were permitted to live in Chan Santa Cruz. Ordinary families visited the place, in a sort of rotation, to attend the needs of the priests. The Indians developed an organization, built around the ceremonial center, complete with a High Priest

and a Master Spy. The High Priest's mission was obvious; the Master Spy's function was to keep the Mayan military leaders informed about the whites' activities.

Once they were secure mentally, the Mayas turned to mundane things: how to gain military strength. Across the border in Belize were British traders, just the other side of the Hondo river. The Mayas bought arms and ammunition from them. What did the traders care? To them it was simply a civil war. To pay for the arms, the Mayas sold mahogany; or they robbed haciendas.

In 1857, it is apparent, the Talking Cross gave the word: it was time for action. The Master Spy had done his work, too. The Mayas knew the time was ripe: there was rivalry between Mérida and Campeche; there was squabbling among the whites. The Mayas also knew that Tekax was sympathetic to Campeche. The omens were good, so the Indians put on captured army uniforms and marched to Tekax, proclaiming they had come to liberate the town from Mérida. The killing began. The followers of the Talking Cross went on the march against town after town and in three years they had captured or killed 4,000 whites.

The Inevitable End

An uneasy truce lasted for 40 years, from 1860 to the end of the century. There was no peace, but no war. Neither side was strong enough to deliver a major blow. Turn now to the Porfiriato. After Porfirio Díaz took power in 1876 and gained control of the country, he turned his attention to the Yucatán. It was intolerable, he believed, that a tribe of Indians would not acknowledge his rule.

It was just a matter of time until the Mexican government would ensure it. An army under General Ignacio Bravo set out to end Mayan resistance. Bravo was methodical. Then, too, his army was equipped with repeater rifles and artillery. His troop laid down a railroad line and built roads as they advanced. No worry then about supplies. The guns blew up the Mayan barricades. The end was inevitable. The federal troops destroyed Chan Santa Cruz. So much for the Talking Cross. Díaz sent criminals and political dissidents to eastern Yucatán.

Relief of a Spanish conquistador with his foot on a Maya's head; at the Casa Montejo, Merida.

Lucrative Sisal

Once the Indians had been quelled, the economy of the Yucatán picked up, thanks to henequen. It took a while to determine what would grow nicely there, though they should have asked the Mayas. They had been growing henequen for years. Henequen is a drought-resistant cactus. The pulp is scraped from the leaves and the fiber woven into rope. After 1875 demand for henequen shot up. Production increased by ten-fold between 1879 and 1916. By then the fiber became known as sisal, named for the only port in northwest Yucatán.

Sisal became a thriving industry mainly because the Indians did the work. It was in reality slave labor and that was one of the better-kept secrets of the Díaz regime. In 1908, John Kenneth Turner, an American journalist, documented the working conditions on the sisal plantations.

In 1915, President Venustiano Carranza dispatched General Alvarado and 7,000 soldiers to the Yucatán on a monetary mission. Carranza needed money for his fight against that pair of troublesome rebels, the revolutionists Pancho Villa and Emiliano Zapata, "The Scourge of the South." Alvarado extracted millions of pesos from the wealthy plantation owners.

Another threat to the élite manifested itself in the person of Felipe Carrillo Puerto, the local governor, a Socialist who turned the Mayas into what artist Diego Rivera called "the best organized workers in the country." Carrillo Puerto set up "leagues of resistance," which were a combination of labor union, political club, and educational and cooperative center. Change came about; the wealthy Yucatatecans were forced to accept it. Carrillo Puerto issued a decree that abandoned haciendas were liable for expropriation and that tore it. He was assassinated by conservatives who hated him for his agrarian reforms.

Another populist leader, Tomás Garrido Canabal, also made his power felt. He inspired ambivalence: love or hate. Governor of Tabasco, he fought the Catholic Church, and alcohol. He was characterized as a man who believed "neither in God, nor his race, nor in his country, traditions, or culture, not in his family, his father, his mother, in the law, social, political or economic institutions, nor in honor, reputation, self-esteem, any doctrines or principles." Indeed a harsh judgment, but after all he was the man who exiled his own father for getting drunk. He forbade the making of alcohol in his state and the sale of it. He closed down the churches in Tabasco; he permitted to serve only priests who were willing to marry.

Yucatán Today: Oil, Sulphur and Tourism

And what now of this part of Mexico?

There is great hope. It lies in the munificence of nature—the three letter word, OIL. Tabasco always lived at poverty level. It grew crops; many people existed at a subsistence scale. Now there is oil, and big dreams. As in southern Veracruz and Campeche, Tabasco is filled with men drilling for oil. Oil has changed the way of life. Towns are crowded; there's money floating around, inflation rides high. Prices have gone up; there is pollution. So oil wealth brings with it deep concern, too.

In the state of Veracruz, the oil boom has not had quite the same effect. Poza Rica in the north has had oil for decades. Southern Veracruz produces almost all of Mexico's sulphur. Still, Veracruz, with a population of 6 million, including 350,000 Indians, remains essentially an agricultural state. It tops all other Mexican states in growing sugar cane, potatoes, beans, chile, pineapple and oranges. It is second in production of coffee, corn and cocoa.

The Yucatán is still Mexico's leading producer of henequen, though it has lost its world monopoly. Sisal is now grown in both Tanzania and Brazil. The Yucatán has more than a million inhabitants and it is slowly improving its standard of living. The tourist dollar is one reason. There are many pure Mayas. They now have land on which to grow corn and beans and they also raise cattle.

Quintana Roo, which has the smallest population of any state in Mexico (less than 100,000), was separated from the Yucatán in 1902. Quintana Roo became a state in 1974. Under President Cárdenas about half of the usable land was given to the poor. Still, much of the state is underdeveloped; it lacks commerce and industry. As tourism thrives so will its fortune. It is staking a lot on the attractions of Cancún, Cozumel and Isla Mujeres.

Reflecting o▮ the country's 'oil-rich' futu▮

Excursions Into Veracruz, Yucatán And Quintana Roo

Veracruz and the Yucatán peninsula are almost next-door neighbors, but they are in sharp contrast to each other. There are the mountains of western Veracruz and the flat limestone plain of northern Yucatán; the rains of Tabasco and the almost-never-wet eastern Quintana Roo on the Caribbean; the rich agricultural land in Veracruz and the thin soil of the Yucatán. Veracruz has been linked by road to Mexico City since earliest colonial days, whereas many Yucatán roads have been laid down only in the last two decades. There is also the contrast in affluence: the wealth of the oil-boom towns of Tabasco, and the poverty of subsistence farmers of Quintana Roo.

Old and New Sun Gods

This big and dazzling region has many attractions for the visitor. It is best to see the highlights the first time around, then come back and savor it again. There is the traveler's proven axiom: Return trips often are more fun. Of course, the magnet is the Mayan ruins and the sun-soaked beaches of Quintano Roo, south and east of the Yucatán. There is no reason not to combine both: say, a tan from Cancún, and a side trip to the Mayan ruins at Chichén Itzá.

Much of the trip is along a coast road; seldom will you be more than an hour's drive from water, either the Gulf of Mexico, or the Caribbean. A car will give you the freedom to set your own schedule and work out your own pace. This is especially true in the Yucatán, where many sites are close to one another. Be sure to buy Mexican auto insurance and don't drive at night except in emergency.

Starting points? Tampico, Veracruz, Villahermosa, Mérida, Cancún? Take your choice. There are frequent airplane flights and car rentals are available. Make sure, though, that you have hotel reservations during the holidays and during the tourist season. It rains a lot in Veracruz and Tabasco; November to March is the best time to travel there. It can get a bit chilly. In the Yucatán the rains usually come from May to September, while the "northers"—wind and

Preceding pages, a pristine beach at Quintana Roo; and at left, a colorful visitor on a Mayan stele. Below: On the beach at Cancún.

rain in devilish combination—strike occasionally from September to May. But except for a few places in Tabasco where it never seems to stop raining, the odds are for good weather in the winter. The Yucatán's rainy season consists usually of a heavy shower in the afternoon, then pleasant, though a bit humid, weather the rest of the time. The beaches of Quintana Roo are almost always sunny.

Hotel rates in the tourist areas are higher during the mid-December to Easter season and sometimes in July and August as well. Except for Cancún and a couple of oil-boom towns, you can usually find inexpensive lodgings everywhere—if you can manage to speak a little Spanish.

Pyramids and Pole Dancers

Tampico, at the southern tip of Tamaulipas, is a logical starting place for a trip through Veracruz. It's a typical port town, a bit raffish, not very pretty, but with plenty of excitement and good seafood. Nearby the huge new port area of **Altamira** is under construction. The Tampico region has oil refineries, good hunting and fishing.

You cross the **Pánuco river** going south and you are in the state of Veracruz and there's not much of interest until you reach **Poza Rica,** another oil center. Nearby is the archeological site of **Castillo de Teayo,** not really a castle as the name suggests, but a pyramid. It was probably built by the Toltecs, then taken over by later groups. The bell on top obviously is not pre-Columbian but was mounted in comparatively recent times to serve the villagers.

Southeast of Poza Rica, the town of **Papantla** is the center of Mexico's vanilla industry. The town is famous for its *voladores,* who perform a daring pole dance. Close to Papantla is the archeological site of **El Tajín,** which, unfortunately, is heard of but not often seen. Granted it's a bit out of the way, but it is well worth the seeing. The archeologist J. García Payón spent 38 years working at this site. The most interesting structures are the **Pyramid of the Niches** and the ball court with its beautiful sculptured panels. El Tajín was a religious center from about the year 300 until around 1100.

From Papantla there are two routes to the port of Veracruz. Either you can go down the coast or travel inland by the

El Tajín's Pyramid of the Niches.

mountain road. The coast road starts at **Tecolula.** Nearing Veracruz you pass near **Zempoala** (also spelled Cempoala), an archeological site of secondary importance. Cortés landed near here and this was the first town he saw in Mexico. It then had 30,000 inhabitants and conducted the grim ritual of human sacrifice. Near the ruins of Zempoala is the town of **Antigua,** which was the first Spanish settlement in New Spain. The local people will show you an old house, said to have belonged to Cortés, and a church, the foundation of which, it is claimed, is the oldest in Mexico.

The inland route from Papantla takes you on a 2,300-meter (7,545 feet) climb from **Tlacopayan** to **Tezuitlán,** some 100 kilometers (65 miles) away. Cool off here in the handsome plaza; look at the colonial architecture and the homes of the influential, carved ingeniously out of the face of the mountain. Yes, they have TV aerials and garages.

Orizaba, the Star Mountain

The next stop is **Jalapa** (also spelled **Xalapa**), capital of Veracruz, and home of a well known university. The town is built on hills, but it's not to be compared with Rome. Often it's drizzling out; locals call the rain *"chipichipi."* If it is clear, you will get a spectacular view of snow-capped **Orizaba,** Mexico's highest mountain (5,654 meters, or 18,551 feet). It is the third highest peak in North America, after Mt. McKinley in Alaska and Mt. Logan in the Yukon Territory. Some call Orizaba by its pre-Hispanic name—Citlaltepetl (Star Mountain). It is said that the first climbers to scale the mountain were American soldiers in 1848, who were part of General Winfield Scott's invading army. If you intend to try the climb, it is well to have had experience in mountain climbing and even then you need a guide.

Juárez Park in Jalapa is a good place to take your ease. At the archeological museum is a large outdoor park with excellent sculpture of the Totonacs, Olmecs and Aztecs. From Jalapa it's all downhill to Veracruz.

Another good way to get to Veracruz is via the main highway east out of Mexico City, through **Puebla** and the city of **Orizaba.** You might like to visit Orizaba's famous **Monctezuma brewery** where the famous Dos Equis, Tres Equis and Supe-

A distant, snow-capped Pico de Orizaba.

rior brands of beer are brewed. Nearby is Tuxpango falls.

Veracruz Café Society

Out of Orizaba you pass **Fortín de las Flores,** which has a quaint plaza, and, of course, flowers. Then on to **Córdoba,** one of the centers of Mexico's coffee industry. Take a side trip to a coffee plantation. From Córdoba it's a gradual 1,000-meter (3,280 feet) drop to the tropical port of **Veracruz.** Except at *Carnaval,* accommodations are no problem in Veracruz. Relax and play the role of the Veracruzan. They sit, day and night, around a cafe on the **Plaza de Armas** and listen to the talk and look at the people and watch the fountain.

Listen to marimba combos. Eat the local seafood—*huachinango a la Veracruzana* (red snapper, that is, in a thick tomato sauce). Or oysters on the half-shell and exotic shrimp soup. Do try the local tropical fruit; have a strong coffee and a cigar. Maybe you'd even like to play a game of dominos in a cafe. Stroll around, admire the wood and stucco buildings with their overhanging balconies. See the old **La Parroquia** church and the arched

portals of the **Municipal Palace.** Take the waterfront walk—along the **malecon**—down to the port and the sailors' bars. Or take a ride out to the island fort of **San Juan de Ulua.** At dusk across the bay the lights of Veracruz awaken and the place is twinkling.

From Veracruz you head for **Alvarado** and **Tlacotalpan,** a few kilometers up the **Papaloapan river.** At Alvarado the **Port Authority Cafe** serves a scrumptious seafood at budget prices. Tlacotalpan was founded by the wealthy of Veracruz who wanted to get out of reach of pirates. It's a charming town, full of pastel colors and graceful arches. People are friendly; room and board are inexpensive. A riverside location brings an added bonus. Bring your camera or your watercolors.

Back on the main road as you follow the curve of the Gulf, you will reach the Tuxtla towns: **San Andrés Tuxtla** and **Santiago Tuxtla.** Stop at Santiago Tuxtla and examine the giant Olmec heads in the main plaza. **Lake Catemaco** is a few minutes out of Santiago. In exaggeration, the locals call the place the "Switzerland of Veracruz," but it is a pretty spot with a 16-kilometer (10 miles) long lake. Two mountains, both called **San Martín,** flank

The port of Veracruz at the turn of this century.

244

the lake. You can ride in a boat to **Teota-pan falls** and to the **Coyame springs.** If you are of adventurous bent, try *chango-con*, a dish of monkey meat.

The Monumental Grandeur Of La Venta and Palenque

The boom towns (oil and sulphur) of **Coatzacoalcos** and **Minatitlán** are the next major cities. A huge port complex is under construction. Most travelers make tracks for Tabasco. On the outskirts of **Villahermosa,** capital of Tabasco, is **La Venta,** a great archeological center. All of La Venta's 28 enormous sculptures were removed from their former sites when oil was discovered there. You cannot but be moved by the subtle mastery exhibited in stone by those marvelous sculptors of Meso-America. But be prepared: take insect-repellent with you to fight the bugs.

Do take in the **Tabasco Museum of Anthropology** in downtown Villahermosa. This is the pet project of the top flight poet-archeologist, Carlos Pellicer. The museum has a reputation second only to the incomparable National Museum of Anthropology in Mexico City. The Tabasco museum houses excellent pieces of Olmec, Mayan and Toltec

sculpture and full-scale reproductions of Mayan paintings from Bonampak.

You can go to Campeche via **Frontera** and the coast road or you can take an alternate route to **Palenque,** inland in northern Chiapas. Palenque, of course, is another of the monumental archeological sites of Mexico. At Frontera, you cross the two-kilometer-wide estuary of the **Grijalva** and **Usumacinta** rivers which drain central Chiapas. The coast road continues to the ferry landing at **Za-catal.** From there boat ferries go to **Ciudad del Carmen** on the western tip of a narrow, 32-kilometer (20 miles) long island, also called Carmen. **Carmen** is a thriving city and has been tagged the "Oil Capital of the Mexican Gulf." Hotel rooms are at a premium; the shrimp is great but expensive. The beaches out of town are said to be a shell-collectors' paradise. For some 200 years the **Laguna de Términos,** the body of water between the island and the mainland, was a pirates' hangout. At the other end of the island, **Puerto Real,** there is another ferry crossing to **Isla de Aguada** on the mainland. From here it's an easy, coast-hugging hop to **Campeche,** capital of the state of Campeche.

he port
f Veracruz
day.

If you take the more frequented route out of Villahermosa, it's a two or three-hour drive to Palenque. In Palenque there are hotels and restaurants. The archeological site is about eight kilometers (five miles) away in the rain forest.

'El Palacio!'

John Stephens, an American who explored the ruins, wrote of his first impressions when he saw the place: "Our Indians cried out, 'El Palacio!' and through the opening in the trees we saw the front of a large building, richly ornamented with stuccoed figures on the pilasters, curious and elegant; trees growing close against it, and their branches entering the doors; in style and effect unique, extraordinary and mournfully beautiful." He was so thunderstruck by the sight that he fired off his remaining rounds of ammunition in jubilation.

At Palenque are some of the most exquisite and detailed sculpture of the Mayan civilization. Some of it is in stone; most in stucco. Take, for example, the **Temple of the Inscriptions,** a pyramid. In 1949 the Mexican archeologist Alberto Ruz Lhullier discovered that the stone on top of the structure seemed to be a sort of cap, and was meant to be lifted. So he did and came upon a rubble-filled passageway. About a meter and a half (five feet) under the base of the pyramid, he found a royal tomb, covered by a stone lid weighing 4½ metric tons. Using truck jacks, Ruz and his crewmen lifted the massive stone and found underneath a skeleton—probably that of a priest-ruler, who wore a mosaic jade mask. Certain pop archaeologists have said that a bas relief figure on this heavy stone lid is that of an astronaut who visited this site in ancient times.

On one side of the pyramid is the **Temple of the Foliated Cross.** The entire area is fascinating. You will probably agree with Ruz who said that "it would have been difficult to choose a more appropriate place for a work worthy of the gods."

Next to the Temple of the Inscriptions is the **Palace,** a structure which features a unique four-story tower which may have been used as an observatory. Its walls are embellished with delicately detailed stucco panels, and its courtyards have low walls decorated with mysterious

A stucco portrait of a ruler priest, at right; and below Palenque's Pyramid of the Inscriptions.

stone sculptures and glyphs, many of which have never been deciphered.

From Carmen island the coastal road goes on to **Champotón.** It was there that in 1517 Spanish blood was shed for the first time in Mexico when an expedition under Francisco Hernández de Córdoba fought the Mayas. Córdoba was wounded and died shortly after in Havana. From Champotón it's an easy 62-kilometer (40 mile) drive along the coast to **Campeche city.** Campeche has retained much of its colonial character. There's a Franciscan cathedral that took almost 200 years to complete (1540 to 1705). The problem was pirates. The town funds went into building fortresses and great walls to protect the residents from marauders from the sea, and they didn't have the money to finish the cathedral. Under the cathedral's main altars is a passageway to the forts—so that the congregation could depart in a hurry to safety.

'The Jukebox' And 'The Flying Saucer'

Some of the fortresses and sections of the wall are still standing. The **Baluarte (bastion or fort) Soledad** now houses the archeological museum which contains lovely Mayan figurines from the island of **Jaina.** The **Baluarte San Carlos** is a regional handicraft center. Two of the town walls are still standing: the **Puerta de Tierra** and the **Puerta del Mar**—the land and sea entrances. Just out of town the **Baluarte San Miguel** overlooks the sea and the town. In days of old the moat was filled with alligators.

Campeche also has some intriguing architecture. Locals refer to the **Palacio de Gobierno** as "The Jukebox" and the **Chamber of Deputies** as "The Flying Saucer." Talk about futuristic design.

Campeche developed in colonial times, thanks to the export of logwood, a rare and valuable source of dye. Campeche's chief exports now are lumber, honey and shrimp. Don't leave without trying *camarones en ajaco,* a spicy shrimp stew. Other specialties include *congrejo moro* (stone crab) and *pan de cazón* (shark cornmeal).

When you head for Mérida, you should visit the nearby site of **Edzna,** which is dominated by a five-story pyramid sometimes called the **Great Acropolis.** A massive stairway leads to the top.

Just before reaching the Yucatán, you arrive at the village of **Bolonchen de Rejon.** Three kilometers (1.8 miles) out of town is an immense subterranean cave, 70 meters (200 feet) underground. You need a guide to explore it.

Into Ancient Yucatán

Now into the Yucatán—Mayaland. First **Kabáh,** on the main highway, a small but delightful introduction. There you can view the **Temple of the Masks,** whose façade is covered with inlaid stonework representing masks or deities. The **Arch of Kabáh,** which has been compared to a Roman triumphal arch, once marked the path of a sacred road leading to the ceremonial center of **Uxmal.** Of *Puuc* (hill) style construction, the site is characterized by fine cut stones, almost mosaic-like, in horizontal panels used as decoration on the buildings.

On a side road near Kabáh is **Sayíl,** another site which offers fine examples of the Puuc style. The buildings date from the post classical period; that is, from the 9th Century. The three-level palace has about 100 rooms and rows of impressive columns.

Detail of mosaic Quadrangle of Nuns in Uxmal.

Back on the main road it's 32 kilometers (20 miles) to **Uxmal,** another of the superb Mayan archeological sites. It's worth spending a full day there. Outside the complex are excellent if somewhat expensive hotels. When it comes to intricately-carved but harmonious stonework, taut with simple line, but rich in detail, Uxmal cannot be surpassed. Uxmal means "thrice built" in the Mayan language, but, in fact, archeologists have found as many as five different construction periods represented here.

The work at Uxmal started in the classical period, in the 6th and 7th centuries. Some of the sapodilla-tree lintels (horizontal crosspieces over doors, windows, etc.) are still in place and have endured through all those years. Sapodilla wood is fantastically tough; the climate is relatively dry. For inlaid stonework no place in Mexico surpasses what Uxmal has.

Reserve some extra time to visit the site's **Pyramid of the Magician,** a pyramid with unusual rounded corners that purportedly was built overnight by a dwarf who had magical assistance. Also very worthy of excursion time is the nearby **Palace of the Governor** which has what has often been called *the* most beautiful Mayan facade. This façade has some 20,000 hand-carved stones fitted in geometric friezes. The Mayan expert Sylvanus Morley called this palace "the most magnificent, the most spectacular single building in all pre-Columbian America." (For more information see the book's sections on pre-Columbian history and art.)

By making a short detour from the main road to Mérida, you can inspect **Labná,** and its splendid archway. Stop at the village of **Ticul,** which has for sale hats, footwear, ceramics and jewelry. The nearby town of Mani has a huge church and convent, a place where once Bishop Landa burned hundreds of priceless Mayan writings which he called "lies of the devil."

Mérida—Mexico's 'Paris'

Mérida once liked to think of itself as the "Paris of the Western World." Of such are the ravages of time. At the turn of the century, thanks to profits made from the sale of henequen, a fibre used to make rope with, the city claimed there were more millionaires per capita in Mérida than in any other place. These wealthy ones spent much of their time in

An overview of Uxmal, featuring the Nunnery and Pyramid of the Magician.

Paris (France) and in New York City. They built fabulous homes in Mérida and lived in high style.

The most pleasant way to see Mérida is from the seat of a horse-drawn carriage, called a *calesa*. Drive along the Avenida Itzaes into **Centenario Park** and see the huge **Monumento a la Patria**, featuring a bas relief interpretation of Mexico's history. Look at **La Ermita**, a Moorish-style gate built in the 17th Century. It is one of the last two such structures which remain out of 13 such gates erected in the 17th Century. (The other remaining gate is the **Arco de San Juan**.)

The Zócaló or **Plaza de Independencia** is in the center of town. It is the site of a great Mayan temple and pyramid. The Franciscan **Church of the Tercera Orden** is built largely from rubble taken from Mayan ceremonial buildings. Inside the cathedral is an interesting panoramic painting, depicting a formal visit made by Tutul Xiu, the Mayan ruler of Mani, to the conquistador Montejo. On one side of the Zócala is the **Municipal Palace**. Just off the main plaza is **Montejo House**, which is open to the public. The residents are descendants of the first Spaniards.

There's lots of good shopping in Mérida: *guayabera* men's shirts, embroidered women's *huipil* blouses, panama hats, footwear. The panama hats, most of which are made in Campeche, have a fine, silky texture. Do visit the **Mercado Muncipal**, the city market. Usually there are plenty of hotel rooms in Mérida, and, at last count, 18 car-rental agencies. During Mardi Gras/Carnaval, however, the place is deservedly crowded. Everyone comes to see the *jaranas*, or Yucatán folk dancing.

Be careful about the spicy food; you may or may not be able to take it. It can set your throat on fire. If *chile habanero* is used, it may even be too much for the most *macho* of appetites. Often the chile is served in a separate dish so you can apply it with care. There are excellent game dishes—deer, wild pig. Best of all is the *pibil*-style of cooking—meat, baked with spices in an underground oven, and wrapped in banana leaves. León Negra is an excellent local black beer. "X Tabentum" is one of the names given a Mayan drink made of fermented honey and flavored with anise. A non-alcoholic alternate is *horchata*, a delicious thirst-quencher which has a milled-rice base, flavored with vanilla.

Before leaving Mérida for Chichén Itzá and points east, take a quick trip north if you can. The port of **Progreso** lies a few kilometers away. Just off the road is the site of **Dzibilchaltún**, one of the oldest continuously occupied settlements in the Americas. People have lived here since 1500 B.C. The best known structure is the **Temple of the Seven Dolls**, named for the figurines found there. Some of the buildings have elaborate façade ornamentation. You can have a look and then take a dip in the big **Xlaca cenote** (ceremonial well), from whence have come thousands of art objects. Yes, it's all right to go swimming there. Just be sure to wear a decent bathing suit.

Chac Mool of Chichén Itzá

Chichén Itzá is located less than two hours' drive—120 kilometers, or 75 miles—east of Mérida. It's a place that should be seen. You will note that there are droves of visitors, all bearing cameras. Try to get there early. It is built on the grand scale. There is little of the classical Mayan refinement and for good reason. The architects were Toltecs who arrived in the Yucatán in the late 10th

The main pyramid at Chichén Itzá, 1904.

Century. They left behind their version of warriors, eagles and plumed serpents and they introduced the worship of Quetzalcóatl (called Kukulkan in Mayan). They made Chichén Itzá their capital.

El Castillo, an impressive pyramid, dominates the site. The passageway is open only a few hours a day so it's just smart to get there early. Next to the pyramid is the complex of the **Temple of the Warriors.** Hundreds of columns representing plumed warriors were used to hold up the roof. On top of the stairway, between two massive stone snakes, reclines probably the most photographed man in the Americas. He is the *chacmool,* (the word comes from the Mayan words for "claw" and "red"), a receptacle for receiving the hearts of sacrificial victims.

The cenote is a short walk away. From the well have been recovered the bones of children, under age 12. They, too, were sacrificed to the gods. The cenote also has yielded thousands of artifacts; amazingly, some came from as far away as Panama.

One of the most fascinating structures at Chichén Itzá is an ancient Toltec **ball court.** This sacred ball-playing court, the largest of its kind, has low relief sculptures showing how the losers of games here were decapitated.

The oldest buildings at Chichén date from the year 432. Chichén was the religious center of the Itza branch of the Mayas. The site was occupied and abandoned several times but the cenote was always maintained as a place for pilgrimage. It was thoroughly explored by underwater experts in 1960 and 1961.

Near Chichén Itzá is the **Cave of Balancanche,** an exciting place to explore if you are in good condition. Stalactites and stalagmites form what the Mayans call a sacred *ceiba* tree. Hotels near Chichén are expensive. Budget-minded travelers stay in **Vallodolid,** some 48 kilometers (30 miles) away. Vallodolid prides itself on the blue blood of its inhabitants. In town, look at the 16th Century Franciscan **Church of San Bernardino** and take a swim in the cenote near the center of town.

Pink Flamingos

North of Vallodolid is **Río Lagartos** on the coast. The town's chief attractions are the thousands of pink flamingos. There is

Chichén Itzá's main pyramid today.

an inexpensive hotel in town and good tarpon fishing nearby.

From Vallodolid, most travelers head for the beaches of Quintana Roo. Following highway 180, you reach the Caribbean coast at **Puerto Juárez,** close to Cancún. From near Puerto Juárez, you take a ferry to **Isla Mujeres,** so called because many female figurines were found there by the Spaniards. Twenty years ago you could sleep on the beach and eat your fill of fresh fish for three pesos a day. Isla Mujeres is still a nice place. Relax in the sun, but be careful because the sun is strong. You should know that there's no way to get an instant suntan. It is acquired, slowly but surely, over a period of time. The main ingredient is patience.

You can hire a boat to visit the turtle pens or take you to an undersea coral garden called **El Garrafon** (The Jug) and **El Dormitorio** (The Dormitory), a pirate ship graveyard under 10 meters (30 feet) of clear water. A bit farther along is **Contoy island,** a bird refuge.

Golden Cancún

Ah, **Cancún!** An expensive place with the most incredible fine-sand beach. Cancún is the Mayan word for "pot of gold." Visitors will enjoy what the place advertises: luxurious hotels, good service, excellent food, and, oh, those beaches! It's sunny almost all the time. For golfers, there's a Robert Trent Jones-designed course, one of the few public golf courses in Mexico. Many hotels have tennis courts. There are Mayan ruins in the cleared jungle near the sound end of the island. The Bank of Mexico decided by computer that Cancún was *the* place to build a luxury resort and there it glows. Cancún island is 19 kilometers (12 miles) long, narrow, and connected to the mainland by two short causeways. Most of the hotel staff are multilingual.

About 64 kilometers (40 miles) south of Cancún, the coastal highway goes to **Playa del Carmen** from where you can take a boat to **Cozumel island.** There are also frequent air flights to Cozumel. Cozumel, the Island of the Swallows, was sacred to the Mayas. It was a center for pilgrimage to pay tribute to the moon goddess, Ixchel. Later, it was an important trade port. When Cortés came by, some 40,000 Indians lived on the island. Today only half as many live there permanently. Once pirates, such as Henry

Le Club Méditerranée Cancún.

Morgan and Jean Lafitte, relaxed there, between making their rounds.

Cozumel is about 19 kilometers (12 miles) off the mainland. The island boasts some of the clearest water in the world, with visibility often reaching some 70 meters (200 feet) deep. **Palancar reef,** a skin-divers' delight, is nearby. Hotels can arrange for you to take a "Robinson Crusoe" cruise. If you're lucky you'll catch a fat lobster for lunch.

An Underwater Museum
And Sacred Causeways

Not far away is **San Miguel,** which has a row of hotels. You can rent a scooter and buzz around to see the place. On the mainland off Cozumel, **Akumel** is headquarters for the **Mexican Underwater Explorers' Club.** It is open to the public. Just offshore is an **underwater museum.** Nearby, at **Xel-Ha,** is a large natural aquarium. All you need to join the fun is a mask and flippers. The underwater view is absolutely stunning, even for the most jaded.

Continuing south, you will see more Mayan ruins. **Tulum** is a low-keyed but spectacular location, overlooking the

Caribbean. A fortified city, it is the only town in Mayaland enclosed by a wall. Once it was an important port of trade. A temple of frescoes stands in the middle of the complex.

Just south of Tulum, a side road leads to **Cobá,** another Mayan city. Once it was a trade center with 50,000 inhabitants. There is a pyramid and a ball court. The city was set in a five-lake area with sacred causeways connecting it to outlying centers. Farther south, the main road goes to **Felipe Carrillo Puerto.** You can cut back inland to Mérida, or keep going south to **Bacalar,** once a fortress town. The nearby lagoon is ideal for a swim. Wear your mask and fins and have a look below. Enchanting. Nearby **Chetumal** is just across the border from the now independent country of Belize. Chetumal offers bargains in its duty-free shops.

From Chetumal a recently paved road cuts across the base of the Yucatán peninsula. Some 55 kilometers (35 miles) out, a side road from **Francisco Villa** leads to **Kohunlich,** a recently discovered site (first located by thieves) with giant stucco masks and a vast area paved over by Mayas for collecting rain water.

A Mayan site at Cancún.

MOUNTAINOUS OAXACA, AN OUTDOOR MUSEUM

Oaxaca is Indian country *par excellence*. Though the Zapotec and Mixtec Indians, the founders of the ancient civilization of the area, still dominate the state, there are 16 other groups living there as well, each linguistically and culturally different from the other. No other Mexican state can lay claim to such diversity.

Oaxaca is one of the poorest states of Mexico. Because the people have engaged in slash farming and indiscriminate lumbering, erosion is devastating. There is not enough land to go around: often small to begin with, the plots keep getting divided among a man's heirs, and now some are minuscule. To supplement what they earn from farming, many Oaxacans have become artisans and craftsmen. They sell their pottery, weaving and leatherwork in the marketplace.

Life is hard in these hills. Small wonder then that when people drink the fiery *mezcal*, they say, *"Para todo mal mezcal y para todo bien también."* (Mezcal goes with all that is bad, and with all that is good, as well.") The harsh life of the mountains also sharpens the edge of violence. A machete often springs to life with devastating effect. There is indeed truth in the words inscribed on some machete blades: "You won't find a cure in a drugstore for the bite from this snake."

Many Oaxacan communites are isolated. Health services are inadequate. The most famous of the nature healers, Maria Sabina, who is still living, used mushrooms with hallucinogenic property to cure illness. From plants used by the Indians, more than 200 different medicines have been made, including birth-control pills.

Before the Spanish arrived, the Aztecs had conquered parts of what is now Oaxaca and set up a colony. There are more than 4,000 archeological sites of which only about 800 have been surveyed to any extent. Someone once suggested putting a roof over all of Oaxaca and calling it a museum.

Spaniards founded the city of Villa de Antequera de Guaxaca, now called simply Oaxaca, the capital, in a location which commands a fertile valley. At some 1,500 meters altitude, the climate is splendid; it never gets too hot or too cold. In the 17th Century, the English friar Thomas Gage remarked that "there was no place I so much desired to live in while I was in these parts as in Oaxaca..."

Benito Juárez and Porfirio Díaz, perhaps the two most famous Mexicans, were both natives of Oaxaca. The economy is based mainly on agriculture: coffee, rubber, pineapples, tobacco and sugar. Thers's a lot of lumbering and a sugar mill in operation but not much else. And, of course, there is mezcal. Indeed some people consider Oaxaca as a colony for the rest of the country.

Mineral Waters, Hot Baths And 'Trees of Life'

How to get there? It's 548 kilometers (341 miles) from Mexico City to Oaxaca city. There are several ways of going. By road or railroad. All roads pass by mountain scenes of great beauty. You can go by way of Cuernavaca, Cuautla and Izúcar de Matamoros, or start with Puebla, then go south to Izucar and pick up the Pan American highway. Another route from Puebla takes you through Tehuacán, famed for its mineral waters and hot baths.

Preceding pages, a group of Tzeltal officials; at left, Atzompa pottery; and below, in Mitla, circa 1925.

If you drive through Puebla, then go to **Izúcar** and see the town of **Atlixco**, known for its bandstand and tiled benches. In September a dance festival is held there. Izúcar is a center for ceramics, including the "tree of life" candelabrum. Farther down the road is **Acatlán**, also famous for ceramics.

A short distance over the border from Puebla into Oaxaca is the town of **Huajuapán de León**. Annual fairs are held there on May 19 and July 23. Down the road is **Yanhuitlán**, at the head of a fertile valley. Stop at the church-convent which dates back to colonial times. The church is now undergoing extensive restoration but the convent with its paintings is worth seeing.

Then on to the capital city of Oaxaca. From Oaxaca the road to **Tehuantepec** is hazardous; you must drive carefully. Tehuantepec is known for its gracious women who dress elaborately. Do not pester them with your camera.

Another challenging drive is the road from Oaxaca to **Tuxtepec** and the Gulf coast. Parts of the road often are shrouded with fog; you will encounter lumber trucks. The road goes through **Guelatao**, Juárez's birthplace. Near **Ixt-**lán is one of the biggest gold mines in Mexico. Along the way is a rich agricultural area.

Oaxaca has 480 kilometers (298 miles) of Pacific coastline. There are excellent beaches, quiet lagoons and good surfing. The road from Acapulco in Guerrero state to **Salina Cruz** in Oaxaca is fully paved. Once the bridge is finished between Puerto Angel and Salina Cruz, the whole stretch will be in good shape year-round. As of now (1982), you must drive your car aboard a small barge which ferries you across the river where the bridge is under construction.

Puerto Escondido, on the coast, is the most developed of Oaxaca's seaside resorts. You can get there by plane from Oaxaca. Though the place is not Acapulco, nevertheless there are comfortable hotels (often full during holidays) and many restaurants offering good seafood at reasonable prices.

Puerto Angel is a bit more rustic, but you still can find passable accommodations, especially in a hillside hotel overlooking the bay. But at La Ventosa beach, 11 kilometers (7 miles) from Salina Cruz, you may have to sleep in a hammock.

Puerto Escondido.

258

Baroque Oaxaca City

Oaxaca city is the perfect place in which to get acquainted with Indian cultures of the south. Here too are some of the best examples of colonial architecture. The roads to Oaxaca are good, if winding. It requires some nine hours driving time to negotiate. The scenery en route is gorgeous. The city of Oaxaca has good hotels in all price ranges but they tend to get crowded during Christmas, Easter week and other holidays. The best is the **Hotel Victoria** ($40–$75 for a double room). Another fine place is the **Hotel Presidente**, located in a renovated former convent. You can dine in restaurants or eat at foodstalls.

Start your tour of the city by dropping in at the local tourist office. Ask if any fiestas are coming up. The biggest bash of the year takes place in July. This annual Lunes del Cerro (Monday of the Hill) is a festival of Indian music and dance. Performances are held in an open area on a hill called **Cerro del Fortín** on on the edge of town. There are band concerts almost daily in the **Plaza de Armas,** the zócalo, or central square. You can buy handicraft from the Indians who come to town to sell their wares, chiefly hand-woven woolen rugs or *sarapes* (ponchos). Don't be afraid to bargain. It's expected.

Oaxaca has fine baroque colonial architecture. For example, the church of **Santo Domingo** with its ornate facade and incredible interior. The polychrome reliefs and golden decorations will overwhelm you. Next to the church is the former convent which houses the **regional museum** with treasures from the famous Tomb 7 of Monte Albán, such as gold jewelry and finely carved bone and jade. There are shops nearby where you can buy excellent gold-plate copies of the artifacts in the museum.

Drop in at the **Rufino Tamayo Museum** and see the galleries. The cathedral on the zócalo is worth inspection. It was begun in 1535; it collapsed during an earthquake in 1696 and had to be rebuilt, which took until 1728. On one side of the cathedral is a clock that is 250 years old and whose wooden works still keep good time. Don't neglect the basilica of **Our Lady of the Solitude**, the patroness of the city. The museum at the back of the basilica is open from 10 a.m. to 2 p.m. Two

Oaxaca's baroque church of Santo Domingo.

huge markets are a few blocks from the zócalo. You can sample local cuisine at the foodstalls for budget prices. They'll cook you a piece of meat and you can eat it in a fresh tortilla. Try a drink of the Aztecs—a cup of frothy chocolate. Bargain for glazed green pottery, natural black earthenware, jewelry, clothing, leather goods, *rebozos* (shawls) sarapes and rugs. Don't be discouraged if the price quoted sounds high. It will come down quickly when you start bargaining. You should be able to count in Spanish. Know your numbers. That's the first step.

Sometimes even knowing Spanish is not enough. The Indians of the mountain villages often speak only their own language. But look around—there's usually someone who can speak Spanish. It's nice to know, too, that money can't buy everything in Oaxaca. A visitor asked the saleslady to put more chicken in his sandwich. He said he was more than willing to pay twice the usual price. She told him bluntly that just because he had the money didn't mean he could buy someone else's food.

Coyotepec Clayware

Atzompa (Tuesday Market) is famous for its green-glazed ceramics. Some of the designs are centuries old. But the clever potters also are gifted with a touch of fantasy: they turn out toys, animals, and decorative objects, some as tall as a meter and a half. The Coyotepec clayware is easily recognizable: it's always black. Would you like a whistle in the shape of an animal? Or perhaps a mezcal container? Here's your place.

Teotitlán del Valle, just off the main road, is the best known of the villages in Oaxaca producing wool weaving. The store often is in the front of the house; in back the male members of the family may be busily spinning thread carded by their women. Patterns, sizes and colors are infinite. Motifs range from traditional geometric forms to portraits of Che Guevara, copies of pre-Columbian sculpture or even of paintings by Picasso and Miro. Visit the old **colonial church.** Embedded in the walls are stones with ancient Indian carving.

At nearby **Tlacolula** is a 16th Century church, and also the best of the Sunday markets in the region. Again, have your telephoto lens ready.

The town (and around town) is a mezcal center. It's one of the best places to get the top quality *mezcal de pechuga*. Not only does it contain the usual cactus base, but also fruit and chicken go into the making of the drink. Other types of mezcal are flavored with herbs and, sometimes, with a worm that lives in the mezcal cactus plant.

Santa María del Tule is just off the main roads which lead to Teotitlan del Valle and Tlacolula. The main attraction in Santa María is a cypress tree, 50 meters (164 feet) in diameter, and presumably 2,000 years old.

Mitla is a few miles past Tlacolula. Here you will find excellent embroidery and weaving. Mitla is also the site of one of the most intriguing archeological centers in the region. Most ceremonial centers were abandoned after the Spanish conquest, but not Mitla. It remained active well into the 16th Century. The buildings with their carefully fitted stones amazingly resemble the geometric frieze of Greek buildings of antiquity. Even the catacombs where the priests were buried are worth a visit. Next to the site is a church built of stones taken from pagan buildings. Just off the plaza is the **Frissell Museum,** which has artifacts on display and local handicrafts for sale.

Oaxaca Indians.

260

Everything is labeled in Spanish and in English—the museum is a research center for the University of the Americas.

Monte Alban's 'Dancers'

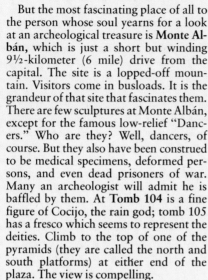

But the most fascinating place of all to the person whose soul yearns for a look at an archeological treasure is **Monte Albán,** which is just a short but winding 9½-kilometer (6 mile) drive from the capital. The site is a lopped-off mountain. Visitors come in busloads. It is the grandeur of that site that fascinates them. There are few sculptures at Monte Albán, except for the famous low-relief "Dancers." Who are they? Well, dancers, of course. But they also have been construed to be medical specimens, deformed persons, and even dead prisoners of war. Many an archeologist will admit he is baffled by them. At **Tomb 104** is a fine figure of Cocijo, the rain god; tomb 105 has a fresco which seems to represent the deities. Climb to the top of one of the pyramids (they are called the north and south platforms) at either end of the plaza. The view is compelling.

The archeology-buff also will find several other worthy sites near Oaxaca city.

There is **Zaachila,** a place where the natives for years made it a point to drive away the inquisitive; **Yagul,** perched on a hill; and the partially excavated sites of **Lambityeco** and **Dinzu.**

Cuilapan is worth visiting for its early colonial church and convent. The building was never completed. There is a series of arches curving gracefully to support a roof that was never built. The walls are the tomb of the last Indian nobles of the area. Cuilapan is now insignificant, but once it was a center for the production of *cochineal,* a scarlet dye made from a fried insect. Under the Spanish, the export of the dye was strictly controlled. It was used as a base for magenta hues in Europe, even in the "red coats" of the British Army.

For the adventurous—and those in good physical condition—Oaxaca offers some fascinating sidetrips into nearby mountainous areas where many Indian groups live in relative isolation. From the city of Oaxaca you can take second (or lower) class buses to villages that are several jolting hours away. You will ride squeezed and betwixt local animals and natives, but the grand vistas enroute are worth the discomfort.

The fine mountaintop archaeological site of Monte Albán.

SPECTACULAR CHIAPAS, AT ROAD'S END

Chiapas, the tail on the body of Mexico, was a meeting ground—the boundary of Olmec and Mayan pre-historic cultures. There is little but archeological conjecture about the pre-history of the region, though it may have been the cradle of the earliest Olmec civilization. There are the Mayan ceremonial centers in Chiapas: Palenque, Bonampak, and Yaxchilan in the lowland forests, and Toniná and Chinkultik in the highlands.

With the breakup of the classic Mayan culture, the Chiapa Indians came to dominate the area, conquering such Mayan tribes as the Zoques, the Tzotziles and Tzeltales. Some sources believe the original Chiapanecos came from Paraguay; others think they came from Nicaragua and still others believe they came from central Mexico.

The Aztecs conquered parts of Chiapas toward the end of their relatively short control of central Mexico. Within a few months after the defeat of the Aztecs, Chiapans sent emissaries to Cortés with word that they would submit to Spanish rule. But shortly after, they changed their minds. To persuade them, Cortés sent an armed force under Luis Marín in 1523. That worked for a while but when Cortés was busy elsewhere (in Honduras, for instance), Chiapas took the opportunity to revolt again. In 1528 in came Diego de Mazariegas to punish the natives and make the conquest irrevocable.

There is not much information on the three centuries of Chiapas colonial history. At times, Mexico controlled the territory; most of the time Guatemala did. The agriculturally rich southeastern part of the state, called the Soconusco, which specialized in the production of cocoa, was administered directly by the Spanish crown but depended on Guatemala for judicial procedure. The Catholic Church in Chiapas, run mainly by Dominicans from 1544, formed part of the diocese of Oaxaca.

During these early years beautiful baroque churches were built, especially in San Cristóbal. The Indians were compelled to do heavy labor and pay tribute. They rebelled several times. Father Bartolomé de las Casas, though himself a slave-owner, defended the Indians and won their love as well as the hate of the Spanish. Because of his devotion, the name of the old capital eventually was changed from Ciudad Real to San Cristóbal las Casas.

Independent Isolation

At first, Chiapas decided to side with Mexico and its first emperor, Iturbide. But when he was eased from power (and later executed), Mexico reneged on its terms of independence from Spain and Chiapas decided to withdraw from the Mexican federation, as did Guatemala and the rest of Central America. After a few years of confusion the Chiapans by plebiscite decided to go back into the Mexican union. The isolated region of Soconusco did not make up its mind to rejoin Mexico until 1841. Of course, there were good reasons to rejoin. First, the Church was for it and that counted for a lot. Second, because of the backward state of the economy, union with Mexico made good sense.

Porfirio Díaz crushed any rebellion that might have flared in Chiapas. He tried to open up the country to foreign capital and interests. He encouraged Germans from Guatemala to settle and grow

Diego de Mazariegas, conquistador of Chiapas.

coffee. A railroad was pushed through along the coast, which opened up marketing possibilities. The capital was moved from San Cristóbal to Tuxtla in 1892 because the residents didn't support Díaz in one of his elections.

When revolution put Madero in power, fighting erupted between the San Cristóbal and Tuxtla factions. At first the San Cristóbal forces had the upper hand; they did some killing and some pillaging under their leader, Jacinto Peréz, who was called "Pajarito," or Little Bird. The Tuxtla men, who were better armed, eventually triumphed and cut off some ears of the losers as a warning. Little Bird was executed to prevent a possible new uprising.

And as is usual after all the excitement, things settled down into their old patterns. It was not until the regime of Lázaro Cárdenas that agrarian reform came to pass in Chiapas. Many large estates were broken up and land handed to the peasants who had worked that land for generations.

Chiapas is where the road ends. The Pan-Am highway leaves Mexico here and goes on into Guatemala, a troubled spot perhaps best left off the visitor itinerary.

Not for the Faint-Hearted

Chiapas is beautiful but its steep, switch-back roads are not for the faint-hearted. There is the panorama of mountain, rivers, waterfalls; the place is spectacular. The Pan-Am highway and a road network within the state provide a vast area for the traveler to explore.

The two main road axes into Chiapas both start in the Tehuantepec peninsula at Tapachula and run in roughly an east-west direction. One follows the Pacific coast and the other the Pan-Am highway. The Pan-Am climbs to the state capital of Tuxtla Gutiérrez, then runs east to San Cristóbal de las Casas before dropping down to the Guatemalan border. A north-south highway connects the oil-rich region of Reforma and Villahermosa, capital of the state of Tabasco, with Tuxtla Gutiérrez. A paved road connects Palenque with San Cristóbal.

Coffee is the main crop. Cotton is also grown, along with corn, wheat, sugar cane and fruit. The cane is used mainly to produce alcohol. Chiapas is a land of a variety of climates. In some areas there is almost continuous rain throughout the year. The rain, in the main, begins in May

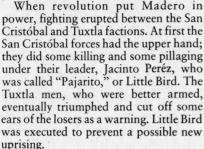

Canyon of the Grijalva River.

and ends in October. July and August are the wettest months. The best time to visit? December, January and February.

The best places to start your adventure in Chiapas is at **Tuxtla Gutiérrez** and **San Cristóbal.** If you want to see the western and southern parts of the state, it's best and much more convenient to have your own transportation.

Palenque, perhaps the most beautiful of the Mayan ceremonial complexes, is in northeast Chiapas and it's easier to get there by following the Gulf coast highway from Veracruz to the Yucatán. The other two important Mayan sites, **Yaxchilán** and **Bonampak,** are in the heart of the rain forest. You have to charter a small plane to reach them, either from Villahermosa or Tuxtla Gutiérrez. (In early 1982, a 5-passenger plane rented for $200 an hour, plus $40 an hour waiting time. Total flying time for the roundtrip is about 3 hours.) During the dry season only, you can reach Bonampak, by truck from Palenque either to **Lacanjá** or **Echeverría** on the **Usumacinta River,** upstream from Yaxchilán. You will have to possess a strong spirit of adventure or be a fervid archeology buff, however. Your Spanish should be adequate. Bring a hammock, mosquito net, food and water-purifying tablets. This is an adventure, as we said. Remember, the road shown on the map between **Montebello Lakes** and Bonamapak does *not* exist—it was never more than a thought in some planner's mind.

Yaxchilán is famous for its intricate stucco roof *combs* (baroque decorations). Bonampak has, by far, the best Mayan paintings. It was discovered by Giles Healy, a young American, in 1945. Another American, Charley Frey, also has laid claim to the discovery. Be that as it may, the paintings are artistic treasures with a lively sense of color.

From Arriaga you reach **Tonalá,** supposedly the hottest place in Chiapas. From here you can drive to **Paredón** on the **Dead Sea,** which is really a lagoon with excellent fishing, and calm water for year-round swimming. There are no hotels but plenty of seafood places. An alternative to Tonalá is a quick 19 kilometer (12 mile) drive to **Puerto Arista,** where the well-to-do of Chiapas have weekend homes. Again, there are no hotels but plenty of restaurants. **Ramon's** will rent you a hammock for a modest sum. In winter, be sure to bring a light blanket.

Celebrants at the fiesta of San Sebastian in Chiapas de Corzo.

264

The seafood is great and inexpensive.

Tapachula, a few kilometers from the Guatemalan border, is sometimes called the "Pearl of the Soconusco." It is a clean city, the center of the region's banana, cotton, cacao and coffee plantations. People of German origin run the coffee plantations. During the Díaz administration, the Germans moved from Guatemala to Chiapas and bought large tracts of virgin land for coffee planting. Coffee is grown from 650 to 1,500-meters (2,130 to 4,900 feet) elevation. The Germans did much experimenting and did well with their enterprise and thus gave the economy a strong push. When they were interned during World War II, coffee production dropped drastically. Germans are still around, but they keep a low profile. Of course, many are Mexican citizens and the names of the plantations have been localized. Still there is the town of Nueva Alemania (New Germany) in the coffee-growing district near Tapachula. The Soconusco area of Chiapas is one of Mexico's chief sources of coffee, the country's main agricultural export, ranking third in world production, behind Brazil and Columbia.

From Tapachula, you backtrack to **Huixtla,** start an incredible climb, then drop along highway 190 which follows the Guatemalan border to the main crossing point at Ciudad Cuautémoc. It's well worth the drive for the scenery alone, but don't try it at night. There are checkpoints along the way where customs agents stop travelers. They are looking for contraband drugs, arms, and illegal Guatemalan immigrants. Because of political trouble in Guatemala, Mexico has had to deal with increasing numbers of illegal immigrants.

Shortly after you enter the mountainous region, you will reach **Ciudad Cuauhtémoc** (no hotels). If you plan on going to Guatemala have your visa ready. Cross before 1 p.m., or between 4 p.m. and 6 p.m. Most problems, however, can be resolved by the payment of an extra "fee."

Ciudad Cuauhtémoc is at the end of the Mexican part of the Pan-Am highway, which begins at Ciudad Juárez, just over the Texas border. If you follow the Pan-Am going west, you will climb to the Chiapas central highlands and, across a broad valley, you will see Guatemala's imposing mountains, looking hazy in the distance. Before reaching the town of Comitán, there's a turnoff to the Monte-bello Lakes and the archeological site of Chinkultic.

Tuxtla has no major attractions. There is plenty of hotel space. The main square recently had a face-lift: the cathedral was renovated and there are new municipal buildings. A new and popular attraction here is the cathedral's German-like glockenspiel that features musical movements, by the 12 apostles at every hour. The anthropology museum in **Madero Park** is interesting as is the municipal zoo. There's a kilometer-long walk at the zoo, with animals on both sides. There are some of the sleekest jaguars you ever will see. It's all worth a leisurely visit. It's also worth exploring the environs of Tuxtla. On top of the list is the **Sumidero,** a lookout point in the cliffs over 1,000 meters above the **Grijalva river.** Volkswagen minibuses called *combis* leave Madero Park whenever they fill up and take you up the highway which deadends at the Sumidero. A restaurant is located at the end of the road, overlooking the spectacular canyon.

Just west of Tuxtla there is a turnoff on the Pan-Am to **Chicoasén,** some 40 kilometers (25 miles) away on a well-paved road. The dam was completed late in

Indian girl, Chiapas.

1981 and is one of Mexico's largest. Just after you reach a tunnel and come out above the dam, there's a turnoff marked "Mirador" (Lookout). A couple of kilometers takes you to a spectacular view point. On one side you see the imposing canyon of the **Grijalva** (the Sumidero is farther back at the top of the cliffs); on the other side is the top of the dam, with an artificial lake in between. There are buses from Tuxtla to Chicoasén.

A 15-minute combi ride from Tuxtla takes you to the town of **Chiapa de Corzo.** The principal attraction is a 16th Century Moorish-style structure over the public fountain. Chiapa de Corzo was the site of the first Spanish settlement in Chiapas, later abandoned because the place is too hot. The **Santo Domingo Church** stands a block from the plaza. A huge, white 16th Century structure, it seems to be in mourning for a departed past.

Chiapa de Corzo has a lacquerware museum. Crafts (mainly embroidered clothing) are for sale in shops along the plaza. The place is the main point of departure for an exciting 2- to 2½-hour motorboat roundtrip through the Sumidero canyon to the Chicoasén dam. Bring

a hat, please, and suntan lotion and a wide-angle lens. As you move up the canyon, the walls become steeper, sometimes rising 1,000 meters (more than 3,200 feet) straight up. The water is placid; the rapids used to be fierce but the dam tamed them.

Cool Off at San Cristóbal

The logical step from Tuxtla is to drive or take a bus for a ride of about 80 kilometers (50 miles) and cool off at the 2,300-meter (about 7,500 feet) elevation of **San Cristóbal de las Casas.** If Tuxtla seems mundane and without character, San Cristóbal, a city of 40,000, displays plenty of colonial charm. It is full of Indians wearing traditional dress. On arrival, you should check at the local visitors office in the municipal building on the main plaza. They know all about hotels, road conditions, local festivities and other attractions. They will also give you a good map. There are many clean, inexpensive hotels and you can get good meals at reasonable prices. Many young foreigners fall in love with the place and stay for weeks. San Cristóbal has a leisurely pace; it is cool and healthy. The

The Church of Santo Domingo in San Cristóba[l]

town was founded in 1528 and churches dominate the architectural scene. The best is **Santo Domingo**, begun in 1547. Its baroque façade is intricately beautiful. The interior is filled with excellent *retablos* (religious paintings). The pulpit is perhaps the best in Mexico. On one side of the church you will often see Indians weaving or doing embroidery; while on the other is a one-time convent, which contains an Indian artisan cooperative shop and a colonial museum. Cultural events are held here.

The façade of the cathedral on the main square is not as ornate as the church of Santo Domingo's but its Tuscan style is worth inspecting. It has baroque retablos and an ornate pulpit. Another church, the **Carmen Church**, is plain in comparison with her two proud sisters but boasts excellent wood carvings and an unusual Moorish-style tower.

The most interesting thing to do in San Cristóbal is to watch people. Chamula Indians wear long white woolen tunics; their civic leaders wear black tunics. Male Zinacantecans wear reddish-pink tunics and hats with colorful ribbons. If a man is married, he ties the ribbons down tight. If he is single he lets the ribbon

wave in the breeze announcing that he's available. If you want to buy anything, it is prudent to check the price in one of the downtown shops or at the cooperative in the former convent. Be prepared to bargain. The best purchases are woolen and cotton clothing. You can buy pottery and leather goods, both of which are specialities of the area. There are also amber items (fosilized pine resin), but it takes a good eye to distinguish originals from fakes.

Mirror-Bearing Saints And the Blue Water Cascade

San Juan Chamula, some 9½ kilometers (6 miles) from San Cristóbal on a paved road, is the best known and most accessible of the Indian centers. Upon arrival, report to the local visitors office in the municipal building. Upon payment of a small fee, you will be issued a permit to photograph the church and an escort will be assigned to make certain that you do not take photos inside the church. The church is filled with saints with mirrors around their necks, apparently to show how they see the world. People are there praying to the saints and sometimes they are in tears. Obviously, they do not want to be photographed at a time like that. Do *not* try to sneak a shot.

In San Cristóbal, to photograph people in the street, you should either catch them with a long telephoto lens; or politely ask them if you can take a photo of them and offer to pay them for it. They are justified in asking for a small fee. After all, *they* are the main attraction in town, but the profit is made by the airlines, the hotels, restaurants and tour operators. The low man on the totem pole deserves at least a share.

The nearby village of **Zinacantan** is reached by taking the same paved road that goes to San Juan Chamula, but you branch off to the left. If you're lucky you may be there during the fiesta of San Sebastian. Then the town is full of red tunics and beribboned hats; people are dancing; people are drinking. (No photos, unfortunately, are allowed.)

If you want more spectacular scenery, you can drive or bus to **Tenajapa,** some 29 kilometers (18 miles) away. There's excellent weaving, embroidery, and brocaded crafts in Tenajapa. Try to be there for Sunday market.

The road to Palenque, which is being built, passes breathtaking sights. You go

one white erons on the acific coast; following o pages, asked erformers at e fiesta San ebastian.

by the Indian village of **Oxchuc,** then the Mayan ruins of **Toniná.** There a hilltop pyramid dominates the valley. Out of Ocosingo, the road starts to wind through vegetation-covered steep slopes and then you begin to catch a glimpse of the river, which later comes rumbling down the **Cascada Agua Azul.** That is, the Cascade of the Blue Water, one of the most spectacular of Mexico's natural beauties. The water rushes down a series of natural mineral deposits. During the dry season the water is turquoise-blue, hence the name. It is not so fetching during the rainy season. Then eroded soil turns the water dull brown. From Agua Azul, you are but a short way to Palenque.

Clay Animals, Fiery Spirits And Montebello's 60 Lakes

Out of San Cristóbal the Pan-Am highway running toward the Guatemalan border passes the **Amatenango del Valle.** There the Tzeltal women specialize in making beautiful unglazed pottery, which is fired in the pre-Columbian way. They do not use a baking oven; they simply light a pyre around sun-dried clay vessels. These natural colors will not fade, but the pottery is not as hard as pottery fired in high-temperature kilns.

Farther down the road, you come to **Comitán,** known for fiery liquor, steep streets, and ears of corn that measure almost half a meter long. There is a pleasant plaza, orchids, good hotels. If you like, stay overnight, or push on to the more pristine if rudimentary accommodations at the lakes of **Montebello.** From Comitán it's an easy hour's drive to the lakes, of which there are some 60. They are of different colors, from light blue to almost blue-black. All are located in peaceful settings. A path takes you to a limestone arch, the **Arco de San José.** A few kilometers back on the paved highway, there's a dirt road which leads to more lakes, including the **Tziscao.** You can stay at a dormitory-style hotel. A bit farther back on the highway, there's a turnoff to the archeological site of **Chinkultic,** where a pyramid looms high over the valley. As you are then very close to the Guatemalan border, do not panic if you see a roadblock, manned by soldiers with automatic weapons. They probably just want to look for illegal weapons.

PRE-COLUMBIAN ART: DISQUIETING STRENGTH

The art produced in Mexico before the conquest (1521) remains one of the most fascinating branches in the vast realm of man's imagination. At the same time ancient and exotic, and, to the modern taste, refreshingly contemporary and attractive, Mexican art of the Indian times is both visually handsome and conceptually intriguing. Both the art lover and the historian-archeologist find in it an endless source of wonder.

Created in isolation, with no close connection with external influences, Mexican Indian art offers a remarkable level of quality and unity. Like Egyptian and Chinese art, Mexican art provides a feeling of permanence and variety and freshness.

Pre-Columbian art is widely accepted today but this was not always so. At first Europeans misunderstood Mexican art—they recoiled in disgust. Sometimes they were even horrified by it. The Spanish conquerors thought it was the work of the devil and they had no qualms about destroying it. They appreciated only jewelry, for obvious reasons. Mexican art was considered inferior, childish, ugly to the point of monstrosity. This attitude prevailed for a long time and in a subtle way exists even today. The average Mexican finds it impossible to place on the same level of reverence the art of the Indians and the beautiful pictures and sculptures in Europe's museums and churches.

For Mexicans the appreciation of pre-Columbian art was part of the process of the growth of nationalism. Both national identity and cultural pride found a prestigious symbol in the neglected art of the Indians. The feeling was more political than esthetical, implying not so much enjoyment, but reverence for those forms of art.

Miracles of the Gods

Indian shapes can be found universally in Mexico today—in interior decoration, architecture, jewelry, coins, clothing design, even in advertising. But that does not necessarily mean that pre-Columbian art is *liked* and enjoyed. However, there is a growing acceptance of Indian art. It has ceased to be a "curiosity"; people in Mexico are discovering this incredibly rich treasure of beautiful and

Preceding pages, a Huichol Indian concentrates on the intricacy of a growing yarn painting; left, a huge Olmec head with puzzling Negroid features.

meaningful, though strange, shapes, which are the homage paid to forgotten old gods with unpronounceable names. Most Mexican pre-Columbian art is religious art. Its purely visual and formal values are rich and its power of suggestion strong.

Acceptance of this art is credited first to eccentric foreigners who fell under its spell. One of the earliest was Sir Edward King, viscount of Kingsborough. Obsessed with the codices, or books, made by the Indians, he spent his fortune reproducing them. The American journalist John Lloyd Stephens and the splendid British artist Frederick Catherwood teamed up to record their experiences exploring the Mayan cities. It is one of the classics of Mexican art: *Incidents of Travel in Central America, Chiapas and Yucatán.* Many writers have visited the old sites and left their impressions: Aldous Huxley, André Malraux, D. H. Lawrence, Jacques Soustelle, B. Traven, Evelyn Waugh.

Although the highland area, the *altiplano* of central Mexico, seems more suitable for human survival, in actuality it does not have rich soil and the primitive agriculture of that day could not provide sustenance for a growing population. Yet against all odds, many cultures did flourish and left countless monuments as tribute to their genius. Mexican Indian art is the product of small, isolated tribesmen who inhabited a difficult country. Art flourished after an agricultural base was established to support the society.

Consider the technique of producing pre-Columbian art. Remember that the Indians did not have any iron tools with which to carve their sculptures or erect their pyramids. Yet working without shaping tools or machines they produced some of the most polished and spectacular works of art in the world. There is nothing "primitive," technically speaking, about pre-Columbian art. Sometimes the virtuosity, such as that exhibited by the crystal rock jewelry or obsidian mirrors, is incredible. No wonder skill in the art was considered one of the moral virtues, one of the ways to religious fulfillment.

The Olmecs were the originals. Their development dates from the year 1500 B.C. The colossal heads they produced—strong, silent, expressive—present the earliest portrait of American man. They are mysterious since they have negroid features. On the other hand, the Olmec figurines represent an Asiatic-looking people, all of which serves to

compound the mystery of the Olmecs.

According to Laurette Séjourné (*Burning Water*), symbolic language was first developed by the Olmecs, and, afterward, spread all over Mexico. The Olmecs developed a strong, centralized organization closely identified with religion. The chief god was the Jaguar, who apparently served as a symbol of the Earth. He is abundantly represented as a combination of man and beast, and that was the beginning of the fantastic gallery of Mexican gods, hybrids of man and animals, or perhaps humans hidden behind a baroque disguise of symbolic imagery. Pre-Columbian Indian art is religious, obsessively so.

Consider, first, the pyramid. This beautiful, simple and strong architectural shape that is so assertive and forbidding among the Aztecs, so eloquent and spiritual in Teotihuacán, and so exquisite and baroque among the Maya, is an Olmec invention. In the beginning a pyramid was a simple mound covered with roughly cut stone. It was placed in front of an open square where platforms were built. From the beginning it had a purpose, or rather, a multipurpose. First, it was a bulky pedestal to elevate a small temple where the priests could pray and perform their rituals.

Those Mexican temples were simple rooms but cleverly placed on top of the pyramid. Sometimes there was some extra space and they served as an astronomical observatory. It was in the temples that human sacrifice took place. Sometimes the steps ascending the pyramid were made slippery with the blood of humans.

The pyramid also performed another function, apparently a symbolic one. It was, curiously enough, the magical equivalent of a mountain. This may sound strange, but from a ritual point of view it is clear. We know that in primitive religions the mountain has often had a strong symbolic appeal. Even in the Judeo-Christian tradition there is Sinai, Zion, Tabor, Golgotha. The mountain is the point of contact of earth and heaven, the doorway to the sky. It is the natural dwelling place of the gods. Hidden sometimes by cloud, every now and then it erupts unpredictably. The mountain, surely, is one of the universal symbols of mankind. So, in Mexico great effort was put forth to construct an artificial mountain.

The Indians built thousands of artificial mountains; that is, pyramids, some plain and homely, some proud and magnificent. It was never easy to do; remember their crude implements. But they went into the jungle and up the high valleys and there they built their mountains, silent and indestructible. These were not primarily burial places and do not seem to possess the same precise and meaningful geometry of the great Egyptian pyramids. Nor are they very sophisticated from an engineering point of view. They are little more than huge mud mounds covered with stone, but nevertheless they are among the most intriguing, and even exciting, buildings of mankind, and they still possess the power to strike the observer with awe.

The first Mexican pyramid was built by the Olmecs at La Venta, which is not a very impressive or beautiful place, but still is a good example of a city with a ceremonial center.

Mexican cities were built in accordance with a precise plan of astronomical layout. Around those sophisticated centers people lived in humble, makeshift towns. From the beginning there was that curious arrangement between man and the gods. People lived in basic simplicity; the gods enjoyed the best of both worlds. The tradition seems to endure: Mexicans often combine a penchant for making their buildings rich and impressive, while at the same time disregarding personal comfort. It appears they agree with Oscar Wilde: the most necessary things in life are luxuries.

The Olmecs started the art of sculpture in stone. They also developed the "minor" arts which Mexicans so cherish: the making of fine jewelry and ceramics. In Mexico some of the most beautiful creations of art are the work of the potter or the goldsmith. The Olmecs left experiments in clay, both in pure ceramics; that is, vases and pots, as well as sculptural ceramics. They were the first to use as material for jewelry, the "green stone,"—that is, jade, translucent, mysterious, spiritual.

Using jade, the Olmecs carved those marvelous figurines which are on exhibit at the Museum of Anthropology, those with mask-like faces. The mask is a Mexican art specialty. Produced most likely for funerary use, the Mexican mask does not portray a person, nor is it a playful variation of the human face, but rather it is something like a portrait of wisdom. For centuries stone carvers sought to reproduce, not human features, but a spirit of serenity depicting a man who has struggled to become his own master.

Ancient, Abandoned Cities

Mexico is a country of ancient, abandoned cities. The most famous is Teotihuacán.

What has been unearthed of the city of Teotihuacán proves it is the great example of the Mexican ceremonial center. The city was

Coatlicue, the Aztec goddess of the Earth and mother of the ferocious Huitzilopochtli, a god of the sun and war who received human sacrifices.

composed along a wide street, or succession of plazas, known as *Micaotli,* or the Avenue of the Dead. Micaotli is one of the most beautiful urban axes in the world. It starts at the huge square known as the citadel, with the pyramid of Quetzalcóatl covered with masks. At the other end of the avenue is the Pyramid of the Moon and its neighbor, the Quetzalpapalotl palace, an ornate building recently restored. Centrally located along Micaotli is the sovereign of all Mexican pyramids, the Pyramid of the Sun. It is a perfect example of classical pre-Columbian architecture, simple but not boring. Though not impressive in size (225 meters, or 738 feet at the base), it manages to convey a feeling of grandeur that no other pyramid in Mexico can achieve. Perhaps this is due to its clever design of inclined planes and proportions.   In contrast to the rich and refined art of the Mayas, or the strong, almost brutal art of the Aztecs, the art from Teotihuacán achieves that perfect simplicity associated with classicism.

After the fall of Teotihuacán around the year 800, there came a period of decline in Central Mexico life until the Aztecs founded their capital city, Tenochtitlán. During that period other centers prospered, then fell. Such was the fate of Tula, Xochicalco and Texcoco. From the point of view of art, Tula, 128 kilometers (80 miles) north of Mexico City, deserves special treatment. The main building at Tula, the Temple of the Warriors, is crowned with four Atlantean figures, nearly 3 meters high. These warrior figures are among the most famous examples of pre-Columbian sculpture. Supposedly they are the entrance columns or caryatids of a long-ago-destroyed temple. They represent a remarkable accomplishment, blending sculptural expression with the simple geometry of the column. The face of each warrior bears a hieratic expression, more a mask than a portrayal of a human face.

From the sculpture we learn how the men of that civilization dressed: in loin cloth, sandals and a feather hat. (In winter, a toga-like cotton cape was added.) Their simplicity of dress contrasts with their elaborateness of jewelry.

Soul of the Poet, Heart of the Barbarian

The Aztecs not only were brave warriors and competent merchants, they were also among the most sensitive of artists. The great paradox is that they blended the soul of the poet with the heart of the barbarian. They were devotees of the cruel ritual of human sacrifice, tearing out the hearts of humans to appease the gods. From the beginnings of time, the Indian religions believed in human sacrifice as a bribe to induce the gods to stay on the job and keep the world spinning. And yet this horrid custom is expressed in the arts. Aztec architecture and sculpture convey a disquieting strength, verging at times on brutality. It is amazing that those old carved stones still give out the impression of blood and sacrifice.

In contrast with the happy beauty of the Mayas or with western Mexican art, the Aztec forms portray deep, violently moving beauty. Undeniably, there are barbaric undertones. Some hint of 20th Century art, even reminding the beholder perhaps of the stark, screaming heads in Picasso's "Guernica." The Aztec gods, no doubt, were among the ugliest in the world. Take that major figure in Aztec art and religion, Coatlicue, as an example. She was the mother of the Aztec God of Sun and War, Huitzilopochtli. In her youth Coatlicue was a sort of Mexican Cinderella girl, in charge of the realm of the gods, the girl who swept up behind them. Once, while at her task, she shaped with her broom a tiny, beautiful ball of feathers. This she put in her apron, and thereupon became pregnant.

Her monumental stone portrait is more than 2½ meters high (8½ feet), an Aztec masterpiece. It was found in the 19th Century when workmen opened a ditch for a water main. Coatlicue is the quintessential Aztec monster-god. Her statue exudes a preternatural strength and a sense of the tragic. Basically, the sculpture is the body of an old woman, with flaccid breasts. That's all we can see of her body. (Mexican art is not concerned with the human body as an object of beauty.) The rest is covered with an arrangement of symbols. Instead of a head, there is a pair of rattlesnake heads forming a horrible face. (The explanation: the rattlesnake is one of the suggestive symbols of changing Earth, a creature that changes its skin regularly.) Coatlicue's chest is covered with the hearts and hands of those who were sacrificed on the altars. Her arms are in the shape of serpents; her navel is hidden behind a skull. She is known as Our Lady of the Serpent-Skirt. Horrible, to be sure, but most effective. Even if you do not like it; even if you recoil, you cannot but be impressed. In its own strange way, the sculpture is beautiful.

The strength of Aztec art is exemplified by two sculptures at the Museum of Anthropology. They are minor works of art and not famous, but they are superb. One is a receptacle shaped like a jaguar. Its Aztec name is Ocelocuauhxicalli, a jaw-breaker. On the back of the sculpture is a cavity in which sacrificial hearts were placed. The carving is about a meter high, of stone, the body smooth and rounded, incredibly strong and simple. Yet the jaws, which bare enormous teeth, inspire the same sense of terror and awe that you feel on viewing the Coatlicue sculpture.

Xiuhcóatl, which is in the same museum, is a fire serpent who is crowned with stars. He is the chap who escorted the Sun in his daily rounds. Of impressive size (3 meters), the Xiuhcóatl is a strong and skillful composition of rounded shapes creating circular movement. Its center is the circle of the serpent's eye whose geometric simplicity emphasizes the almost abstract quality of the sculpture.

Strength is also the quality present in that most celebrated of Aztec works of art: the Sun Stone or Aztec Calendar. This giant monolith (almost 4 meters in diameter) is like the condensation of Aztec astronomic knowledge. There are countless interpretations of its hidden meaning. At the center it exhibits the face of the impassive Sun God, who is surrounded by successive rings containing astronomical symbols. The last ring is formed by two fire serpents facing each other.

Apart from their magnificent sculpture, the Aztecs were extraordinary potters, jewellers and painters. Their books—the codices, on deer skin—are among the most beautiful ever produced. But perhaps the greatest masterpiece of Aztec art was the city they built in the middle of the lake, the proud center of their empire.

Gifted Western Ceramicists

The Indians of western Mexico left little sculpture or architecture, no painting and no ceremonial centers of importance. Indeed western Mexican art is just a collection of pots and small sculptural ceramics. But what a happy collection! In a land of gifted ceramicists, the Westerners are an odd group. Lacking the refinement of the Mayans or the technical sophistication of the Oaxacans, the work of the potters of the West is distinctive, thanks to simplicity and cleanliness of design and to the joyfulness the art expresses. Such a feeling of joy was absent in old Mexican art which devoted itself to religion and cosmic preoccupations. The art of the West, in contrast, seems to busy itself with everyday life and the small joys and pleasures inherent in everyday living. For instance, a number of tiny sculptural groups (the term is misleading since the figurines that make up these groups are little more than kindergarten clay-modeling) depict scenes from the life of common people in the villages. A good number show a small house, a fire, and people gathered around; obviously they are engaged in that most human and universal of occupations—gossiping. Other clay figures show people doing just about everything, including making love.

Erotic art, however, is practically absent in old Mexico. No sculpture or figure of Venus or Apollo is to be found. Sex obviously was a strictly controlled commodity. One of the most common models for western Mexican art was the dog. Or rather the Mexican dog, the *itzucuintl,* the only dog of Mexico. That fellow was plump and hairless, and, it is said, very tasty. He managed to be the chief attraction at many a banquet and so he is practically extinct. In western Mexico they took him as a model for the delightful figurines that are among the masterpieces of Indian ceramics.

Tajín's Pyramid of the Niches

The Huastecs, who inhabited the northern half of the region, left one of the most magnificent sites of pre-Columbian Mexico: Tajín. Now covered with jungle, Tajín apparently was a major metropolis around the year 500. The main surviving structure is the Pyramid of the Niches. Around 18 meters high (about 60 feet), the pyramid is adorned with 365 niches which lend richness to its appearance. Although it is not certain just what the purpose of the niches was, in the niches were placed braziers and the smoke from these woodburners gave the pyramid a fantastic look.

Little is known of the Huastecs and the Totonacs. However, the art objects they left are mysterious but magnificent. They are the so-called "palms," "axes" and "yokes." The palms apparently were breastplates, cumbersome and uncomfortable, while the axes and yokes relate to a ballgame. But what a ballgame! The game was a mixture of ritual and sport. It was played at practically all ceremonial centers in ancient Mexico. The best preserved field—it is shaped like the letter "H"—can be seen at Chichén Itzá in the Maya country. The players used a heavy rubber ball slightly larger than the modern day softball. They could hit the ball only with their knees, hips and elbows. The ball had to be passed through a stone ring, placed high on one of the walls surrounding the grounds. The ballgame, it is assumed, was a symbol of astronomical movement. The losers, it was said, paid a fearful price. They were enslaved or sacrificed.

The masterpiece of Huastec sculpture is also at the Museum of Anthropology. It is the figure of a young man, believed to be Quetzalcóatl, the ancient deity, tall, slender, elegant. There is a delightful contrast between the half of his naked body which is unadorned, and the other half which is delicately carved.

The Totonacs lived in the southern half of the region which is present-day Veracruz. Though no major ceremonial center survives, they left an impressive contribution to the art of Mexico, especially in their smiling figurines. They are three-tenths of a meter high (1 foot) and are among the enigmas of Mexican art. Nobody knows for sure what these little men are supposed to be. They are not unlike the gnomes of European folklore. However, the smiling tiny fellows from Veracruz seem more like naughty children. But that smile! It could be anything from the ironical to the moronical. But they are smiling, and that's good.

The ceramists of Veracruz had great skill. At the Museum of Anthropology is the magnificent sculpture in clay of the oldest god in the Mexican pantheon: Xiuhtecuhtli or the old god of fire, who was also known as Huehuetéotl. He is hunched, and it is easy to explain his weariness. The man is toting an enormous brazier on his head. He is a good example of the skill the Mexican artists showed in portraying natural grace in ceramics, which contrasts with the rigid, solemn architectural design of most of the stone sculpture.

Oaxaca is one of the poorest and most Indian of Mexican states and therefore one of the most colorful. It is the seat of two major pre-Columbian cultures: the Mixtec and the Zapotec. The Mixtecs and the Zapotecs together make up the art of Oaxaca and especially the art contained in that ceremonial center high on a mountain top, Monte Albán. The architecture is of a refined classicism. No ornamentation was added to the precise geometry of the pyramids and platforms forming the city. Though the buildings of Monte Albán may seem less picturesque than those of Teotihuacán, the blend of sky, mountain and architecture makes for a magnificent beauty. It was at Monte Albán that Alfonso Caso made one of the greatest discoveries in Mexican archeology. The contents of the burial places he unearthed show that the Mixtecs probably were the best jewellers of old Mexico. The treasures from Monte Albán can be seen in the museum of Oaxaca, housed in the old Dominican monastery of Santo Domingo. Here the art of Mexico perhaps even comes up to the level of achievement of the art of China and the art of India.

On display is another museum in Oaxaca, which was donated by the artist Rufino Tamayo, is a most attractive collection of pre-

Columbian art: products of Mixtec and Zapotec potters, whose main speciality was funerary urns. In nearby Oaxaca is another major center, Mitla, built by the Mixtecs and celebrated for the cut-stone mosaics which cover its walls. The mosaic design is apparently geometrical, but actually deals with that most important of Mexican themes: the crawling snake.

Mayan Pyramids and Palaces: Habitable, Ceremonial, Artistic

For the hurry-up-and-see-it-all-quickly, the Mayan world can be compressed into three all-important centers: Palenque, Chichén Itzá and Uxmal. There the observer will find the features that make Mayan art so distinctive and different from the rest of Mexican art. The differences are obvious. For example, architecture. The Mayan pyramid is considerably more vertical than its counterparts in other parts of Mexico. This verticality is emphasized by the importance given to the temple built at the top, which the Mayans usually crowned with a tail and an elaborate crest.

Mayan "palaces" are habitable buildings placed in the ceremonial centers. A feature of the Mayan construction is the decorated wall with small doors as the only opening. Another unique feature of Mayan architecture is the remarkable pieces of sculpture known as *stelae*. Tall and free standing, the *stelae* were time milestones. They were raised periodically to mark the passage of time. Time and its measurement were the great obsessions of the Mayan culture. They developed a complex double calendar to pursue their calculations of time, back into the far past and forward into the far future. Astronomy and the measurement of time were important to all Mexican cultures, and as far as that goes to any agricultural society, but to the Mayans that pursuit became the main concern of the privileged and sophisticated priestly caste.

The Mayans excelled in all artistic techniques. They produced some of the most exquisite ceramics of old Mexico: elaborate funerary urns, delicately painted vases and figurines with almost a Chinese refinement. To experience the greatness of Mayan art one must go to Palenque, Chichén Itzá and Uxmal. Palenque, located in the Gulf coastal area, is the most accessible of the old empire sites. It has a remarkable beauty, both architecturally speaking and because of the tropical setting. Palenque offers some of the best Mayan buildings, palaces and pyramids. The "Palace" is perhaps the most complex of antique Mexican buildings, with vaulted galleries, open courts and a four-story stone tower, which

One of the Huastec masterpieces, this adolescent image is believed to be that of the young Quetzalcóatl. It is slender, refined and cleverly wrought.

was probably used for astronomical purposes. The most important pyramids are those of the Sun, the Cross and the Inscriptions. All of them exhibit the peculiar verticality of Mayan pyramids and the richness of design of the temples. Though small (usually one to three chambers), the Mayan temple is elaborate in form with a sloped roof, a crest or comb crowning and delicate carving.

The Palenque Cross

The Temple of the Inscriptions yielded a surprise. By chance, in 1952, the Mexican archeologist Alberto Ruz discovered a burial chamber in the temple. That led to the speculation that Mexican pyramids were, like the Egyptian pyramids, a place for burial and not merely the base for a temple, as previously had been thought. The treasure in the burial chamber contained two marvels. One is the tomb slab itself, which is beautifully carved. The other is a masterpiece of sculptural portrait, showing a young man with a long and aristocratic Palenque nose. He is wearing a lovely feather hat. The sculpture is at the Museum of Anthropology.

In the Temple of the Cross the archeologists found a giant carving of a cross that is much like the Christian cross. Naturally, this led to speculation that somehow Christianity was being preached many years before the Spanish came to conquer. Perhaps even by Quetzalcóatl himself. In any case, the Palenque Cross is one of the most beautiful carvings the Mayans left.

Uxmal, in the flat Yucatán, is an open city and it contains two of the jewels of Mayan architecture. One is the Pyramid of the Magician, so called because of the tale that a magician built it in a single night. The other is the Nunnery Quadrangle, next door.

The pyramid is a majestic structure, more than 38 meters high, with rounded ends and a proud, soaring staircase that leads to the elegant temple on top. Less spiritual and restrained than the Pyramid of the Sun in Teotihuacán and not as well polished as the Castle in Chichén, it has, nevertheless, an unsurpassable elegance, standing in point of balance between stark classicism and excessive baroque. The Nunnery was named by the Spaniards because it reminded them of a convent, with its spacious central court around which are four long galleries. Each gallery has several doors leading into dark, undecorated rooms. The exterior is formed by two horizontal stripes. The lower one is plain; the upper one is highly decorated with abstract looking serpentine motifs. The Nunnery reaches perhaps the perfection in this balance between the sim-

ple and the ornate. It has been influential in modern architecture. The American architect Frank Lloyd Wright designed several houses in this Mayan style.

Chichén Itzá in northern Yucatán is the best example of a curious cultural cross-breeding. The Mayas were invaded by a group of Toltecs; from central Mexico; thus Mayan art absorbed all the characteristics of simplicity and roughness of central Mexican art. The hybrid style that resulted might not please the purist but it is certainly attractive. The outstanding structure in Chichén is the Castle, a pyramid in strong and simple central Mexican style but with the verticality and grace of Mayan architecture. It was built in honor of our old friend Quetzalcóatl, who is known in the Yucatán as Kukulcán.

Another structure in Chichén, The Warriors, is deservedly famous for it contained the two famous pieces of Mayan/Toltec sculpture. One is the so-called *chac-mool*, a reclining figure, upon whose chest apparently offerings were placed. This sculptured form came from central Mexico, as interpreted by the skilled hands of the Mayans. The chac-mool is flanked by the other masterpiece: a pair of sculptured columns of feathered serpents.

Of course, Chichén Itzá had pure Mayan structures before the arrival of the Toltecs. The large sacred cenote, for example, had already been a sacred pilgrimage site for centuries. The *caracol* (snail), thus named for its spiral interior staircase, was an astronomical observatory with precisely located windows which corresponded most exactly to sacred positions of celestial bodies, especially the sun and Venus.

Astronomy and astrology, especially of the local variety, probably lost some of its importance with the arrival of the Toltecs, who placed more value on warfare and sacrifice, in curious contradiction to Quetzalcóatl-Kukulkán's original teachings. Excellent bas-relief sculptures at Chichén Itzá show an eagle and a jaguar, each devouring a human heart (the most appreciated offering to the gods of central Mexico). This blood and sacrifice theme is carried on in low relief sculptures that flank the ceremonial ball court at Chichén Itzá, the largest and best restored of its kind in Mexico. According to the most acceptable interpretations, these carvings depict the decapitation of the captain of the losing team. The pre-Columbians took their ball games seriously. Indeed, life, art and religion were inseparable elements of Mayan life.

This head is from one of the *atlantes* stone sculptures at Tula. These tall columns, perhaps representing Quetzalcóatl, were roof supports.

THE MURALISTS—IMPASSIONED RENAISSANCE MEN

Mural painting is Mexico's greatest contribution to contemporary art. A cultural product of the Revolution, mural painting flourished in Mexico well into the 1950s. The work of Diego Rivera, David Alfaro Siqueiros and José Clemente Orozco astounded the world.

Murals were painted in Mexico as far back as in pre-Columbian times, but the murals of the Revolution are something else again. They are explosive. They were extemporaneous, but were probably influenced by the work of José Guadalupe Posada (1852–1913), whose stark engravings have been described by the

made Rivera an offer he couldn't refuse. He said, Why not use the walls of the ministry on which to paint murals? That was the beginning of the mural-on-the-wall syndrome.

Rivera had just returned from Europe where he had been in touch with avant garde movements, such as cubism. Curiously, though, the most important influence on him was not contemporary at all, but came from Italian renaissance painting, from artists such as Paolo Uccello. Uccello's "La Battaglia di San Romano" is one of the sources of Mexican mural painting.

author-researcher Kate Simon as "masterly fierce." Posada's macabre *calaveras* (skulls) for the popular press were authentic Mexican, a far cry from the way artists of the era used foreign models. Posada employed black humor and incisive line. He laid the groundwork for a whole school of artistry which was vigorous, obsessively nationalistic, and a curious blend of the simple and the baroque.

Rivera—the Fiery Founder

The Big One was Diego Rivera (1886–1957), the founder of the mural movement in Mexico. Once the regime of Porfirio Díaz was overthrown, Jóse Vasconcelos, minister of public education in the Obregón cabinet,

Rivera painted murals at the Anfiteatro Bolivar and at the Ministry of Education in the 1920s. Highlights of his remarkable career include frescoes at Chapingo (1927), at the Cortez Palace at Cuernavaca (1930), New York's Rockefeller Center (1933), the National Palace (1935), and at the Prado hotel (1947). Rivera is a contradictory painter. He arouses deep feeling. An ideologist (he was a Communist, but was expelled from the party), he is not at all a political artist, but a true sensualist in the tradition of Paul Gauguin, Douanier Rousseau and even Pieter Brueghel the Elder.

Notwithstanding all these influences, which are hotly denied by nationalist critics, Rivera was deeply Mexican in his love of color and soft shapes and in his strong identification with the Mexican Indian. An excellent draftsman and watercolor artist, he created an image of a sweet, primitive Mexico, inhabited by brown, tender-loving girls and dreamy children carrying huge bouquets of flowers. Naturally, there was sentimentality in all of this.

Rivera himself was also colorful—he was the stuff that makes the front page. He was a source of gossip. His detractors said he was an accomplished liar, humorist and womanizer. Naturally, he became notorious. As the French say, he loved to *"épater la galerie,"* or

queiros volunteered for the Spanish Civil War; he took part in labor struggles and was imprisoned several times. His paintings reflect his ideological drive, his taste for bold action, and even for violence.

Siqueiros's paintings are so massive and muscular that they become a sort of imprisoned sculpture. Indeed, he experimented with a combination of painting and sculpture which he called *"esculptopintura."* He was also a constant innovator; he kept trying new materials and techniques. Perhaps his best murals are those in Chapultepec Castle, which

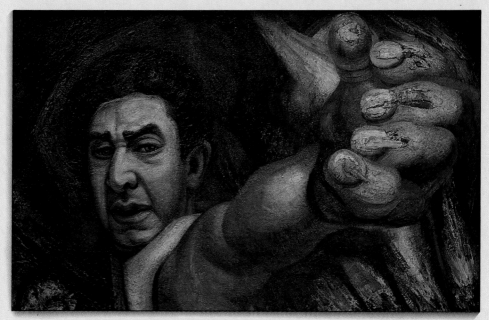

shock the multitudes. A blasphemous example: he wrote on his mural in the Prado hotel that "God does not exist." The words caused such an uproar that they had to be expunged. Rivera made millions. He built one of Mexico City's strangest homes, which he called the Anahuacalli, a sort of Aztec-surrealist building which housed his studio and art collection.

Siqueiros—the Ideologue

Siqueiros (1899–1974), in contrast to Rivera, was a strong man of action. A participant in the Revolution, he was a political activist all his life. He was involved in an attempt which failed to assassinate Leon Trotsky. Si-

offer a baroque and powerful interpretation of Mexican history. His works at the Palace of Fine Arts are among the best of his easel paintings.

Orozco—the Master

Orozco (1883–1949) often is considered the best of the big three. He is a tragic and passionate artist. A political skeptic, a biting satirist, and yet at bottom an idealist who was deeply disturbed by the sordidness of history, he used the mural to convey his troubled feel-

Preceding pages, "Catharsis" by Orozco; left, Rivera's "Liberated Earth" eulogizes Mexico's land reform; above, Siqueiros' powerful self-portrait.

ings. In a sense he is the *true* muralist of Mexico. At heart Rivera was an easel painter and Siqueiros a *sculpteur manqué.*

Orozco may be said to be the least Mexican of the muralists. He is interested in the universal and, though a keen observer of things Mexican, his message transcends the national picture and can be understood by everyone. In many ways he may be associated with the German expressionism of such artists as Max Beckmann, Otto Dix, and Käthe Kollwitz. They were described as savagely objective; they reacted forcefully to the horrors of war and the hypocrisy of society. Orozco, always an outspoken man, denounced the Mexican Revolution as a bloody farce that resulted in new servitude for the masses.

The first important Orozco mural was painted in the early 1920s at the National Preparatory School. Stark and simple, it still showed some influence from early Italian renaissance painting. At the Escuela Preparatoria, he achieves nonetheless moments of grandeur, especially in "The Trench," a powerful image of war and human struggle. On the staircase of the same building, Orozco painted "Cortez y la Malinche," the naked bodies of the Conqueror and his woman. The painting makes a clear statement about the relationship between Spain and Mexico, between conqueror and conquered, a theme which he returned to many times.

From 1927 to 1934, Orozco lived in the U.S. and painted murals for Pomona College, Dartmouth and the New York School for Social Research. He observed the cultural life of the times which he described in his bitter "Autobiography," and in letters to his friend and fellow artist, Jean Charlot. Back in Mexico, he painted "Catharsis," at the Palace of Fine Arts, in which the central figure is a colossal whore—the symbol of corruption. Orozco also produced many paintings, drawings and watercolors on the subject of prostitution. He viewed the brothel as the place of ultimate horror.

In the late Thirties he painted his greatest works, in Guadalajara—in the Palacio de Gobierno, the Paraninfo and on the walls and ceilings of the Hospicio Cabañas. Here he is at the peak of his power, covering straight and curved surfaces with fiery reds and stark blacks, paying homage to Father Hidalgo, denouncing political manipulation, searching for deep and universal symbols.

Tamayo, Coronel, Charlot, O'Gorman

Beside the grand three, there are others of note. Rufino Tamayo, born in 1899, is one. Never political, he soon abandoned realism for poetically simplified forms. He's a case totally apart. Tamayo's murals are unabashedly decorative. They play with cosmic and domestic symbology (the stars, cats, women) and are indifferent to the interpretation of history as told by *los tres grandes,* Rivera, Siqueiros and Orozco.

Pedro Coronel is another muralist who explored much the same ground as Tamayo. His murals are perhaps the best painted nowadays. But mainline Mexican mural painting is ideological or, at least, folkloreish and never is far removed from realism. In this regard we should mention others, such as Fernando Leal, Xavier Guerrero, José Chávez Morado, Roberto Montenegro, Raúl Anguiano, Manuel Rodríguez Lozano, Alfredo Zalce and Jorge González Camarena.

Jean Charlot, born in Paris in 1898, was one of the forerunners of the modern Mexican mural and he left an interesting body of work. His "Massacre in the Main Temple," a mural completed in 1923 on the stairway of the west court of the Escuela Preparatoria has been identified as the first fresco painted in Mexico since colonial times. Charlot was interested in archeology and he collaborated with the great historian of the Mayan culture, Sylvanus G. Morley. He also produced fine field studies of archaeological finds at Chichen Itzá, Yucatan, and at Cobá, Quintana Roo. Charlot later painted in the U.S. and helped, with his works and writings, to popularize mural painting there during Franklin Roosevelt's early days as president. Charlot later moved to Hawaii.

Juan O'Gorman, a painter and architect, transformed the mural into a sort of panorama of miniature scenes. Though modern, his paintings are anchored in Mexico's 19th Century popular art. He is famous chiefly for his murals which decorate the Central Library Building in University City in the capital. Constructed with colored stone, these giant mosaic-murals describe the culture of the world. They create a baroque texture, surprisingly innocent and fresh.

The contemporary mural in Mexico seems to be trying to follow the many paths of modern art, with different degrees of success. But, in truth, the Mexican mural sprang forth out of passions engendered by the Revolution and, for all practical purposes, that emotion is gone and done with. The followers of the three great ones keep repeating the same old formula, but what, in Rivera, Siqueiros and Orozco was a statement delivered in heat and passion, now has become, through repetition, sheer rhetoric.

Orozco's monumental portrait of Hidalgo, the great liberator, brandishing the fire of rebellion. This mural is in the Palacio de Gobierno, Guadalajara.

MEXICAN CRAFTS—INSPIRED, COLORFUL VISIONS

When does a craft become an art? When it is unique? When the product it produces sells for more than $10,000 at a New York art auction? When you put a frame around it and distinguish it with a spotlight? As a very loose definition, let us say that it becomes a craft if it makes things for common people's daily use and, incidentally, may even be good to look at.

The first crafts of Mexico were the making of weapons used for hunting, and baskets for carrying wild edible plants. Archeological excavations show that man used a variety of interlaced fiber to carry things with. These findings date back some 10,000 years. Around 6,000 B.C., man first planted corn and used stone implements to crush it. Those were the crude antecedents of the *metate* and the *mano*, which are still used today to grind corn. At about the same time man began to domesticate corn and improve the plant. He also began to improve the quality of his baskets to carry corn in. He wove vegetal stands so tightly that they could hold water without leaking.

At the Tianguis:
Utilitarian Charms

Perhaps about 4,500 B.C. a chap with great imagination covered a basket with clay, then hardened the clay in fire, and made pottery. That was quite a creative leap forward. You could cook with pottery; it could hold liquid indefinitely. It seèmed almost routine that man then began to decorate clay vessels, thus adding a non-utilitarian charm to a household item. A neighbor saw what he had done and tried to go him one better. Who can resist the desire to excel?

Soon man began to make weavings from maguey fiber, tree bark and native cotton. Many of the techniques and designs used in basket-making, pottery and weaving are still in use today. So are the same materials. They all go back to before the first complex Mexican civilization which began around 2,500 B.C. The discovery that wet clay could be shaped, then fire-hardened, led to the making of the first religious figurines. Those were the replicas of naked women with huge breasts, which were found in great quantities in Tlatilco, outside Mexico City. All the while

Left, a mask from Guerrero reflects both Indian and Spanish roots; above, the devil plays a happy role, smiling as he performs one of his odd tricks.

new crafts were springing up. Mankind always has had an inordinate curiosity. Most crafts had to do with things needed for daily use, obviously. But other craftsmen dedicated themselves to making luxury items for the leisure class: gold jewelry, feather mosaic "paintings," fine cotton weaving, exquisite lacquered vessels, beautiful figures of polished jade, and monumental stone and clay representations of the deities.

When the Spaniards came to Mexico, they found the native artisans well organized according to their specialty. They were selling

their wares at great Indian markets called *tianguis*. (The word is still used today.) None surpassed the fabulous Tlatelolco in Tenochtitlán, the Aztec capital which became Mexico City.

The Spanish wrought profound changes in all domains of life, including the crafts. They introduced new techniques, such as the use of the wheel in pottery-making, and the use of metal tools. The Spaniards needed items which were too expensive to import from Spain: furniture, saddles and bridles, woolen weaving, household items. In 1529, a lay brother, Pedro de Gante, established an arts and crafts school in Mexico City for the Indians. In Michoacán, Bishop Vasco de Quiroga introduced new techniques for working copper. He also showed the Indians such new products as iron ware and lacquer.

On the heels of the Conquistadores came Spanish craftsmen who taught their specialties to Indian apprentices. The natives learned quickly and soon competed with their former instructors. For a long time, however, native craftsmen were looked down on; everything Spanish was considered superior. But then came independence and a spirit of nationalism swept Mexico and the creative pendulum swung the other way. For a while Indian craft was exalted and Spanish work denigrated. Cuauhtemoc, king of the Aztecs, was a hero; Cortes, a villain.

Humble Artisans

In 1921, President Alvar Obregon opened a crafts exhibition, the first such official recognition given the native artisan. The great muralists, David Siqueiros, Jose Clemente Orozco and Diego Rivera, praised the humble crafts. All of this hype had its effect. Middle-class Mexicans started to buy it; so did the American visitors. They still do. There is a fly in the ointment, however. Because there are so many middlemen who get their cut, the craftsman who turns out the product seldom does well.

Artisans in Mexico might be divided roughly into four classes. The majority are farmers or laborers who work at their craft part-time to supplement their income. Usually they make everyday things. Then there is the craftsman who works fulltime. He usually lives in the city or town and either has his own shop or works for someone who does. He fashions items that are both decorative and useful, and he also makes cheap stuff that visitors like to buy. The souvenir trade, in other words. Then there are those engaged in large-scale commercial production who study the market and mass-produce their work to fill a need. The last group is the unemployed city worker who lives by his wits. He uses the cheapest of materials—paper, wire, wood, cork—to make toys, trinkets, or geegaws. Do not frown on his endeavors. Often he is amazingly skilled, marvelously imaginative, ingeniously effective. It is not an exaggeration to call him an artist.

Mexico's various regions specialize in certain items. Sometimes the same village has made the same item since pre-Columbian times. If it is something that catches the public's fancy, then it is mass-produced. The biggest concentration of craftsmen is found in central and southern Mexico. In many state

capitals there is a *Casa de Artesania* where you can buy the specialties of the region, albeit at higher prices than is customary in the marketplace, or from the craftsman himself. The north of Mexico is not known for its crafts, but there are exceptions, such as the ironwood animal carvings of the Seri Indians, the wide woolen belts of the Tarahumara Indians, and the sarapes made in Saltillo, Coahuila and Zacatecas.

In Tepic, Nayarit and Guadalajara, the Cora and Huichol Indians sell woolen belts and bags, embroidered clothing and yarn paintings. Tlaquepaque, a suburb of Guadalajara, offers ceramics, including fine copies of pre-Columbian pieces, blown glass and furniture. The town of Tonalá, near Guadalajara, specializes in pottery. Market days are Thurs-

days and Saturdays. In Guadalajara, the huge market of San Juan de Dios sells much handicraft, but don't forget to bargain.

Delicate Rebozos, Sarapes
And Woven Palm Leaves

Aguascalientes is known for its *deshilados* (hemstitch) and embroidery. The best time to buy and have fun is during the yearly wine festival, beginning in April to May 5. San Luis Potosi is famous for its fine silk *rebozos,* so delicate and compressible you can slip the silk through a wedding ring. In the area known as La Huasteca (parts of San Luis Potosi, Puebla and Veracruz), Indians weave a white traditional woman's cloak `(quechquémetl)` with cross-stitch embroidery. They also weave rugged and inexpensive wool bags and cactus fiber items. Guanajuato offers fine pottery; San Miguel de Allende sells sarapes, cane containers, piñatas for children's festivals and paper masks; and Querétaro is famous for its semi-precious stones and silver jewelry. In nearby Tequisquiapán, craftsmen make baskets, stools you can take apart, and sarapes. Usually you can buy it all in the colonial town of San Juan del Río. In Mezquital valley in Hidalgo, the Otomi Indians use handlooms to weave rebozos and belts. They also make reed containers. The town of Ixmiquilpan makes tremendous bird cages in the shape of cathedrals. The town and state of Tlaxcala, where wool was first woven in New Spain, is still a center of weaving. Sarapes are a specialty of Pablito Pahuatlán are the best examples. A kind of thick paper, *amatl,* is made from tree bark and local sorcerers use the paper for casting their spells. Reed baskets—made in Puebla—are the most frequently purchased items by tourists. Thirty to forty boxcars laden with baskets go to Tijuana monthly.

Michoacán probably has the greatest variety of crafts in Mexico. Many craftsmen and artisans live near Lake Pátzcuaro. You can reach most of the villages thereabouts by car or bus or do your buying in Pátzcuaro town. On November 2, the Plaza de Don Vasco becomes a center for craftsmen. In a nearby former convent, called the "House of the Eleven Patios," artisans work year-round and sell their products to the public. Here again certain towns boast a specialty: Santa Clara

the house. Coastal Veracruz, meanwhile, produces silver and coral jewelry, and woven palm-leaf items.

Puebla state boasts riches in the variety and quality of its crafts. Talavera ceramics, household crockery and glazed tiles are made in the capital. In Tehuacán and Tecali onyx is cut. The "Tree of Life" baroque ceramic decorations, often seen on travel posters, are made in the town of Acatlán, especially by Heron Martínez, and in Izúcar de Matamoros by the Flores and Castillo families. Puebla is also famed for its textiles; over the centuries the Indians have kept making their traditional clothes. The embroidered blouses of Cuetzálan and the bead-decorated blouses of San

del Cobre (also called Villa Escalante), copperware; Paracho, guitars; Tzintzuntzan, burnished ceramics; Quiroga, painted wood bowls and household items; Ihuatzio, reed mats and basketry; Patamban, exquisite green-glazed pottery; and Uruapan, masks and lacquerware. There are two places in Morelia, capital of Michoacán, where you can also buy some of the best of the state's handicraft. There is the Casa de Artesaniás, located in the former convent of San Francisco, and the convention center, a typical Tarascan wooden house.

Left, a 19th Century water jug with pre-Columbian influences. The man's tears are symbolic of rain. Above, a Huichol woman weaves a belt on a loom.

Gourd Bowls and Jaguar Masks

South of Mexico City, the state of Morelos concentrates on the sale of its craft production in Cuernavaca, a tourist-oriented town. You can buy locally made, colonial-style furniture, wooden bowls, combination jewelry and sarapes, and palm-leaf strip basketry. The village of Huejapan, in the municipality of Tetela del Volcán, produces sarapes and Indian clothing. The adjoining state of Guerrero specializes in pottery. The town of Olinalá produces the most beautiful lacquerware in Mexico—gourd bowls, wooden trays, jaguar masks. Taxco is world famous for its silver jewelry. Near the Pacific coast and the border of Oaxaca, the Amuzgo Indians of Xochistlahuaca, in the vicinity of Ometepec, are known

for their fine blouses, called *huipiles,* many of which are woven from rough cotton *(coyuche).* In the tropical towns of Xalita, Toliman and San Agustín de las Flores, the Huapanec Indians paint flowers, animals and abstract designs, using bright, fluorescent paint on the bark paper which is made in San Pablito Pahuatlan, in the state of Puebla.

Over the border in Oaxaca, the Zapotec Indians make elaborate blouses with tiny flowers and miniature dolls which hold the pleats together. So intricate is the work that the artisans say, as a challenge: *"Hazme si*

Above, a ceramic "Tree of Life" from Metepec, a theme loosely based on the Bible; right, a mestizo shapes a hat from a rolled cactus fiber called *ixtle.*

puedes"—that is, "Make one like me, if you can." The blouses and wrap-around skirts of Yalalag are dyed with natural colors. No analines for them. Yalalag also produces silver crosses.

The Mixtec coast is known for its carrying nets. Cuilapan produces wooden animals in bright colors and assorted shapes. Near the city of Oaxaca, the village of San Bartolo Coyotepec makes a traditional burnished black pottery. In Santa María Atzompa they make ceramic animal figures. Teotilán del Valle produces Mexico's best sarapes, either in traditional pre-Columbian designs or as copies of famous modern art paintings. In the town of Oaxaca, artisans make exact copies of the intricately beautiful Mixtec jewelry found in the tombs of Monte Albán. Market day in Oaxaca city is Saturday. There are important fiestas in December where much local craft is sold.

Chiapas produces woven woolen clothing, worn by the Indians of the highlands. The clothing is for sale in the villages and at market on Sunday in San Cristóbal de las Casas, as well as in the cooperative of Sna. Jolobil in the former convent of Santo Domingo. The town of Chiapa de Corzo is known for its lacquerware, especially the masks used in the festival of San Sebastián. Ametenango produces traditional pottery, which is fired without an oven. The Tzotzil village of San Juan Chamula makes much of the woolen clothing sold throughout the state, as well as guitars and harps. The Yucatán produces the county's best hammocks, made either from cactus fiber or from cotton. The best Panama hats come from Bekal in Campeche. Quality mahogany and cedar furniture is made in Mérida, Valladolid and Campeche.

The state of Mexico also has many crafts. The town of Metepec produces the polychrome ceramic "Tree of Life." Wool sarapes are woven in a number of villages. Lerma produces baskets. Using orange-tree wood, Ixtapán de la Sal carves household utensils and decorative animals. Toluca is known for silver work, chess and domino games, made of leather, bone or wood.

Mexico City produces modern jewelry. The capital has many gifted craftsmen, some whose imagination seems boundless. They can produce art objects from plastic, bottle caps, rubber bands or wire. Popular TV characters are made from foam rubber and painted in garish colors. A model of a children's hero comes with rubber-ball springs emerging from his head. There is the work of the Linares family who make figures of Judas, which are burned on Holy Saturday. They also make sophisticated papier-mâché figures.

FIESTAS: CELEBRATIONS OF SADNESS AND JOY

To understand the Mexican fiesta think of Mexican history and its mix of peoples. Mexican history is full of blood and tears. Mexico's people are partly mestizo, partly Indian, partly Spanish. The culture is old, yet new; it has retained to some degree the traditions of the past. The background of fiesta is Indian and Spanish, but condiment and spice have been added. There is some modern influence, chiefly from America; some folklore influence, from places as far away as France, and, unbelievably, even China. That is the mold out of which fiesta came.

On the whole, the Mexican is not a happy hombre. At least not in the effervescent way that the Cariocas of Rio de Janiero are said to be. Generally, the Mexican is grave and sedate and life for him is serious. Sometimes he even verges onto the gloomy. Nor are Mexicans usually outwardly expansive; they tend to silence and introversion.

Sacred Theatrical Performances

The Indian fiesta was religious in character. Not until the Conquest did things liven up and become human. Somberness dominated. That was only natural. After all, the Indian festival had as its central element human sacrifice. Pre-Columbian man lived in a hostile world, ruled by gods who were indifferent to man's fate. Like the gods of ancient Greece, they had to be bribed to keep them content and not vindictive. Unfortunately, the Mexican gods were addicted to human blood. The Indians of ancient Mexico performed human sacrifice in a most ritualistic way. It almost verged on the artistic—a sort of sacred theatrical performance, but the blood was real.

At some of the celebrations the people ate the flesh of the humans they had sacrificed. But drink was forbidden—only senior citizens were permitted to get drunk. Perhaps it was construed as a reward for longevity. When the Spanish came they brought to festival more pleasures: bullfighting, horse racing, sports, dance, gambling, drinks—for everybody. Those same revelries are now ardently pursued at fiesta time.

Mexican fiesta today is associated with Catholic festivities. Indeed, fiesta is two-sided: human enjoyment and religious practice. There are the masses, the religious processions, the reciting of rosaries, the chanting of novenas. As an example, the *Feria de San Marcos* is celebrated for 10 days every year, starting on St. Mark's day, April 25th. San Marcos is the patron saint of Aguascalientes city. This feria has been celebrated there since 1604 and apart from religious rites, it has attractions such as musical serenades, flower battles, bullfights, mariachis, cockfighting, and much drinking of the wines of Aguascalientes.

Mexicans like to gamble and it goes on unabated. It's a chance at fiesta to win or lose a bundle. They take their gambling seriously. At the *palenques* (palisades), where cockfights are held, the doors are closed once an event starts. Why? So that bettors can't duck out if they run up a gambling debt. And, of course, there's the betting on horse races. Everyone likes to have a "flutter," as the English say. The horse racing is not Churchill Downs or the Pimlico. Often it's a primitive affair, really, with two horses running *(carreras parejeras)* along an improvised dirt track.

Who foots the bill for a fiesta? Well, usually someone who is chosen by the community for the honor. A fiesta patron is called a butler, a deputy, or a district attorney. Whatever the title, the chosen one sometimes spends a large share of his capital to sponsor the event, but he obtains from his largesse the gratitude of the people and even a lifetime of prestige.

Fiesta-goers wear their best traditional dresses. The women adorn themselves with big gold earrings, bracelets, rings, and such. They put on ribbons, lace, bright-colored silk. It produces what might be said to be a baroque effect. They do it up big especially in Oaxaca. Sometimes a well-off woman will tote around pounds of gold on her person. She throws more light than a 150-watt bulb. It should be said at this point that Mexicans, generally speaking, are indifferent toward comfort and not much concerned about saving pesos for a rainy day, but they do love the display of riches.

Fiesta takes place in mid-town, in the church and in the square and streets surrounding the square. A marketplace springs up instantly. Someone installs a wheel of fortune, or a merry-go-round. (These accouterments accompany fiestas from town to town. It's their life-long vocation.) At the marketplace are the *lotería* and *los antojitos*. The lotería is a Mexican version of that mesmeristic pastime

Left, a "conchero" dancer performing in a festival for the Virgin of Guadalupe.

called bingo. The cardboards are decorated with traditional figures: the devil, the moon, the soldier, the drunkard, the dandy, the watermelon, death. The man in charge *(el gritón)* calls out the name of the card from a stack he has shuffled and the first person to complete the figures on his cardboard cries out: *"Lotería!"* and all the others groan. It is a game played all over the world—from Europe to the Orient. What makes lotería so creative a game is the way each gritón describes the figures. Death, for example, becomes "The one that will take us all." The moon is "The one who goes out by night." The drunkard is the "Chap who does not give a damn." The descriptions vary with the imagination of the caller.

Los antojitos mexicanos are the favorite for the biggest celebration of all, Christmas. Posadas (inns) commemorate the journey of Mary and Joseph to Bethlehem, trying to find an inn that will receive them. In Mexico people used to take part in an informal procession behind the images of the Holy Pilgrims, chanting songs about their quest for a room *(pedir posada)*. Afterward, there were games, such as the breaking of *piñatas*. (A piñata is a clay pot filled with candy and fruit, hanging from a moving rope. It is broken by a blindfolded child wielding a stick.) The piñata may be beautifully decorated with colored shreds of paper and hanging ribbons.

Nowadays the posadas have become more sophisticated. Following the procession come dancing and drinking. Some families are trying to preserve the old traditions which were

dishes of Mexican cooking which enliven every fiesta. Most are made of corn, cooked in many ways. Antojitos are deeply fried and heavily spiced and calorie-laden, but so what? This is fiesta. You can start dieting next week. Among the most popular dishes are *tamales, buñuelos, sopes, atole, tacos, tostadas, pozole, enchiladas, menudo, mixiotes, quesadillas, memelas,* ad infinitum.

Among the patriotic fiestas the most important take place around September 16th, Independence Day. There are the parades, the *"Grito"* or proclamation, speeches, fireworks, etc. Religious celebrations are more elaborate, though it seems they are losing their clout in the big cities.

The *Posadas* are fiestas preparing the way

meant for the enjoyment of the children.

On Christmas, Mexicans have a big dinner, attend midnight mass, and nowadays, because of the influence of the giant from north of the border, they also have a decorated Christmas tree in their home and they exchange gifts. In the old days they put up a *nacimiento*—a miniature clay replica of Bethlehem and the stable where Christ was born. Gifts were given, but only to the children, and not on Christmas but on January 6th, the day the Magi gave their present to Jesus. At dinner on that day a huge doughnut-shaped cake is

Above, a Nahua wears a headdress to honor St. Francis of Assisi. Right, the crucifixion is reenacted at Ixtapalapa on Good Friday.

served. Inside the cake is hidden a figurine. The one who finds it has the honor of paying the expenses for a fiesta which is held on February 2nd, the *Candelaria* feast.

New Year's eve used to be a sort of Thanksgiving day for Mexicans. It had a touch of melancholia, a whiff of the nostalgic. It has since become a happier day, even a bit boisterous. There is dancing and drinking and the air is full of great expectation for the new year.

Lent and Holy Week

In February or March is the beginning of Lent, preceded by *Carnaval* or Mardi Gras. Though the carnival celebration is an old custom in Mexico, it was important only in the port cities—mainly in Veracruz and Ma-

precisely at 10 in the morning, the presumed hour of heaven's opening. The Judas replica can be tiny and toylike, or big and sculptured. Judas is painted in bright colors. Sometimes the villain of the moment is portrayed in the Judas head: Adolf Hitler, for example, during World War II.

Corpus Christi day was one of Mexico's most important fiestas in colonial times. The processions were elaborate; the preparations lavish. Children were taken to church, dressed as Indians and carrying tiny straw donkeys. Feasts are held to honor other saints: Joseph, Francis of Assisi, Anthony of Padua, John the Baptist, Philip of Jesús. The latter is the first Mexican saint. In addition there are celebrations in honor of the Virgin: the Assumption, the Immaculate Conception, and

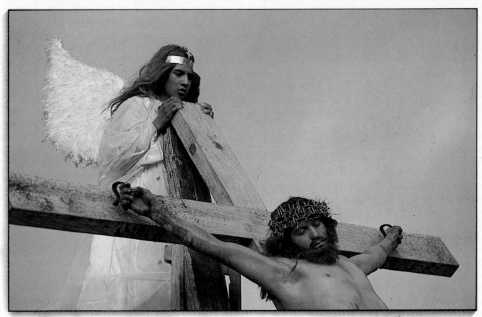

zatlán. There are parades, all-night dancing, all-night drinking and masked balls. Everyone does a lot of repenting. They all go to church to be reminded that man is mortal.

Lent, however, is not really a season of fiesta. It is supposed to be a time of penitence and prayer. Lent is also a chance to savor new dishes and to enjoy the splendors of the usually dry and sunny Mexican spring. The Holy Week used to be tightly controlled. Noise was forbidden. People stayed home and attended all the religious functions. They had to visit seven churches on Maundy Thursday. Good Friday was traditionally a day of fasting and silence. On Saturday, "Judas" was burned in effigy. Mexicans used paper figurines, wrapped in firecrackers, which they set off

local celebrations, such as Guadalupe, Talpa, Zapopan, de la Salud de Pátzcuaro, de los Remedios, etc.

November 2nd, the Day of the Dead, is a religious ceremony of special importance. People go to the cemeteries to visit their *muertitos,* to put flowers on the graves, pray and weep. Indians symbolically place food on the graves for the dead, and the living drink to their memory. This day brings forth all sorts of things related to death: primarily skulls and skeletons—painted, drawn, sketched or made in sugar candy or of pastry. These *calaveras* (skulls) might seem grotesque, but Mexicans do not think of them in terms of the macabre. They look upon such things calmly and with a touch of wry humor.

Antonio, a full-blooded Tarascan Indian, stood up in the round-bottomed canoe, with his trusty spear in his hand. The slightest indiscreet move would tip the canoe over into the cold water. Lithe as a ballet dancer, Antonio moved quickly and let fly his spear at a wild duck about to land on the surface of the water. The spear hit home—the duck fell thrashing into the water. Antonio paddled over and picked the bird up. Smiling, he said, "Now when my father comes home from the land of the dead, he will be happy." When alive, Antonio's father loved baked duck.

Quixote tilting his lance at a windmill; he is a bullfighter, a bicyclist, even a bride. Children are given toys that familiarize them with death. At the fiesta people exchange candy skulls. Death often bears a title. In folk songs and popular poetry, Death is referred to as "the bald one," "the slim one," or "the one with his teeth always showing." (There's a very strong drink called *levanta muertos*—literally, "the raiser of the dead.")

The Indian attitude toward the souls of the dead springs from the Nahua-speaking peoples of pre-Columbian Mexico. They did not

The Ultimate Liberation

The Fiesta of the Dead is one of Mexico's strangest rituals, but oddly it has its counterpart in other places in the world. The fiesta follows Indian tradition and is celebrated in central Mexico, chiefly by Tarascan, Nahua, Totonac and Otomi Indians. The mestizo has a quiet defiance of death; he takes it in stride, he sort of has a cocked-hat attitude about it. Mexicans look upon dying as one more misfortune to contend with, but they also regard it as the ultimate liberation. They joke about it. In popular art, Death is described with irony or sarcasm, which express the joy, the pain and the tribulation of humankind.

Death assumes human features—he is Don

think the skull was a symbol of death but a symbol of life. A skull did not inspire horror. On the contrary, it symbolized the promise of a new life. It was one of the most popular forms of ornament. In modern Mexico the skull is used in humorous drawing, in toys, and candy.

Indians who celebrate the Fiesta of the Dead believe the souls of the dead return each year to visit their living relatives. The relatives make sure to provide a feast with the deceased's favorite food (Antonio's father's baked duck, for example), and they even sup-

Above, relatives of a beloved deceased keep a graveside vigil on the night of November 2; right, sugar skulls, a sweet reminder of our mortality.

ply the departed one's soul with his favorite booze.

At Antonio's house the table was set for the Fiesta of the Dead. Naturally, the baked duck had a place of honor—right below a photograph of the departed man. Candles were lit; there was a profusion of flowers, and especially the yellow *cempoalzúchil,* which resembles the marigold. The night before Antonio had gone to his brother Pablo's house for the festival of the "little dead," dedicated to children who had died. An altar had been set up; there were toys and candy, so that the souls of

toasts to the "health" of the departed soul. At one corner of the cemetery stood an altar, bearing a photograph of "Tata" (father) Cardenas, the late President Lázaro Cárdenas, who came from this state and is much beloved.

At about 4 in the morning one of the candles fell over onto the baked duck. Probably a gust of wind blew it over. That served to reassure Antonio—it was proof that his father's soul, in fact, had returned and had accepted gratefully the offerings, and especially the baked duck. Antonio smiled as he thought

the children, who had become little angels, would have a good time when they returned to visit their parents and relatives.

At six next evening the bells of the church began to "call the dead." Every 30 seconds the bell rang and it went on until sunrise next morning. Just before midnight, Antonio and his brother's family left their homes. At the cemetery hundreds of candles glowed. Antonio and Pablo covered their father's tomb with offerings of food, drink, incense, candles and flowers. It is believed that the returning soul will find his way back to the grave by the light of the candles and the smell of the incense. The hours of devotion to a memory went by in silence, punctuated by the tolling of the church bells. Naturally, they drank numerous

about it, but there were tears on his cheeks.

Came the dawn and the people returned home, carrying the food which they had placed on the grave. They ate and drank heartily. They danced, and sang and got drunk. Having remembered the dead, they delighted in still being alive.

The ancients of Mexico believed in the indestructability of a vital force and its transcendence after this life. The Indians did not believe in the eternal life of the individual soul but in the survival of an abstract collective force in which humans as well as animals and plants participated. The world was conceived as an eternally repeated cycle of death-life-death where all destruction had in itself the seed of a new birth.

MUSICA MEXICANA—OF POETS AND SINGERS

You've heard of mariachi music, even if you've never been to Mexico. The players wear tight pants and dark jackets with silver buttons and decorations and big, filigree and felt hats. They plan a variety of string instruments and maybe a trumpet or two.

You've also probably heard of *ranchero* music that goes back to the Spanish *romances* or chivalric ballads. In Mexico they became *corridos* and they sang of heroes and villains, *bandidos* and *pistoleros,* catastrophic events, politics, current events, and, of course, love. The themes are treated with varying degrees of stoicism, pathos, humor and mockery.

In popular music, the *machismo,* which one comes to expect from the manly Mexican, is muted. Of course, in ballads about revolutionaries, such as Pancho Villa and Emiliano Zapata, the machismo is up front, where it counts. There are old favorites: The hombre who always does what he pleases because his word is law. Or the hombre who tells about his forthcoming execution. He has killed his best friend and the woman who done him wrong with his best friend. He has no regrets; he fears nothing. He says that in the afterlife he will seek out the pair he murdered—and kill them once again. A very macho man.

There is a small audience in Mexico for classical music, usually in the cities. Still, there have been Mexican composers of international repute who at times have been inspired by folk music. Two stand out: Silvestre Revueltas and Carlos Chávez.

Noble Musical Traditions

Musical tradition in Mexico has its roots in both pre-Columbian Indian and Spanish cultures. Before the arrival of the Conquistadores, the music of the Aztecs was an integral part of their religious rituals, under the patronship of Macuilxochitl, goddess of the five flowers. Music in pre-Hispanic Mexico displayed unsuspected energy and variety. It had to be performed, like the dance, in a plaza, on a platform, or on a pyramid. Priests, nobles and even kings took part.

Netzahualcoyotl, king of Texcoco, near Mexico City, was a poet and a fine singer. He encouraged the composers in his court who narrated the glories of his lineage and the history of his kingdom. Many of the songs dedicated to the gods have survived. Manuscripts and codices with rhythmic annotation were set down by the Spanish friar Bernardino de Sahagún in the 16th Century. They are the first examples of scored music in the Americas. The songs generally were accompanied by the *huehuetl* and the *teponaztli,* both of them percussion instruments, as well as by rattles, flutes, conch shells and grooved bones.

The huehuetl was a drum, supported on a tripod. It was made of a hollowed log, one end of which was covered by deerskin. The drummer, who was standing, played with his bare hands. The teponaztli was also made of a hollowed-out log. The player used two drumsticks, tipped with rubber. In some villages of Hidalgo, Veracruz and Tabasco both the huehuetl and the teponaztli are still considered sacred instruments and are used to accompany the old-time rituals.

The ancient wind instruments were sophisticated: reed and clay flutes, multiple flutes, ocarinas, whistle jugs and conch shell trumpets. In funerary rites, it was common to associate the sound of the conch shell with the sound of mourning.

Fray Juan de Torquemada left an excellent description of pre-Columbian song and dance incorporated into religious rites. He wrote: "At the beginning of a dance three or four Indians blow shrill whistles. Other instruments come in, sounding a low tone, gradually growing louder. When the dancers hear the instruments play, they begin to sing and dance. At first the songs proceed at a slow pace, in a deep tone. When one song is finished (and it may seem very long because of its slow pace, although none lasts more than an hour), the instruments change their tone, and the leaders begin another chant, a little more lively, and rising in pitch. In this manner, the songs continue as though changing the voice from a base to a tenor."

Musical instruments for ceremonial use in Mexico-Tenochtitlán were kept in a sacred place called Mixcoacalli. A large number of musicians were employed in the service of the temples; men dedicated themselves to the study of songs and dances. So important was music to the Indians that a missionary wrote that conversions came about more readily through music than through preaching.

A violin player provides music for "conchero" dancers: his instrument bears the image of the Virgin of Guadalupe.

Colonial Influences

Musicians who served in the Aztec temples were employed, following the Spanish conquest, in the churches. While enjoying their ancient prerogative of being exempt from paying tribute, they demanded the right to participate in the most colorful of the colonial ceremonies. The earliest school to teach music to the Indians was founded three years after the conquest by Friar Pedro de Gante. Soon after, New Spain started making its own organs and other secular instruments. Instruments used in the Renaissance and during the baroque period were made in Mexico, starting in the 16th Century. Some, such as guitars, violins and harps, became the specialty of certain villages. So did large church organs.

tias, who served from 1617 to 1667.

The secular music of the Renaissance arrived aboard the galleons from Spain. Out of the Caribbean and ports of the Gulf of Mexico came rhythms and musical forms that mixed Latin, Mediterranean, Arab, African and Indian music. From out of all this mélange came the tango, the rumba, the fandango, the *chaconne,* the *saraband,* the *cumbé,* the *habanera,* the bolero and the *danzón.* Exciting rhythm, all of it. It set your feet a-tapping.

During its 300 years as a colony, Mexico was treated to all kinds of music. In 1711, Mexico City played host to the first opera composed and performed in the New World, *"La Parténope,"* by Manuel de Zumaya. During late colonial times, the corrido, accompanied by guitar and harp, became the most pop-

The Indians learned music surprisingly quickly. An early missionary marveled that "at the beginning they did not understand anything nor did the old instructor have an interpreter. In a short time they understood so well that they learned not only plain chants but also the songs of the organ and now there are many choirs and singers who are skillful in modulation and harmony, learning everything by heart." In Tlaxcala an Indian composed an entire mass by himself.

The most pretigious job open to a musician in New Spain was that of musical director of the cathedral in Mexico City. Many of the directors were noted composers of religious music; competition for the job was intense. The first Indian to win the post was Juan Ma-

ular musical form. It related an event out of the ordinary.

Mariachi groups were first formed in the 18th Century and they now play all over the country but seem to be most popular in Jalisco and central Mexico. The name comes from either the French word *marriage,* for wedding, or the Galician word *marriagero,* for a musician who plays at a wedding. At first the players used only string instruments. Later, trumpets were added for pizazz.

During the 19th Century the waltz came into popularity. The new music spoke of the triumph of the War of Independence. Naturally, it had a melancholic flavor. Major composers such as Macedonio Alcalá, Juventino Rosas, Ricardo Castro and Felipe Villanueva gave form to the Mexican version of the waltz. They combined originality, nostalgia and melodic imagination. The *jarabe* of Jalisco, the *sandunga* of Oaxaca, the *jarana* of the Yucatán, and the *pirecua* of Michoacán accompany dances. The texts are in Spanish, Tarascan, Mayan or Zapotec.

The *marimba* is most popular in Chiapas, Oaxaca and Tabasco. These xylophone-type instruments with big wooden keys are played by four persons using rubber-tipped batons. The soloist carries the tune; the other three divide the secondary melody in counterpoint. It was traditional that all players came from the same family and could play waltzes, *paso dobles*, boleros and even excerpts from operas. The marimba presently is sometimes accompanied by a saxophone, gourds and per-

which protest the treatment of wetbacks in the U.S.

The bolero is probably the most popular type of music in the cities. Its origin goes back to the Andalusian bolero, but is enriched by the beat of the tropics imported from Cuba. It takes pleasure in nostalgia. Agustín Lara, the most famous composer of boleros in this century, is able to combine clear and voluptuous writing with audacious rendering. The songs often are dedicated to the women in a gallant's life. Some of the best known titles of the 1930s and '40s are "The Lady Adventurer," "Sell Dearly Your Love" and "I'm in Love."

Tropical bands often play in the dancehalls. Usually the players play percussion instruments—bongos, *tumbadoras, güiros*— rattle-gourds, guitars, pianos, marimbas and

cussion drums.

Wind instruments characterize the music of Indians from Oaxaca, Querétaro, Michoacán and Morelos. Their repertory, aside from marches and waltzes, intrudes into the classical field, though at the same time keeping its solemn, traditional character. The musical bands of the far north are generally composed of guitars, accordions, contrabass and drums. Often you hear a central European flavor, which is evident in the waltzes, mazurkas and polkas. The repertory consists of popular music, *huapangos*, and even, these days, ballads

Left, a mariachi singer concludes a heart-breaking love song; and above, a girl twirls into a folk dance that keeps her country's musical traditions alive.

at times even electric organs. Rock from the U.S. has gained popularity in recent years, and some heavy metal quartets in Mexico City nearly knock the paint off the city's colorful walls.

Perhaps as a reaction against this trendy American invasion there has been a recent revival of interest in folkloric music. This genre attracts a middle class audience—sometimes appearing at concerts dressed in colorful Indian clothes—that favors genuine artists such as Cuco Sánchez, Chavela Vargas or Tehua. They appreciate nostalgic and rural musical forms such as the old *corridos* and sad love songs. They also like to relate to Mexican music as a part of an overall Latin American artistic expression.

H. Iriarte dibujó.

Lito. de M. Murguía y Cª

EL RANCHERO

CHARROS—MEXICO'S GOLDEN RANCHEROS

To define the Mexican *charro* as merely a cowboy is to do him an injustice. Although there are some likenesses, there are marked differences between the two, in style, appearance, and how they perform. Naturally, the charro objects to a superficial comparison, and so probably does the cowboy.

Charro Chronicles

The charro has his roots in Spain from whence came his horses, the cattle he works, and the dress he wears. When Hernán Cortés

horses and cared for them. They had all the time in the world to practice with the lasso, and to teach their horse new tricks. It is no exaggeration to say that the best of them became as superb a horseman as the gaucho of the Argentine or the Cossack of the Don river.

The Mexican horsemen developed a skill of their own—*colear,* or grabbing the bull by the tail. It was a maneuver to show the animal who was boss. That indefatigable chronicler of things Mexican, Madame Calderón de la Barca, described in 1840 how "they (charros) proceeded to amuse us with the colear of the

landed in Mexico, he had a troop of 16 cavalrymen and that introduced the horse to Mexico. Those horsemen were Cortes' most effective strike force; they made a tremendous impression. When Cortés led an expedition to Honduras, one of his horses died on the way. The Mayas thereupon deified the horse. That shows the esteem the horse was held in.

During colonial times, all Spaniards were obliged to own a horse. A royal decree, issued in 1528, forbade the Indians, under penalty of death, from riding a horse, even if they were of the nobility. Over the years cattle was introduced into Mexico and since the Indians were needed to work the cattle, they had to be allowed to ride horses. For both sport and exercise, as well as their daily work, men rode

bulls, of which amusement the Mexicans throughout the whole republic are passionately fond. They collect a herd; single out several (animals), gallop after them on horseback; and he who is most skillful, catches the bull by the tail, passes it under his own right leg, turns it round the high pummel of his saddle, and wheeling his horse around at right angles by a sudden movement, the bull falls on his face. Even boys of ten years old joined in this sport."

What did she think of the charros? "It is impossible to see anywhere a finer race of men

Left, a 19th Century engraving of a hacienda owner dressed in colonial-era finery; above, felt hats that can cost more than $500 are *de rigeur.*

than these rancheros—tall, strong and well-made, with their embroidered shirts, coarse sarapes and dark-blue pantaloons embroidered in gold. . . . their games of skill and trials of address are manly and strengthening, and help to keep up the physical superiority of that fine race of men, the Mexican rancheros."

Charros made fine cavalrymen in the wars Mexico fought. At the battle of the Alamo, charros lassoed and captured Texans. In the fight against the French, galloping charros snagged cannon with their lassos and turned them over. And who could resist Pancho Villa's "Golden Ones" as they rode into battle? (Well, General Alvaro Obregón, for one. He stopped them by digging trenches, putting up barbed wire, and firing machine guns.)

The skilled work that the charros did in the

charros to travel abroad were the 12 men who took part in Buffalo Bill's Wild West shows in the U.S. Their leader, Vicente Oropeza, was known as the world's greatest artist of the lasso.

Urban Charros

After the expropriation of many large cattle ranches during post-revolution days, the charro lost status. Since then, the charreria has been developed by what one might call "the cowboys of the city." In other words, in an urban setting. It has become what many consider to be the only truly national Mexican sport. The biggest *lienzo charros* (charro rings) are in Mexico City and Guadalajara where the city dudes hold weekly competition from 11 a.m. to 2 p.m. on Sundays. The event

field led only naturally to competition, and then to sport. It all originated on the cattle ranges. Roping, tying, riding, branding. Was there ever men with more endurance? They could work all day from sunup to sunset, stay up very late to dance the *jarabe,* then get up at dawn next day for another day's work in the field.

For years bullfighting and *charrería* were intimately associated. Indeed, aficionados of both the *fiesta brava* and the charros claimed as their own the great Ponciano Díaz, who was a bullfighter and a charro *extraordinaire.* This famous torero (by the way, only in the opera "Carmen" is a bullfighter called a toreador) was the first to charge admission for a charro performance. The first group of

is known as a *jaripeo.*

The show starts with horsemen riding abreast to salute the judges and the public. This may remind you of the opening of a bullfight. The first event, called *cala de caballo,* demonstrates the mastery of rider over horse. The rider comes full gallop down a passageway and brings his horse to an abrupt stop inside a white, chalk-powdered rectangle. The rider turns his mount round and round—to the right, to the left—all the time staying within the marked-off rectangle. To top it off, he walks his horse backwards out of the ring.

Then comes the *coleadero*—the thriller. A bull comes charging out of a chute and down the passageway into the ring. Up gallops our hero, the charro, who grabs the bull by the tail, and then tries to throw him off balance and roll him over on his back. Points are given for how swiftly the charro can perform the task and how neatly he makes the bull fall and roll over. Sometimes the rider ends up with a section of the bull's tail in his hand. He waves it at the fans.

The next series of events are performed in a circular space in front of the spectators. Aside from bronco-bucking and bull-riding (the riders hang on with both hands), everything is now work with the lasso. The charro is a magician with the rope. After making his flourishes with the lasso, the mounted rider throws down the loop in front of the bull. His teammates induce the bull to venture into the loop; thereupon the rider pulls the rope tight around both the animal's legs and hauls him down.

The most spectacular event takes place near the end of the competition. Three riders drive a wild horse around the edge of the ring. The fourth member of the team stands about 3 meters (10 feet) from the side of the arena, leaving enough room so that the wild horse and the riders will pass between him and the wall. After the riders and the horse have galloped a few times around the edge of the ring, the man on foot starts twirling his lasso. Then, with incredible, split-second timing, he jumps through a loop in his lasso and in the same breath drops a loop on the ground in front of the horse who will come thundering by. When the hind legs of the horse are inside the loop, the charro on foot jerks his lariat, slips the knot tight, and wraps the rope around his back. The slack is hauled in; the charro leans back, digs in his heels, and brings down the wild bronco, who is not at all pleased with these developments. The crowd is, though. They go wild. It's an amazing feat. Try that, one of you gauchos!

Usually, this performance is followed by the *paso de la muerte*—the pass of death wherein a charro jumps off his galloping horse onto the back of a wild horse. It is what is known in the trade as changing horses in midteam.

The ladies have their own events, called *escaramuza charra*. They dress, naturally, in charra style, and mount their horses side-saddle, so as not to lose the "attractiveness of their exquisite feminity," as one gallant Mexican writer put it. They are extremely adept at riding. The show sometimes closes with the dancing of the *jarabe tapatío*, a folk dance out of Jalisco, which is, as every Mexican knows, the favorite dance in charro country.

Left, a charro jumps through his looping lariat before proceeding to lasso a wild horse; above, young ladies focus on the charro's amazing feats.

Charro Chic

Charros tend to be romantic and conservative. They idolize women. Usually, they are fervent nationalists. Naturally, they are devoted to horses. They love to eat well and drink heartily. A charro who does not drink is almost as rare as a cook or journalist who does not drink. Teetotaling charros are suspect.

Charros sometimes seem peacockish. They may spend a fortune on their outfits, or on equipment for their horse. As they say in Mexico, they "throw the house out of the window" in their splurging. There is a charro saying: "We're all made of the same clay, but a well-dressed dandy is not the same as a well-dressed charro."

Here are some charroisms, straight out of the horse's mouth:

"A horse to fill your legs, a fighting cock to fill your pocket, and a woman to fill your arms."

"A horse, a fighting cock and a woman should be chosen along blood lines."

"There are three kinds of idiots: those who drink with their employees, those who ride without a bridle, and those who dance with their own wives."

There is an aura of nostalgia about the charros, a wish to return to a golden past when everyone knew their place in society. Their machismo is up front—men with their horses perform daring feats to impress demure and well made up ladies.

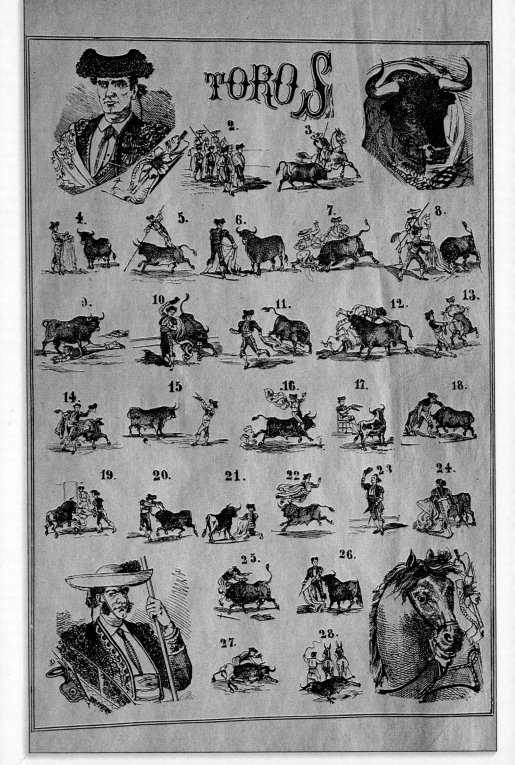

TOROS

BULLFIGHTING—¡OLÉ!—LA FIESTA BRAVA

January 5th, 1840: The scene is altogether fine, the address amusing, but the wounding and the tormenting of the bull is sickening, and as here the tips of his horns are blunted, one has more sympathy with him than with his human adversaries. It cannot be good to accustom a people to such bloody sights.

Yet let me confess, that though at first I covered my face and could not look, little by little, I grew so much interested in the scene, that I could not take my eyes off it, and I can easily understand the pleasure taken in these barbarous diversions by those accustomed to them from childhood.

—Madame Calderón de la Barca, the Scottish wife of the Spanish ambassador to Mexico, in Life In Mexico.

Many people are appalled when they see a bullfight for the first time. They say it's terribly unfair; the bull always dies. They think the bullfighter seldom loses. They don't know that one out of four bullfighters will be crippled in the course of his career, and that one out of ten will be killed by the bull. And, of course, most bullfighters are gored, sometimes a great many times. Also, few who are not bullfight fans know that now and then a bull who has fought the good fight can be *indultado*—that is, pardoned or forgiven. He no longer will fight in the bullring; he is retired to pasture and will spend the rest of his life eating, sleeping and at stud. It is hoped that his sons will inherit his courage.

Ernest Hemingway said there are two kinds of spectators at the bullfight: those who identify with the bull and those who identify with the bullfighter. The crowd at a bullfight may be unruly, even savage. Muralist David Siqueiros called the spectacle "the dance of the butchers." He was, it is plain, not an *aficionado*.

Yet the pageantry at a good bullfight has no equal: it's more dazzling, in fact, than even the Superbowl. Don't think of it as a sport, but rather as an art form. The chief character, lurking in the wings, is death. The second most important character is not on stage; he can't be seen. He must be felt. He is fear. The fear that any mortal feels when he faces death. The fear the bullfighter must master before he masters the bull.

The Sport of Nobles

Bullfighting probably began in Crete (frescoes depict it on Cretan walls). There, acrobats grabbed the bull by the horns and somersaulted over his back. In the Middle East the bull was an object of worship. Perhaps that idea found its way to Spain through the Greek colonies established there. The Arabs who ruled parts of Spain for centuries may have introduced a form of bullfighting. In the Middle Ages, it was the sport of nobles. They rode a horse and, armed with a short lance, they took on the bulls. One pope decreed that a bull could fight only once. The pope reasoned correctly that a single encounter taught the bull something. A second go-round might prove fatal to the bullfighter. In 1567, Pope Pius V threatened to excommunicate all nobles who permitted bullfighting. But, in vain; it was too thrilling a spectacle; the Spanish high-born found it fascinating. It was such a splendid way to show your courage, and, incidentally, stay in shape between battles.

Some accounts say that the first bullfight in Mexico took place in 1526 to celebrate Hernán Cortés' return from his expedition to Honduras. There was certainly a bullfight on St. Hippolyte's day, August 13, 1529, organized by that *bandido* of the Conquistadores, Nuño Beltrán de Guzmán, to commemorate the Spanish capture of the Aztec capital in 1521.

Throughout the three centuries that Spain ruled Mexico, bullfights were held regularly to commemorate religious and civic celebrations; the canonization of a saint; the arrival of a new viceroy; the inauguration of the sanctuary of the Virgin of Guadalupe; the birthday and coronation of a Spanish monarch; the signing of a peace treaty.

Although the Catholic Church often decried against the spectacle, still the clergy always occupied their reserved boxseats at the corrida. Obviously, they did not think the spectacle would be damaging to their morals.

Bullfights were held in make-shift arenas until 1788 when the first permanent plaza was built in Mexico City. Originally, bullfighters fought on horseback. The first instance of someone getting off his high horse was in 1680, and thereafter the bullfighters fought

An old print, attributed to Posada, enumerates various skills of bullfighting; though the basics came from Spain, Mexican bullfighting has its own style.

on foot as well as from a horse. In the Yucatán, mounted bullfighters used an enormous cape to taunt the bull with. It was not until 1769 that bullfighters were paid for their services. Up until then, apparently, they fought for the honor. Now and then a spectator, caught up in the fever, leaped over the barrier and into the bullring and squared off vaingloriously in front of the bull. Finally, strict laws were passed to discourage these interlopers: a year's exile for nobles, two months' imprisonment for common Spaniards, and 100 strokes of the lash for all the others.

Madame de la Barca is notable for her descriptions (See Precede) of bullfighting in the old days. She wrote that "the matadores would throw fireworks ... adorned with streaming ribbons, which struck on his (the

prohibited bullfighting. That restriction was lifted by Porfirio Díaz, who knew he would win points with bullfighting fans. President Venustiano Carranza also banned the *fiesta brava*. However, once he was assassinated bullfighting went on again. No recent presidents have been rash enough to even consider prohibiting bullfighting. They attend enthusiastically at least one corrida a year, in honor of the Mexican Army.

The first superstar among the bullfighters was Bernardo Gaviño. He caught Madame de la Barca's eye. She described his "dress of blue and silver which was superb and (which) cost him 500 dollars." Once, on his way to Chihuahua for a bullfight, Gaviño and his party of 64 were attacked by Comanches. The battle lasted from 9 a.m. to 4 p.m. that day. Only

bull's) horns, (and) as he tossed his head, enveloped him in a blaze of fire. Occasionally, the picador (horseman) would catch hold of the bull's tail, and passing it under his own right leg, (would) wheel his horse around, force the bullock to gallop backwards, and throw him on his face."

Valiant Toreros:
'Intelligent, Dry, Dominating'

President Benito Juárez attended bullfights. In fact, his wife organized a bullfight with the help of the Committee of Patriotic Ladies to raise money for the resistance against the French and the imposed emperor, Maximilian. But after the Mexican triumph, Juárez

three whites, including Gaviño, survived. But that did not deter the valiant torero. He kept his engagement and fought a good fight (the parish priest of El Paso del Norte who saw the performance died of a heart attack from the excitement). Gaviño kept fighting the bulls for more than 50 years. In fact, he fought until age 75 when he was gored by a bull in Texcoco and died from the infection. Otherwise, who knows how long he might have gone on fighting bulls?

Torero Ponciano Díaz was both a great bullfighter and a superb horseman. He was able to work his fans up to such a frenzy of excitement that in 1902 they burned down the arena at Puebla. Díaz toured Spain in 1889 and demonstrated his horsemanship. He used a Mexican method of placing the *banderillas,* the barbed darts thrust between the shoulders of the bull. Mounted on his horse, he used both hands. He delighted the Spanish crowd with his *charro* (cowboy) clothes, and his superb, bristling mustache. He was the only unshaven torero ever allowed in Spain.

Mexico has nurtured a number of great bullfighters: Rodolfo Gaona y Jiménez, immortalized by his *par de Pamplona,* a perfectly planted set of banderillas; Fermín Espinosa Saucedo, who fought in the classical Spanish style, which is described as intelligent, dry and dominating; Pepe Ortiz, who performed *à la baroque,* kneeling in front of the bull.

Few Spanish or Mexican women ever have taken up bullfighting. It is generally a mascu-

and gold embroidery. Behind them come their assistants, then the picadors, and then the ring attendants with their mules. They will haul away the dead bulls.

Mandar, Parar and Templar In a Three-Act Play

The ring *presidente* waves his handkerchief and the first bull rushes in. He is looking for a fight. He weighs upwards of some 500 kilos (1,100 pounds)—a raging muscular combatant, moving along like an express train. Those horns! They are the cynosure of all eyes. Sometimes dirt is thrown on his back. When he runs along the dirt flies off. It emphasizes how swiftly he can move.

The play unfolds in three acts.

line province. A few American women have tried bullfighting with modest success. There's no denying its popularity. There are 225 permanent arenas and 500 improvised ones in Mexico. Plaza de Mexico in Mexico City can seat 50,000; it's the biggest bullfighting arena in the world. The season runs from the end of November to March or April. Some good bullfights are performed in the summer in arenas in cities along the U.S. border. Some nortéamericanos have caught the fever.

The show starts promptly at 4:30 p.m., even if the clock has to be turned back. The opening parade is led by a bailiff who formally asks the authorities for permission to hold the corrida. Three toreros follow, resplendent in their *traje de luces*—suits of light—all silk

Act 1: The torero watches while his assistants handle the bull with their capes. Then he takes a few turns himself to test the animal's behavior. How does he run; which way does he hook his horns? The torero uses a heavy gold-and-silk cape and will perform the best known "Veronica" pass (so named for the lady who wiped Christ's face). The picadors ride in. They push their heavy lances into the big hump of muscle on the bull's back. The *picadores* usually stab twice to expose the "cross" where the bullfighter will thrust his sword in the death stroke. Exit picadors, leav-

Sighting meticulously, the torero takes aim at the small vital spot between the bull's shoulders. That is the place he should penetrate for a clean kill.

311

ing a raging but weakened bull on stage.

Act 2: The torero's assistants, or sometimes the bullfighter himself, plant three pairs of banderillas into the bull's hump. The bandillero runs to the bull, plants the darts, leans on them, and dexterously gets out of the way of the charging animal. The bull is furious and bleeding profusely.

La Hora de la Verdad

Act 3: The Moment of Truth. *La Hora de la Verdad.* The torero asks permission to kill the bull and dedicates the kill to his lady friend, or to some other charming señorita, or to a compañero, or to the crowd, or to Pedro Pérez, or to anyone else he may feel like dedicating the bull to. He then has 16 minutes to dispatch the

sword can penetrate cleanly and sever the artery to the heart or puncture the lung. The bull drops to his knees and usually dies at once. Sometimes, though, a coup de grâce has to be delivered by means of a dagger wielded by one of the torero's assistants.

The torero's reward depends on his performance. He can be awarded an ear, two ears, two ears and the tail, and sometimes even the hoof of the bull. If the bull has fought with their customary courage, his body is dragged around the ring by a team of not-too-happy mules. The torero walks around the ring in triumph. He is showered with hats, flowers, cushions and wineskins, which his assistants toss back in the general direction from whence they came.

bull or be ordered from the ring in disgrace. The torero works his magic on the bull with his heavy cape, going through a series of daring passes, working even closer to the horns. That is when his capework is sternly appraised by people who are experts in the art of such an appraisal.

The torero then switches to a smaller flannel cape. (Bulls are color blind; they go for anything that moves. It doesn't have to be red.) Often the torero will maneuver the beast in front of the judges or in front of his lady friend. When the bull has been sufficiently weakened so that his head droops, the torero aims along his sword and plunges it, going over the horns, between the shoulder blades, and into the "cross," the place where the

End of Act 3. The curtain falls.

This performance is repeated six times. Two bulls are assigned each torero. Aficionados and judges look for the following points: *mandar,* or how much mastery the torero shows over the bull; *parar,* or how well the torero stands: is he straight, firm, with feet firmly planted? Unyielding and not leaning toward the bull to fake audacity? And finally, *templar,* or the timing of the torero, the slow, rhythmic motion he uses to give the bull maximum time to hook him. And, of course, how clean was the kill.

Above, planting bandilleros from horseback requires impeccable split second horsemanship; right, a young bullfighter and impresario strut.

THE QUEEN OF MEXICO

Día de la Raza

October 12 is of special significance to the Mexican. It is called Día de la Raza—the Day of the Race, meaning to convey the idea that on this day the mixture of cultures and races which resulted in Mexico began. In the United States, this same day is called Columbus Day in honor of the first white to discover the Americas. But this is of minor importance to the Mexicans, who feel that the Americas were already discovered by their indigenous inhabitants.

When the Spaniards arrived, they were shocked by the sight of paganism, especially the ritual offering of human sacrifices (in which the still beating hearts were ripped out of the victims in order to give strength to the Sun). In order to eradicate the old religion, the conquistadors tore down the temples and built churches; in the process they burned priceless documents. However, they discovered, an edifice does not guarantee devotion. Many of the Indians continued to worship their old gods; they simply gave them different names. This kind of theological eclecticism is still practiced by several Mexican Indian tribes. The priests understand.

The sight was enthralling: on their knees in the plaza more than a hundred young men moved haltingly along, pushing bicycles. They were engaged in an act of faith and self-mortification. They had been riding their bicycles for days to come to this place, and now, on their knees in supplication, they went the last torturous stretch.

Why were they doing it? What could kindle such devotion in these times when men mock religion? In Mexico, the answer was obvious. They were paying a call on the Virgin of Guadalupe, the patroness of Mexico. She is synonymous with Mexico. Born from the fusion of the Spanish and Indian ways of life, she represents the Catholic, as well as the pre-Columbian religions. She is the symbol of nationalism; the symbol of the racial and cultural mix that is Mexico.

Except for the Vatican, the Shrine of the Virgin of Guadalupe in the Federal District is visited by more people than any other religious site in the Christian world. Some 6 million devouts arrive every year. The trail to the

site is lined with orange peels and taco stands. The pilgrims carry wreaths and wax flowers.

There are some 1,500 pilgrimages made every year. Business groups—ranging from General Motors of Mexico to Pepe's Clear Soups—send devotees. Sometimes a whole village will arrive. One day there may be just a dozen or so of the faithful—on another day, 100,000. An office in the basilica directs large-scale movements. They coordinate things as meticulously as a military landing on a beach. Some of the faithful walk from remote parts of Mexico; they are on the road for

days. Others walk only the last five kilometers, down the Calzada de Guadalupe.

Ask an old man why he has come and he says: "Señor, I have a hard life. A lot of work and very little money. But whenever I really need anything, I've always asked the Little Virgin and she has always helped me. I am grateful to her. Now that my wife is sick, I have come to ask the Virgin to cure her."

A Tent in the Sinai

The old home of the Virgin was built in 1694. But it had become too small; it was cracking; the foundation was unstable. Indeed it leaned at a sharper angle than even the Leaning Tower of Pisa. It was time for a new

Preceding pages and left, "conchero" dancers perform for the Virgin of Guadalupe; above, a Posada engraving documents the Virgin's 1531 visit.

home. The new basilica was conceived by the architect Pedro Ramírez Vasquez, the same man who designed the National Museum of Anthropology in Mexico City, a building that has won the admiration of the world. The basilica is meant to convey the idea of a tent in the Sinai, used by the biblical Abraham. It conforms to the directives of the Second Vatican Council under Pope John XXIII and seeks to combine religious spirit and ritual. It took more than 20 months to build the imposing 11,000-square-meter (36,000 square feet) temple and it cost well over $10 million. The new basilica can hold 10,000 pilgrims, and when the doors are open another 20,000 can look in.

The scene on the inauguration day (October 12, 1976) of the new basilica and the

Sahagun set out to rectify what the Church considered a melancholy state of affairs. He reasoned that Catholicism could be implanted only by first understanding, then eradicating, the gods of the Indians. He found, of course, that the Aztec deities were a complex lot. The most important of the goddesses was known by the names of Cihuacóatl (the Serpent Woman); Coatlicue (Serpent Skirt); Chicomecóatl (Seven Serpents), or, as was most common, Tonantzín—Our Mother. She was the goddess of earth, of spring and maize. A temple was dedicated to her atop a hill called Tepeyac on the outskirts of the Aztec capital of Tenochtitlán. Naturally, she became a rival of the Virgin.

The Spaniards themselves were also religious fanatics. Among the "gods" they

transfer of the sacred image from the old shrine to the new was hectic. More than half a million people attended. A visitor described it. He said many people fainted from the crush. During the ceremony someone thoughtlessly slammed shut the doors, trapping those inside. Outside people hammered on the doors to get in. Inside women screamed, children cried out in fear, men shouted. It became hard to breathe in that writhing mass. People surged back and forth. To trip and fall down would have been disaster. People would trample on you. Women became hysterical, begging the Virgin to save them. Then, suddenly, the doors swung open and with ashen faces and breathing hard, the people escaped.

In the 16th Century, Father Bernardino de

brought along, none was more important than their own Virgin of Guadalupe, who, according to legend was carved by St. Luke and appeared miraculously in Spain. She was associated by the Spanish with their reconquest of the Iberian peninsula from the Moors. Her shrine was built in Extremadura, Cortés' home. After surviving the sting of a scorpion in Mexico, Cortés, in gratitude, presented the Spanish Virgin of Guadalupe with a scorpion of gold. Gonzalo de Sandoval, one of Cortés' captains, brought with him to Mexico a copy of the Spanish Virgin of Guadalupe. During

Above, a group of pilgrims complete the last leg of their arduous journey on their knees; above, floral offerings to the Brown Virgin by visiting devotees.

the siege of Tenochtitlán, he set up camp on the bottom of the hill of Tepeyac where stood Tonantzín's temple. No doubt, the haughty Spaniard ejected the Indian goddess and substituted his own.

The Juan Diego Miracle

It was not long after the conquest that all the Indians who lived in or near the capital had been converted to Christianity, peacefully, if possible, but by force, if necessary. What happened next is accepted by all the faithful in Mexico, though there is no documentary proof. It is the story of the birth of a story. Early one morning in 1531, a newly converted Indian named Juan Diego, a simple man of the soil, was walking on the hill of Tepeyac when he heard a sweet voice calling

ordered Juan Diego to gather up the roses in his cactus-fibre mantle and take them to the archbishop. And he did. He threw down the roses at the archbishop's feet, and, miracle of miracles, the image of the Virgin dramatically appeared on the rough cloth of his mantle. That was the proof positive. And—in theory, at least—that is the same piece of cloth which is now preserved at the Basilica of the Virgin of Guadalupe. It has retained its design, impervious to the centuries.

Franciscan monks sought to make sure no one could be confused by the legends inspired by the Virgin of Guadalupe and the old deity of the Aztecs, Tonantzín. There were problems: the Virgin's shrine was located at the site of Tonantzín's former temple. Also, the tone of the Virgin's skin was brown, almost an

him. It was the Virgin Mary. She informed him she wanted a temple built at that place so that everyone could worship and adore her. Juan Diego did not lose his cool.

"Why me?" he asked boldly. "Why do you not ask one of the powerful Spaniards?"

The Virgin did not explain but she told Juan Diego to relay her message to Archbishop Zumaragá, and he did. As was to be expected, the archbishop scoffed. But next day the Virgin again appeared before Juan Diego, and the day after, once again. Finally she understood that Juan Diego had to bring the archbishop some proof: he had to establish his credentials. So the Virgin commanded some roses to bloom, which of itself was a miracle since roses had never been seen there before. She

Indian brown. There was also the date of celebration. The pre-Columbian festival for Tonantzín was held on the first day of the 17th month of the Aztec ritual calendar. That corresponded to December 22 on the Julian calendar, which was used in Mexico until 1582. At that time Pope Gregory XXIII subtracted 10 days from the calendar date in order that it align better with the solar cycle. So, December 22 became December 12—the day when all Mexico holds ritual for the Virgin of Guadalupe.

Rays of Divine Love

The first undisputed written evidence of the miraculous apparition dates from 1648—117 years after it all happened. This is a book by

Miguel Sánchez, called *The Image of the Virgin Mother of Guadalupe Miraculously Appearing in Mexico*. It is based on a copy of the "Codex Valerianus," purportedly dating back to 1531 and written in the Nahuatl language, which recounts the Juan Diego story. But more important obviously than "factual" evidence was the psychological attitude of the creoles, Spaniards born in Mexico. They were a frustrated people; they were, in effect, second-class citizens in the country of their birth, having to take second place to Spanish-born subjects when it came to position and rank and prestige. The élite who ruled came directly from Spain, armed by royal decree. And they regarded the creoles as second-class residents of an inferior land.

The Virgin of Guadalupe helped make ble epidemic which had killed 40,000 people. It was only natural that the Virgin of Guadalupe became associated with Mexican pride and nationalism. When Father Hidalgo cried out for independence, his cohorts raised the banner of the Virgin and their rallying cry was, "Death to the Gachupines. Long live the Virgin of Guadalupe." (Gapuchine was a term of ridicule applied to Spaniards.)

During the struggle against Spain, the Virgin of Guadalupe was awarded the rank of general. When Mexico won her independence, she was elevated to preeminence. Political leaders casually tossed off her name— they knew she touched on a feeling in the heart. Emperor Iturbide founded the Imperial Order of Guadalupe. The name of the first president of Mexico was Guadalupe Victoria.

amends. By her appearance before a humble Indian, she showed her favor to the entire Mexican nation. Now the people could lay claim to be the "chosen people." This helped balance the ledger and restore confidence. In the eyes of the creoles this placed Mexico on equal footing with Spain. As early as the 17th Century, the writer Sigüenza y Gongora presented Mexico as a land warmed by the rays of divine love, a preeminent people, second to none.

A Venerated Symbol

In 1629, the Virgin of Guadalupe, the faithful believe, stopped the inundation of Mexico City. In 1736, her image was said to have appeared and to have brought to an end a terrible dictator, Porfirio Díaz, had the Virgin crowned Queen of Mexico. And at the same time she was the patroness of Emiliano Zapata who fought Días. No politician would dare raise his voice against the Virgin of Guadalupe. She is sacrosanct.

In 1921 some anarchists planted a bomb under the altar of the Virgin. The bomb exploded—miraculously, the Virgin's image was unharmed. She was protected by a statue of Christ that was blown into pieces. It was, of course, what one would expect from a miracle-worker.

Above, a conchero wearing a mirror-studded fantasy headdress reflects his faith; right, a pilgrim wears a personal vision of the Virgin of Guadalupe.

TRAVEL TIPS

Getting There

BY AIR

Mexico City can be reached by direct flights from many cities in the U.S., as well as major cities in Europe, Canada, and Central and South America. The American airlines, most of which serve several Mexican cities in addition to Mexico City, include American, Continental, Frontier, Hughes Airwest, Northwest Orient, Pan American, Texas International, United and Western. European carriers include Air France, Aeroflot, Alitalia, British Airways, El Al, Icelandic, Iberia, KLM, Lufthansa and Swissair. Mexico City is also served by Air Canada and Canadian Pacific, Egyptair, Japan Airlines and Singapore Airlines. Some of these carriers fly to other Mexican cities, particularly Acapulco and Guadalajara. If you cannot fly direct to your destination, connections can be made with Aerómexico or Mexicana, which have numerous domestic flights. Both Aerómexico and Mexicana also fly to the United States.

Since domestic flights are less expensive, some travelers from the United States choose to fly to a border city such as San Diego, El Paso, Laredo or Brownsville, then cross the border and take a Mexicana or Aerómexico flight to their destination. Please see the section about air travel within Mexico.

BY SEA

Round-the-world cruise ships frequently include Acapulco and Mexico's Caribbean resorts on their voyages. From the United States, a variety of one- to three-week cruises is available. Caribbean cruises departing from New Orleans, Tampa, Miami and Fort Lauderdale may stop at Cancún and Cozumel. Numerous cruises along the west coast of Mexico originate in Los Angeles; some can be boarded also in San Francisco, Portland, Seattle and in Vancouver, British Columbia. These west coast voyages may stop at Acapulco, Ixtapa/Zihuatenejo, Manzanillo, Puerto Vallarta, Mazatlán, and in Baja, Cabo San Lucas and Ensenada.

In general, this is a slow, comfortable and expensive way to get to Mexico. Little time is left for travel within Mexico. Travel agents are a good source of information on cruises.

Traveling to Mexico in your own boat requires clearance papers, obtained at a Mexican Consulate or through a marine customs broker before you leave home. You must present them at your ports of entry and departure; sanitary inspection will also be made at the port of entry. In addition to the clearance papers for the boat, each passenger and crew member needs a multiple entry tourist card (see the section on Immigration). The boat and all passengers and crew must leave Mexico at the same time.

BY RAIL

Railroads can be a good way of traveling in Mexico, but are not recommended as a way of getting to the country. If you travel by rail from the United States or Central America, you must transfer at the border to the Mexican national railroad system. This can be inconvenient and time-consuming, and it is difficult to arrange reservations and ticket purchases until you arrive at the railroad station in Mexico. Few travel agents handle reservations on Mexican trains because they are run by the Mexican government which pays no commissions to travel agents. See the "Getting Around" section about rail travel within Mexico.

Once you are in Mexico, you can make reservations by going to the train station from which you will depart a few days in advance (except holiday periods!). You can also make your reservations from another train station, provided it is on the same railroad line as your journey.

If you want to make stop-overs and you can be definite about the amount of time at each intermediate destination, buy the whole set of tickets initially. Be sure to check the dates on each ticket, as well as the type of accommodations. If you can't plan the whole trip in advance, just go to buy your ticket as soon as you know when you want to leave that town – at least the day before.

The only sure way to get train seats before you arrive in Mexico, or before you arrive in an area served by the railroad line you want to travel on, is to have a friend in the appropriate place who will go to the station and buy your tickets for you.

BY BUS

Bus travel within Mexico has many advantages, and those travelers coming from the United States have the option of making their entire journey by bus. However, unless you live near the border or have a great deal more time than money, flying to the area you want to visit and then using buses is a better

In this amazing NASA photo of Mexico, the eye of 1980s big hurricane can be seen winking at the storm's center as it swirls toward Mexico's Gulf coast. Also visible in this satellite-eye view of Mexico is a second, weaker hurricane, Hurricane Isis, which is seen here spiralling off the southwest-Pacific Ocean coast of Baja California.

bet. Bus tours are available through both Greyhound and Continental Trailways. For more information about bus travel refer to the "Getting Around" section.

BY CAR

Many Americans also drive to Mexico, particularly those living in the border states. Although generally more expensive as a means of travel within Mexico than taking buses or trains, driving is cheaper than flying and offers more flexibility of travel plans than any other mode.

MAP SOURCES

Maps are not available in gas stations in Mexico, so it is advisable to obtain those you will need in advance. In the past, *Baedeker's Mexico* (Prentice-Hall) has included an excellent, fold-out road map. Those published by National Geographic Society and Rand McNally may be useful for trip planning but will not be adequate as driving maps. Try a map specialty store, if you live

in a big city, or write to one or more of the following, asking for a list of maps pertaining to the area of your trip, along with prices and ordering information:

Mexican Government Tourism Office
405 Park Avenue
New York, NY 10022
Guia Roji, S.A.
Calle Republica de Colombia # 23
Mexico City 1, Mexico

(Publishers of a road atlas, the *Atlas Turistico de Carreteras*, and an extremely detailed map of Mexico City.)

American Map Company
1926 Broadway
New York, NY 10023

(U.S. distributors for the *Patria* series of maps; you could also write to Libreria Patria, S.A., at Cinco de Mayo # 43, Mexico City, Mexico. Patria maps are available for each state, and they are excellent driving maps; their Mexico City map is not as easy for the foreign traveler to understand as either the *Guía Roji* or the DETENAL map).

If you haven't the time or inclination to attempt mail-order, bookstores in large Mexican cities carry these maps. American gas stations and bookstores near the border should also have Mexico maps. Most maps, however, are out of date.

There are many things you should consider before you take off for a driving tour of Mexico; more detailed information is available in the "Getting Around" section.

Travel Essentials

VISAS & PASSPORTS

Travelers from most countries will need a valid passport with visa, smallpox vaccination certificate, and a tourist card to enter Mexico. British subjects do not require a visa; Canadian citizens need neither the visa nor the smallpox certificate, just a passport

and a tourist card. U.S. citizens, because of special agreements between the countries, need only the tourist card. There are three exceptions to this: naturalized U.S. citizens, who must have either naturalization papers or a U.S. passport; those traveling on business, who need a business visa; and children, who will be discussed on page 325. U.S. citizens can visit Mexican border towns for up to 72 hours without even a tourist card.

A visa can be obtained from a Mexican embassy or consulate in your home country, or from a Mexican embassy in some other country if you are already away from home.

Tourist cards can be obtained in advance from Mexican embassies, consulates and National Tourist Council Offices (see lists at the "Tourist Information" section), as well as from travel agents and airline companies. To order the card by mail, request a DT-54 form and enclose a self-addressed, stamped envelope. Allow plenty of time, but be aware that if you don't enter Mexico within 90 days after the card is issued, it becomes invalid. If you want a multiple-entry tourist, you must obtain it from a Mexican consulate, three passport-type photographs will be required. Otherwise, only proof of citizenship is required; send a photocopy of your birth certificate, passport or voter registration.

Most travelers from the U.S. get their tourist cards from the immigration officials at the border. Even if you already have the card, you must sign it in the presence of the border official, and have him stamp it. You will need to present proof of your U.S. citizenship (birth certificate, passport, voter registration or military I.D. – *not* a driver's licence). If you fly into Mexico, you'll go through this procedure upon landing. Don't forget to bring three passport-type photographs if you need a multiple-entry card: for example, if you're on a sailboat or cruise ship with several Mexican ports of call.

When you first enter Mexico, the immigration official who stamps your tourist card will decide how long you can stay: 30, 60, 90 or 180 days. Since getting an extension is a hassle, ask for more time than you think you will need. However, it is impossible to predict whether the border official will give you what you want. His decision is based in part on how you look.

Once you're in the country and you feel you have an insufficient amount of time on your tourist card, it is possible to have the card renewed for a longer time. This is a time-consuming procedure, so begin at least a week before your expiration date. You must go to an office of the Immigration Department; there is one in most major towns. In Mexico City, the office is at Albaniles # 19 (tel: 571-3020). You must fill out a form, then take it to another office where they will want to see how much money you have. They will only count traveler's checks in your name – not cash. Approval takes five working days, after which you can pick up the card or have it mailed to you anywhere in Mexico. Another option, if you are near a border, is to cross into the United States or Guatemala, then renew your tourist card on re-entry into Mexico.

Keep your tourist card with you at all times when traveling in Mexico, even though you may never have to show it except at the checkpoints just south of the border. You will have to return the card to Immigration upon leaving the country. If you lose the card, report the loss immediately to the nearest Mexican Tourism Office. These offices are in the state capitals; they are listed in the "Tourist Information" section. In Mexico City, you can get help from the Immigration Department (address given above) or from the central National Tourism Office at Masaryk # 172, Colonia, Polanco. You can telephone them at 250-0123; English is spoken.

Children over 15 years of age must have their own proof of citizenship and tourist card. Those under 15 may be included on the tourist card of one parent, but it is not a bad idea to have separate cards issued for them: if your child is listed on your tourist card, you cannot leave Mexico without the child. This could cause problem if the child were hospitalized, for example. If the other parent is present, you can apply to the Immigration Department to have the child transferred to the other parent's tourist card.

Any traveler under 18 years of age who is not accompanied by parents must have a notarized affidavit, in duplicate, stating that the minor is permitted to travel in Mexico. The affidavit should be signed by both parents, or by the legal guardian. If the parents are not in the same place, each should prepare a separate affidavit. When a minor is accompanied by only one parent, they should have an affidavit from the other parent giving permission.

Unless you are flying into Mexico, don't plan to enter the country at night. Waiting for a border official to wake up is a waste of your time, and, having been inconveniently disturbed, he is not likely to accommodate your request for a 180-day tourist card.

MONEY MATTERS

The Mexican currency is the peso, which is divided into 100 centavos. Bills are issued in 10, 20, 50, 100, 500, 1,000, 5,000 and 10,000 peso denominations. Coins are 5, 10, 20 (used for pay telephones) and 50 centavos, and 1, 5, 10, 20 and 100 pesos.

The same sign, $, is used for pesos as for U.S. dollars. Don't panic when you sit down in a restaurant and see nothing on the menu cheaper than $2,000! Frequently the abbreviation *Dlls* after the amount is used to indicate dollars.

In border towns patronized by large numbers of daytrippers from the U.S., many visitors use American currency instead of changing their money. Stores in such places – Tijuana being the ultimate example – often have price tags showing both pesos and dollars.

Even in these areas they will be better off changing your money, since the stores are unlikely to give you the best rate of exchange. Those going further into Mexico, or staying more than a day, will certainly want to trade their money into pesos; and those coming from other countries must do so. The best place to change your money is at a bank – or at a bank-run exchange counter (labelled *Cambio*) in an international airport. You can also change money at a hotel, or at a money-changer.

The peso has been greatly devalued. At press time, the exchange rate is 2,520-2,580 pesos to the dollar. It may continue to devalue, making Mexico an ever-better bargain for the dollar-bearing traveler. On the other hand, inflation is bringing the prices up. Prices of items and services mainly desired by tourists may particularly increase, to compensate for the losses caused by devaluation. In short, the traveler should use any prices in this book for comparative purposes only. Do not assume that they will still be valid when you arrive.

Try to obtain a current money conversion table. This will save you a lot of computation when you're shopping. They are often available from travel agents, in hotels and in department stores.

The safest way to travel is to bring traveler's checks of a well-known variety, in fairly large denominations, and cash them in banks. If you have multitudes of $20 checks, you will tend to cash them as you go – never at the best rate of exchange. For less than $100, the trip to the bank may not seem worthwhile. On the other hand, don't carry large amounts of cash; Mexican pickpockets are as efficient as those elsewhere.

Major credit cards are widely accepted in tourist areas. Away from the tourist areas and big cities, you may find that only the largest hotels, restaurants and stores accept credit cards. Look for signs, or ask.

WHAT TO WEAR

As with any journey, your Mexico trip requires you to choose clothing appropriate to the climate and social environment you'll be visiting. Mexico's climate is diverse, and you should be at least minimally prepared for the weather of every area you travel through. Check our section on "Climate" for information on the places you'll be. Keep in mind the time of year, and the kind of activities you'll be engaged in: you may be absolutely certain that it is always hot in Baja, but if you go camping there in mid-winter you will discover that the nights are quite cold. Even those who are not camping out should take along a wool sweater when traveling in mountain and desert areas of Mexico in winter. May to October is the rainy season in much of Mexico, and though you can plan around it – plan indoor activities for the afternoon when the rain usually comes – you should bring a folding umbrella and perhaps a lightweight raincoat.

You also have to be at least minimally prepared for each of the different social environments you'll encounter in your travels. Styles of acceptable dress are different in the city, in the country and in resort areas.

In Mexican cities, except the resort cities, dress tends to be rather formal. It's a good idea for a man to bring at least one coat and tie; the more elegant restaurants won't admit you without them. For Mexico City vacations, depending on your choice of activities, you may want to bring a suit, a sports-jacket with a couple pairs of slacks, and a tie or two. If you never go anywhere at home in a suit, don't bring one to Mexico, but do bring slacks and sports shirts. The same principle holds for women. Elegant restaurants will expect you to dress somewhat formally, but if you won't be going to such places you needn't bring fancy clothes. Mexican women in cities tend to dress up more than women in the U.S. and some other countries, but you are not there to impress people. Pants worn by women are perfectly acceptable. Permanent-press or knit dresses and skirts are comfortable in hot weather and easy to pack. Women traveling alone should keep in mind that many Mexican men have unreasonable expectations about foreign women, i.e. that they are likely to be sexually promiscuous. Of course, you have the right to wear what you like, but if you will compromise by trying to avoid clothing that might be taken to be sexually provocative, you will save yourself many annoyances.

The same standards of decency are applied by Mexicans in the country and in provincial towns. No shorts or bathing suits, no shirtless men, and, for women, avoidance of any clothing resembling that worn by Mexican prostitutes. You are less likely to require formal dress, but you still need something in your wardrobe besides jeans. Baggy khakis are cooler than jeans, and easier to hike in. Long-sleeved shirts help prevent mosquito bites and sunburn, though you'll also need insect repellant and sunscreen. A hat will also help keep off the sun. A decade ago, any woman traveling in Mexico needed a hat or scarf (or at least a handkerchief) to cover her head when visiting churches; now this is considered unnecessary. However, your best approach will always be to observe what the people around you are wearing. Remote areas are often conservative, and conservative people often feel most comfortable with people who are not too conspicuous. Appearing bizarre to the local people will gain you nothing, except perhaps the suspicions of the police.

Standards are quite different in resort areas: Acapulco, Ixtapa/Zihuatenejo, Puerto Vallarta, Mazatlán, Cozumel, Cancún, and the beach towns of Baja frequented by California surfers. Shorts and bathing suits are acceptable on the street, even in restaurants (except the formal ones). Dress tends to be high style in many resorts – nothing that you can wear in your home city will be too outrageous to wear in Acapulco. Rarely will a man feel the need for a suit and a tie; bring or buy a *guayabera* shirt, which you can wear over slacks to look a little dressed-up while feeling cool and comfortable. Women often dress up in long, loose embroidered dresses which are also cool and comfortable.

No matter where you plan to travel in Mexico, bring a pair of comfortable walking shoes that are already broken in.

CUSTOMS

On entering Mexico, be aware that the following items are exempt from duties and importation permits. Correspondingly, anything not on the list may be subject to duty, or in some cases, detainment by customs officials. For business travelers, note that portable computers are not on the list and require special permits.

1. Personal articles such as clothing, footwear, and toilet articles, in reasonable amounts.
2. A photo, movie or video-recording camera, including its power source, excepting professional equipment. You can also bring up to 12 rolls of unexposed film or videocassettes and printed or filmed photographic material.
3. Up to 20 different books or magazines.
4. One used sports article, or individual sporting equipment, as long as it can be carried by one person.
5. Up to 20 packages of cigarettes, or 50 cigars or 250 grams of tobacco.
6. Up to 3 liters of wine or liquor (if the person is of legal age.)
7. Medicine (with a prescription from your doctor if appropriate.)

8. One binocular and one photo camera in addition to what's allowed in #2.
9. One portable television.
10. One portable radio or radio/recorder.
11. Up to 20 records or tapes.
12. One musical instrument, as long as it can be carried by one person.
13. One tent and camping equipment.
14. Up to five toys if visitor is a minor. (If you are bringing toys in as gifts, it's a good idea to take the price tag and packaging off.)
15. One set of fishing tackle, one pair of skis, and one tennis racquet.
16. One boat without motor, less and 5.5 meters long, or a surfboard with or without sail. These are allowed if you enter Mexico in a privately registered mobile home, airplane or yacht:
17. One videocassette recorder.
18. One bicycle with or without motor.
19. Household linens.
20. Kitchen, sitting-room, and/or bedroom utensils and furniture.
21. Pets may enter Mexico with you only if you have a certificate of good health, signed by a veterinarian, and a certificate of rabies vaccination, dated within the last six months. Both must be stamped by a Mexican Consul (see the list in the "Tourist Information" section). Before going to all this trouble, consider this: few hotels will accept your pet; airlines and trains will require it to travel in a kennel in the baggage compartment; it will not be permitted on first class buses. Only if you are driving and plan to camp out nearly all the time does it make sense to bring a pet.

When leaving Mexico, don't try to take narcotics or pre-Columbian artifacts. Otherwise, the restrictions that apply are those of the country you next enter; consult Customs in your home country. Travelers from the U.S. are permitted to bring home some 2,700 different items duty-free from Mexico, under the General System of Preferences. The brochure "G.S.P. and the Traveler" is available at the border and by mail from the U.S. Customs Service, Dept. of the Treasury, Washington, D.C. 20229. Another useful brochure is "Customs Hints for Returning U.S. Residents" available at the border and by mail from the Superintendent of

Documents, U.S. Government Printing Office, Washington, D.C. 20402. If you order the brochures by mail, send a self-addressed stamped envelope.

The long list of items that American visitors to Mexico can bring home duty-free includes most of the items that most travelers want to bring back: pottery, folk art, handmade clothing, and so on. For items that are not on the G.S.P. list, each traveler may bring back up to $300 worth of purchases duty-free, as long as they are not expressly limited or prohibited from entering the U.S. Be sure to keep your receipts, to substantiate the value of your purchases. Family members may pool their exemptions.

If you want to bring plants from Mexico into the U.S., write for information to the Import and Permit Section, Plant Quarantine Division, 209 River Street, Hoboken, N.J. 07030.

GETTING ACQUAINTED

TIME ZONES

Most of Mexico is on Central Standard Time year-round. The northern Pacific coast states of Sonora, Sinaloa and Nayarit, along with Baja California Sur, are on Mountain Standard Time year-round. The state of Baja California Norte is on Pacific Standard Time, with a seasonal change to Daylight Savings Time.

CLIMATE

Mexico City, Guadalajara and many other cities of Mexico lie in the central plateau where the climate is temperate year-round. High altitude (1,545 meters, or 5,069 feet, for Guadalajara, and 2,240 meters, or 7,349 feet, for Mexico City) keeps these cities from getting really hot, even in the summer. In an average year, Mexico City's highest temperature will be around 31° C (88° F);

Guadalajara's around 35° C (95° F). In Mexico City, expect temperatures in the upper 20s° C (70s° F) in April and May, in the low 20s° C (70s° F) in the summer and fall, and in the upper 10s° C (60s° F) to low 20s° C (70s° F) in the winter. Summer is the rainy season – in July and August, Mexico City has rain nearly every day – but usually the rain lasts only a couple of hours in the afternoon. It is cool at night: in winter the temperature may fall as low as 0° C (32° F) in early morning and at night.

In southern Mexico and the Yucatán peninsula, the climate varies depending on where you are – some areas are dry, others have nearly 5 meters (about 16 feet) of rainfall a year. High in the mountains it is not nearly as hot as at sea level. In Oaxaca, which is over 1,500 meters (about 5,000 feet) high, the night-time temperature in winter can fall into below 0° C (32° F) but in summer, in mid-day, it occasionally rises nearly to 38° C (100° F). On the peninsula, Mérida's temperature can rise as high as 42.2° C, (108° F); Cozumel's maximum is scarcely above 32° C (90° F), because of being right on the coast. Anywhere in the Peninsula, expect daily temperatures in the upper 20s° C (80s° F) year-round; night-time temperatures seldom go below 16° C (60° F).

Acapulco has daily highs of 27° C (80° F) to 32° C (90° F) year-round, seldom falling much below 21° C (70° F) at night. As with most of Mexico, the rainy season is summer and early fall; there is little rain in the winter. Pacific breezes keep things comfortable.

Further north along the Pacific coast, the temperature is somewhat cooler at night, but otherwise similar. In an average year, the maximum temperature experienced by Mazatlán or Puerta Vallarta will be in mid-30s° C (mid-90s° F). North of Mazatlán, the coast becomes a desert, and summer weather is hotter. In Guaymas, the maximum temperature in an average year is 44° C (112° F). Typical summer temperatures would be in the upper 20s° C (80s° F) to 30s° C (90s° F). The winter is temperate, usually in the 20s° C (70s° F) in the daytime.

Baja has very low rainfall throughout, with what rain there is falling in the late fall and winter months. Temperatures are more comfortable where the land is cooled by sea breezes, as on the southern tip of the peninsula and along the Pacific coast. In an average year Ensenada's temperature will not rise above 35° C (95° F); but San Felipe, on the Gulf of California coast, may go up to 48° C (118° F). The desert is cold at night.

Northern Mexico is largely desert. The days are very hot in summer – well over 38° C (100° F) – except up in the mountains. It is cold in winter, when it may go below freezing at night. As you go east toward Monterrey, the climate is more moderate and less dry, but still very hot in summer.

CULTURE & CUSTOMS

Every culture has its own morality, and if Mexico were no different from your home you would probably not be going. Our comments here are intended to help you avoid misunderstandings which could be unpleasant, or even painful. (If you want something which really helps you to understand the Mexican culture: turn to our list of Suggested Readings, especially the section entitled "Mexicans on Mexico".)

One of the most common sources of misunderstanding is the disparity between Mexican and foreign women in terms of dress and behavior. A completely respectable American or European or Asian woman will wear clothing on the street which, if worn in Mexico, would signify sexual availability. Since many Mexican men believe that foreign women are in fact sexually available (Mexican women – with the exception of prostitutes – seldom being available outside of marriage), the misunderstandings which arise can be most unpleasant for the woman traveler – especially if she is traveling alone, or with another woman. Groups of three or more are much less likely to be bothered, and women with men are unlikely to receive more than whistles. Even if you enjoy the attention and flattering comments, be careful not to respond to any overtures unless you mean to follow through. If you don't enjoy the attention, you can minimize your discomfort by following severing rules. Don't make eye contact. Don't respond to compliments by strangers on the street – don't smile, don't say thanks, don't glare or make nasty remarks. Just walk on. Go with groups whenever possible. If you want to take a long walk and you're traveling alone, try to recruit congenial fellow-travelers to come along.

Observe the wide differences between respectable Mexican women and prostitutes, and try to adjust your dress and behavior accordingly.

Women traveling in Mexico, with or without men, should also be aware that some Mexican drinking establishments admit only men. Bars in hotels and restaurants, cocktail lounges and many other bars admit women, but true *cantinas* do not. *Pulquerias* not only don't admit women, they don't admit men who are strangers (in general). See the following "Drinking Notes" section for more information.

If you see two Mexican men hugging one another, don't assume they are homosexual. Hugging, *abrazos*, is normal behaviour between good friends. In the same way, girls will walk with their arms around one another's waists; nothing is implied except friendship. Incidentally, homosexuality between consenting adults is not illegal in Mexico, although it can lead to blackmail and other forms of persecution. Pornography is illegal, but prostitution is not, as long as the girl is not a minor.

Mexicans take nudity very seriously. Avoid any public exposure that might offend people. As mentioned in "What to Wear", shorts are considered indecent by many Mexicans, and the same goes for shirtless men. If you are caught in the nude by someone who seems upset about it, don't try to laugh it off – apologize and put some clothes on. The alternative could be arrest.

Another good way to get arrested is to buy marijuana from strangers (or smoke it in public). Marijuana has a different history in Mexico than in the United States; until fairly recently, most Mexicans associated it almost exclusively with criminals. Near the Guatemalan border, and in remote areas elsewhere in Mexico, you can expect to have police descend on your car for a search.

Most travelers would like to go beyond simply avoiding arrest – to be polite, by Mexican standards; to be gracious, even. In addition to the usual methods of behaving politely, you can improve the impression you make by shaking hands frequently. Mexicans shake hands not only when first introduced, but whenever they meet again, and when they take leave of one another. Another good habit is to say "*Salud*" when anyone sneezes (it's like Gesundheit); when someone says *salud* to you, always reply, *Gracias!*

A few warnings about the Mexican version of politeness. Mexicans believe it is less rude to accept an unwanted appointment or invitation, then fail to appear, than to refuse the invitation. Don't be too offended by being stood up in this way. Most travelers needn't be warned that Mexicans are not always strictly punctual, since this habit has become so famous. As in any country, some of the things people say are strictly for politeness and should not be taken literally. When you ask a Mexican where he is from, he will often give the name of the town, followed by "*donde tiene su casa*". This means "where your home is", implying that "my home is your home". Don't take him up on this; he is only being polite.

TIPPING

In restaurants, the usual tip is 15 percent; no tip is expected in inexpensive eating places that do not cater to tourists.

Porters and bellhops are tipped 75 to 100 pesos per suitcase. The same is appropriate for a taxi driver who helps with your luggage; otherwise, there is no need to tip taxi drivers.

Gas station attendants are usually given a small tip, even if they don't wash your windshield or check your oil (you must ask for these services). Many Mexicans ask for 98 pesos worth of gas, then give the attendant 100.

Boys who guard your car when you park on the street may be given 10 to 20 pesos; be sure to remember what the boy looks like or you may feel compelled to tip the whole group surrounding the car on your return. Parking lot attendants are tipped 20 pesos.

In barber shops and beauty salons the usual tip is about 20 percent of the bill.

Tour guides are tipped according to the amount on the bill and the quality of their performance.

Keep in mind that many people in Mexico depend almost exclusively on tips for their livelihood.

ELECTRICITY

Sixty-cycle alternating current is standard in Mexico, as in the U.S. There are occasional power shortages, and the current may be weak or fluctuating, especially in remote areas. If you are bringing electric appliances, bring along an extension cord as well to insure that you will be able to use them conveniently.

BUSINESS HOURS

If you need to have money transferred to you while you are in Mexico, or to transfer money to someone who is in Mexico, ask your home bank which bank in the relevant Mexican city they have dealings with, and have the funds transferred there.

Banks are open 9 a.m. to 1:30 p.m., Monday through Friday. The main offices of some banks are open Saturday mornings until noon. Offices are generally open 9 a.m. to 2 p.m., then close for dinner and siesta, reopening from 4 p.m. to 6 p.m. Men of importance, whether in government or the private sector, seldom are available before 10 a.m. Stores open at 9 a.m. or 10 a.m. and stay open until early evening, perhaps 7 p.m. or 8 p.m.; some close from 2 p.m. to 4 p.m.

HOLIDAYS

January 1	New Year's Day
February 5	Constitution Day
February 24	Flag Day
March 21	Birthday of Benito Juárez
(date varies)	Easter
May 1	Labor Day
May 5	Battle of Puebla
May 10	Mother's Day
September 1	President's State of the Union Message
September 16	Independence Day
October 12	*Dia de la Raza* (Columbus Day)
November 20	Revolution Day
December 25	Christmas

January 6, *Dia de Santos Reyes*: the traditional day for giving Christmas gifts.

January 17, *Dia de San Antonio Abad*: day for blessing the animals.

January 18 in Taxco, Guerrero: *Fiesta de Santa Prisca*.

January 20 in Chiapa de Corzo, Chiapas: *Fiesta de San Sebastian*. In Leon and Guanajuato, Guanajuato: fair.

February 2, *Candelaria* feast.

(date varies) *Carnaval* during the week before Lent, especially in Acapulco, Guerrero; Mazatlán, Sinaloa; Mérida, Yucatán; Huejotzingo, Puebla; Tepotztlán, Morelos; and Veracruz.

(date varies) Semana Santa, Holy Week.

Beginning February 5 in Zitacuaro, Michoacán: fair.

Beginning March 1 in Durango, Durango: fair.

Beginning March 10 in Huachinango, Puebla: dance of the flying men.

April 5 in Ticul, Yucatán: fair.

Beginning April 20 in Tuxtla Gutiérrez, Chiapas: fair.

April 23, Aztec Day of Tezcatlipoca.

Beginning April 25 in Aguascalientes, Aguascalientes: *Fiesta de San Marcos*.

Beginning April 29 in Puebla, Puebla: fair.

Beginning May 1 in Morelia, Michoacán: fair.

Beginning May 2 in Cuernavaca, Morelos: fair.

Beginning May 3 in Valle de Bravo, Mexico: fair

(date varies) Corpus Christi Day; dance of the flying men at Papantla, Veracruz.

Beginning May 20 in Tecoh, Yucatán: Festival of the Hammocks.

Beginning May 31 in Tehuantepec, Oaxaca: crafts fair.

Beginning June 13 in Uruapan, Michoacán: fair.

Beginning July 1 in Huamantla, Tlaxcala: fair.

Beginning July 7 in Comitán, Chiapas: fair:

(date varies: usually the last two Mondays in July) In Oaxaca, Oaxaca: *Lunes del Cerro* (Indian festival.)

Beginning August 1 in Saltillo, Coahuila: fair.

Beginning August 8 in Mérida, Yucatán: fair.

August 15, many towns have fiestas.

Beginning September 1 in Tepotztlán, Morelos: fair.

Beginning September 6 in Zacatecas, Zacatecas: fair.

Beginning September 10 in Chihuahua, Chihuahua: fair.

September 14, Charro Day.

(date varies: late September) In San Miguel de Allende: fiesta on the Saturday following *Dia de San Miguel*.

October 4, *Dia de San Francisco* – many towns have fiestas; in Cuetzalán, Puebla: coffee growers' fair.

Beginning October 4 in Pachuca, Hidalgo: fair.

October 12 in Guadalajara, Jalisco: fair.

November 1-2, Day of the Dead.

Beginning December 1 in Compostela, Nayarit: fair.

December 8, *Dia de Nuestra Señora de la Salud*; in Pátzcuaro, Michoacán: fair.

Beginning December 7 in Taxco, Guerrero: silver fair.

December 12, *Dia de Nuestra Señora de Guadalupe*

December 18, *Dia de Nuestra Señora de la Soledad*; in Oaxaca, Oaxaca: fair.

COMMUNICATIONS

If you read Spanish, you might compare *El Excelsior* (jammed-packed, if cumbersome), *UNOmasUNO, La Jornada,* (both left-leaning) and *El Financiero* (more business-oriented). *Tiempo Libre,* issued on Thursdays, gives a week's listings of cultural activities in Mexico City, as well as updated information on museum exhibits and hours. In English, *The News* is a right-leaning daily aimed at English-speaking foreigners, available at most hotels and newsstands in touristed cities. There is also the excellent *Mexico City Journal,* issued weekly, with feature articles on contemporary Mexican issues. *Time* and *Newsweek* are readily available. Various weekly and monthly publications in English, containing mostly travel information and advertisements, are to be found in hotels and travel agencies.

RADIO & TELEVISION

Mexico has numerous radio stations, both FM and AM, ranging from *mariachi* music to rock 'n' roll. All broadcast in Spanish, with the exception of two English language stations in Mexico City. Radio VIP (AM 1560) is a CBS affiliate; Stereo Best (FM 105) is an NBC affiliate.

All television broadcasts in Mexico are in Spanish except late-night movies in English. If you watch sports events originating in the U.S., you can listen for the English narration beneath the louder narration of the Mexican sportscasters. Various American serials are shown, with Spanish dubbed in; you can try to read the actors' lips. Your best bet is to forget about T.V. until you get home.

POSTAL SERVICES

Post offices are usually open 9 a.m to 7 p.m. Monday through Friday, and 9 a.m. to 5 p.m. Saturday. Some close for siesta, approximately from 1 p.m. to 3 p.m. Post office hours vary, especially in smaller towns; many will be closed Saturday afternoons. Registered mail must be picked up before 5 p.m. on weekdays, before noon on Saturday.

To send a letter within Mexico costs between 3-500 pesos, depending upon where it's going. An airmail postcard or letter, up to 10 grams, can be sent to the U.S. or Canada for 1,100 pesos, and to Europe for 1,300 pesos. Be sure to mark it *Correo Aereo*. Surface mail is quite slow. Check at the post office for rates to other countries. Sending packages out of Mexico involves a lot of paperwork; go to the central post office of a large town, and have the package registered. It's much easier to have stores mail your purchases to your home. Most large stores are experienced with this and are reliable. Keep in mind that Christmas is a bad time for mailing any packages and expect delays and some losses at that time of year.

The surest way to receive mail in Mexico is to have it sent to a hotel at which you have a reservation, marked "Please hold for arrival". You can receive mail at post offices if it is addressed to *Lista de Correos*, with your last name in capital letters and underlined. When you go to the post office where you are expecting mail, look or ask for the *Lista*. The postal clerk will need your name, the date of the list and the number next to your name on the list, and some identification. Mail addressed to *Lista de Correos* will be held 10 days before being returned to the sender. If you leave town before receiving mail that you know is on the way, fill out a change-of-address form and leave it (or mail it).

Packages sent to people in Mexico are subject to customs duty, which can be substantial. It's best not to send anything except books.

TELEGRAPH

You must go to a telegraph office, *Oficina de Telégrafos*, to send a telegram; you can't telephone it in from your hotel. The office will usually be open from 9 a.m. until early evening on weekdays, possibly closing for siesta in early afternoon, and will be open Saturday morning if not all day Saturday. If rapid delivery is important, ask for urgent service (*urgente*); regular service (*ordinario*) is less expensive. Write out your message and the address of the recipient clearly to minimize errors.

To receive a telegram in Mexico, if you are not staying at a hotel or home where it can be sent, have it addressed to you at *Lista de Correos* (to receive it at the post office) or at *Lista de Telégrafos* (to receive it at the telegraph office).

TELEPHONE

Since the 1985 earthquakes, calls made at public telephones (easily sighted in Mexico City by their bright orange shells) have been free. A few newly-installed phones charge 200 pesos, however. The only long distance calling possible on these phones is collect calling (dial 09 for the long distance operator.) For directory information in Mexico City, dial 04 and get your Spanish ready; the operators do eventually answer.

For most travelers, the least expensive

way to make long distance calls will be to go to the *Larga Distancia* office – there's one in almost every town. You should write out the area code and number, the city and country, and if the call is to be person-to-person, write the person's name clearly. Specify *persona a persona*; station-to-station is called a *quien contesta* (literally, to whoever answers). When the operator puts your call through, your name will be called and you will be assigned to one of the phone booths: "*Señor Müller, cabina dos!*"

When calling collect, (*por cobrar*), be aware that if the answering party refuses to accept the call you will be charged for a one minute call.

The operator in your hotel will place long distance calls for you, but usually a surcharge will be added to the bill.

Long distance calls can be dialed direct from Mexico to the U.S. and most other countries, but only from private telephones. If you want to know the cost of the call you are making so you can repay the friends whose telephone you are using, you will need the services of an operator – and will not, therefore, get the cheaper direct-dial rates. For those who are in a position to dial direct, the prefix for calls within Mexico is 91 (followed by the area code and number); for calls to other countries, the prefix is 95. To reach the long distance operator for calls within Mexico, dial 02; for the international long distance operator, dial 09. The international long distance operator (*Operador Internacional*) speaks English.

A 39 percent tax is added to all outgoing calls, so if possible have your family, friends or business associates telephone you rather than vice-versa.

EMERGENCIES

MEDICAL ADVISORIES

Take it easy for your first few days. Many travelers arrive in Mexico City jet-lagged from a long flight, then spend their initial days walking for miles, eating and drinking heavily and immersing themselves in unfamiliar customs – all of this in the low-oxygen environment of a smoggy, high-altitude city. Their ability to resist disease takes a plunge, and the infamous result is the so-called Moctezuma's revenge.

Besides keeping yourself in shape to fight off the unfamiliar bacteria, you can help by trying to avoid too much exposure to sources of the bacteria.

DRINKING WATER

As in many other parts of the world, water in Mexico may be contaminated. All hotels and restaurants catering to foreign travelers will provide purified water. In restaurants, ask for *agua purificada*. If you are in any doubt about the purity of the *agua purificada* – for example, in an inexpensive restaurant catering to working-class Mexicans only – ask for *agua mineral* (mineral water), or drink beer, soft drinks, or fruit juice. Be aware of the difference between fruit juice, *jugo*, and fruit drink, *agua fresca*, which is made with water – probably not purified. Brush your teeth with the same water you drink. Wash fruits and vegetables with purified water, or peel them. If you are camping out or traveling in remote areas, be prepared to purify water yourself: either boil it 20 minutes or more (depending on altitude), or use halazone tablets, following the directions on the bottle. One final reminder: it does no good to obtain pure beverages if they are served with impure ice, or in glasses which have not been washed in hot water with detergent (or in purified water). This is a good reason to stick with bottled beverages, drunk out of the bottle.

USEFUL DRUGS

There are plenty of pharmacies (*farmacias*) in Mexico, but it is a good principle to bring along the basic items you will need to keep healthy and deal with medical problems that arise. With regard to Moctezuma's revenge, Kaomycin is frequently recommended as a cure; it has an antibiotic to kill the bacteria. Symptoms may be relieved by Kaopectate (Kaomycin without the antibiotic), Lomoti (anti-diarrhea), or Paregoric (fights both diarrhea and stomach cramps, but is an opiate). Whether or not you take a drug, be sure to lie down and drink lots of fluids.

An alternative treatment is recommended by the U.S. Center for Disease Control (CDC). You'll need two clean glasses, a cup of fruit juice (8 ounces, about one-fourth of a liter), half a teaspoon of honey, a pinch of salt, a quarter teaspoon of baking soda and a cup of boiled or carbonated water. In one glass, mix the water and baking soda; in the other glass, mix the fruit juice, honey and salt. Sip from one glass, then the other. Believe it or not, this relieves the diarrhea (as well as dehydration). The CDC suggests that you not turn to antibiotics unless you have a high fever or blood in the stool, and does not recommend the old standby drugs, Lomotil and Paregoric, for sufferers.

Many diseases that are uncommon further north are present in the subtropics and tropics, and you should consider protecting yourself against them. Before you go, renew your tetanus protection if necessary, and ask your physician whether you should have a typhoid booster shot. In Mexico, avoid going barefoot in areas where many people walk barefoot; some foot infections are common in parts of Mexico. Bring along a good insect repellent and use it, because many diseases are carried by mosquitos and other insects. Check the labels before you buy: the repellent with the highest percentage of N-Diethyltoluamide is the strongest one. Keep in mind that if the smell is really awful, you won't use it – perhaps one not quite so strong will be better for you.

Bring with you aspirin; something for treating minor wounds (rubbing alcohol,

hydrogen peroxide, iodine); bandaids; halazone tablets to purify water (if you think you might need them); any prescription drugs you need, along with their prescriptions; and a good sunscreen lotion.

Hikers should also bring an ace bandage, gauze bandages and adhesive tape. If you'll be traveling through cactus country, bring a pair of tweezers and a candle. When you encounter the kind of cactus spines that are too fine to tweeze out, light your candle. Pour melted wax over the afflicted part (Careful! Some candles have room for the wax to cool a bit, and these work better than narrower candles). When the wax solidifies, pull it off. The tiny spines will come out, embedded in the wax.

SUNBURN PREVENTIVES

Burning yourself to a lobster hue in your first two days will not result in a quick bronzy tan. On the contrary – you'll be damaging your skin for nothing. The quickest routes to a good tan are 1) build up your exposure time gradually, avoiding the midday sun (11 a.m. to 2 p.m.), and 2) use a good sunscreen lotion with PABA. Sunscreens now have numbers on the labels: an "SPF" (Sun Protection Factor) of 2 means you can take twice as much sun before you begin to burn. Most people will find an SPF between 5 and 10 to be sufficient protection for tanning without burning. SPF 15 lotion is a sunblock. Read the label – only a few brands specify that the sunscreen will stay on your skin during and after your swim. A small tube of lip sunscreen is also a good idea.

MEDICAL SERVICES

If you need a doctor, ask your hotel for a list of English-speaking physicians (or dentists) in the area; any hotel catering to foreign travelers will have such information. In Mexico City, you can call the embassy of your home country (see list in "Tourist Information") and ask if they know of a doctor, who speaks your native language. In other cities, ask at the government Tourism Office. If you are in a remote area you will have to depend upon a hotel manager, innkeeper or anyone you can find who seems appropriate to give you a referral. It may not be possible to reach a doctor who speaks your language, so an interpreter may have to be found.

Both Mexico City and Guadalajara have hospitals that cater to the English-speaking foreigner.

Mexico City
Hospital Ingles – ABC
Calle Sur 136, # 201 (at the corner of Observatorio)
Colonia Americas
Mexico 18, D.F. 01120
Telephone 277-5000

Guadalajara
Hospital Mexico-Americano
Colomos # 2110
Guadalajara, Jalisco
Telephone 41-3141

GETTING AROUND

DOMESTIC TRAVEL

For domestic flights there are two major airlines, Aerómexico and Mexicana. Both have reservations offices in a number of cities; not all are listed here. Telephone numbers may be changed, so check at your hotel if necessary.

Airfares are the same whether you fly Mexicana or Aerómexico, on routes served by both; sample fares, in post-devaluation pesos are as follows. Prices do not include the 15 percent tax.

Mexico City to:	
Acapulco	112,143
Cancún	298,730
Chihuahua	289,641
Guadalajara	124,357
La Paz	296,403
Mazatlán	207,209
Mérida	237,858
Monterrey	177,196
Puerta Vallarta	160,914
Tijuana	327,073
Tapachula	196,055

On domestic flights, each passenger is permitted to check two bags, with neither weighing more than 70 pounds and with total weight not exceeding 110 pounds (50 kg). You are also permitted one carry-on bag, small enough to fit under a seat, and a garment bag.

You can write for an Aerómexico timetable from their office at Reforma 445, Mexico City, Mexico 5, D.F. For Mexicana, write to Balderas 36, 12th floor, Mexico City, D.F., Mexico. In Mexico, domestic airline tickets and information are available at the ticket desks in airports, at travel desks in many hotels, and through travel agents.

DOMESTIC AIRLINES

Aerómexico ticket offices in various cities in Mexico (numbers in bold are Aerómexico offices at the airport):

Acapulco
Av. Costera M. Alemán No. 286, tel: 516-25, 516-00, **400-35/85, 406-16**
Av. Costera M. Alemán No. 1252, tel: 470-09, 472-24

Aguascalientes
Calle Madero No. 474, tel: 702-52, 703-56, **724-04**

Bahias de Huatulco
Apto. Int. de Bahias de Huatulco, tel: **403-28, 403-35**

Campeche
Aeropuerto Intl. de Campeche, tel: **666-56, 656-78**

Cancún
Av. Coba No. 80 Supermanzana 03, tel: 411-86, 410-97, **427-28, 426-39**

Chihuahua
Victoria No. 106, tel: 15-6303 con 5 líneas, **12-2695, 12-7196**

Cd. Juárez
Av. Lincoln No. 759, tel: 13-8089, 13-8298
"Zona Pronaf", tel: 16-6959, **17-3095, 17-7227**

Cd. Obregon
No Reelección No. 509 Ote., tel: 321-90, 330-36 y 454-42, **640-95, 613-55**

Culiacan
A. Rosales No. 77 Pte., tel: 537-72/82/92, 316-31, **411-94, 427-45**

Durango
Juárez 201-B Sur, tel: 128-13, 126-52 y 283-36, **808-28, 806-49**

Guadalajara
Av. Corona No. 196, tel: 14-5400, 13-6990, **89-0028, 89-0163**
Condoplaza Local 20, tel: 21-7518, 21-7619
Vallarta, tel: 1458-8, 25-2612 y 25-2342,

Guaymas
Aquiles Serdán No. 236, tel: 202-66, 201-23, 272-33, **271-11, 232-66**

Hermosillo
Boulevard Navarrete No. 165, tel: 682-06, 682-59, **607-72**

La Paz, B.C.
Paseo Alvaro Obregón entre, tel: 200-91/93-216-36, **203-66, 203-67**
Hidalgo y Morelos, tel: 276-36

Leon
Madero No. 410, tel: 662-26, 318-07, **405-74, 489-78**

Los Mochis
Gabriel Leyva 168 Nte., tel: 525-70, 525-80, **529-50, 525-75**

Manzanillo
Centro Comercial "Carrillo Puerto" Local 107, tel; 212-67, 217-11, **324-24**

Matamoros
Alvaro Obregón No. 21, tel: 307-01/02, 652-25, **376-50**

Mazatlán
Av. Camarón Sabalo No. 310, tel: 411-11, 416-21, **203-66, 203-67**
Local 1 y 2, tel: 416-09, **234-44, 235-33**

Mérida
Av. Paseo Montejo No. 460, tel: 27-9000 con 6 líneas, **24-8576, 24-8554**

Mexico, tel; 207-8233 con 60 líneas
Oficina Aeropuerto, Aeropuerto Internacional de México

Oficina Insurgentes, Insurgentes Sur No. 724 P.B.
Oficina Satelite, Manuel E. Izaguirre No. 2
Oficina Reforma/Colon, Paseo de la Reforma No. 76
Oficina Reforma/Mississippi, Paseo de la Reforma 445 P.B.
Oficina Relox, Centro Comercial "El Relox" Av. Insurgentes Sur No. 2374 Locales 34 y 35 San Angel
Oficina Lindavista, Montevideo No. 303 Local A Col. Lindavista
Oficina Presidente Chapultepec, Motel El Presidente Chapultepec Av. Campos Eliseos No. 218
Information, arrivals and departures, tel: 762-4022

Monterrey
Av. Lázaro Cárdenas No. 2499, tel: 40-0617 y 44-63-99, **44-7720/30/40**
Pte. Cuauhtémoc y Padre Mier, tel: 44-4181

Oaxaca
Av. Hidalgo No. 513 Centro, tel: 637-65, 610-66 y 632 29, **640-55, 628-44**

Puebla
Av. Juárez 1514-A, tel: 32-00-13/14/15/83/84

Puerto Vallarta
Juárez No. 255, tel: 258-98, 212-04 y 200-71, **210-55**

Reynosa
Guerrero No. 1510, tel: 211-15, 224-40, **300-40**

San Jose del Cabo/Los Cabos
Zaragoza e Hidalgo s/n, tel: 203-98, 205-98, **203-99**

Tapachula
2a. Av. Norte No. 6, tel; 620-50, 639-21, **625-32**

Tijuana
Av. Revolución No. 1236, tel: 85-2230, 85-8681, **83-2700, 82-4169**

Torreon
Blvd. Independencia No. 565 Ote., tel: 13-6477, **17-7080**

Villahermosa
Periférico Carlos Pelicer, tel: 269-91, 215-28, **416-75, 209-04**
Camara No. 511, tel: 295-54, 243-89

Zihuatanejo
Calle Juan N. Alvarez No. 34, tel: 420-18, 420-19, 420-22, **422-37, 426-34**

Mexicana ticket offices in various cities in Mexico:

Acapulco
Edif. La Torre de Acapulco, tel: 4-68-90, 4-69-43, **4-18-15**
Cost. M. Alemán No. 1252, tel: 4-81-92
Lobby del Hotel Las Hamacas, tel: 2-02-58, 2-30-83
Cost. M. Aleman No. 239, tel: 2-48-92
Aeropuerto Int'l Juan N. Alvarez

Bahias de Huatulco
Hotel Posada Binniguenda Hab. 116, tel: 4-00-77/78, **4-02-28/08**

Cancún
Av. Coba No. 39, tel: 4-14-44/23/32/11-54, **4-27-40**

Cd. Carmen
22 x 37 Edifico "Jaber", tel: 2-11-71/25, **2-09-76/2-11-88**

Coatacoalcos
Corregidora No. 401, tel: 2-65-59, 2-65-60

Cozumel
Av. Gral. Rafael E. Melgar Sur 17, tel: 2-01-57, 2-02-63, **2-04-05/2-01-33**

Cuernavaca
Hidalgo No. 26, tel: 12-36-81/91
Plaza Cathedral Cuernavaca. Mor., tel: 14-12-65

Guadalajara
Mariano Otero 2353, tel: 47-17-31 ext. 4020
Av. 16 de Septiembre No. 495
Av. González Gallo No. 1090
Plaza Patria, Zona H Local 6, tel: 47-22-22 con 30 líneas
Centro Comercial Las Torres Av. 8 de Julio 1896 Locales 28 y 27 Zona C
Zona Rosa López Cobila y Marsella
Apto. Int'l. Miguel Hidalgo, tel: **89-01-19**

Hermosillo
Rosales No. 35 Esq., tel: 7-11-03, 7-11-81, **6-00-88**
Noberto Aguirre, tel: 7-10-55

Huatulco
See Bahias de Huatulco

Ixtapa/Zhuatanejo
See Zihuatanejo

La Paz. B.C.
Av. Alvaro Obregón No. 340, tel: 2-49-99, 2-40-10/09, **2-43-88**

Leon, GTO.
Blvd. A. López Mateos No. 401 Ote., tel: 4-95-00/12, 6-15-19, 6-03-08, 6-28-78

Manzanillo
Av. México No. 382, tel: 2-19-72, 2-17-01, 2-10-09, **8-20-59**

Mazatlán
Paseo Claussen 101-B, tel: 2-77-22 c/4 líneas, **2-28-88**
Centro Comercial Balboa, tel: 3-62-02
Locales 4 y 5, tel: 3-55-54
Calz Camarón-Sabalo
Apto. Int'l. Rafael Buelna, tel: **2-56-66**

Mérida
Calle 58 No. 500 x 61, tel: 24-66-33 c/6 líneas, **23-69-86**
Paseo de Montejo Calle 56-A No. 493, tel: 24-74-21 y 23-05-08

Mexicali
Av. Fco. I. Madero No. 832, tel: 53-54-01/02/03, **52-93-91**

Mexico, tel: 6-60-44-44 con 105 líneas
Oficina Aeropuerto, Edificio Torre P.B.
Oficina Amberes, Reforma y Amberes
Oficina Camino Real, Hotel Camino Real Locales No. 21, 22 y 23; Calle Lebnitz No. 100
Oficina Coyoacan, Div. del Norte No. 2591
Oficina Ejercito Nacional, Ejército Nacional y Calderón de la Barco No. 359
Oficina Insurgentes Sur, Insurgentes Sur No. 753; Locales A y B
Oficina Juárez, Juárez y Balderas
Oficina Lafragua, Paseo de la Reforma No. 51

Oficina Lindavista, Montevideo No. 303 Local "A", Col. Lindavista

Oficina Lomas, Reforma Lomas 110 ler Piso, Lomas de Chapultepec

Oficina Perisur, Centro Comercial Perisur Locales, 192 y 193 Insurgentes Sur y Periférico Sur

Oficina Presidente Chapultepec, Hotel El Presidente Chapultepec, Av. Campos Eliseos No. 218

Oficina Relox, Centro Comercial "El Relox", Av. Insurgentes Sur No. 2374, Locales 34 y 35 San Angel

Oficina Satelite, Plaza Satélite Locales H 281 at 287

Oficina Universidad, Av. Universidad No. 936-A Locales, A.B.C.-1

Oficina Vallejo, Calz. Vallejo No. 1111, Esq. con Av. de las Torres

Oficina Xola, Av. Xola No. 535

Oficina Zocalo, 16 de Septiembre No. 82, Gran Hotel Cd. de México

Groups, tel: 6-60 36-66 con 20 líneas

Information, arrivals, departures, tel: **5-71-88-88**

Lost and found, tel: 5-71-03-54/31-18

Minatitlan

Av. Hidalgo No. 117-Bis, tel: 4-00-26 4-14-82, **2-59-48**

Monterrey

Hidalgo 922 Pte., tel: 44-11-22

Cuauhtémoc No. 716 Nte., tel: 74-14-74/77

Hidalgo 498 Ote., tel: 45-64-22/82

Bajos Hotel Ancira

Apto. Int'l. Mariano Escobedo, tel: **45-08-11/71**

WATER TRANSPORT

Ferries run between Baja California and the mainland, and between the Caribbean islands of Cozumel and Isla Mujeres and the Yucatán peninsula. The latter are mainly passenger ferries, traveling short distances. The Baja ferries make long journeys across the deep Gulf of California, allowing the traveler to see both the peninsula and the mainland without making the extremely long and hot drive around the Gulf.

For these long-distance ferries, check to make sure you have the latest schedule information and plan your trip accordingly; the ferries don't run every day. If you are on the Mexican mainland and want to take a ferry to Baja, ask at your hotel for ferry information, preferably a few days before you want to leave. If you are coming from the U.S., ask your travel agent or the insurance agent at the border for a current ferry schedule.

If you are planning ahead, the best course is to write for information and reservations to the central ferry office: Oficina Central de Transbordadores, Tlaxcala 151, ler piso, Colonia Condesa, Mexico D.F. The telephone number is 584-8051. Telephone numbers for local ferry offices follow:

Puerto Vallarta	(322) 204-76
Mazatlán	(678) 170-20, 22
Guaymas	(622) 223-24
Santa Rosalia	(685) 200-13, 14
La Paz	(682) 511-56
Cabo San Lucas	(684) 300-79
Topolobampo	(681) 256-42, 203-20

At the time of going to print, the ferry service from Puerto Vallarta to Cabo San Lucas is not in service.

Rates for the ferry running from La Paz to Mazatlán, are: 26,000 for a cabin; 12,000 for Tourist class; and 6,000 for Salon class. These are one-way fares and don't include any meals. However, food is available on the ferries.

The northern-most route connects Santa Rosalía with Guaymas, leaving Guaymas at noon on Sundays, Tuesdays and Wednesdays, to return the same day with at 11 p.m. departure from Santa Rosalía. Don't forget to double-check schedule information, since an unplanned three-day layover in Santa Rosalía could be very tedious.

Reservations and schedules are not a problem for the frequent, short-distance ferry trips from the Yucatán peninsula to offshore islands. The passengers-only ferry to Cozumel departs from Playa del Carmen three times a day; if you are driving, there is a parking lot near the ferry landing. If you want to take your car onto the island – which is not a bad idea, for Cozumel is fairly large – the departure point is Puerto Morelos, further north. This ferry goes each direction *once a day*.

For the shorter trip to Isla Mujeres, you can take a car ferry from Punta Sam or a passenger-only ferry for Puerto Juárez. The latter runs several times a day; again, parking is available if you are leaving your car on the mainland. Alternatively you can drive right onto Cancún over a causeway. There are no ferries are available to Isla Contoy, a bird refuge favored by fishermen and snorkelers as well as bird-watchers, but you can charter a boat.

PUBLIC TRANSPORT

The visitor to Mexico can move around with ease and comfort using the various forms of public transportation. The bus, train, subway services have extensive routes throughout the country and their fares are reasonable.

TRAINS

For those who want to see a lot of the countryside, trains are a more relaxing alternative than driving, and more comfortable than buses. If you have a long way to go and don't want to fly (or can't afford to fly), trains and probably your best bet, provided there's track to where you are going. Although they don't go everywhere like the buses do, there are some 15,000 miles of track in Mexico; you can get to any area, and

take a short bus ride to your ultimate destination. In general the scenery will be better than that along the highways, and some of the most spectacular scenery in North America – the Barranca del Cobre, or Copper Canyon, in the state of Chihuahua – is accessible only by rail.

Prices are low, due to government subsidy. As with buses, second-class trains are not a good choice for most foreign travelers: they will be very hot or very cold, the seats very uncomfortable, the bathrooms very inadequate, and so on. The price is hardly worth it. On major routes, there are also notable differences between train runs, and corresponding differences in prices. It is worth scheduling around the higher priced ride. For example, to travel from Mexico City to Guadalajara, you can take the regular train at 10,945 pesos, first class; 6165 pesos, second class, or you can take *El Tapatio* which costs 28,525 pesos for a first class seat, 53,620 pesos for a bed and 107,240 for a suite. This ride will get you there more quickly and smoothly than the regular runs.

Various sleeping-car options are available, and are well worth their prices for long

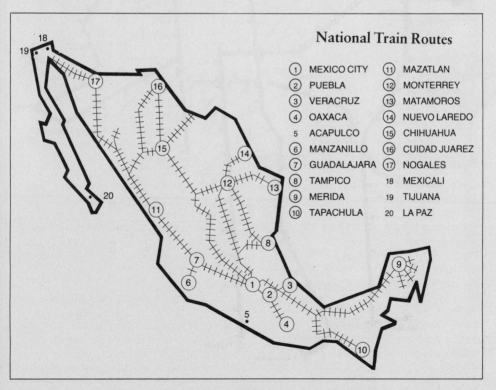

National Train Routes

① MEXICO CITY	⑪ MAZATLAN
② PUEBLA	⑫ MONTERREY
③ VERACRUZ	⑬ MATAMOROS
④ OAXACA	⑭ NUEVO LAREDO
5 ACAPULCO	⑮ CHIHUAHUA
⑥ MANZANILLO	⑯ CIUDAD JUAREZ
⑦ GUADALAJARA	⑰ NOGALES
⑧ TAMPICO	18 MEXICALI
⑨ MERIDA	19 TIJUANA
⑩ TAPACHULA	20 LA PAZ

trips. The Pullman cars are those retired from the U.S. railroads as rail travel fell off there, and they are fairly well maintained. Still, don't expect everything in your compartment to work. The cheaper Pullman option is a one-bed *camarín*; when the bed is folded up into a seat, the toilet is usable. Most couples will not find the bed big enough for two. More space is available in a *camarín doble* (double compartment) or *alcoba* (a suite with three or more beds). The *alcoba* also has a shower. Considering that you save the cost of a hotel, prices are low. For example, a *camarín* on the Mexico City-

Zacatecas night train costs 65,990, and an *alcoba*, 131,980.

On some trains there are also dormitory cars (*dormitorios*) with curtained-off beds that are less expensive than the Pullman compartments. When you make your reservation you can choose an upper or a lower bunk (*cama alta* and *cama baja*, respectively); upper beds are the cheaper ones.

Reservations are advised; at vacation times, especially Christmas and Easter, reservations are essential. Since the railroads are government-owned and no commissions are paid to travel agents, obtaining your

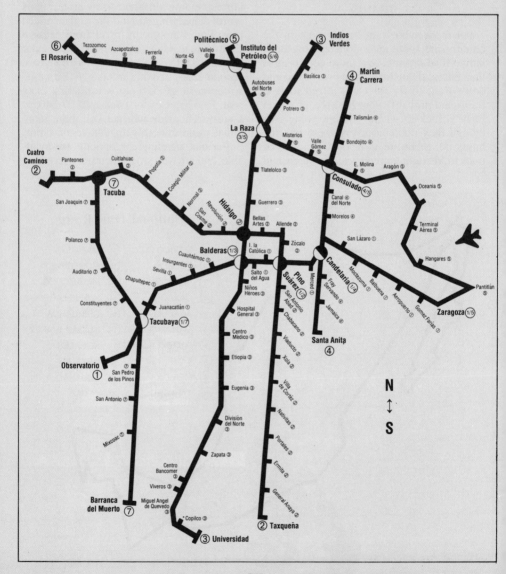

reservations before you arrive in Mexico can be difficult. You can try writing for information, schedules and fares to:

Ferrocarriles Nacionales de Mexico
Departamento de Tráfico de Pasajeros
Estacíon Central de Buenavista
Insurgentes Norte
Mexico 3, D.F.

The telephone numbers are 547-1084, 547-1097. This is a busy office and you may not get a prompt answer. If you receive the information you need, send a certified check or cashier's check to purchase the tickets. Specify whether you want them sent to you (be sure there is sufficient time) or held for you to pick up. If some of your tickets are for children, make the appropriate adjustments: children between 5 and 12 travel for half-fare, those under 5 travel free.

SUBWAYS

Mexico City has an excellent subway system. If it goes where you want to go, you may want to try it. There is less danger of getting lost than when riding the bus, and several of the stations are interesting.

Two cautions about riding the Metro. Don't do it at rush hour. Don't plan on using it for a trip to the airport or bus station with all your luggage, or for coming home after a successful shopping trip: no package larger than a briefcase is permitted, and that's one briefcase per rider.

The Metro has just been expanded, with the last lines still under construction.
Line 1 runs east-west through downtown and past Chapultepec Park; it gets you to the airport and two bus stations, the Central Camionera de Oriente and the Central Camionera Poniente. **Line 2** runs from Cuatro Caminos, near the bull ring, to downtown and then south to Taxqueña, near the Central Camionera Sur. **Line 3** runs from Indios Verdes south to the University. **Line 4** runs north-south also, further east. **Line 5** runs from Pantitlan in the east, where it meets Line 1, northwest past the airport and the Central Camionera del Norte. **Line 6** runs east-west in the northern part of the city. **Line 7** runs north-south in the western part of the city, past Auditorio (a good place to start seeing the museums and Chapultepec

Park), to Barranca del Muerto.
Subway fare at press time is 100 pesos per ticket, a definite bargain.

BUSES

One can go virtually anywhere in Mexico on the bus, and the price is low. Hundreds of bus companies crisscross the country, their vehicles ranging from the very clean, modern and fast to the opposite extreme. Most foreign travelers will prefer the first-class buses, which are air-conditioned and have a toilet in the back. First-class buses stop only at major centers, while others may stop whenever someone flags them down. If you are going to a remote area you will need to take a second- or third-class bus, but use a first-class bus to get the general area more quickly. The trip from Mexico City to Guadalajara, for example, takes about 9 hours even on a first-class bus, but costs only about $10. On long hauls, drivers usually stop at meal-times (especially around 2 p.m.).

Another advantage to first-class buses is that seats are assigned. You get the best view from near the front of the bus; the center provides the smoothest ride, the back the bumpiest. For night travel a seat on the right side is preferable, away from the glare of headlights. An afternoon trip in hot country is more comfortable if you're on the side away from the sun. Generally you can purchase the right to use the seat next to yours, for your bags or to stretch your legs, for half the price of an additional ticket.

Reservations are a bit of a problem. You cannot reserve a seat by telephone. You cannot buy a round-trip ticket, nor can you buy a ticket to your ultimate destination with stop-over privileges. At busy times of the year, make reservations for your trips well ahead. Especially around Christmas and Easter, buses are very crowded and you should reserve your seat at least two weeks in advance. If you make several stops, buy your seat for the next segment of your trips as soon as you arrive in a place – otherwise, you may have to stay a day or two longer than you intended.

If you are traveling from the United States, Greyhound or Trailways will arrange your reservations from the border as far as Mexico City, or for a tour of the country. In Mexico City, the Greyhound office at Reforma # 27 will handle reservations for several Mexican bus companies. Their telephone numbers are 535-4200, 535-2618. Trailways is at Av. Morelos # 110, room 408, telephone number 592-3376. There is also an agency called Mexicorama near downtown Mexico City (in the Zona Rosa, at Londres # 161, suite 48, tel: 533-2047, 533-2047) which will help you with bus tickets. They also speak English.

Otherwise, bus reservations must be made and tickets purchased at the bus stations, in person. In most cities, the bus station is conveniently located. In Mexico City, you must go to one of four stations; all are well away from downtown to avoid traffic problems. Buses for the northern part of the country – beyond Manzanillo on the Pacific side, or beyond Poza Rica on the Gulf side – use the Central Camionera del Norte, at Av. de los Cien Metros # 4907. Central Camionera Sur handles buses for points south and southwest of Mexico City, such as Taxco, Acapulco and Zihuatanejo. Its address is Av. Taxqueña # 1320. Other buses westward use the Central Camionera Poniente, at Avenida Sur 122, south of Observatorio Blvd. in Colonía Tacubaya. Buses to the east and southeast, including the Yucatán peninsula, use the Central Camionera de Oriente at Zaragoza # 200, near the airport. Since the bus stations are in outlying areas, you may want to take a taxi; as a bonus, the taxi driver can probably tell you which of the many bus companies at that terminal will take you to your destination.

Baggage is limited to 25 kg on first-class buses (about 55 pounds), but the limit is not usually enforced. On second-class buses there is virtually no limit, although you may have to load it yourself. Live baggage is also permitted on second-class buses: this includes pigs and chickens on their final journeys as well as your pet parrot or poodle.

City buses are often convenient for the traveler without a car, and in Mexico City – where driving is a nightmare for the foreign traveler – they are highly recommended. The fare is quite low, 3 pesos at press time. In addition to the regular city buses, Mexico City has special Rota 100 (Route 100) buses which travel only on the system of *Ejes Viales* or main thoroughfares. This makes them more efficient; they are also more comfortable and more clearly labeled.

TAXIS

Mexico has a bewildering variety of taxis. Fares are generally low, but we recommend that before getting in, you should tell the driver your destination and ask the fare: *Cuanto cuesta*? To get some idea what is reasonable, ask the desk clerk at your hotel, or a friend or acquaintance.

The only Mexico City taxis that are truly convenient for the non-Spanish speaking traveler to use are those waiting outside hotels. Drivers often speak English. Their fares are roughly comparable to those of taxis in the U.S. – very expensive by Mexican standards. You can get a guided tour at an hourly rate; if you speak no Spanish, be sure you can comprehend the driver before you hire him.

Somewhat less expensive are the *sitio* taxis, which work out of cab stands. You can telephone them to pick you up, but you will need to speak some Spanish to do so. Frequently, all their cabs are busy; some *sitio* stands accept advance reservations.

Many of the cruising taxis are Volkswagen beetles. These charge about half as much as hotel cabs. Be warned: it is virtually impossible to hail a cruising cab if it is raining, or during rush hours (7 a.m. to 10 a.m., 4 p.m. to 9 p.m.).

The cheapest cabs are collective taxis, *colectivos*. Those called *peseros* travel only on set routes, using the main thoroughfares. They are large American cars with a green stripe painted down the side. The driver will take two passengers in front, four in back – sometimes more. You will be charged according to the length of your ride, up to 500 pesos.

Special colectivos carry passengers leaving the bus stations of Mexico City. Tickets are sold in the bus stations for rides in these taxis. The first passenger to get in determines the direction the cab will go; the driver will then wait for a full load before leaving. During holiday periods, there is a mad rush for each taxi as it pulls in to the loading zone; you may just as well give up and pay the premium for a private cab.

If your Spanish is good, or you can get someone to help you, and you want to do some touring in Mexico City, try to settle on an hourly rate with a taxi driver. The legal rate at press time is 8,000 pesos, but you may have to do some looking to find a taxi driver willing to charge by the hour.

Leaving the airport, porters will shuttle you over to the taxi stand. Buy your ticket according to the city zone you're traveling to – and don't pay the cabdriver more, unless you want to give him a tip.

PRIVATE TRANSPORT

Exploring Mexico by car is a popular option, especially for Americans who drive their own cars over the border. This needs a special permit, obtainable free from the border guards and valid for 30, 90, or 180 days. Single- and multiple-entry permits are available. You will need proof of ownership, like your auto registration. If you are staying less than 72 hours and not driving beyond the border region, you don't need a permit.

If you drive a rented car into Mexico, or one belonging to a friend, you'll need a notarized statement of permission to drive the car in Mexico, signed by its owner.

Your regular driver's license is valid in Mexico, as long as you drive your own or a rented car. To drive any other car with Mexican plates, you'll need a temporary permit obtainable from the Dirección General de Tránsito. There are offices in major cities; in Mexico City, the office is at the Plaza de Tlaxcoaque.

Before you drive in Mexico, buy special comprehensive Mexican auto insurance. Get coverage for liability, property damage and theft, at a minimum. Your regular insurance does not cover you in Mexico, but your home agent may be able to arrange the policy for your through a Mexican company. Mexican auto insurance is easily purchased in any border town. Buy a policy for the longest period you might stay; if you leave the country sooner, you can arrange for a pro-rated partial refund.

Such special insurance is vital because Mexican law is based on the Napoleonic Code – guilty until proven innocent – and if you have an accident, you could be jailed until the fault is established. With the insurance, damages will be paid regardless of fault. When you buy the policy, get names and addresses of the company's adjustors in the areas you will travel in, and contact the adjustor immediately if you are met with an accident. It is recommended that you leave the scene of the accident quickly, however much it may offend your sense of decency; likewise, it is advised that you not stop to help if you witness an accident. Instead, notify the nearest "Green Angel" patrol you see, or – if there are injuries and no "Green Angels" in sight – notify the police. All of this is to avoid medical malpractice suits that may result from well-intentioned first aid.

The "Green Angels" are government employees in green trucks patrolling major highways. They are ready to offer first aid, minor repairs to your vehicle, or an emergency supply of gas and oil. You pay only for the parts used and for gas and oil. The "Green Angels" operate daily from 8 a.m. to 9 p.m. except Tuesdays, when they start at noon. Most of them speak some English. In time of need, just raise your hood and wait.

If you don't drive into Mexico, you may want to rent a car while you're there. There are agencies in most cities and resorts. You'll need to be at least 25 years old and to have a major credit card as well as a valid driver's license. During busy vacation periods, advance reservations are necessary. Costs vary according to location and type of car, beginning at about $30 per day plus 20¢ a kilometer for a standard transmission Volkswagen without air-conditioning (1989). Prices jump to $40 a day plus 25¢ a kilometer in Mexico City, Cancún, Mérida and Oaxaca, and to $60 a day plus 20¢ per kilometer (with 200 free km) in Acapulco, Cozumel and Mazanzanillo.

If you drive your own car into Mexico, you must also leave with it. This is to prevent you from selling it – at a handsome profit, since importation taxes keep auto prices high. To leave without your car in an emergency, you can post a bond with Mexican customs officials or leave the car with them at the airport; a storage fee will be charged.

The car may also be left at the Registra Federal de Automóviles, Calzada de Tlalpan # 2775, Mexico 21, D.F.

Whether the car you drive is your own or a rented one, certain precautions are necessary. Always carry water for the radiator, a jack and spare tire (or two, in rugged and remote country), fuses and any other spare parts that might need replacement – even if you're not prepared to do the repair yourself. You can count on the Green Angels for mechanical know-how but not for the fan belt specific to your make and model (and remember, away from the main roads you may be on your own). Have your car tuned up and checked before you leave for Mexico, to prevent problems. Fortunately, since problems do arise, Mexican mechanics are familiar with American-made autos as well as some foreign-made cars, especially Renaults and Volkswagens. Mechanics are to be found in nearly any village, as well as at the ubiquitous Pemex gas stations.

The Pemex stations are a government monopoly. Leaded and non-leaded gasoline and diesel fuel are available. Some attendants are reputed to overcharge customers by failing to set the pump at zero before pumping your gas, so be alert. The gas stations don't accept credit cards.

Don't drive at night in Mexico. Animals seem to have suicidal urges that lead them to sleep on highways at night, and there are many other hazards that your headlights reveal when it is too late to avoid them.

ROAD SIGNS

Many road signs are of the international variety, easy to guess at. Others assume a knowledge of Spanish. If you don't understand a highway sign, slow down and be prepared to stop. On the following page is a collection of the most common signs. Meanwhile, some key words:

Alto	Stop
Despacio	Slow
Peligro	Danger
Precaución	Warning
Ceda el paso	Yield right of way
Puente angosto	Narrow bridge
Curva	Curve
Transito;	One way:
Circulación	usually on an arrow.
Estacionamiento	Parking; usually abbreviated E, with E meaning no parking.
Vado	Dip; in wet weather, a ford.
Conserve su derecha	Keep right
Altura maxima	Vertical clearance (in meters)
Ancho libre	Horizontal clearance (in meters)
Manaje despacio, neblina	Drive slow, fog (seen on toll booths – lights up when the warning applies).
Una hora; Dos horas	One hour, two hours (parking time limits, printed beneath a large circled E).

If you encounter a policeman directing traffic, the signals are as follows: if he is facing toward you or away from you, stop; if he is sideways to you, go.

If you park illegally you may return to find your license plates missing. Usually the policeman will be nearby and you can retrieve them by offering him some money. The same technique is effective if you

Principal Mexican Road Signs

           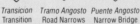

| *Doble Circulacion* Two Way Traffic | *Glorieta* Rotary Intersection | *Transicion* Transition | *Tramo Angosto* Road Narrows | *Puente Angosto* Narrow Bridge | Stop | *Yield* Right of Way | Inspection | Speed Limit (km) | *One Way* Traffic |

          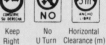 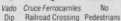

| *Altura Maxima* Vertical Clearance (m) | *Camino Derrapante* Slippery Road | *Pendiente* Hill | *Vado* Dip | *Cruce Ferrocarriles* Railroad Crossing | No Pedestrians | Keep Right | No U Turn | Horizontal Clearance (m) | No Left Turn |

| *Trabajadores* Workmen | *Escuela* School Zone | *Zona de Derrumbes* Slide Area (Watch for Falling Rocks) | *Semaforo* Traffic Light | *Ganado* Cattle | Do Not Pass | Do Not Enter | One Hour Parking | Parking Limit | No Parking |

commit a minor traffic violation. Try to think of it as an on-the-spot fine, rather than as a bribe.

If you drive to Mexico City, your best chance of avoiding parking violations is to leave your car in the garage of your hotel. You will want to do this because, bad as parking is in Mexico City, driving is even worse. You can rent a car and driver or take taxis, buses or the subway.

WHERE TO STAY

HOTELS

When planning a trip to Mexico you must decide if you will spend every night in a hotel, or spend part (or all) of your time camping out. If you will be staying in hotels you should make reservations in advance for your accommodations (a) every night during holiday periods, especially around Christmas and Easter but also on national holidays; (b) every night that you will be in a major tourism areas, especially during the summer; and (c) every night if you have special needs, such as accommodations that accept dogs or other pets in the rooms.

Hotels in Mexico number in the thousands, and range from luxurious rooms in some of the world's most opulent hotels, which you may pay more than US$100 per night, to small rooms in modest inns for which you may pay 20-30,000 pesos per night. The latter are fine for those with a tight budget and plenty of time, but they do not pay commissions to travel agents and you will find it difficult or impossible to make reservations in advance. You may have to depend on your Spanish to help you find them: *Donde hay un hotel economico*? (Where is there an inexpensive hotel?) If you are planning to use this type of hotel, you should be prepared either to pay more in time of need, or to camp out.

There are several good sources of infor-

mation for campers, whether you have a trailer or a tent. The *Rand McNally Campground and Trailer Park Guide*, available in bookstores, lists many Mexican campgrounds. You can also order campground directories from K.O.A. (P.O. Box 30558, Billings, MT 59114); from Climatic Data Press (P.O. Box 413, Lemont, PA 16851); and from *Margarita* (Apartado Postal 5-599, Mexico 5, D.F.). For these, your best bet is to write well in advance inquiring about the current price; specify that your interest is in Mexico. You may want to buy *The People's Guide to Camping in Mexico* written by Carl Franz, and published by John Muir Publications, which is available in bookstores. You can also seek information from the A.A.A., from the company from which you buy your Mexican auto insurance, and from offices of the Mexican National Tourist Council (see list in the "Tourist Information" section). Keep in mind that campgrounds, like hotels, can be very crowded at peak tourist season.

Assistance in choosing hotels is available from the National Tourist Council offices in Mexico and abroad, and from travel agents. Following is a partial listing, drawn by kind permission from the *Directorio Industria Turistica National*. Note: *gerente* means manager; *Apartado Postal* refers to the post office box number; *cuarto* and *habitacion* both mean room.

AGUASCALIENTES

Hotel Colonial
Aguascalientes: Cabon San Lucas
Av. 5 de Mayo No. 552, tel: 535-77. Sr. José Dávila-Esparza, gerente. 44 cuartos.

Hotel Francia
Madero y Plaza Principal, tel: 560-80. Sr. Juan Andrea B., gerente. 88 cuartos.

Las Trojes
Blvd. Campestre y Carretera a Zacatecas, tel: 617-26. 104 cuartos.

Medrano
Blvd. José Ma. Chavez 904, tel: 555-00. 69 cuartos.

BAJA CALIFORNIA

EL ROSARITO

Rosarito Beach Hotel
Km. 27 Carr Tijuana-Ensenada, Apartado Postal 202, tel: 2-11-06 y 2-11-26. C.P. Hugo Torres Charbert, gerente general, tel: 6-62-25. 135 cuartos.

ENSENADA

Estero Beach Hotel
Apartado Postal No. 86, tel: al 04. Sr. Antonio Novelo, gerente.

Hotel Motel Cortés
López Mateos No. 1089. Apartado Postal 396, tel: 8-23-07 al 09. Sr. César Maza, gerente. 62 cuartos.

MEXICALI

Holiday Inn
Blvd. Benito Juárez, tel: 66-13-60. Sr. Juan J. Díaz de Sandi, gerente general. 124 cuartos.

Hotel Lucerna
Blvd. Juárez No. 2151, tel: 54-10-00, telex: 56719. C.P. Roberto Rojas, gerente general. 200 cuartos.

Motel La Siesta
Calzada Justo Sierra No. 899, tel: 54-11-00. Sr. José Luna Pérez, gerente propietario. 83 cuartos.

TECATE

Motel El Dorado
Av. Juárez No. 1100, tel: 4-11-01. Sr. Guillermo Vélez, gerente. 42 cuartos.

TIJUANA

El Conquistador Motor Hotel
Blvd. Agua Caliente South 700. Apartado Postal 2491, tel: 81-79-55. Sr. Octavio Dominguez, gerente. 110 cuartos.

Paraiso Radisson
Blvd. Aguacaliente 1, tel: 81-72-00. 200 cuartos.

BAJA CALIFORNIA SUR

BUENA VISTA

Rancho Hotel Beuna Vista
Domicilio Conocido. Sr. Theodore White, gerente. 45 cuartos.

CABO SAN LUCAS

Hotel Twin Dolphin
Bahia Sta. Maria s/n. Apartado Postal No. 52, tel: 3-01-40. Sr. Cándido H. Garcia, gerente general. 46 cuartos.

GUERRERO NEGRO

Hotel El Presidente
Paralelo 28, ubicado en la Carretera Transpeninsular a 320 km de Cataviña. 24 cuartos.

LA PAZ

Gran Hotel B.C.S.
Calle Rangel s/n, tel: 2-39-00 y 2-38-44. 248 cuartos.

Econhotel Palmira
Carr. a Pichilingue s/n, tel: 2-40-00, telex: 052-218. Sr. Raúl Rodríguez Gil, gerente general. 120 cuartos.

Hotel Perla
Alvaro Obregon No. 1570, tel: 2-07-77. Sr. Lic. Sergio Trujillo Venegas, gerente general. 100 habtiaciones.

LORETO

Hotel El Presidente La Pinta
Propietario Nacional Hotelera. Apartado Postal 28. Prolongación calle Fco. 1. Madero. Sr. Ernesto Torrestleal, gerente general. 48 cuartos.

SAN IGNACIO

Hotel El Presidente San Ignacio
Edificio Sta. María Av. López Mateos y Castillo, tel: 8-30-01. 28 cuartos.

SAN JOSE DEL CABO

Hotel Presidente
Blvd. Mijares, tel: 2-02-32. 250 cuartos.

Calinda Aquamarina
Blvd. Mijares, tel: 2-00-77. 99 cuartos.

CAMPECHE
CIUDAD CAMPECHE

Hotel Baluartes
Av. Ruiz Cortines s/n. Apartado Postal 286, tel: 6-39-11. Sr. Evelio Segovia Franco, gerente. 102 habitaciones.

Hotel El Presidente
Av. Ruiz Cortines No. 100. Apartado Postal 251, tel: 6-22-33 y 6-46-11. Arq. José Elías Selen, gerente general. 120 cuartos.

Hotel Alhambra
Av. Resurgimient, tel: 6-68-00. 100 cuartos.

CIUDAD DEL CARMEN

Hotel Isla Del Carmen
Calle 20-A No. 9, tel: 2-2350. Sr. Roberto Ongay, gerente. 96 cuartos.

ESTADO DE COAHUILA
MONCLOVA

Hotel Chulavista
Av. Frontera No. 100. Col. Guadalupe, tel: 3-02-11. Sr. J. Fernando Núñez Calderón de la Barco, gerente.

Hotel Gil Cantu
V. Carranza No. 410, tel: 3-04-1. Sr. David A. Quintero Alvarez, director general.

Motel Kalionchiz
Carretera 57 entre Mérida y Allende, tel: 3-25-11. Sr. Jorge Kalionchiz Manu, gerente.

PIEDRAS NEGRAS

Hotel Autel Rio
Padre de las Casas 121 Norte, tel: 2-10-80. Sr. Roberto Mijares, gerente. 60 cuartos.

Casa Blanca
Carretera 57 y Av. Brisas, tel: 2-46-46. 71 cuartos.

Motel 57
Av. E. Carranza No. 805, tel: 2-12-20. Sr. Homero Niño Portales, gerente. 73 cuartos.

La Quinta Motel, S.A.
Av. E. Carranza No. 1205, tel: 2-21-02 Lic. Manuel García Bermea, gerente. 44 cuartos.

SALTILLO

Camino Real
Blvd. Fundadores Km. 865, tel: 4-15-15. 117 cuartos.

San Jorge
M. Acuna 240, tel: 3-06-00. 130 cuartos.

Eurotel Plaza
Blvd. V. Cerranza, tel: 2-64-72. 45 cuartos.

TORREON

Hotel Calvete
Av. Juárez y Ramón Corona, tel: 2-03-78. Sr. Marcelo Torres, gerente. 97 cuartos.

Hotel Palacio Real
Morelos No. 1280 Pte. Apdo. Postal 346, tel: 6-00-00. Sr. Lic. José J. Hernández, gerente general.

CHIAPAS
PALENQUE

Mision Palenque
Domicilio Conocido, tel: 502-41. 144 cuartos.

Hotel Palenque
Av. 5 de Mayo No. 15, tel: 5-01-03. Sr. José Vicente Castellanos A., gerente. 65 cuartos.

Centro Turistico-Cultural Chankah
Km. 31.5 Carretera a Las Ruinas. Apartado Postal 26, tel: 500-14. Sra. Magali G. de Romano. 12 junior suites.

TAPACHULA

Hotel Loma Real De Tapachula
Apartado Postal 241, tel: 6-14-40 al 45. Sr. Carlos Riveroll Cinta, gerente. 62 cuartos.

Kamico Hotel
Prolong. Central Orienta, tel: 6-26-40. Sr.
Carlos Moguel, gerente general. 55 cuartos.

TUXTLA GUTIERREZ

Hotel Bonampak
Blvd. Belisario Dominguez No. 180, tel:
320-50 con 6 líneas directas. Sr. Ing. Iván
Pedrero Gutiérrez, gerente. 100 cuartos.

Hotel La Mansion
1a. Poniente Norte 221, tel: 2-21-51 y 2-21-
63. Sr. Federico de la Cerda Serrano, gerente
general. 34 cuartos.

Hotel Palace Inn
Blvd. Belisario Dominguez 1081. Tuxtla
Gutiérrez, Chis, tel: 2-43-43 y 2-48-90. Sr.
Jalil Abraham P., gerente general.

CHIHUAHUA

CIUDAD JUAREZ

Calinda Juárez
Hnos. Escobar 3513, tel: 13-7250.
111 cuartos.

Colonial Las Fuentes
Av. Lincoln 1355, tel: 13-5050. 186 cuartos.

Hotel De Luxe
Lerdo y Galeana No. 300 Sur. Apartado
Postal 238. tel: 15-0082 Sr. Alfonso Mur-
guia Chavez Jr., gerente general. 71 cuartos.

CHIHUAHUA, CHIH.

Hotel Cabanas Divisadero Barrancas
El Divisadero, Chih. Apartado Postal 661,
tel: 2-33-62 y 5-65-75. Sra. Ivonne Sandoval
A., propietaria. 34 cuartos.

Hotel El Presidente
(Nacional Hotelera) Libertad No. 9, tel: 16-
06-06, telex: 034-858. Sr. Leon A. Joanis,
gerente. 84 cuartos.

Hotel Victoria
Av. Juárez y Colón. Apartado Postal 19, tel:
12-88-93 al 96. Sr. Eustacio Granados, gerente. 130 cuartos.

DISTRITO FEDERAL

Hotel Benidorm
Frontera 217, tel: 584-9899. 146 cuartos.

Can Cun
Donato Guerra 24, tel: 566-6488. 90 cuartos.

Century Zona Rosa
Liverpool 132, tel: 584-7111. 143 cuartos.

Galeria Plaza
Hamburgo 195, tel: 211-0014.

Krystal Zona Rosa
Liverpool 155, tel: 211-0092. 335 cuartos.

Maria Christina
Lerma 31, tel: 566-9688.

Hotel Nikko
Campos Eliseos 204, tel: 203-4020.

Parsiso Radisson
Cuspide 53, Parques del Pedregal, tel: 533-
1195.

Park Villa
Gral. Comez Pedraza 68, tel: 515-5245.

Hotel Polanco
Edgar Allen Poe 8, tel: 520-2085. 78 cuartos.

Hotel Del Prado
Marina Nacional 399, tel: 254-4400. 376
cuartos.

Hotel Sevilla Palace
Reforma 105, tel: 566-8877. 414 cuartos.

Suites Hamburgo
Hamburgo 9, tel: 566-1477. 22 cuartos.

Suites Sylmar
Tabasco 259, tel: 514-5637. 14 cuartos.

Hotel Ambassador
Humboldt No. 38, tel: 518-01-10, telex:
017-76-276. Jacobo King, gerente. 169
cuartos.

Hotel Aristos
Paseo de la Reforma 276, tel: 211-0112.
Amine Awwad, director general; Sr. Alejan-
dro Trigos, gerente. 324 cuartos.

Hotel Bamer
Av. Juárez 52, tel: 521-90-60. Sr. Roberto Martínez, gerente. 111 cuartos.

Hotel Bristol
Plaza Necaxa 17, tel: 533-60-60. Sr. Enrique Lambel, gerente.

Hotel Camino Real
Maríano Escobedo 700, tel: 545-6760. Sr. Juan Berthelot, director general. 700 cuartos.

Hotel De Cortés
Hidalgo No. 85, tel: 585-03-22. Sr. Sebastián Rincón Gallardo, gerente. 27 cuartos.

Hotel El Presidente Chapultepec
Campos Eliseos No. 218, tel: 250-77-00. Sr. Bruno R. Lugani, director general; Sr. Jorge Muñúzuri, gerente. 753 cuartos.

Hotel El Presidente Zona Rosa
Hamburgo No. 135, tel: 525-00-00. Sr. Jean Francois Nogueras, director. 128 cuartos.

Hotel Estoril
Luis Moya 93. México 1, D. F., tel: 585-68-77 y 521-97-62. Raúl Arredondo Aguilar, gerente general. 150 cuartos.

Holiday Inn Crowne Plaza
Paseo de la Reforma No. 80, tel: 566-77-77. Sr. Julio Vázquez, director general. 631 cuartos.

Gran Hotel De La Cd. De México
16 de Septiembre No. 82. Apartado Postal 80057, tel: 510-40-40, telex: 017-73069. Sr. Guillermo V. Solórzano, gerente general. 94 cuartos y 27 suites.

Hotel Geneve
Londres No. 130, tel: 525-15-00. Bajo la dirección de Quality Inns.

Holiday Inn Aeropuerto Internacional
Blvd. Puerto Aereo No. 502, tel: 762-40-88. Sr. Federico Schlitter, gerente general. 350 cuartos.

Hotel Maria Isabel Sheraton
Paseo de la Reforma No. 325, tel: 211-0001. Sr. Philippe Gerandeau, director general. 850 cuartos.

Hotel Majestic
Av. Madero No. 73, tel: 521-86-00. Sr. Sebastián Rincón Gallardo, gerente.

Hotel Metropol
Luis Moya No. 39, tel: 510-86-60. Sr. Sony Mizrahi, gerente. 165 cuartos.

Hotel Ritz
Madero No. 30, tel: 518-13-40. Sr. Pablo de Orta, gerente. 140 cuartos.

Hotel Romano Diana
Rio Lerma No. 237, tel: 525-77-65. Sr. Victor Manuel Lara Pardo, gerente. 166 cuartos.

Hotel Suites Del Parque
Dakota 155. Col. Nápoles, tel: 536-14-50. Sr. Ernesto Escamilla, gerente general.

Hotel Vasco De Quiroga
Londres No. 15, tel: 546-26-14. Sr. Larry Murphy, gerente. 50 cuartos.

Suites Amberes
Amberes No. 64, tel: 533-13-06. Sr. Pablo Ibarra, gerente.

Suites Orleans Hotel
Hamburgo No. 67, tel: 533-66-80. Sr. Héctor Navarro, gerente. 42 suites.

COLIMA

MANZANILLO

Villas Del Palmar
Apartado Postal No. 646, tel: 3-0575. 186 cuartos.

Hotel Club Santiago
Playa Miramar, tel: 3-04-12 Manzanillo. Col. Sr. Juan Manuel González, gerente general. 150 cuartos.

Hotel Las Hadas
Apdo. Postal No. 158. Peninsula de Santiago, tel: 3-00-00, telex: 68-2661. Sr. Felipe Chiu, gerente general. 200 cuartos.

Hotel Playa De Santiago
Balneario de Santiago, Apartado Postal No. 90, tel: 3-0344. Sr. Hector Ochoa, gerente. 106 cuartos.

ESTADO DE DURANGO

DURANGO

Hotel El Presidente Durango
20 de Noviembre No. 257, tel: 1-04-80, telex: 066-33. Sr. Luis H. Madariaga A., gerente general. 100 cuartos.

Hotel Casablanca
Av. 20 de Noviembre No. 811 Pte., tel: 1-35-99. Sr. Francisco Durán Alba., gerente general. 46 cuartos.

Gran Hotel Matar
Progreso 112 con Av. 20 de Noviembre, tel: 1-44-12. Sr. Pedro J. Mátar, director general; Sr. Rafael E. Alza, gerente. 75 cuartos.

ESTADO DE GUANAJUATO

ABASOLO

Hotel Balneario Spa "La Caldera"
5 de Mayo y Guerrero, tel: 3-00-20, 3-00-21 y 6-00-16. Sr. Alfonso Cortés O., gerente. 60 cuartos.

CELAYA

Hotel El Cid
Blvd. López Mateos 1548 Pte., tel: 2-29-62. Sr. Luis López Altamirano, gerente.

Posada Santa Monica
Km. 36.5 Carretera Celaya-Salvatierra, tel: 3-02-69. Sr. Guillermo Ortiz V., gerente.

COMANJILLA

Hotel Balneario De Comanjilla
Tel: 2-00-91. Lic. Harold Gabriel, gerente. 130 cuartos.

GUANAJUATO

Hotel Castillo De Santa Cecilia
Camino a Valenciana s/n. Apartado Postal 44, tel: 2-04-85 y 2-04-77. Fernando Martínez, gerente general. 100 cuartos.

Hotel Hosteria Del Frayle
Sospeña 3, tel: 2-11-79. Sra. María Elena Perez Gil de Reyes, gerente. 33 cuartos.

Hotel Hacienda De Cobos
Calle Subterranea. P. Hidalgo No. 3 y Av. Juárez 153, tel: 2-03-50. 40 cuartos.

Hotel Parador San Javier
Plaza San Javier, tel: 2-06-26. Lic. Guillermo Vera, director; Sr. Mario Aguado, gerente. 100 habitaciones.

Hotel Real De Minas
Nejayote No. 17, tel: 2-14-60. Sr. Cosme Vera, gerente. 175 cuartos.

Hotel San Diego
Jardin de la Union No. 1, Apartado Postal No. 8, tel: 2-13-00, 2-13-71 y 2-14-99. Lic. Ricardo Muñoz G., gerente general. 55 habitaciones.

Hotel Valenciana
Carretera a Dolores Hidalgo Km. 3, Apartado Postal 180, tel: 2-07-99. Sra. Berta T. de Quevedo, gerente. 44 cuartos.

IRAPUATO

Hotel Real De Minas
Portal Carrilo Puerto No. 5, tel: 6-23-80. Sr. Rodolfo Vera, gerente. 100 cuartos.

Hotel Flamingo
Blvd. Díaz Ordaz No. 72, tel: 6-36-66. 40 cuartos y 2 suites.

LEON

Hotel Condesa
Portal Brave No. 14, Apartado Postal 14, tel: 3-11-20. Sr. Guillermo Vera, gerente 130 cuartos.

Hotel Leon
Madero 113, Apartado Postal 597, tel: 4-10-50. Lic. Alejandro Ascencio Hernández, gerente. 91 cuartos.

Hotel Real De Minas
Blvd. A. López Mateos, tel: 4-36-77, telex: 012-688. Sr. Bernardo Aguado, gerente. 140 habitaciones

Motel La Estancia
Blvd. López Mateos s/n. Conjunto Estrelia, Apartado Postal 759, tel: 6-3939. Lic. Carlos Alvarado Zavala, gerente. 49 cuartos.

SALAMANCA

Salamanca, A. C. Hotel Trevi
Hidalgo No. 221, tel: 8-07-97. Salamanca.
Gto. Lic. Arturo R. Aguayo Durán, gerente.

SAN MIGUEL ALLENDE

Villa Jacaranda
Aldama 53, tel: 2-1015. 11 cuartos.

Hotel Aristos
Calle Ancha de San Antonio No. 30, tel: 2-01-49 y 2-03-92. Sr. Jorge Alcalá, gerente. 60 cuartos.

Hacienda Taboada, S. A.
Apartado Postal No. 100. San Miguel de Aliende, Gto, tel: 2-08-88 y 2-08-50; tel: en Mexico, D. F. 559-93-52 y 559-93-96. Elba Sandra Blanco D Geddes, directora. 81 cuartos.

Hotel Mision De Los Angeles
Km. 2 Carretera San Miguel-Celaya, tel: 2-10-26. Sr. R. Jurado, gerente. 70 cuartos.

Motel La Siesta
Carretera de San Miguel Allende a Celaya, Apartado Postal 72, tel: 2-02-07. Lic. Raúl Araiza, gerente. 100 cuartos.

Posada De San Francisco
Plaza Principal No. 2. Apartado Postal 40, tel: 2-00-72. Sr. Ramón Zavala Ramírez, gerente. 50 cuartos.

ESTADO DE GUERRERO

ACAPULCO

Hotel Bali Hai
Av. Costera M. Aleman 186, tel: 2-63-36. 121 cuartos.

Hotel Condotel Club Del Sol
Av. Costera M. Aleman s/n, tel: 5-66-00. 286 cuartos.

Hotel Impala
Fragata Yucatán, tel: 4-22-01. 31 cuartos.

Hotel Sand's Acapulco
Av. Costera M. Aleman s/n, tel: 4-22-60. 62 cuartos.

Hotel El Tropicano
Av. Costera M. Aleman 510, tel: 4-11-00. 137 cuartos.

Acapulco Princess
Playa Revolcadero. Apartado Postal 1351, tel: 4-31-00. Sr. Adalberto Stratta, vice-presidente y director general. 777 cuartos.

Auto Hotel Ritz
Av. Magallanes s/n. Apartado Postal 257, tel: 5-80-23. Sr. Tim Campion, gerente general. 103 cuartos.

Hotel Acapulco Malibu
Costera Miguel Alemán No. 20, tel: 4-10-70 al 74. Sr. Victor Andrade, gerente general. 80 cuartos a la orilla del mar.

Hotel Continental Acapulco
Costera Miguel Alemán s/n, tel: 4-09-09. Sr. Dieter Obermann, gerente general.

Hotel Caleta Acapulco, S. A.
Playa de Caleta, Apartado Postal 76, tel: 3-99-40, telex: 016-811.

Hotel Condesa Del Mar
Av. Costera Miguel Alemán s/n, Apartado Postal 933, tel: 4-28-28. Sr. Jorge A. Liberman, gerente general. 505 cuartos.

Hotel Elcano
Av. de las Palmas del Parque y Fracc Club Deportivo, tel: 4-19-50. Sr. Antón Elorriaga Bilbao, gerente. 140 cuartos.

Hotel El Mirador Plaza
Quebrada No. 74, tel: 2-11-11 y 3-11-55, telex: 16-833. Sr. Francisco Medina. gerente general. 133 cuartos.

Hotel El Presidente Acapulco
Av. Costera Miguel Alemán s/n, tel: 4-17-00. Sr. Manuel Garza S., gerente general. 407 cuartos.

Hotel Fiesta Tortuga
Costera Miguel Aleman No. 3675, tel: 4-88-89. Sr. Alberto L. Chia, gerente general. 250 cuartos.

Hotel Calinda Acapulco
Costera Miguel Alemán 1260, tel: 4-04-10. Sr. Karl Hummer, gerente. 366 cuartos.

Hotel La Palapa Acapulco
Fragato Yucatán No. 210, tel: 4-53-63. Sr. Antonio Tovar, gerente general. 340 suites.

Hotel Brisas
Carretera Escénica No. 5255, Apartado Postal 281, tel: 4-16-50. Sr. Willi Dietz, gerente general. 300 casitas, 250 piscinas.

Hotel Maris
Av. Miguel Alemán y Magallanes, tel: 2-28-00 y 2-52-91. Sr. Armando Bahena Ch., gerente. 84 cuartos.

Hotel Maralisa
Apartado Postal 721. Enrique El Esclavo s/n, tel: 4-09-77. Sr. Josee Muñóz, gerente general. 90 cuartos.

Hotel Paraiso Marriott
Costera Miguel Alemán s/n. Apartado Postal 504, tel: 2-41-40. Sr. Rodolfo Navarrete, director general. 442 cuartos.

Hotel Pierre Marques Princess
Playa Revolcadero, tel: 4-20-00. Sr. Alfonso R. Rocha, gerente. 340 cuartos.

Hotel Plaza Hyatt Regency Acapulco
Av. Costera Miguel Alemán No. 666, Apartado Postal 656, tel: 4-28-88. Sr. Fred Lederer, gerente general. 694 cuartos.

Hotel Posadi Del Sol
Costera Miguel Alemán No. 1390, Apartado Postal 808, tel: 4-10-10 al 20. Sr. Arturo Funes, gerente general. 180 cuartos.

Hotel Ritz Acapulco
Costera Miguel Alemán s/n, Apartado Postal 259, telex: 016-813. Sr. Tim Campion, gerente general. 300 cuartos.

Hotel Villa Los Arcos
Monterrey No. 195, tel: 4-22-80, 81 y 82. Acapulco, Gro. Francisco Silva, gerente general. 150 cuartos.

Hotel Villa Vera Racquet Club
Lomas del Mar 35, tel: 4-03-33. Sr. Georg Korber, gerente general. 71 suites y Jr. suites.

La Torre Playasol
Costera Miguel Alemán 1252, Apartado Postal 1756, Acapulco, Gro., tel: 4-80-50, telex: 016-847. C.P. Alfonso Salgado R., director general; Javier Gorozpe C., director de ventas.

IXTAPA ZIHUATANEJO

Villa Del Sol
Playa La Ropa, Apartado Postal 84, tel: 4-22-39. 21 cuartos.

Hotel Aristos-Ixtapa
Apartado Postal 42, tel: 4-22-67 y 4-27-50. Sr. Eduardo García Dávila, gerente general. 226 cuartos.

Hotel Catalina
Playa La Ropa, tel: 4-20-32 y 4-21-37, Zihuatanejo, Gro. Sr. Samuel Elizalde G., gerente.

Hotel El Presidente Ixtapa
Blvd. Ixtapa s/n, tel: 4-20-13. Sr. Diego de Cosslo. director. 304 cuartos.

Holiday Inn Ixtapa
Blvd. Ixtapa s/n. P.O. Box 55, tel: 4-23-96. Henry S. Berberian, gerente general. 238 cuartos, 6 suites.

Hotel Riviera Del Sol Ixtapa
Complejo Turistico, tel: 4-24-06. Sr. Alejandro Espejo Martínez, director; Sr. Carlos Sandoval Bernal, gerente ddministrativo.

Hotel Viva Ixtapa
Playa el Palmar Ixtapa, tel: 4-23-41. Sr. Manuel García Hernández, gerente general. 110 cuartos.

TAXCO

Hotel De La Borda
Cerro del Pedregal No. 2, tel: 2-00-25 y 2-02-25. Sr. Manuel Sadi González, gerente. 171 cuartos.

Holiday Inn Taxco
Fracc. Lomas de Taxco, Apartado Postal 84, tel: 2-13-00. Sr Victor J. Medrano Mearquez, gerente general. 159 cuartos.

Hotel Posada De La Mision
Cerro de la MisiEon No. 32, Apartado Postal 88, tel: 2-21-98. Sr. Henry Berger Schmidt, gerente. 100 cuartos.

ZIHUATANEJO

Hotel Calpulli
Plaza de la Ropa, tel: 4-21-66. Sr. Roberto Marroquin, gerente. 42 cuartos.

Hotel Posada Caracol, S. A.
Playa La Madera, Apartado Postal 20, Zihuatanejo, Gro., tel: 4-20-35 y 36. Sr. Gustavo Cosío Villegas, gerente general. 60 cuartos.

ESTADO DE HIDALGO

TULA

Hotel Lizbeth
Melchor Ocampo No. 200, tel: 2-05-98, 45 y 598. Sr. Mario Argáez García, propietario. 38 cuartos.

ESTADO DE JALISCO

GUADALAJARA

Aranzazu
Av. Revolucion 110 Pte., tel: 13-3232. 500 cuartos.

Diana
Agustin Yanez 2760, tel: 15-0919. 185 cuartos.

Fiesta Americana
Aurelio Aceves 225, tel: 25-3434. 402 cuartos.

Guadalajara Sheraton
Av. Ninos Heroes y 16 de Sept, tel: 14-7272

Quinta Real
Av. Mexico 2727, tel: 15-2507. 53 cuartos.

Hotel De Mendoza
Av. Carranza 16 Esq. Av. Hidalgo, Apartado Postal 1-2453, tel: 13-46-16, telex: 068-2683. Sr. Alberto López Codina, gerente general. 104 cuartos.

Hotel El Tapatio
Blvd. Aeropuerto No. 4275, Apartado Postal 2953, tel: 35-60-50. Sr. Carlos Siliceo, gerente general. 207 cuartos.

Hotel Fenix Best Western
Av. Corona No. 160. Apartado Postal 1-1151, tel: 11-57-14, telex: 068-2885. Sr. Enrique R. Azmitia, director. 26 cuartos.

Hotel Genova
Av. Juárez No. 123, tel: 13-75-00 y 13-19-94. Lic. Enrique Ramos, director general. 139 cuartos.

Gran Hotel
Morelos No. 2244, tel: 15-09-65 y 15-63-14. Sr. Stephano Ghersi, gerente. 95 cuartos.

Las Pergolas Gran Hotel
Morelos 2244, tel: 15-01-86, Guadalajara. Jal José Aguilar, gerente general. 200 cuartos.

Guadalajara Sheraton
Av. Niños Héroes y 16 de Septiembre, tel: 14-72-72. Sr. Emilio Haro, gerente general. 222 cuartos.

Hotel Roma
Av. Juárez No. 170, Apartado Postal 159, tel: 14-86-50, telex: 068-1704. Inq. Guillermo Martínez, director y gerente general. 180 cuartos.

CHAPALA

Brisas De Chapala-Guadalajara
Km. 39 Carr. Guadalajara, tel: 5-2771. 42 cuartos.

Motel Chula Vista
Apartado Postal 75 6 97, tel: 5-22-13. Enrique Rojas M., gerente.

PUERTO VALLARTA

Buenaventura
Av. Mexico 1301, tel: 2-3742. 210 cuartos.

Bugambilia Sheraton
Carr. Aeropuerto 999, tel: 2-3000. 501 cuartos.

Camino Real
Km. 3.5 Carr. P.V.-Chamela, tel: 2-0012.
250 cuartos.

Castel Pelicanos
Km. 2.3 Carr. Aeropuerto, tel: 2-0650.
153 cuartos.

Fiesta Americana
Km. 2.5 Carr. Aeropuerto, tel: 2-2010.
77 cuartos.

Krystal Vallarta
Av. de las Garzas s/n, tel: 8-1459.
457 cuartos.

Molino De Agua
Ignacio L. Vallarta 130, tel: 2-1907.
65 cuartos.

Oro Verde
Rodolfo Gomez 111, tel: 2-5553.
162 cuartos.

Playa De Oro
Av. de las Garzas 1, tel: 2-0348. 392 cuartos.

Plaza Las Glorias Calinda
Km. 2.4 Carr. Aeropuerto, tel: 2-2224.
217 cuartos.

Plaza Vallarta
Km. 2.5 Carr. Aeropuerto, tel: 2-4448.
363 cuartos.

Hotel Camino Real Puerto Vallarta
Playa de las Estacas. Apartado Postal 95, tel:
2-00-02, telex: 06503. Sr. Werni Elsen,
gerente general. 250 cuartos.

Hotel Garza Blanca
Playa Palo Maria, tel: 2-10-23 y 2-10-83,
telex: 06518. Salvador Fernández, gerente.
44 suites; 22 frente al mar, 18 chalets y 6
villas.

Hotel Holiday Inn
Apartado Postal 555, tel: 2-17-00. Sr. Francisco Almeida, gerente general. 230 cuartos.

ESTADO DE MEXICO

IXTAPAN DE LA SAL

Hotel Ideal
Blvd. San Roman Sur 809, tel: 3-0486.
26 cuartos.

Hotel Ixtapan
Plaza Gaspar, tel: 3-0304. 245 cuartos.

Vista Hermosa
Blvd. San Roman s/n, tel: 3-0092.
14 cuartos.

Hotel Kiss
Av. Las Jacarandas Esq. Benito Juárez, tel:
20 Sr. Oscar Kiss, director. 22 cuartos.

TOLUCA

Del Rey Inn Hotel
Km. 63 México-Toluca, tel: 5-36-55. Sr.
Amulfo Martínez, gerente general.
35 cuartos.

Hotel Plaza Morelos
Aquiles Serdán 115, tel: 592-00 con 3 líneas.
Martha Lara de Pavón, gerente. 38 cuartos.

VALLE DE BRAVO

Los Arcos
Fco. Glez. Bocanegra 310, tel: 2-0042.
25 cuartos.

Loto Azul
Av. Toluca s/n, tel: 2-0796. 32 cuartos.

Golf Motel Avandaro, S. A.
Dom. Conocido. Valle de Bravo. Edo. de
Méx, tel: Lada 91726-200-03. Reserv. en
México: 536-77-26. Lic. Margarita Zamora
M., gerente. 30 bungalows.

ESTADO DE MICHOACAN

MORELIA

La Mansion De La C. Real
Av. Madero Ote. 776, tel: 3-2856.
66 cuartos.

Hotel Alameda
Av. Madero Pte. y Guillermo Prieto, tel: 2-20-23 y 24. Sr. Raul Sandoval Castro, gerente. 75 cuartos.

Hotel Morelos
Av. Acueducto y Jardin Morelos, tel: 2-12-48 y 2-44-99. Lic. Angel David Legaria, gerente. 82 cuartos.

Hotel Villa Capri
Madero Pte. 2069, tel: 2-25-37. Srita. Concepción Tena Orozco, gerente. 45 cuartos.

Hotel Villa Montana, S. A.
Calle Patzimba. Colonia Vista Bella, Apartado Postal 233, tel: 2-25-88 y 2-22-75. Srita. Margarita Murillo, gerente. 65 habitaciones.

Hotel Virrey De Mendoza
Matamoros No. 16, tel: 2-06-33 y 2-49-40. Sr. Javier M. Pérez, gerente. 52 cuartos.

Mansion Acueducto
Ave. Acueducto No. 25, tel: 2-33-01. Sr. Julio Gómez Sáenz, gerente. 36 cuartos.

PATZCUARO

Hotel Meson Del Cortijo
Av. Alvaro Obregón y Glorieta de Tanganxuan, Apartado Postal 202, tel: 2-12-95. Lic. Rafael S. Orozco, gerente. 23 cuartos.

Hotel Y Motel Posada De Don Vasco
Av. de las Américas No. 450, Apartado Postal 15, tel: 2-06-94, 2-02-27 y 2-02-62. Sr. Francisco G. Polo, gerente. 70 cuartos.

Operadora De Hoteles Del Bajio Hotel Meson Del Gallo
Dr. Coss No. 20, tel: 2-14-74. Sr. Julio Gómez Sáenz, gerente. 25 cuartos.

PLAYA AZUL

Hotel Delfin
V. Carranza s/n, tel: 6-0007. 25 cuartos.

URUAPAN

M. De Cupatitzio
Parque Nacional s/n, tel: 3-2060. 76 cuartos.

Hotel Pie De La Sierra
Km. 4 Carretera Uruapan-Carapan, Apartado Postal 153, tel: 2-15-10. Sr. Eduardo Ceballos, gerente. 43 cuartos.

Hotel Victoria
Cupatitzio No. 11, tel: 2-15-00 con 3 líneas. Uruapan. Mich., Ing. Héctor Amaro Salazar, gerente.

ESTADO DE MORELOS

COCOYOC

Hotel Hacienda Cocoyoc
Apartado Postal 300, tel: 2-0-00. Sr. Carlos Limón, gerente general. 204 cuartos.

CUAUTLA

Hotel Cuautla
B. 19 de Febrero 114, tel: 2-7233. 76 cuartos.

CUERNAVACA

Hotel El Presidente
Narbo 58, tel: 13-3968. 99 cuartos.

Hotel Casino De la Selva
Leandro Valle No. 1001, tel: 2-47-00. Sra. Lilia Suárez, gerente. 300 cuartos.

Hotel Las Mananitas
Ricardo Linares No. 107. Tel 2-46-46. Sr Rubén Cerda. gerente. 15 cuartos.

SAN JOSE DE VISTA

HERMOSA

Hotel Hacienda Vista Hermosa
Apartado Postal 127, tel: LD300 en Jojutla, Morelos. Sr. Leopoldo Olivares, gerente. 100 cuartos.

TEQUESQUITENGO

Paraiso Ski Club Y Hotel
Lago de Tequesquitengo, Morelos, tel: (LA734) 2-01-10. Sr. Francisco García G., gerente. 37 cuartos.

ESTADO DE NAYARIT

TEPIC

Hotel Fray Junipero Serra
Av. Mexico y Lerdo de Tejada, tel: 2-25-25. Sr. Marco Antonio Escobedo, gerente. 85 cuartos.

ESTADO DE NUEVO LEON

MONTERREY

Hotel Colonial
Hidalgo Ote. 475, tel: 43-6791. 67 cuartos.

Monterrey Plaza Holiday Inn
Av. Constitucion 300 Ote., tel: 44-6000. 390 cuartos.

Hotel Ambassador
Hidalgo y Galeana. Apartado Postal 1733, tel: 42-20-40, telex: 038-875. Sr. Luis Canavati Fraige, director general. 256 cuartos.

Hotel Rio
Padre Mier 194 Pte., tel: 42-21-90. Ing. Agustin Zorrilla, gerente. 290 cuartos.

Gran Hotel Ancira
Plaza Hidalgo, tel: 43-20-60, 43-20-69, 43-17-70, telex: 038-872. Sr. Arturo Renán Carcaño, gerente general. 300 cuartos.

Hotel Jolet
Padre Mier y Garibaldi, Apartado Postal 10, tel: 40-55-00.

Hotel Chipinque
Meseta Chipinque. Garza García No. 295, tel: 78-11-00 y 78-12-04. Sr. Fernando Alpuche, gerente general.

ESTADO DE OAXACA

OAXACA

Calesa Real
Garcia Vigil 306, tel: 6-5544. 77 cuartos.

Hotel El Presidente
(Exconvento de Santa Catalina). 5 de Mayo No. 300, Apartado Postal 575, tel: 6-06-11. Sr. Luis Tarasco, gerente general. 91 cuartos.

Hotel Margarita
Calzada Madero No. 1254, Apartado Postal 25, tel: 6-40-85. 53 cuartos.

Hotel Mision De Los Angeles
Calzada Porfirio Díaz No. 102, tel: 6-15-00, telex: 18850. Sr. José Juan Fuentes R., gerente 140 cuartos.

Hotel Victoria
Carretera Panamericana Km. 545, Apartado Postal 248, tel: 6-26-33, telex: 018-824. Sr. Carlos Gutiérrez, gerente. 151 cuartos.

PUERTO ANGEL

Hotel Soraya
Domicilio Conocido, tel: 11. 31 cuartos.

Hotel Angel Del Mar
Domicilio Conocido (Playa Paraíso). Sr. Rubén Gomez, gerente. 42 cuartos.

PUERTO ESCONDIDO

Castel Bugambilia
Av. Benito Juárez, tel: 2-0133. 1100 cuartos.

Hotel Las Palmas
Alfonso Pérez Gasga, s/n, tels: 2-02-30 y 2-04-69. Sr. Guillermo Campos Barquera. Puerto Escondido, Oax.

Hotel Paraiso Escondido
Calle Union No. 10, tel: 44. Lic. Javier Ruiz, gerente. 25 cuartos.

Hotel Rancho El Pescador
Carretera salida a Acapulco, Apartado Postal 45, tel: 43. Sr. Enrique Ortega, gerente. 38 cuartos.

ESTADO DE PUEBLA

PUEBLA

Gran Hotel Del Alba
Hermanos Serdan 141, tel: 46-0555. 437 cuartos.

Hotel Colonial
Calle 4 Sur No. 105, tel: 42-49-50. Ing. Salvador Ortiz, gerente; Sr. Roberto Ramírez, Subgerente. 81 cuartos.

Hotel Meson Del Angel
Av. Hermanos Serdán No. 807, Apartado Postal 649, tel: 48-21-00, telex: 178-1287. Sr. Eduardo Lastra, director general. 122 cuartos.

TEHUACAN

Hotel Mexico
Maximino Avila Camacho No. 101, tel: 2-00-19. Sr. Felipe Bello, gerente. 90 cuartos.

ESTADO DE QUERETARO

JURICA

Hotel Jurica
Carretera a San Luis Potosi. Km. 219, Apartado Postal 338, Querétaro, Qro., tel: 2-10-81. Sr. Guillermo Rivera Sarti, gerente general. 200 habitaciones.

QUERETARO

Hotel Amberes
Corregidora Sur 188, tel: 286-04. 140 cuartos.

Casablanca
Constituyentes 69 Pte., tel: 620-67. 66 cuartos.

Hotel Impala
Zaragoza y Colón No. 1, tel: 2-25-70. Sr. Manuel Abascal, gerente. 108 cuartos.

Hotel Holiday Inn
Carretera Constitución y Pino Suárez, tel: 4-12-02. Sr. David Páez, gerente general. 175 cuartos.

SAN JUAN DEL RIO

La Mansion Galindo
Km. 5 Carr Amealco, tel: 200-50. 166 cuartos.

TEQUISQUIAPAN

Cortijo Querencia
Av. Juárez s/n, tel: 301-11. 65 cuartos.

Hotel Balneario "El Relox"
Morelos 8, tel: 30-066. Sr. Carlos Manuel Jiménez, gerente. 80 cuartos.

Hotel Las Delicias
5 de Mayo No. 15, tel: 301-80. Sra. Yolanda Moreno de Morales, gerente. 69 cuartos.

ESTADO DE QUINTANA ROO

CANCUN

Hotel Krystal
Zons Hotelera, tel: 3-1133. 250 cuartos.

Hotel Club Mediterranee
Zona Hotelera, tel: 4-2900. 306 cuartos.

Hotel Cancún Sheraton
Zona Hotelera, tel: 3-1988. 474 cuartos.

Hotel Aristos Cancún
Zona Hotelera, Apartado Postal 450, tel: 3-00-11 al 18. Sr. Antonio Alvarez, gerente. 229 cuartos.

Hotel Camino Real
Punta Cancún Apartado Postal 14, tel: 3-0100. Sr. Abelardo Vara, gerente. 251 cuartos.

Hotel Cancún Caribe
Tel: 3-0673 con 7 lineas, telex: HCCCME-07306. Warren R. Brogile, director general; Daniel Diamant, gerente. 205 cuartos. Oficinas en Mexico: Liverpool 123-F., tel: 533-1301/02 y 533-4111/12.

Hotel El Presidente Club De Golf Cancún Y Condominios Kin-Ha
Blvd. Cancún B (Zona Turistical), Apartado Postal 451, tel: 3-02-00 al 04. Sr. Luis Baena de la Torre, director general. 337 cuartos.

Hotel Playa Blanca
Apartado Postal 107, tel: 3-03-44. Sr. Ricardo Pérez A., gerente. 160 cuartos.

Villas Verano Beat
Sección Turistica, Apartado Postal 432, tel: 30-781 al 24. 56 suites.

COZUMEL

Hotel Sol Caribe
Zona Hotelera Sur, tel: 2-07-00. 220 cuartos.

Hotel Cabaras Del Caribe
Playa Santa Pilar, Apartado Postal No. 9, tel: 2-00-17. Sr. Pedro Armin Caamal. Reservaciones y Ventas. 60 cuartos.

Hotel Mayan Plaza
Playa Santa Pilar Apartado Postal 9, tel: 2-00-72, 2-0411. Sr. Pedro Armin Caamal. Reservaciones y Ventas. 94 cuartos y 14 suites.

Hotel El Cozumeleno
Playa Santa Pilar Apartado Postal 53, tel: 2-03-44. Lic. Joaquin Domínguiz, propietario; Sr. Raúl Arredondo, gerente. 84 cuartos.

Hotel El Presidente
Costa Residencial, tel: 2-03-22. Sr. José Maria Lecca, gerente general. 192 cuartos.

Hotel La Ceiba
Playa Paraiso, tel: 2-03-79, telex: 075-708. Sr. Francisco Morales, gerente. 42 cuaratos.

Hotel Mara
Playa San Juan, Apartado Postal 7, tel: 2-03-00, telex: 075-843. Lic. Maria Elena Borge, gerente. 50 cuartos.

ISLA MUJERES

Hotel El Presidente Caribe
Islote Yunque Pta. Nte., tel: 2-01-22. 101 cuartos.

Hotel Berny
Juárez y Abasolo, tel: 2-00-25, 41 cuartos.

Hotel Posada Del Mar
Playa Norte de Isla Mujeres, tel: 2-00-97. Lic. Carlos Azarcoya, gerente. 48 cuartos.

ESTADO DE SAN LUIS POTOSI

CIUDAD VALLES

San Fernando
Km 454, Carretera Mexico-Laredo, Apartado Postal 97, tel: 2-01-84. Sr. Rafael Aguirre, gerente. 61 cuartos.

Hotel Valles
Blvd. México-Laredo No. 36 Norte, tel: 2-00-50 y 2-00-22. Cd. Valles, S. L. P. Sr. Tomas Osuna Salinas, gerente.

SAN LUIS POTOSI

Hotel Panorama
Av. V. Carranza 315, Apartado Postal 659, tel: 2-17-77. Sr. José Antonio Cortés, gerente. 140 cuartos.

Motel Cactus
Carretera 57 Apartado Postal 393, tel: 2-17-77. Sr. Rogelio Aguirre, gerente. 106 cuartos.

MATEHUALA

Motel Las Palmas
Km. 617. Carretera Central, Apartado Postal No. 73, tel: 2-00-01 y 02. Sr. Jesús Trejo Marín, gerente. 94 cuartos.

ESTADO DE SINALOA

CULIACAN

Econhotel Executivo
Blvd. Madero y A. Obregón, tel: 3-93-00 con 15 líneas. Sr. Ramón Saucedo, gerente general. 240 cuartos.

LOS MOCHIS

Santa Anita
Leyva e Hidalgo, tel: 2-00-46. 133 cuartos.

Hotel Florida
I. Ramirez y G. Leyva, Apartado Postal 103, Los Mochis, Sin., tel: 2-03-58. Lic. Alfredo Avilés Aguerrebere, gerente general. 50 cuartos y 16 suites.

MAZATLAN

Hotel Camino Real
Runta del Sabalo. Apartado Postal 538, tel: 3-11-11, telex: 066-855. Sr. Alfredo González, gerente general. 170 cuartos.

Hotel El Cid
Av. Camarón Sábalo s/n, Apartado Postal 884, tel: 3-33-3, telex: 66874. Sr. Guillermo Bernal, gerente general. 120 cuartos.

Hotel Hacienda Mazatlán
Av. del Mar y Calle Flamigos, Apartado Postal 135, tel: 1-69-89, telex: 06688-80. Sr. Enrique Jimenez, gerente. 176 cuartos.

Holiday Inn Mazatlán
Camarón Sábalo No. 696, tel: 3-22-22 y 2-17-44. Sr. Miguel A. Díaz, gerente general. 206 cuartos.

Hotel Playa Del Rey
Calzada Camarón Sábalo No. 51, Apartado Postal 501, tel: 3-46-11, telex: 066873. Dr. Roberto Romero, director general. 166 cuartos y 50 condo apartamentos c/servicio de hotel.

Hotel Playa Mazatlán
Playa Las Gaviotas, Apartado Postal 207, tel: 3-44-55, telex: 066848. Sr. Mario López Milan, gerente general. 360 cuartos.

Hotel Las Arenas
Apartado Postal 309, tel: 2-00-00. Mazatlán, Sin. Sr. Jose Maria Hernández, director general. 60 cuartos.

Oceano Palace
Av. Camarón Sábalo s/n, Apartado Postal 411, tel: 3-06-66, Mazatlán, Sin. Gilberto del Toro, gerente general. 140 cuartos.

ESTADO DE SONORA

BAHIA DE KINO

Posada Santa Gema
Domicilio Conocido, tel: 4-55-76. 14 cuartos.

Hotel Posada Del Mar
Blvd. A. L. Rodríguez y Veracruz, Apartado Postal 314, Hermosillo, Son, tel: 4-41-93. Lic. Santiago Garcia de la Garza. Propietario. Sr. Raúl Gutiérrez Ramirez, gerente. 48 cuartos.

GUAYMAS

Club Mediterranee
Bahia San Carlos, tel: 6-00-70. 430 cuartos.

Hotel La Posada De San Carlos
Bahia de San Carlos, Apartado Postal 57, tel: 6-00-15. Sr. Juan Manuel Alcántara, gerente. 150 cuartos.

Hotel Playa De Cortés
Bahia Bacochibampo, tel: 2-01-21. Sr. Ernesto Aguitar, gerente. 150 cuartos.

HERMOSILLO

Holiday Inn
Blvd. Kino 369, tel: 5-11-12. 218 cuartos.

Norotel Pitic
Blvd. Kino y Ramon Corral, tel: 4-45-70. 144 cuartos.

M. Calinda
Rosales y Morelia, Apartado Postal 619, tel: 3-89-60 y 3-28-25. Lic. Fernando Gándara, gerente. 120 cuartos.

Hotel Kino, S. A.
Pino Suárez 151 Sur., Apartado Postal 113, tel: 2-45-99. Sr. Armando Bernard, gerente. 90 cuartos y 12 apartamentos c/cocina.

Hotel San Alberto
Serdán y Rosales, Apartado Postal 181, tel: 2-18-00. Sr. Diego Redo, gerente. 126 cuartos.

NAVAJOA

Motel Del Rio
North entrance to city. Postal address Box 228, Navajoa, tel: 2-03-31. Lic. Serigio Zaragossa. 75 cuartos. Hunting and fishing information.

ESTADO DE TABASCO

VILLAHERMOSA

Exelaris Hyatt
Av. Juárez 106, tel: 3-44-44. 211 cuartos.

Hotel Manzur
Madero 422, tel: 2-24-99. C.P. Adalberto T. Manzur, gerente general. 116 cuartos.

Hotel Maya Tabasco
Av. Grijalva 907, Villa Hermosa, Tab, tel: 2-11-11. 140 cuartos.

Hotel Villa Hermosa Viva
Paseo Tabasco 1201, tel: 2-55-55. Sr. Lic. José Luis Arriaga, gerente general. 260 cuartos.

ESTADO DE TAMAULIPAS

MATAMOROS

Hotel El Presidente
Alvaro Obregón 249, tel: 2-92-40.
120 cuartos.

Holiday Inn
Av. Alvaro Obregón 249, Apartado Postal
1101, tel: 2-36-00 y 2-43-50. Sr. José Luis
Mojica García, gerente. 120 cuartos.

TAMPICO

Hotel Camino Real
Av. Hidalgo No. 2000, Apartado Postal 453,
tel: 3-88-11, telex: 014886. Sr. Fernando G.
Rosette, gerente general. 100 cuartos.

Hotel Posada De Tampico
Carretera Nacional Km 22, Col. Loma del
Chairel Apartado Postal C-71, tel: 3-30-50,
telex: POSAME 014704. 130 cuartos.

Hotel Inglaterra
Díaz Mirón No. 116, Oriente, Apartado
Postal 26, tel: 2-56-78 y 2-44-70. Sr.
Gilberto Sámano, gerente. 126 cuartos.

NUEVO LAREDO

Hacienda Motor Hotel
Operado por Provincial de Hoteles, S. A.
Reforma No. 5530, tel: 4-46-66. Sr. Juan
Manuel Vasconcelos, gerente general.

ESTADO DE VERACRUZ

FORTIN DE LAS FLORES

Hotel Ruiz Galindo
Calle 7 No. 210, tel: 3-00-55, Fortin de las
Flores, Ver. 153 cuartos.

VERACRUZ

Puerto Bello
Blvd. Avila Camacho 1263, tel: 31-00-11.
110 cuartos.

Hotel Emporio
Paseo del Malecon Esq. Xicoténcatl, tel: 32-
00-20. Sr. Jorge A. Alvarez, gerente general.
207 cuartos.

ESTADO DE YUCATAN

CHICHEN-ITZA

Hotel Mayaland
Chichén Itzá, tel: 1-91-12. Sr. Fernando
Barbachano. director general. 60 cuartos.

Hotel Mision Chichén Itzá
Pisté, Yucatán, tel: 04. Sr. Ignacio Echauri,
gerente residente. 42 cuartos.

MERIDA

Casa Del Balam
Calle 60 No. 868x67, tel: 21-94-64.
54 cuartos.

Hacienda Inn
Av. Aviacion 709, tel: 21-16-80. 68 cuartos.

Holiday Inn
Paseo Montejo y Av. Colon, tel: 25-68-67.
213 cuartos.

Hotel Autel
Calle 59. No. 546, tel: 24-21-00. Sr. Jorge
Torre, gerente general. 71 cuartos.

Hotel El Castellano
Calle 57 No. 513, tel: 3-01-00. Sr. Francisco
J. Gancedo S., gerente. 170 cuartos.

Hotel Maria Del Carmen
Calle 63 No. 550, Apartado Postal 411, tel:
23-91-33, telex: 075-843. Srita. Teresa
Borge, gerente. 100 cuartos.

Hotel Mérida Mision
Calle 60 No. 491, tel: 23-95-00, telex:
075836. Sr. Guillermo Bolaños Cacho. 150
cuartos.

Hotel Montejo Palace
Paseo de Montejo No. 483, Apartado Postal
961, tel: 24-76-14, telex: 075872. Sr. José
Luis Guasch, director deneral. 90 cuartos.

Hotel Paseo De Montejo
Paseo de Montejo No. 482, Apartado Postal
961, tel: 3-90-33, telex 075872. Sr. José Luis
Guasch, director general. 92 cuartos.

UXMAL

Hotel Mision Uxmal
Carretera a Campeche, Uxmal, Yuc., tel: 02.
Sr. Jesús Morcillo, gerente residente. 50
cuartos.

ESTADO DE ZACATECAS

ZACATECAS

Hotel Aristos
Lomas de la Soledad s/n, tel: 2-17-88. Sr.
Isaac Pérez, gerente general. 102 cuartos.

FOOD DIGEST

WHAT TO EAT

As the following essay makes clear, eating
can be one of the greatest delights Mexico
offers to the foreign traveler. It can also
become a tiresome necessity when the traveler is short of cash or desperate for a familiar meal. Mexico's eating establishments
range from the extremely elegant to the very
humble. How to choose among the latter,
how to find a satisfying meal at a small
price?

Restaurants that would be in English be
called coffee shops, snack bars or cafes will
in Mexico be labelled *cafe, fonda,
merendero, comedor* or *loncheria.* The loncheria may specialize in sandwiches, *tortas.*
In any of these, the food will be inexpensive;
in some, it will be very good indeed; in some,
it will be contaminated. The safest course is
to look carefully before ordering. If no effort
is being made to keep the counter clean or the
flies away from the food, chances are good
that the customer will ingest unwanted bacteria with the meal. Some travelers avoid
eating in the marketplace, arguing that a
regular restaurant is safer. However, the
fondas in the market have the advantage that
you can see the kitchen and the food before

committing yourself. In these stalls, there is
likely to be no menu; simply ask, *"Que
hay?"* – "What is there?"

In these modest establishments you will
have to order in Spanish. The most important
phrases are listed in our essay on "Language"; keep a dictionary handy for guess-
ing at the nature of the foods available.

What to do if you find most Mexican food
far too hot? If it's already in your mouth,
reach for the bread, not the water. Beer also
helps. If you are ordering a meal, the key
word is *picante* – spicy – not *caliente*, which
means hot only in temperature.

Many a traveler who is adventurous at the
midday and evening meals wants only the
familiar for breakfast. For such travelers, we
offer the following translations of breakfast
staples, with the warning that you should
still expect the unexpected.

eggs	*huevos*
omelet	*tortilla de huevos*
scrambled eggs	*huevos revueltos*
fried eggs	*huevos estrellados*
boiled eggs	*huevos tibios*
bacon	*tocino*
ham	*jamon*
oatmeal	*avena*
toast	*pan tostado*
plain bread, not toasted	*pan Bimbo*
buns	*bolillos*
butter	*mantequilla*

MEXICAN FOOD

Mexicans believe their cuisine is number
three in the world – surpassed only by
French and Chinese foods. They make the
claim quietly; they are not given to bragga-
docio about things Mexican. But *de veras*,
indeed, Mexican cooking is amazingly rich
and varied, a great blend and with a distinct
personality.

Like so many other things in Mexico,
Mexican food is the result of centuries of
encounters and blendings of cultures and
peoples. The most important of these meetings came when, for the first time, the Indians and the Spaniards looked upon each
other's food – and were revolted. In time,
however, they came to like each other's
cooking and began to experiment in mixing
one with the other. Thus Mexican cuisine
evolved: Indian food enriched with many

things from Europe. Each people made its contribution: the Indians brought to the Mexican table exotic, tropical fruits and herbs, hot chili, cacao, avocados, and that tasty bird the Americans claim as their exclusive property – the turkey. Plus the two essential staples: corn and beans, the soul of Mexican food. The Spanish brought meat and poultry, cheese and wheat, oil and wine. They contributed a style of cooking which was solid and substantial Mediterranean, not nearly as subtle as French cooking or Italian cooking, or even Turkish cooking, but certainly meant to appease the appetite. They were great feeders, the old-time Spaniards.

Africa sent along the blessing of coffee. Spices and that sensual fruit, the mango, came aboard ships from China and the Philippines. (In colloquial Mexican-Spanish, a mango describes satisfactorily in a single word the charms of a pretty girl. That's the high regard in which Mexicans and all discriminating folk hold that marvelous fruit.)

So the great blend that turned out to be Mexican cuisine is better than either Indian or Spanish food, though it may not be as healthful nor organic as the mainly vegetarian diet of the Indians nor as devastatingly nutritious as the food from Spain. Ah, yes, Mexican food is horribly fattening and has a strong personality, but at its most exquisite it has great refinement and subtlety.

THE LOWLY TACO AND THE PRINCELY MODE

To understand Mexican cuisine you must take into account two basic divisions – geographical and social. Begin with social. Obviously, the wealthy and completely spoiled *hacendados* with their armies of servants did not eat the same food their peons ate. The poor man's tacos and *pozole* are a world apart from the princely *mole* (see p. 146). Princely? Indeed. A good mole takes all of the patience and energy and ingenuity of all the women in the household for two days. Mole is basically turkey or chicken covered with sauce, but as Rostrand said of his hero, Cyrano de Bergerac, "He made a gesture, but what a gesture!" What a sauce!

Unfortunately, the most elementary type of Mexican cooking is the one that travels best and, sad to say, the so-called Mexican restaurants in the U.S. serve food that would embarrass any good *cocinera*, or woman cook. It's also true that it's not easy to find good Mexican cooking even in Mexico. You have to be lucky, if you're a visitor. Or get yourself a good guide. Only a few places, such as Fonda del Refugio, San Angel Inn or Las Delicas in Mexico City offer the good old dishes – *manchamantel*, a pork dish (the word means "tablecloth stainer", because the bright red sauce which goes with the dish makes a flaming mark on the tablecloth), *pepian* (sesame paste), *romeritos*, spinach-like vegetable or *sopa de lima*, a fruit soup. Yes you can find delights in the provinces as well, but you need a guide.

The prestige of Mexican haute cuisine is based naturally on sophisticated recipes, but that does not mean that plain cooking cannot be tasty and even enthralling. Just as simple cooking everywhere – fresh food, simply prepared – is delicious. Say, a good taco made with a hot, small, white and soft *tortilla*. Beans are good, no matter how you prepare them, from the simple boiled *frijoles de la olla* to the multi-fried and spiced *frijoles refritos* (refried), which is the traditional final dish before dessert and coffee in any Mexican meal worth its chili.

To speak of regional cooking in Mexico you must make this basic division: the North, the Central Highlands, Mexico City, Puebla and Michoacán, the Gulf Coast, Oaxaca and the Southeast, and Yucatán.

That brings up Tex-Mex and Cal-Mex cooking and let us dispose of it instantly. This is a cooking that has emerged as a result

of contact between Mexico and the U.S. It includes Texas chili con carne, the "red ink" which Texas are world authorities on and which apparently most Texans ingest with their mother's milk. The Mexican with subtle taste buds finds such old recipes of the American Southwest somewhat primitive and is amazed at how Americans sometimes interpret Mexican dishes.

Let us hasten to say, however, that some American dishes have been introduced with great enthusiasm into the Mexican home. Of course, the food is mexicanized: the hot dog, enriched with onion, tomato, cream and *chiles jalapeños*; and a New York-cut steak, but with a side of frijoles refritos. Hang the calories.

SWEATING SOUP AND BABY GOAT

Let us speak of Mexican regional cooking. Start at the top, with the north. This is the poorest region for cooking. It is pioneers' cooking, nutritious, but simple and un-spiced. Its main assets are *tortillas de harina* (flour tortillas), grilled meat, black coffee and beer. (Beer is just the right drink with Mexican food. Few wines can do the job.) But even the sparse northern cooking offers such delicacies as *caldo sudador* (sweating soup) from Sinaloa and Sonora, which is a solid shrimp soup, abalone, turtle soup, and in Chihuahua the great cheese soup, practically a Swiss fondue, to be eaten with clean-tasting flour tortillas.

Monterrey, the booming city of the north, offers a specialty, *cabrito* (baby goat), grilled and greasy but, oh, so tasty, which you wash down with another local institution, cold Carta Blanca beer.

In the Highlands you can choose dishes that range from Indian subtle to Spanish vigor. Highlands cooking includes many varieties of traditional dishes, such as po-zole, tamales and enchiladas, also chicken cooked many different ways, regional sweets, and fruits, from standard papaya and guava to juicy cactus fruits such as *tunas* and *pitayas*. Mexicans like to eat fruit with a bit of lemon – not the tame lemon of the U.S., but the stronger and more acidy Mexican *limón*. Mexicana also favor the avocado in their cooking.

Mexican meals differ from American-style meals, naturally. Breakfast may be the same – orange juice, eggs, coffee. But would an American early in the morning eat *menudo* (*tripe á la mode de Cuernavaca*), *chilaquiles* (hot shredded tortillas with heavy cream), or *carne ranchera* (hot beef 'n' beans), chocolate and sweet rolls?

COMIDA Y CENA

The Mexican midday meal, *la comida*, is a much more serious affair than the light American lunch. (Serious is an important world in Spanish and often it is applied to food by serious eaters). The Mexican lunch-eon is a caloric disaster but an exquisite taste treat: tequila with *sangrita* apéritif, some *botanas* (snacks), *sopa aguada* (thin soup), *sopa seca* (dry pasta soup), meat or chicken (two or three variations), beans, dessert and *cafecito*. The gourmand may add a dollop or two of French cognac to the demitasse to give it authority.

The comida is accompanied either by beer or *aguas frescas*, fruit waters. The most popular are flavored with jamaica, lemon, tamarind or *chia* seeds. Mexicans never drink coffee with the comida. Both tortillas and French-style bread are served with each dish because each dish demands its own company, and while eating informally Mexicans like to make tacos with all the dishes spread out in front of them.

The third major meal of the day (in the old days there was also a mid-morning and a mid-afternoon snack, just to keep up a person's strength) is the *cena*, which is served anytime between 7:30 p.m. and mid-night. It can be Chapter II of the comida, complete with apéritif and dessert. But usu-ally Mexicans prefer something a big lighter – a cup of chocolate with a sweetroll, or a glass of milk with sweetened squash, or maybe just a plate of beans or something left over from the comida. There is a Mexican proverb that deals with the situation (indeed there is a Mexican proverb to cover nearly *all* situation); "Breakfast like a king, lunch like a prince, and dine like a pauper." It makes gustatory sense.

The Highlands offer some remarkable dishes. That includes, of course, the cuisine of Mexico City. As heirs to Aztec cooking, the cooks in Mexico City utilize everything edible, including maguey worms which are eaten dead or alive, blanketed in a hot sauce and tucked into a taco. How does it taste? Not bad. Those *Gusanos de Maguey* are as crunchy as a snap-crackle-pop American cereals.

MEXICO CITY FAVORITES AND PUEBLA'S MOLE POBLANO

Think of *huitlacoche* when you think of exotic Mexico City dishes. It is a fungus which grows on corn – tacos and crepes are made with it. Huitlacoche is a distant relative of an Aztec dish. In days of yore the formidable Aztecs, who were bound to a tiny island in a lake, had to eat anything they could find. Another Mexico City favorite is a soup made of *flor de calabaza* (squash blossoms). Capitalinos also like to use *epazote*, a parsley-like, but stronger herb which housewives use to flavor everything from soup to beans.

Among the great dishes of Mexico City are the following: *Caldo Tlapeño*, a most respectable soup, prepared with pasilla chili, chicken and avocado; *romeritos*, akin to spinach, served during Christmas with dry shrimp and sauce; and *memelas*, baroque *tortas* (sandwich) that are served with cream, mustard, chili peppers, tomato, onion, avocado, meat, chicken or sardines.

Puebla is the home of the *mole poblano*, the queen mother of Mexican recipes. The dish was invented by a colonial nun whose convent wanted to impress a visiting bishop, who apparently was a serious (that word again) *gastrónomo*. Her recipe contains variations upon spices and chili peppers and Mexican cooking chocolate. It is Mexico's celebration dish. Other regions may offer a mole, but Puebla's is unique.

Similar to mole, but milder, is *pepián*, which is lighter in color and less a chore to digest. Both mole and pepián are eaten with plenty of tortillas and, if possible, washed down with a rich, dark beer.

From Puebla, too, comes an Indian delicacy known only to discriminating feeders – *mixiotes*, a sort of barbecue, wrapped in maguey leaves and cooked in earthen ovens.

Jalisco and Michoacan boast important regional cooking. Nayarit has splendid seafood. Jalisco is famous for its *pozole*, one of Mexico's oldest dishes. It is a soup – struggling to become a stew – and is made with pork and hominy corn, garnished with onion, lettuce, radish, oregano, and chili sauce with a few subtle drops of lemon.

From Michoacán come *corundas* and *huchepos*, the local tamales, and the white fish from Patzcuaro, which has acquired national fame.

FROM COASTAL VERACRUZ: SEAFOOD AND MACHO BANANAS

The Gulf coast – mainly Veracruz – offers a rich menu. The seafood is great – better than that of the Pacific. Beautiful Veracruz, as the Veracruz people say. Nothing like it anywhere. They are the Gascons of Mexico. Veracruz cuisine is superb, with strong Spanish influence. They make use of the produce of the neighborhood – such as the giant tropical *macho* banana, which they eat fried. The best known dish is the *huachinango a la Veracruzana* (red snapper, Veracruz style), a classic with tomato sauce, olives, and capers. Veracruz boasts the most delicious fruit in Mexico: great pineapple, aromatic mangoes. At one time a restaurant in Veracruz served only meals prepared with fruit.

An odd feature to Veracruz cooking is black beans, refried several times. They are used in combo with magnificent tamales, made with macho bananas and stuffed with beans.

Seafood? Well, fish in Mexico is not popular generally speaking, and Highlanders seem to have an ingrained dislike for it, which is absurd in a country with such a tremendous coastline. On the other hand, shrimp and oysters are revered. Mexican *marisquerías* (seafood restaurants) seem to be full all the time. Alas, Mexicans, too, seem to have been taken in by the story of the aphrodisiac quality of those fruit of the sea, oysters, shrimp, octopus, eels, abalone and crab. Unfortunately, Mexicans like to joke, 1982 oysters are not as "potent" as those of 20 years ago.

Oaxaca, whose cooking experience goes back to pre-Columbian times, has a remarkable cuisine. Its famous dish is *mole negro*, an even more substantial variety than the Puebla mole. Oaxaca tamales, wrapped in banana leaves, are bigger and more elaborate than the Highland variety. (By the way, the proper way to eat tamales is with *atole*, a corn gruel sweetened with chocolate or strawberries). The marketplace in Oaxaca is one of the treasures of the land, but you've got to know your way around.

Many Mexicans associate Oaxaca with cheese. It's an essential ingredient in the *quesadilla*, a taco made of melted cheese, to which anything out of the cook's imagination can be added: avocado, beans, potatoes.

CURIOUS YUCATECAN CUISINE

Yucatán cooking has inspiration that goes back through the centuries to the Maya. Oddly, in comparatively recent times another element has been added to the old mix: Lebanese cooking. It came from Lebanese immigrants. Curiously, some of the best restaurants in Mérida offer both Yucateco and Lebanese dishes.

Yucatán cooking claims such outstanding dishes as *cochinita pibil*, a spiced pork dish, and *papadzules*, stuffed tortillas. There is a magnificent soup made with *limas*, that most subtle of Mexican fruits. Beer aficionados rate Yucatán beer as the best in the country – both the light Montejo, and the dark and rich Leon Negro.

Another Yucateco-International dish is *queso relleno*, or stuffed Dutch cheese (the red ball kind). It is somewhat akin to minced meat but with a full Maya flavor.

Venison is another Yucatán delicacy, but it's scarce and expensive. Among other exotic dishes eaten in Mexico are baby shark, lizard, and dog. The latter is the almost extinct Mexican hairless, called the *itzcuintli* (Chihuahua). It once served as the *pièce de résistance* at many a pre-Columbian royal banquet.

We have spoken of some of the exotic, and, naturally, expensive dishes that are adventures in eating. But how about the ordinary household? Somehow the Mexican housewife with her modest income often performs a miracle. She transforms pizza, spaghetti, omelettes or chicken soup into something unmistakably *mexicano*. It's the little bit of tomato, chili pepper, or avocado that makes the difference.

For Mexicans, cooking is a bond to its ancient culture. That is why in the great eating places of New York, of Paris, of Rome, the Mexican businessman has been known to carry on his person a small envelope. In it is a little chili pepper, which he may sprinkle unobtrusively into his food, "so that the meal will taste like something."

DRINKING NOTES

Mexicans tend to drink copiously at fiestas and in times of great calamity or great good fortune. Otherwise, they are a relatively sober folk. Beer is very popular as an accompaniment to the heavy *comida* in mid-afternoon, and you would be well advised to adopt this custom. It compliments Mexican flavors and helps take the bite out of chili peppers. Mexican beers are excellent, as good as any in the world. Try drinking canned beer in local fashion: squeeze lemon and sprinkle salt on the lid of the can.

Wine is rarely drunk, although there are vineyards in some areas of Mexico. Some Mexican wines are good and others are not, but all tend to be rather expensive. Imported wines, especially French wines, are quite expensive in Mexico.

Unless you go to bars that cater to foreigners, you may not be able to get your favorite cocktails prepared with the usual brands of liquors. Rather than frustrate yourself trying to obtain the familiar, why not turn to Mexico's deservedly famous liquor, tequila? (For insight into proper tequila-drinking methods, turn to page 161.)

Besides beer and tequila, the drinks popular with middle-class and upper-middle-class Mexicans are *Cubas* (or *Cuba libres*) and "highballs," both made with Coke and rum. Poor people are more likely to drink grain alcohol made from sugar cane, often mixed with soft drinks.

You may also want to try some of the more esoteric Mexican beverages. There are other liquors, besides tequila, made from varieties of the maguey plant; the genetic term is *mezcal*. The most traditional of Mexican drinks is *pulque*. For better or worse, you will probably not have a chance to try it. Made from a type of maguey, pulque is not distilled as are tequila and other mezcals. It must be drunk when freshly fermented, for it cannot be canned or bottled without being ruined. It is highly nutritious (unless diluted with contaminated water) and only mildly alcoholic – about the same as beer. In pre-Columbian Mexico, pulque was reserved for use in ritual and healing. It is still highly valued by Mexicans, although not expensive, and its popularity is why you will have trouble trying to get hold of some.

The other reason is that strangers are not generally welcome in *pulguerias*, the special bars where pulque is drunk. Make friends with a Mexican man and ask him to introduce you; if you're lucky, he may invite you home to drink some special brew. Women, unfortunately, are virtually never allowed in pulquerias.

The *cantina* likewise does not welcome women. In fact, it is sometimes said that you can distinguish a real *cantina* from a bar that calls itself a *cantina* by observing whether women are admitted.

A wide variety of non-alcoholic beverages is available in Mexico. Soft drinks, as a group, are called *refrescos*. You will see familiar and unfamiliar brands. If you want to avoid taking any risks with water but dislike soft drinks, order mineral water (*agua mineral*, often listed on menus by the brand name *Agua de Tehuacan*). Even if you are not a great drinker of soft drinks you might like to try some of the Mexican ones. *Sidral*, which is apple-flavored and *sangria*, a mixed-fruit drink, are both interesting.

Fruit juices, whether ordered in restaurants, in markets or from street vendors, are often freshly squeezed for you. *Jugo* is the word for juice. *Agua fresca* is a fruit juice mixed with a lot of water. It is much cheaper but more risky. *Liquados* are fruit milkshakes, often with eggs added. Order a *coco*, coconut, from a street vendor.

When you are in the mood for authenticity, try *atole* – cornmeal mixed with water and sugar – or *horchata*, made from ground rice or melon seeds and water. Another pre-Columbian drink is chocolate. Try it instead of coffee one morning. If you stick with coffee, you will find that Nescafe (instant) is most often served. Coffee which is brewed comes under the name of *café de olla*. *Café con leche* is mostly milk with a little coffee in it. You may have trouble getting coffee with milk served separately, except in tourist areas.

Culture Plus

CINEMAS

The Mexican film industry has been one of the world's most prolific, and Mexico has provided sites for the filming of innumerable Hollywood Westerns (the Durango area has rather specialized in this).

Not many Mexican films have attained international prominence. Perhaps the most admired by cinema buffs are Luis Buñuel's *Los Olvidados* and *Nazarin*, and Sergei Eisenstein's *Que Viva Mexico* – a classic film focusing on the visual beauty of life in Mexican Indian villages. Other fine films such as *María Candelaria* and *Animas Trujano* have followed Eisenstein's lead in their Indian settings.

A group of vintage Mexican films is now experiencing a nostalgic revival in Mexico – pictures such as *Alla en el Rancho Grande*, *Los Tres García*, *Historia de un Gran Amor* and others, featuring stars such as Jorge

Negrete, Pedro Infante, Pedro Armendariz, Joaquin Pardave, Fernando Soler, María Feliz, Marga López and the enduring Dolores del Rio.

Cantínflas, Mexico's best-known comedian, has many movies to his credit. Cinema experts would perhaps prefer the films that feature the bizarre character *Tin-Tan*, who popularized *pachucos*, those snazzy zoot-suiters of yesterday.

SHOPPING

WHAT TO BUY

Few travelers can resist shopping in Mexico. Indeed, for some shopping may even be the primary purpose of their visit. The range of prices is nearly as wide as the range of craft items available, so take your time and choose wisely.

Serious shoppers should plan to travel extensively in the countryside, because everything is cheaper in the areas where it's made. You may also be lucky enough to be able to watch and photograph the *artesano* at work. We list below a number of craft items, with some of the towns that produce them.

For those whose travels are limited to one or more cities, the range of possible purchases is still quite wide. Items from all over Mexico can be bought at the large markets, especially San Juan de Dios in Guadalajara.

Prices are well above those paid the artisan at the source, but you can bargain the prices down – even where there are signs saying *precios fijos* (fixed prices). Simply ask for a "discount". You'll have to exercise your Spanish, especially your numbers. Begin by asking "*Cuanto vale?*" (How much?) You're under no obligation to bargain if the asking price is ridiculously low! If it's not, make an offer. Half the asking price is the usual offer in a tourist area; perhaps two-thirds the asking price in other cases. Take your time and work down to a mutu-ally-agreeable figure. **Warning**: Once the vendor has come down substantially to meet your price, do not change your mind and walk away! That is poor form.

Handicrafts from all over the country are also available at government-run stores in many cities (see the list in this section). These are not particularly inexpensive stores, and prices are generally not negotiable, but quality is high. The same is true of many shops and boutiques in stylish areas of town, such as Mexico City's Zona Rosa.

As elsewhere, *caveat emptor*. Some specific things to consider: Buy jewelry from a reputable store, never from a street vendor. As a general principle, buy jewelry because you like the design, not because of its silver content. Iron items may be sprayed with paint to imitate copperware. Hand-made clothing may shrink, so buy a larger size if you're in any doubt. Wash such items gently, in cold water. Cotton (*algodon*) will be pure cotton, but wool (*lana*) will often be a blend of fibers. Machine-made embroidery can be beautiful, but not after you've paid a hand-made price for it, so check first by looking at the reverse side. Hammocks should be pure cotton, of thin thread, and tightly woven. Bees-wax on the thread will make it mildew-resistant. Mexico's beautiful green-glazed pottery cannot be trusted to be lead-free, so use it for decoration or for dry items, not for wet or acidic foods.

Other things to note: Pottery can break, and bulky items like furniture or basketry can be tiresome to travel with. Most large stores will pack your purchases carefully and mail them to your home, for a reasonable charge. U.S. travelers should be aware that items mailed will not be counted as part of your three hundred dollars' worth of duty-exempt purchases. Of course, this is not a problem if the items are on the G.S.P. list (see the section on "Customs").

If you are shopping for gifts, you can have these mailed directly to the recipient in the U.S. They will not be counted as part of your duty-exempt purchases. Write GIFT on the outside of the package, and indicate the retail value of the contents. You cannot send perfume, tobacco or alcohol. There is a limit: No one recipient can receive more than ten dollars' worth in one day.

Don't pay high prices for genuine pre-Columbian artifacts. Most will be fakes, though perhaps very well made. Some people make very fine ceramic figures using original types of clay and authentic firing procedures. Should the artifact be genuine indeed, you will not be permitted to take it out of Mexico (nor to import it into many other countries, including the U.S.).

SHOPPING AREAS

Ceramics:

Tlaquepaque, Jalisco	a variety of pottery, including replicas of pre-Columbian pieces.
Tonalá, Jalisco	new innovations as well a traditional styles
Puebla, Puebla	household crockery, tiles, and Talavera ceramics
Acatlán and Izucar de Matamoros, Puebla; and Metepec, Mexico	"tree of life" ceramics
Guanajuato and San Miguel de Allende, Guanajuato	a variety of pottery styles
Tzintzuntzan, and San Miguel de Allende, Guanajuato	burnished ceramics
Patamban, Michocán	green-glazed pottery
Guerrero state	a variety of traditional ceramics
San Bartolo Coyotepec, Oaxaca	burnished black pottery
Santa María Atzompa, Oaxaca	ceramic animals
Amatenango, Chiapas	traditional pottery fired without kilns

Woodworking and Lacquerware:

Bahía de Kino Sonora	Seri Indians' ironwood animals
Uruapan, Michoacán	masks, lacquerware
Quiroga, Michoacán	painted wooden bowls, household items
Ixtapán de la Sal, Mexico	household items and carved animals
Cuernavaca, Morelos	colonial-style furniture, wooden bowls
Olinalá, Guerrero	jaguar masks, gourd bowls, wooden trays, fine lacquerware
Ixmiquilpan, Hidalgo	bird cages
Tequisquiapán, Querétaro	knockdown wooden stools
Cuilampan, Oaxaca	painted wooden animals
Chiapa de Corzo, Chiapas	masks and other lacquerware
Mérida, Yucatán; Valladolid, Tabasco; and Campeche	mahogany and cedar furniture
Paracho, Michoacán	guitars
San Juan Chamula, Chiapas	guitars and harps

Basketry and Fiber Items:

Tequisquiapán, Queretaro	basketry
Lerma, Mexico	basketry
Xalitla, Tolima and San Agusti de las Flores, Guerrer	Huapanec Indians' bark paintings

San Miguel de Allende and Guanajuato, Guanajuato; Puebla, Puebla; and Otomi Indian villages in the Mezquital valley, Hidalgo	cane and reed containers
San Miguel de Allende	paper and papier mache – pinatas and masks
Veracruz coastal area	palm-leaf mats and other items
Ihuatzio, Michoacán	reed mats and basketry
Mixtec area of Oaxaca	net carrying bags
Puebla, Veracruz and San Luis Potosi	Huastecan Indian cactus fiber bags and wool items
Mérida, Yucatán	hammocks
Bekal, Campeche	Panama hats

Woven Wool:

Tlaxcala; Cuernavaca and Huejapan, Morelos; Tequisquiapan, Queretaro; San Miguel de Allende, Guanajuato; Teotitlan del Valle, near Oaxaca City; Saltillo, Coahuila; and Zacatecas	sarapes
Otomi Indians of Mezquital Valley, Hildago; Tarahumara Indians of the Barranca del Cobre, Chihuahua; Cora and Huichol Indians of Tepic, Nayarit; Tzotzil Indians of San Juan Chamula, Chiapas	handwoven belts and clothing

Embroidered Clothing:

Amuzgo Indians near Ometepec, Guerrero, and in Oaxaca	cotton *huipiles* (women's blouses)
Yalalag, Oaxaca	Indian blouses and wrap around skirts, made with natural dyes
San Pablito Pahuatlán, Puebla	beaded blouses
Cuetzalan, Puebla	embroidered blouses
San Luis Potosi	silk *rebozos* (shawls)
Aguascalientes	clothing
Puebla, Veracruz and San Luis Potosi	Haustecan Indian's *quechquemetl*, a cross-stitch decorated women's cloak

Jewelry:

Mexico City	modern jewelry
Taxco, Guerrero; Toluca, Mexico; Yalalag, Oaxaca; Querétaro; Veracruz; Yucatán	silver jewelry
Veracruz	coral jewelry
Querétaro	semi-precious stones
Oaxaca, Oaxaca	replicas of gold jewelry found at Monte Alban

Other Items:

Santa Clara del Cobre (now called Villa Escalante), Michoacán	copperware
Tehuacan, Puebla	onyx
Toluca, Mexico	chess games and dominos

GOVERNMENT CRAFT STORES

In Mexico City:
FONART
Avenida Insurgentes Sur 1630

FONART
Londres 136 (Zona Rosa)

FONART
Londres 6 (Wax Museum)

FONART
Manuel E. Izaguirre 10, (Satelite)

Exposicion de Arte Popular
Av. Juárez # 89

Exposicion Turistico-Artesanal
Av. Juárez # 92

Museo Tienda del Arte Popular de Oaxaca
Av. Juárez # 70

Tiendas Exposicion Michoacan-Queretaro
Glorieta Metro-Insurgents, Locales 14 & 17

Decorart
Pino Suarez # 28

In Guadalajara:
FONART
Av. Juárez # 267-B, Tlaquepaque

Museo Regional de Ceramica
Av. Independencia # 237, Tlaquepaque

Casa de las Artesanias de Jalisco
Av. Alcalde # 1221, Guadalajara

In Other Cities:
FONART
Anillo Envolvente, Lincoln y Mejia, Ciuded
Juárez, Chihuahua

FONART
Constitucion e Iturbide 31, Matamoros,
Tamaulipas

FONART
Edificio la Estrella, Puerto Mexico, Piedras
Negras, Coahuila

FONART
Calle Salazar 1, Cuernavaca, Morelia

FONART
Efren M. Tavera 2, Cuaulta, Morelia

FONART
Manuel M. Bravo 116, Oaxaca, Oaxaca

FONART
Juárez y Zaragoza, Puerto Vallarta, Jalisco

FONART
Hernandez Macias 95, San Miguel de
Allende, Guanajuato

FONART
Alfaro 10, Jalapa, Veracruz

FONART
Agora de Fonapas, Calla 63, Mérida,
Yucatán

FONART
Museo de Arte Popular
Jardin Guerrero 6, San Luis Potosi, San Luis
Potosi

Museo de Arte Popular de Mérida
Calle, 59, # 151, Edificio de la Mejorada,
Mérida, Yucatán

Museo Regional de la Laca
Chiapa de Corzo, Chiapas

FONART
Ex-Convento Santa Rosa, Calle 3 Norte, #
1203, Puebla, Puebla

Casa de las Artesanías de Puebla
Calle 3 Norte, # 1203, Puebla, Puebla

Casa de las Artesanías de Guerrero
Altamirano # 29, Chilpancingo, Guerrero

Casa de las Artesanías de Hidalgo
Av. Juárez, Pachuca, Hidalgo

Casa de las Artesanías de Mexico
Paseo Tolloacan, Netzahualcoyotl, Toluca,
Mexico

FONART
Hernández Macía # 95, San Miguel de
Allende, Guanajuato

Casa de las Artesanías de Guanajuato
Constancia # 7, Guanajuato, Guanajuato

Museo de Arte Popular
Jardin Guerrero # 6, San Luis Potosí, San
Luis Potosí

FONART
Constitución e Iturbide, # 31, Matamoros,
Tamaulipas

Casa de las Artesanias de Cd. Victoria
Torre Gubernamental Cd. López Portillo,
9th floor, Cd. Victoria, Tamaulipas

FONART
Maclovio Herrera # 3030, entre Juárez y
Guerrero, Nuevo Laredo, Tamaulipas

Casa de las Artesanías de Nuevo Leon
Emilio Carranza Sur # 730-A, Monterrey,
Nuevo Leon

FONART
Edificio "La Estrella", Puerta Mexico,
Piedras Negras, Coahuila

Casa de las Artesanías de Zacatecas
Ortiz Mena # 405, Col. Diaz Ordaz, Zacatecas, Zacatecas

Museo Regional Huatapera
Domicilio Conocido, Uruapan, Michoacán

Museo de la Danza, la Mascara y las Culturas Populares
27 de Septiembre y Manuel Gallardo,
Colima, Colima

FONART
Anillo Envolvente, Lincoln y Mejia, Cd.
Juárez. Chihuahua

Museo de Arte Popular de Chihuahua
Reforma # 5, Chihuahua, Chihuahua

Museo Regional del Noroeste
Dr. Caliza # 16, Hermosillo, Sonora

Museo Regional del Arte Seri
Fraccionamiento Kino, Residencia Seri
Bahia de Kino, Sonora

FONART
Av. Revolucion # 1020-A, Tijuana, Baja
California Norte

FONART
Av. Lopez Mateos # 1306, Construcciones
Pronaf, Locales 15, 16 y 17, Ensenada, Baja
California Norte

SPORTS

FISHING

Fishing is permitted in Mexico's lakes, rivers and dams, and along its 5,000-odd miles of coastline. Annual fishing tournaments are based in La Paz, Guaymas, Mazatlán, Puerto Vallarta, Barra de Navidad, Manzanillo and Acapulco on the Pacific Coast; in Tampico, Veracruz and Cd. del Carmen on the Gulf of Mexico; and in Cancún and Cozumel on the Caribbean. Most tournaments are in May and June.

Fishing seasons and regulations vary from one area to another, and from one season to another, so you should write in advance for specific information before finalizing your plans. The government department to write to is the Departamento de Pesca, Oficina de Permisos de Pesca Deportiva, Avenida Alvaro Obregon # 269, Planta Baja, Mexico 7, D.F. Send a large stamped self-addressed envelope and they will send you (in English) information and regulations. If you are already in Mexico, their telephone number is 511-7264, ext. 142. There are also some 150 branch offices of the Departamento de Pesca.

One license will cover you for fresh-water or salt-water fishing anywhere in Mexico. Licenses are issued for periods of three days, one month, three months or one year. You can purchase a license at any Departamento de Pesca office, from any local fish or game warden, or from the Captain of any port or fishing facility.

You may import your fishing gear without any problem, except for harpoons or spearfishing equipment – these are illegal in Mexico.

Mexico abounds with game, but there are numerous restrictions on what you may hunt, on hunting zones and seasons, and on what you may export after you have killed it. Your home country will also have restriction on what you may bring in. Anyone serious about hunting in Mexico should begin planning their trip well in advance. Begin by writing to the Dirección General de la Fauna Silvestre, Aquiles Serdan # 28, 7th floor, Mexico 3, D.F. Send a large stamped self-addressed envelope, and request a hunting calendar and information on hunting regulations. You can also get information from the Mexican Consulate or National Council of Tourism office nearest you.

You may apply for a hunting license at the same time, from the Dirección General de la Fauna Silvestre. Include two passport-sized photographs of yourself. Specify in your letter where you want to hunt, what game you are seeking, and when you plan to come. The basic license fee varies according to whether you want to hunt in one or more states. There are special licenses that you have to get if you want to hunt certain species (fox, ocelot, panther, black bear, antelope or wild lamb).

In addition to these licenses, you will need a license to carry a firearm. Write to or inquire at your nearest Mexican Consulate. Handguns are not permitted.

U.S. residents planning to hunt in Mexico and hoping to bring home that trophies should write (in advance, enclosing a stamped self-addressed envelope) to the U.S. Customs Service, P.O. Box 7118, Washington, D.C. 20044. Ask for the pamphlet called "Pets and Wildlife". You can also get it from your nearest Customs office.

PHOTOGRAPHY

Each traveler is permitted to bring into Mexico one still camera and one portable movie camera, with 12 rolls of film for each. These restrictions are intended to prevent people from importing cameras or film for resale; both cameras and film are quite expensive in Mexico. As long as the quantity of film you are bringing in is not unreasonable, and there is no evidence that you intend to resell it, you will probably be allowed to bring in as much as you will need. By doing so you will save a lot of money. Film is especially expensive in hotel and resort shops.

If you are serious about photography, bring a tripod and any other equipment you have. However, tripods and flashes are not permitted in museums, archeological zones or colonial monuments without a special permit.

You can have any type of film processed in Mexico. For Kodachrome, take the film or have it sent to the Kodak lab in Mexico City. If you take it there yourself, processing takes a few days; if it is sent from elsewhere in Mexico, it will take 10 days to three weeks.

Unless you are spending a lot of time in Mexico, or just can't wait to see your shots, take your film home to have it processed. Meanwhile, try to keep it cool. Cars get very hot, and the glove compartment is an especially bad place for film. Also beware of airport X-ray inspections: one passage through the machine may not ruin your film, but several inspections might do so. Ask to have your camera and film hand inspected.

Photographing Indians can be difficult. You can offer to pay them, but chances are your shots will look terribly posed. If you have a telephoto lens, you may be able to get good pictures without offending people. You can also try using a wide-angle lens, shooting from waist level without looking through the viewfinder. None of these strate-

gies will get you the great photographs you want. The only way to get those is to spend time with the people; be friendly and polite until you and your camera become part of the scenery. Then it may be possible to get excellent and "unposed" shots.

LANGUAGE

Although many Mexicans speak some English, it is good to have basic Spanish phrases at your disposal; in remote areas, it is essential. In general Mexicans approve of the foreigner who tries to speak the language, and they'll be patient – if amused. Pronunciation is not difficult, if you only want to make yourself understood; if you want to sound authentic, practice before you go. The following is quite simplified:

Vowels: **a** as in father
     e as in bed
     i as in police
     o as in hole
     u as in rude

Consonants are approximately like those in English; the main exceptions are:

g is hard before **a**, **o**, or **u** (as in English), but where English **g** sounds like **j** – before **e** or **i** – Spanish **g** sounds like a rather gutteral **h**. **G** before **ua** is often silent, so that agua sounds like awa, and Guadalajara like Wadalahara.

h is silent.

j sounds like the English h.

ll sounds like y.

n sounds like ny, as in the familiar Spanish word *señor*.

q is followed by u as in English, but the combination sounds like k instead of like **kw**. *Que quiere Usted*? (What do you want?) would be pronounced: Keh kee-ehr-eh oostehd?

r is often rolled.

x between vowels sounds like a gutteral **h**, e.g. in México, Oaxaca.

y alone, as the word for and, is pronounced **ee**.

You're likely to want a pocket-sized Spanish-English dictionary, but here are some useful words and phrases:

NUMBERS

1	*uno*	30	*treinta*
2	*dos*	40	*cuarenta*
3	*tre*	50	*cincuenta*
4	*cuatro*	60	*sesenta*
5	*cinco*	70	*setenta*
6	*seis*	80	*ochenta*
7	*siete*	90	*noventa*
8	*ocho*	100	*cien*
9	*nueve*	101	*ciento uno*
10	*diez*	200	*doscientos*
11	*once*	300	*trescientos*
12	doce	400	*cuatrocientos*
13	*trece*	500	*quinientos*
14	*catorce*	600	*seiscientos*
15	*quince*	700	*setecientos*
16	*diez y seis*	800	*ochoscientos*
17	*diez y siete*	900	*novecientos*
18	*diez y ocho*	1,000	*mil*
19	*diez y nueve*	2,000	*dos mil*
20	*veinte*	10,000	*diez mil*
21	*veinte y uno*	100,000	*cien mil*
		1,000,000	*un millon*

COMMON EXPRESSIONS

Please.	*Por favor*.
Thank you.	*Gracias*.
You're welcome.	*De nada*. (Literally, It's nothing.)
I am sorry.	*Lo siento*.
Excuse me.	*Perdoneme*; *disculpeme*.
Yes.	*Si*.
No.	*No*.
Can you speak English?	*Habla Usted Ingles*?
Do you understand me?	*Me comprende*? *Me entiende*?
This is good.	*Esta bueno*.
This is bad.	*Esta malo*.
Good morning.	*Buenos dias*.
Good afternoon.	*Buenos tardes*.
Good night, good evening.	*Buenas noches*.

Goodbye.	*Adios.*	the daily special	*la comida corrida*
Where is.....?	*Donde esta .....?*	May I have more beer?	*Me puede dar mas cerveza, por favor?*
the exit	*la salida*	May I have the bill?	*Me da la cuenta, por favor.*
the entrance	*la entrada*	(to get the attention of a waiter)	*Oigal! Senor! Joven!* (Literally, young man!)
the airport	*el aeropuerto*		
the subway	*el metro*		
the taxi	*el taxi*		
the train station	*la estacion del ferrocarril*	Please call a taxi for me.	*Pidame un taxi, por favor*
the express bus station	*la central de autobuses*	How many kilometers is it from here to…?	*Cuantos kilometros hay de aqui a…?*
the police station	*la delegacion de policia*	How long does it take to go there?	*Cuanto se tarda en llegar?*
the embassy	*la embajada*	What will you charge to take me to…?	*Cuanto me cobra para llevarme a…?*
the consulate	*el consulado*		
the post office	*la oficina de correos; el correo*		
the telegraph office	*la oficina de telegrafos*	How much is a ticket to…?	*Cuanto cuesta un boleto a…?*
the public telephone	*el telefono publico*	I want a ticket to…	*Quiero un boleto a…*
the bank	*el banco*		
a hotel	*un hotel*	Where does this bus go?	*Donde va este autobus?*
an inn	*una posada*	Down! (to yell at a bus driver when you want to get off)	*Bajan!*
a restaurant	*un restaurant*		
a cafe, coffee shop	*un cafe, fonda, merendero*		
the restroom	*el sanitario*	Please stop here.	*Pare aqui, por favor,*
a private bathroom	*el bano*	Please go straight.	*Vaya derecho, por favor.*
a public bathhouse	*los banos publicos*		
the ticket office	*la oficina de boletos*	What is this place called?	*Como se llama este lugar?*
the dry cleaners	*la tintoreria*	I'm going to…	*Me voy a…*
the department store	*la tienda; los almacenes*	bus stop	*parada*
the marketplace	*el mercado*	reserved seat	*asiento reservado*
the duty-free shop	*el duty free*	airplane	*avion*
the souvenir shop	*la tienda de curiosidades*	train	*tren*
		bus	*autobus*
What is the price?	*Cuanto cuesta?*	first class	*primera clase*
It's too expensive.	*Esta muy caro.*	second class	*segunda clase*
Can you give me a discount?	*Me puede dar un descuento?*	ferry boat	*transbordador*
Do you have…?	*Tiene usted…?*	Where is there an inexpensive hotel?	*Donde hay un hotel economico?*
I will buy this.	*Voy a compraer eso.*	Do you have an air conditioned room?	*Hay un cuarto con aire acondicionado?*
Please show me another.	*Muestreme otro (otra) por favor.*	Do you have a room with bath?	*Hay un cuarto con bano?*
Just a moment, please.	*Un memento, por favor.*	Where is the dining room?	*Donde esta el comedor?*
Please bring me, some coffee.	*Un poco de cafe, por favor.*	key	*llave*
Please bring me…	*Traigame por favor…*	manager	*gerente*
a beer	*una cerveza*	owner	*proprietor dueno* (male), *duena* (female)
cold water	*agua helada*		
hot water	*agua caliente*		
a soft drink	*un refresco*	Can you cash a	*Se puede cambiar un*
a menu	*un menu*		

traveler's check?	*cheque de viajero?*
money	*dinero*
credit card	*tarjeta de credito*
tax	*impuesto*
letter	*carta*
postcard	*tarjeta postal*
envelope	*sobre*
stamp	*estampilla*
Where is...	*Donde esta...*
a gas station?	*la gasolinera?*
a repair garage?	*un taller mecanico?*
an auto parts store?	*una refaccion eria para coches?*
Fill it up, please.	*Lleno, por favor.*
Please check the oil.	*Vea el aceite, por favor.*
Please fill up...	*Favor de llenar...*
the radiator.	*...el radiador.*
the battery.	*...la bateria.*
I need...	*Me necessita...*
a jack.	*un gato.*
a towtruck.	*una grua.*
a mechanic.	*una mecánico*
a tune-up.	*una afinaction.*
a tire.	*una llanta.*
a fuse, like this one.	*un fusible, como este.*
The...is broken.	*Ella...está roto*
The...are broken.	*Los/las...estan rotos*

FURTHER READING

HISTORY

Bazant, Jan. *A Concise History of Mexico, from Hidalgo to Cardenas* (Cambridge University Press, 1977). Emphasis on the struggle for land.

Brenner, Anita, and George R. Leighton. *The Wind That Swept Mexico* (University of Texas Press, 1971). Brief account of the revolution, with many excellent historical photographs.

Caso, Alfonso, *The People of the Sun* (University of Oklahoma Press, 1978). Authoritative source on the Aztecs.

Coe, Michael, *The Maya* (Thames Hudson, 1980). A good one-volume summary.

Collis, Maurice, *Cortes and Montezuma.* (Avon, 1978). Good in both style as well as content.

Cortes, Hernan. *Five Letters* (Gordon Press, 1977). Long letters in which Cortes recounts his exploits and justifies his actions to his king.

Davies, Nigel. *Voyager to the New World: Fact and Fantasy* (Morrow, 1979). If you are tempted to subscribe to any of the fashionable theories about the Chinese, Middle Eastern or extra-terrestrial origins of Mexican civilization, read this first.

De Landa, Bishop Diego. *Yucatán Before and After the Conquest* (Kraus reprint of 1941 Harvard University Peabody Museum publication). Written by the same man who burned nearly all the Mayan pictographic accounts. This book is the starting point for all serious research on the Mayas.

De Mexico, Colegio. *A Compact History of Mexico.* This is a summary of the Spanish original, a four volume classic. Excellent for getting the basic facts placed in historical perspective.

De Sahagun, Bernardino. *General History of the Things of New Spain* (12 volumes, University of Utah Press). A gold mine of information about the Aztecs and neighboring peoples, written by one of the early Spanish missionaries.

Diaz del Castillo, Bernal, *The Conquest of New Spain* (Penguin, 1963). This simple soldier's tale, delightful to read, has been corroborated by archeological findings and is now the standard reference on the events of the conquest.

Leon-Portilla, Miguel. *The Broken Spears: The Aztec Account of the Conquest of Mexico* (Beacon Press, 1962). Read this for its contrast with the Spanish viewpoint of Diaz del Castillo. Also good is Leon-Portilla's Aztec Thought and Culture (University of Oklahoma Press, 1978).

Parkes, Henry Bamford. *A History of Mexico* (Houghton Mifflin, 1969). A hefty tome, useful for those with a serious interest.

Peterson, Frederick. *Ancient Mexico* (Capricorn). A good introduction to all the major pre-Columbian cultures.

Prescott, William H. *The Conquest of*

Mexico (Modern Library, 1931). This vivid recounting, based on Diaz del Castillo's story, is a 19th-century gem. Highly recommended.

Reed, John. *Insurgent Mexico* (International Publishing, 1969). Exciting account of the 1910 revolution by the reporter famous for his coverage of the Russian revolution (and the subject of a 1981 film, "Reds"). Lacks perspective, most notably in its hero-worshipping treatment of Pancho Villa.

Sejourne, Laurette. *Burning Water: Thought and Religion in Ancient Mexico* (Shambhala, 1976). Controversial but stimulating. Argues that local religions were manipulated and distorted by the invading Aztecs to serve their political ends.

Soustelle, Jacques, *Los Olmecas (The Olmecs).* For those who can read Spanish or French, this is a scholarly and yet highly readable account of Mexico's "mother culture."

——————. *Daily Life of the Aztecs on the Eve of the Spanish Conquest* (Stanford University Press, 1961) – which is exactly what the title says, and rather fascinating.

Thompson, J. Eric. *Maya History and Religion* (University of Oklahoma Press, 1976);

——————. *The Rise and Fall of Maya Civilization* (University of Oklahoma Press, 1977). Thompson has inherited the mantle of Sylvanus Morley, the dean of Mayan archeology. His explanations are based on decades of excavating Mayan temple complexes.

Womack, John, *Zapata and the Mexican Revolution* (Knopf, 1968). Readable and well-researched; not as exciting as John Reed's account, but more balanced than either Reed's or Martin Guzman's work.

MEXICAN WRITERS ON MEXICO

Casanova, Pablo Bonzalez. *La Democracia en Mexico* (Democracy in Mexico). A very good book, unfortunately not available in English. Analyzes Mexico's social, political and economic institutions and its overall power structure, and assesses the potential for a more active democratic process.

Cosio Villages, Daniel, *American Extremes* (University of Texas Press, 1964). Cosio Villegas has a ten-volume history of Mexico to his credit, but he's also capable of brevity. In these excellent essays, he provides an intelligent perspective on Mexico's problems and its relations with its neighbor to the north.

Gonzalez de la Garza, Mauricio. *Last Call* (no English edition). A scathing critique of Mexico's political institutions. The book has been quite controversial and enormously successful in Mexico (by 1982 there were some 200,000 copies in print).

Paz, Octavio. *The Labyrinth of Solitude* (Grove, 1962). Paz is perhaps the best known (outside of Mexico) of all Mexico's intellectuals. This book is not easy to read, but is a must for those who want to go beyond a superficial understanding of the psychology and culture of contemporary Mexicans.

——————. *The Other Mexico: Critique of the Pyramid* (Grove, 1972).

Ramos, Samuel. *Profile of Man and Culture in Mexico* (University of Texas Press, 1962). A companion piece to Paz's Labyrinth of Solitude. Provides particular insight into the psychology of Mexican Indians and their relations with the dominant mestizo culture. The prose is light with no trace of pedantry.

FOREIGN WRITERS ON MEXICO

Brushwood, John S. *Mexico in its Novel* (University of Texas Press, 1966). Those who want to read more Mexican fiction will find this a useful guide.

Calderon de la Barco, Fanny. *Life in Mexico: The Letters of Fanny Calderon de la Barco, with New Material from the Author's Private Journals*, edited by H.T. and M.H. Fisher (Doubleday, 1966); first published 1913. The author was a Scotswoman living in Spain, whose husband became Spain's first ambassador to independent Mexico. Madame Calderon de la Barco was intelligent and curious, loved to travel, and spoke Spanish fluently. Her memoir is a marvelous book, widely held to be the best of all foreigners' accounts of Mexico.

Casteneda, Carlos. *The Teachings of Don Juan: A Yaqui Way of Knowledge* (University of California Press, 1968); *A Separate Reality* (Simon & Schuster, 1971); *Journey to Ixtlan* (Simon & Schuster, 1973); *Tales of Power* (Simon & Schuster, 1975); *The Second Ring of Power* (1980); *The Eagle's Gift* (Simon & Schuster, 1981). Read these books for their imaginative insights into spiritual experience – but don't believe every word.

Flandrau, Charles Macomb. *Viva Mexico* (University of Illinois Press, 1964); first published 1908. In the same vein as the writings of Madame Calderon de la Barca, but more limited in scope. The style is charming and unhurried, and some of Flandrau's insights into Mexican character are absolute gems.

Gage, Thomas. *Travels in the New World* (University of Oklahoma Press, 1969); first published 1648. One of the few accounts of colonial Mexico that is still worth reading. Gage was a Dominican friar from England who traveled from Veracruz to Mexico City, then through Oaxaca and Chiapas to Guatemala.

Gardner, Erle Stanley, *Hovering Over Baja* (Morrow, 1961); *Whispering Sands* (Morrow, 1981); and others. When he was not writing detective stories, Gardner was a passionate outdoorsman who knew Baja thoroughly.

Greene, Graham. *The Lawless Roads* (William Heinemann, 1950); published in the U.S. as *Another Mexico* (Viking, 1939). Greene tells of his travels in a most entertaining way, even though his accounts of the condition of Catholicism in Mexico are distorted.

Gruening, Ernest. *Mexico and its Heritage* (Appleton-Century Crofts, 1928). A dated but insightful historical analysis.

Gunn, Drewey Wayne. *American and British Writers in Mexico, 1556-1973* (University of Texas Press, 1974). For those who want to read further, this is an excellent resource.

Huxley, Aldous. *Beyond the Mexique Bay* (Vintage; 1960). Erudite observations on the Mayan cultural remains. Mostly concerned with Guatemala, but worth reading if you'll spend a lot of time on Oaxaca.

Krutch, Joseph Wood. *The Forgotten Peninsula* (William Sloan, 1961). Perhaps the best book about Baja.

Lawrence, D.H. *Mornings in Mexico* (Knopf, 1927). Includes several descriptive essays which beautifully express Lawrence's feeling for the country.

Lewis, Oscar. *Five Families* (Basic Books, 1959); *The Children of Sanchez* (Random House, 1961); *Pedro Martinez* (Random House, 1964); and *A Death in the Sanchez Family* (Random House, 1969). Lewis has spent many years studying Mexico's "culture of poverty" and interviewing its members. In these books his informants tell of lives full of adversity met with unexpected strength.

Lumholtz, Carl. *Unknown Mexico: Indians of Mexico* (Rio Grande Press). Lumholtz was one of the last of the great explorer-anthropologists. Read Unknown Mexico as an adventure tale, or for its enormous body of information on the Indians of northern Mexico.

Myerhoff, Barbara. *Peyote Hunt: The Sacred Journey of the Huichol Indians* (Cornell University Press, 1974). Read this if you're fascinated by the Huichols or by religious use of hallucinogens. Myerhoff is mainly concerned with analyzing Huichol religious symbolism.

Reck, Gregory C. *In the Shadow of Tlaloc: Life in a Mexican Village* (Penguin, 1978). Highly recommended account of life in a village in central Mexico. Full of information, like most anthropological studies, but also unusually expressive of the feelings of village life.

Simpson, Lesley Byrd. *Many Mexicos* (University of California Press, 1966). A good historical analysis.

Soustelle, Jacques. Mexico, *Terra India* (no English edition). Soustelle is an anthropologist who writes with humor and humanism. Recommended most highly for those who read Spanish or French.

Steinbeck, John. *The Log from the Sea of Cortes* (Viking, 1951). Steinbeck tells of an expedition to gather biological specimens from the Sea of Cortes off Baja California. Recommended for those who will boat or fish in these waters.

Stephens, John L. *Incidents of Travel in Central America, Chiapas and Yucatán* (Dover, 1969); first published 1841. Stephens and illustrator Frederick Catherwood had many adventures and made remarkable discoveries. Their book was instrumental in arousing scientific interest in the lost Mayan civilization.

Turner, John Kenneth. *Barbarous Mexico* (University of Texas Press, 1969); first published 1908. Contrasts sharply with Flandrau's account, published in the same year. Turner's reporting of misery and death among the slaves working Mexico's tobacco and henequen plantations led many Americans to question Porfirio Diaz's reputation as a benevolent dictator.

Vogt, Evon Z. *Tortillas for the Gods: A Symbolic Analysis of Zinacanteco Ritual* (Harvard University Press, 1976). Good source for those interested in the contemporary Mayan Indians of Chiapas.

Von Humboldt, Alexander. *Political Essay on the Kingdom of New Spain* (A.M.S. Press, reprint of 1811 edition). Unusual in that it's not the work of a British or American writer. Von Humboldt traveled through Mexico in 1803-1804, studying the country's economic resources and pre-Columbian antiquities. His book, the first systematic study of the country, alerted European powers to the great mining wealth of Mexico.

Yates, P. Lamartine. *Mexico's Agricultural Dilemma* (University of Arizona Press, 1981). A good source for those interested in Mexico's land problems.

FICTION BY MEXICAN AUTHORS

Arreola, Juan Jose. *Confabulario* (University of Texas Press, 1964). Highly polished short stories. Some very international, some surprising Mexican.

Azuela, Mariano. *The Underdogs* (New American Library). An excellent novel (based on the author's own life) with insights into the experiences, ideals and frustrations of ordinary men fighting the Mexican revolution.

Fuentes, Carlos. *Where the Air Is Clear* (Farrar, Straus & Giroux, 1971). Considered by some to be the best novel of modern Mexico. The narrator is a rather mysterious man who spends his life listening to and watching fellow inhabitants of Mexico City, of every social stratum, as they attempt to cope with the various conditions of their lives. His outlook is both cynical and simpatico as he considers those who struggle to live and those who waste their lives in frivolity. In *The Death*

of Artemio Cruz (Farrar, Straus & Giroux, 1964), flashbacks reveal the protagonist's life as he is about to die. His memory ranges over the revolution – where he is seen to have been as much coward as hero – and the following years, when he gradually becomes a cynical opportunist, manipulating old revolutionary contacts to build his fortune.

Guzman, Martin Luis. *Memoirs of Pancho Villa* (University of Texas Press, 1965), and *The Eagle and the Serpent* (Peter Smith). Both books are based on the author's personal experiences with Pancho Villa and other revolutionary leaders. Guzman is a good reporter but lacks imagination; he attributes the revolution's success too much to the effectiveness of its leaders, too little to their masses of followers.

Rulfo, Juan. *The Burning Plain* (University of Texas Press, 1967). The Mexico described in these short stories is known to few foreigners. In spare, suggestive prose Rulfo gives the reader a deep understanding of the mestizo culture that was formed and then left behind by the nation's progress. *Pedro Paramo* (Grove Press, 1959), a novel, is headier than Rulfo's short stories, but worth reading twice.

Spota, Luis, *Casi El Paraiso* (Almost Paradise). If you read Spanish and are curious about the kind of novel that is a best-seller in Mexico, read this or another of Spota's many books.

Yanez, Agustin. *The Edge of the Storm* (University of Texas Press, 1963). A great novel, set in a small town in Jalisco just before the revolution. The atmosphere is heavy, the characters complex. They feel change coming, but many cannot understand, and some don't want to try. Also, *Lean Lands* (University of Texas Press, 1968).

FICTION BY FOREIGN AUTHORS

Aiken, Conrad, *Ushant* (Little, Brown, 1952).

Anderson, Sherwood. *Memoirs* (Harcourt, Brace, 1942) and *Letters* (Little, Brown, 1953).

Bellow, Saul. *Mosby's Memoirs and Other Stories* (Viking, 1968).

Bradbury, Ray. *The October Country* (Ballantine Books, 1955); *The Machineries of Joy, especially "El Dia de Muerte"* (Simon & Schuster, 1964); and *The Golden Apples of the Sun* (Doubleday, 1966). Among the short stories in these collection there are some very good ones set in Mexico.

Burroughs, William. *The Naked Lunch* (Grove, 1962), and *The Soft Machine* (Grove, 1966).

Corso, Gregory. *Gasoline* (City Lights, 1956).

Dana, Richard Henry. *Two Years Before the Mast* (Ward Ritchie, 1964).

Ferlinghetti, Lawrence. *The Mexican Night: Travel Journal* (New Directions, 1970).

Ginsberg, Allen. *Siesta in Xbalba* (out of print).

Greene, Graham. *The Power and the Glory* (Viking, 1962). This novel, considered Greene's finest by many critics, takes place in Tabasco during the persecution of the Catholic clergy. Its hero is one of the priests faced with choosing marriage, exile or the firing squad. Greene's insight into his characters and his evocations of life in the jungle and the town are superb, but the picture he gives of Catholicism in Mexico is quite distorted.

Grey, Zane. *Tales of Southern Rivers* (Harpers, 1924).

Hughes, Langston. *I Wonder as I Wander* (Rinehart, 1956).

Kerouac, Jack. *On the Road* (Viking, 1957); *Dharma Burns* (Viking, 1958); *Mexico City Blues* (Grove, 1959); and others.

Kesey, Ken. *Kesey's Garage Sale* (Viking, 1973).

Lawrence, D.H. *The Plumed Serpent* (Knopf, 1951). Lawrence takes on the profound problems – the meaning of life and death, the relations of man to man and woman to man – and argues for a profound change in Mexico – adoption of a new state religion based on the ancient worship of Quetzalcoatl. He does not succeed very well in this enormous undertaking; perhaps no writer could. Lawrence misunderstood the pre-Columbian religions and their modern survivals as well as Mexico's political past and present. With all its flaws this is still one of the very best novels ever written about Mexico.

Lowry, Malcolm. *Under the Volcano* (Lippincott, 1965). Without making any ex-plicit attempt to explain them, Lowry reveals the hidden forces which move Mexico. In this, his only major work, he tells the deceptively simple story of a British Consul who drinks himself to death. It helps to know that the novel is set in 1938, the crisis year when President Cardenas nationalized the oil industry, leading to the cutting of Mexican-British diplomatic relations.

MacLeish, Archibald. *Conquistador*. (Houghton Mifflin, 1932).

Morris, Wright. *Love Among the Cannibals* (Harcourt, Brace, 1957); and One Day (Atheneum, 1965).

Porter, Katherine Anne. *The Collected Stories* (Harcourt, Brace, 1965); and *The Collected Essays* (Delacorte, 1970). In contrast to fellow Catholics Graham Greene and Evelyn Waugh, Porter understood the oppressive role the Church had played in Mexican history. She also understood the new Constitution and Mexico's intricate political machinery. Further, Porter was one of the first to appreciate and document the difference between pre-Columbian and contemporary Indian arts.

Steinbeck, John. *The Forgotten Village* (Viking, 1941); and The Pearl (Viking, 1947).

Traven, B. *The General from the Jungle* (Robert Hale, 1945); *The Rebellion of the Hanged* (Knopf, 1952); *March to Caobaland* (Robert Hale, 1961); *The Bridge in the Jungle* (Hill & Wang, 1967); *The Treasure of the Sierra Madre* (Hill & Wang, 1967); *The Carreta* (Hill & Wang, 1970); and others. No other author has written so much and so well about Mexico as the mysterious B. Traven (his identity is still a matter of some controversy). Although he is best known for *The Treasure of the Sierra Madre*, most of Travern's books are set in southern Mexico, and his knowledge of that area is astounding. His sympathy for the Indians of southern Mexico was so strong that he defended their cruelty as the just result of centuries of oppression. That was not a common opinion at that time.

Waugh, Evelyn. *Mexico: An Object Lesson* (Little, Brown, 1939); also published under the title *Robbery Under Law*.

Williams, Tennessee. *The Night of the*

Iguana (New Directions, 1962).

Williams, William Carlos. *The Autobiography of William Carlos Williams* (New Directions, 1951); also *The Desert Music* (now out of print).

ARTS & CRAFTS OF MEXICO

Baird, Joseph. *The Churches of Mexico* (University of California Press, 1962). An excellent reference on Mexican colonial art, almost all of which is in churches.

Cordry, Donald and Dorothy. *Mexican Indian Costumes* (University of Texas Press, 1968).

Covarrubias, Miguel. *Indian Art of Mexico and Central America* (Knopf, 1957); and *Mezcala: Ancient Mexican Sculpture* (Andre Emmerich Gallery, 1956). Covarrubias is a respected authority on Mexican art.

Dockstader, Frederick, and Carmelo Guadagno. *Indian Art in Middle America* (New York Graphic Society, 1964).

Edwards, Emily, and Bravo Alvarez. *Painted Walls of Mexico* (University of Texas Press, 1966). Treats Mexican murals from pre-Columbian examples onward, with special emphasis on the post-revolutionary masters.

Fernandez, Justino, *Guide to Mexican Art* (University of Chicago Press, 1969). An excellent introduction; rather dry but certainly informative.

Graburn, Nelson H.H., editor. *Ethnic and Tourist Arts* (University of California Press, 1976). Includes articles by anthropologists on three Mexican art forms popular with foreign travelers: the ironwood carvings of the Seri Indians, the bark paintings of Xalitla, and Teotihuacan-area pottery. These articles explain the cultural and economic contexts of these so-called "tourist arts."

Gutierrez. Tonatiuh and Electra. *Popular Art of Mexico* (reprint of a 1960 special issue of the magazine *Artes de Mexico*). Illustrates the crafts of every area of the country. Available in three languages, English, French or Spanish, in FONART stores, Sanborn's bookstores, and museum shops in Mexico.

Martinez Penaloza, Porfirio. *Popular Arts of Mexico* (Editorial Panorama, 1981). A compact and inexpensive book by one of the outstanding authorities on Mexican art. Easily available in Mexico, in English or Spanish.

Ramirez Vazquez, Pedro, and others. *The National Museum of Anthropology, Mexico: Art, Architecture, Archeology, Anthropology* (Abrams, 1968). This is really three books in one. The first is the story of the creation of the remarkable National Museum, written by the men responsible and illustrated with many photographs. The second, written by the museum's curator (Ramon Chan) and a prominent archeologist (Luis Aveleyra), uses excellent photographs of museum exhibits to enrich short essays about Mexico's pre-Columbian cultures. The last section of the book is on the ethnography of Mexican Indians; the essays, written by a museum anthropologist (Demetrio Sodi), are brief but heavily illustrated with interesting photographs.

Ross, Patricia Fent. *Made in Mexico: The Story of a Country's Arts and Crafts* (Knopf, 1960). This is a classic work on the history of Mexico's popular arts, written by an American who lived for many years in Mexico before the large-scale commercialization of the country's craft traditions.

Sayer, Chloe. *Crafts of Mexico* (Doubleday, 1977). Includes step-by-step instructions for making traditional Mexican craft items. Excellent photographs.

Toor, Frances. *A Treasury of Mexican Folkways* (Crown, 1947). Covers folk art, fiestas, music and dance. A classic in its field.

Toussaint, Manuel. *Mexican Colonial Art* (University of Texas). The best textbook on the subject, covering everything worth knowing about colonial art in Mexico. Toussaint's newspaper columns in the 1930's and 1940's brought new attention to Mexican colonial art.

Von Winning, Hasso. *Pre-Columbian Art of Mexico and Central America* (Abrams, 1968). Among coffee-table art books, this one stands out; informative as well as beautiful.

Westheim, Paul. *The Sculpture of Ancient Mexico* (Doubleday, 1963); and others. Westheim's writings on the aesthetics of pre-Columbian art are hard to surpass for insight and clarity.

GUIDEBOOKS

Birnbaum, Stephen, *Mexico 1982* (Houghton Mifflin, 1981)

Carlson, Loraine. *The TraveLeer Guide to Mexico City* (Upland Press, 1981); *The Traveleer Guide to Yucatán and Guatemala* (Upland Press, 1980).

Tucker, Alan, editor. *Fodor's Mexico 1982* (Fodor's Modern Guides, 1981).

Foster, Lynn V. and Lawrence, *Fielding's Mexico,* (William Morrow and Co., 1986).

Franz, Carl. *The People's Guide to Mexico* (John Muir Publications, 1979); and *The People's Guide to Camping in Mexico* (John Muir Publications). Full of funny reminiscences. If you're a do-it-yourself mechanic, get *Franz's Guide to Mexico* for its extremely detailed list of automotive terms.

Hunter, C. Bruce. *A Guide to Ancient Maya Ruins* (University of Oklahoma Press, 1974). Useful if you're serious about visiting archeological sites.

Simon, Kate, *Mexico: Places and Pleasures* (Thomas Y. Crowell, 1979). Not a comprehensive guidebook, but wonderful to read.

Terry, Philip. *Terry's Guide to Mexico* (first published 1922; revised edition 1947). Terribly out-dated, of course, but a classic. The section on gestures in the "Peoples of Mexico" chapter is great.

Wilhelm, John. *Guide to Mexico City* (Ediciones Tolteca, 1971). Wilhelm's knowledge of the city is enormous. His "Handbook for New Residents" chapter is very good.

Wood, Robert D. *A Travel Guide to Archeological Mexico* (Hastings, 1979).

USEFUL ADDRESSES

TOURIST INFORMATION

Before arriving in Mexico you may write for information to the Mexican National Tourist Council. Its main office is at Mariano Escobedo # 726, Mexico 5, D.F. (telephone 533-0540). There are offices in some other nation, including several in the United States. The regional office for the U.S. and Canada is at 405 Park Avenue, Suite 1002, New York, NY 10022 (tel: 212-755-7261). The regional office for Europe is at 34 Avenue George V, 75008, Paris, France (tel: 720-6907 or 720-6911).

In Mexico, each state capital has an office of the Tourist Secretariat (*Secretaria de Turismo*). These offices are listed below. In Mexico City, the main office is at Av. Presidente Masaryk #172, Mexico, D.F. 11587. This office has three useful telephone numbers. For standard information (locations of tourist destinations; date, times and prices of special events) call 250-0123. For any other assistance, call 254-1954 or 545-4613.

There are also two tourist offices at the Mexico City. One, along the far wall of the international area with the shops, is specific to Mexico City. Another, hidden near the taxi stand and customs office, is an outlet of the national tourism service. At last visit, this latter office was far more helpful and ready with information than the Masaryk center.

AGUASCALIENTES:
Av. De Las Americas No. 502
Primer Piso. Fracc.
Las Americas A.P. 1452-C
Aguascalientes, AGS. C.P. 20230
Tel: 91 491, 6 01 23

Circunvalacion Sur Y Mahatma Gandhi
Aguascalientes, Aguascalientes 20230

BAJA CALIFORNIA:
Puerta Mexico. Planta Alta
Linea Internacional
Tijuana, B.C. C.P. 22310
Tel: 91 66, 82 33 47 al 49, 82 33 87

Av. Guanajuato #102-D
Tijuana, Baja California Norte 22150

BAJA CALIFORNIA SUR:
Paseo Alvaro Obregon No. 2130
A.P. 419 LA PAZ, B.C.S. C.P. 23000
Tel: 91 682, 2 11 90, 2 80 19

Plaza De La Constitucion Y 5 De Mayo
La Paz, Baj California Sur 23000

CAMPECHE:
Av. Republica No. 159
Frente A La Alameda
Campeche, Camp. C.P. 24000
Tel: 91 981, 631 97, 6 55 93, 6 25 10

Av. Ruiz Cortines #61
Campeche, Campeche 24000

CHIAPAS:
Av. Central Poniente No. 1498
Esquina 14a Poniente
Colonia Moctezuma
Tuxtla Gutierrez, Chiapas, C.P. 29030
Tel: 91 961, 2 45 35, 2 55 09

Av. Central Poniente #1454
Tuxtla Gutierrez, Chiapas 29030

COAHUILA:
Blvd. Venustiano Carranza
No. 2454 Tercer Piso A.P. 101
Saltillo, Coahuila C.P. 25280
Tel: 91 841, 3 83 22, 3 96 76

Felipe Pescador #651 Altos
Saltillo, Coahuila 25000

COLIMA:
Av. Juárez No. 244 4O PISO
Manzanillo, Colima C.P. 28200
Tel: 91 333, 2 01 81, 2 20 90,
2 20 91 (tourist aid)

Juárez #111
Manzanillo, Colima 28000

CHIHUAHUA:
Edif. De La Unidad Adma.
Municipal "Lic. Benito Juárez"
Av. Malecon Y Francisco
Villa Ciudad Juárez, Chihuahua, C.P. 32000
Tel: 91 161, 4 66 92, 4 01 23, 4 06 07

Av. Malecon Y Francisco Villa
Cd. Juárez, Chihuahua 32000

Oficina Auxiliar De Tourismo
Av. Technoligico No. 7901
Franccionamiento Gloris
Chihuahua, Chihuahua C.P. 31120
Tel: 91 14, 17 89 72

DURANGO:
Av. 20 De Noviembre No. 1006
Poniente, Planta Baja
Durango, Durango C.P. 34000
Tel: 91 181, 1 56 81, 2 76 44

Bruno Martinez #403-305
Durango, Durango 34000

Oficina Auxiliar De Tourismo
Blvd. Miguel Aleman No. 250
Ote. Colonia Las Rosas
Gomez Palacio, Durango C.P. 35090
Tel: 91 171, 4 43 34, 4 15 56

ESTADO DE MEXICO:
Av. Vicente Villada No. 123
Colonia Centro
Toluca, Estado De Mexico C.P. 50000
Tel: 91 721, 4 89 61, 3 03 88,
4 42 49 (tourist aid)

Plaza Fray Andres De Castro
Edificio B Local 112, Toluca, Mexico

GUANAJUATO:
Calle De La Insurgencia No. 6
Guanajuato, Guanajuato C.P. 36000
Tel: 91 473, 2 01 23, 2 01 19, 2 02 44

Galarza #90
Guanajuato, Guanajuato 36000

GUERRERO:
Zona Pacifico Sur.
Costera Miguel Aleman
No. 187, Acapulco, Guerrero C.P. 39580
Tel: 91 748, 5 11 78, 5 10 22

Lic. Nicolas Castillo Diáz, Subcoordinador
5 13 04
5 41 28 (administrative)
5 12 49 (technical info)
5 10 41 (tourist aid)
5 10 93 (rec. humanos)
5 41 34 (tourist aid)
5 15 95 (tourist aid)
5 13 56 (FONATUR)

Prolongacion Pedro
Ascencio No. 4 A.P. 100
Zihuatanejo, Guerrero C.P. 40808
Tel: 91 743, 4 28 35, 4 38 35

Oficina Auxiliar De Tourismo
Av. John F. Kennedy No. 28-9
Barrio De La Mision
Taxco, Guerrero C.P. 40239
Tel: 91 732, 2 15 25

Costera Miguel Aleman #187
Acapulco, Guerrero 39300

HIDALGO:
Carretera Mexico-Pachuca
Km. 85 "Las Cuatro Plazas"
Pachuca, Hidalgo C.P. 42000
Tel: 91 771, 3 95 00, 3 95 66

Victoria #202
Pachuca, Hidalgo 42000

JALISCO:
Zona Occidente
Paseo Degollado No. 50, Plaza Tapatia
Guadalajara, Jalisco C.P. 44100
Tel: 91 36, 14 86 65, 14 85 43
Subcoordinador
Tel: 91 36, 14 83 71, 14 87 53

Av. Lazaro Cardenas #3298
Guadalajara, Jalisco 45040

MICHOACAN:
Santos Degollado No. 340
Altos Colonia Centro
Morelia, Michoacan C.P. 58000
Tel: 91 451, 2 05 22, 2 01 23, 2 84 98

Santos Degollado #357-2
Morelia, Michoacan 58000

MORELOS:
Ignacio Comonfort No. 2 "Altos"
Casa De las Campanas
Colonoa Centro
Cuenavaca, Morelos C.P. 6200
Tel: 91 73, 12 18 15, 12 54 14

Av. Morelos #205-A
Cuenavaca, Morelos 62000

NAYARIT:
Av. Mexico Sur No. 253-A
Primer Piso Esq. Eulogio
Parra Tepic, Nayarit C.P. 63000
Tel: 91 321, 3 09 93

Av. Mexico #253-A Sur
Tepic, Nayarit 62000

NUEVO LEON:
Palacio Federal 3er. Piso
Av. Pte. Benito Juárez Y Corregidor Ciudad
Guadalupe
Monterrey, Nuevo Leon, C.P. 67100
Tel: 91 83, 54 19 22, 24 24 16

Emilio Carranza #730 Sur
Monterrey, Nuevo Leon 64460

OAXACA:
Matamoros No. 105
Esq. Garcia Vigil
Oaxaca, Oaxaca C.P. 68000
Tel: 91 951, 6 01 44, 6 00 45

Garcia Vigil E Independencia
Oaxaca, Oaxaca 68000

PUEBLA:
Av. 13 Sur No. 1303
Colonia San Manuel
Puebla, Puebla C.P. 72580
Tel: 91 22, 40 90 09, 40 92 09,
43 00 47 (tourist aid)

Av. Hermanos Serdan
Puebla, Puebla 72000

PUERTA VALLARTA
Edificio Parian Del Puente
Local 13 Libertad Y Miramar
Puerto Vallarta, JAL. C.P. 48300
Tel: 91 322, 2 25 54, 2 25 55

QUERETARO:
Puente De Alvarado No. 102-4
Colonoa Carretas
Queretaro, Queretaro C.P. 76050
Tel: 91 463, 4 32 73, 2 48 28

Puente De Alvarado #102-4
Queretaro, Queretaro 76050

QUINTANA ROO:
Edificio Fonatur, Av. Coba Y Nader
Cancún, Quintana Roo C.P. 77500
Tel: 91 988, 432 38, 4 34 38

Edificio "Plaza Del Solz"
Planta Alta
Cozumel, Quintana Roo C.P. 77600
Tel: 91 987, 2 09 72

Alvaro Obregon # 457
Chetumal, Quintana Roo

Super Manaza #4
Retorno #8-A, Lote 12
Cancún, Quintana Roo 77500

SAN LUIS POTOSI:
Zona Centro
Jardin Guerrero No. 14
Colonoa Centro
San Luis Potosi, San Luis Potosi C.P. 78000
Tel: 91 481, 4 09 06, 2 15 30

Lic. J. Alberto Gonzalez Karam
Subcoordinador.
Tel: 91 481, 2 21 78

Alende #201
San Luis Potosi, San Luis Potosi 78000

SINALOA
Zona Noroeste
Av. Olas Altas No. 1300, Colonia Centro
Edificio Banco De Mexico
Mazatlán, Sinaloa C.P. 8200
Tel: 91 678, 1 42 10, 1 42 11

Dr. Jorge A. Alvarez Valero
Subcoordinador
Tel: 91 678, 1 42 12, 1 49 66 (FONATUR)

Paseo Clausen Y Zaratoga
Mazatlán, Sinaloa 82000

SONORA:
Blvd. Fray Eusebio Kino
No. 1000 Colonia Pitik
Hermosillo, Sonora C.P. 83150
Tel: 91 621, 4 63 04
Calle Yanez #77
Hermosillo, Sonora 83150

TABASCO:
Av. Gregorio Mendez No. 718-2 Planta Baja
Colonia Centro
Villahermosa, Tabasco C.P. 86000
Tel: 91 931, 2 73 36, 2 74 56

Zaragoza #101 Altos,
Esquina Malecon Y Carlos M
Villahermosa, Tabasco 86000

TAMAULIPAS:
Oaxaca No. 360 Altos
Colonoia Rodriguez
Reynosa, Tamaulipas C.P. 88630
Tel: 91 892, 2 46 60, 2 24 49

Carrera Torres Ote # 708
Cd. Victoris, Tamaulipas 87000

TLAXCALA:
Av. Alvaro Obregon No. 6
Tlaxcala, Tlaxcala C.P. 90000
Tel: 91 246, 2 36 06

VERACRUZ:
Av. Ignacio Zaragoza No. 20
Altos Colonial Centro
Veracruz, Veracruz C.P. 91700
Tel: 91 29, 32 70 26, 32 16 13

Blvd. Mariano Sanchez #1061
Esquina Callejon 5 De Febrero
Veracruz, Veracruz 91700

YUCATAN:
Zona Peninsula
Calle 61 No. 470
Manzana 4A. Del Cuartel
Primero Colonial Centro
Mérida, Yucatán C.P. 97000
Tel: 91 99, 24 94 31, 24 95 42

C.P. Luis H. Alcocer Aranda
Subcoordinador
Tel: 91 99, 24 65 96, 24 53 67
Telex: 753825 CRTPME

Calle 20 #89
Col. Itzimina, Mérida, Yucatán 97100

ZACATECAS:
Blvd. Lopez Mateos No. 923-A
Colonial Centro A.P. 124
Zacatecas,
Zacatecas C.P. 98000
Tel: 91 492, 2 67 50, 2 67 51

Blvd. Lopez Mateos #923-1
Zacatecas,
Zacatecas 98000

DISTRITO FEDERAL:
Zona Metropolitana
Presidente Mazaryk No. 172, 6o. Piso
Colonia Polanco
Mexico, Distrito Federal C.P. 11587
Tel: 91 5, 2 54 00 26, 2 50 85 55 ext: 266

EMBASSIES & CONSULATES

Albania
Cuvier #30, tel: 531-0141.

Argentina
Reforma #1225, tel: 520-9430.

Australia
Reforma #195, 5th floor, tel: 566-3055.

Austria
Campos Eliseos #305, tel: 540-3415.

Belgium
Dante #36, 11th floor, tel: 533-1392.

Bolivia
Mariano Escobedo #724-601, tel: 525-2979.

Brazil
Reforma #453 and #455, tel: 525-0140.

Bulgaria
Reforma #1990, tel: 596-3283.

Canada
Schiller #529, tel: 254-3288.

China (People's Republic)
Rio Magdalena #172, tel: 548-0896.

Colombia
Genova #2-105, tel: 511-8936.

Costa Rica
Av. Avila Camacho #40, tel: 540-0640.

Cuba
Presidente Masaryk #554, tel: 540-6890.

Czechoslovakia
Cubier #22, tel: 531-1837.

Denmark
Campos Eliseos #170, 5th floor, tel: 51-3060.

Dominican Republic
Nuevo Leon #78-201, tel: 528-7785.

Ecuador
Tennyson #217, tel: 545-7041.

Egypt
Ruben Dario #30, tel: 531-9028.

El Salvador
Galileo #17, tel: 531-7995.

Ethiopia
Miguel de Cervante Saavedra #465-602, tel: 577-2238.

Finland
Manuel Avila Camacho #1, 9th floor, tel: 557-8811.

France
Havre #15, tel: 533-1360.

Germany (Democratic Republic)
Horacio #1506.

Germany (Federal Republic)
Lord Byron #373, tel: 545-6655.

Greece
Reforma #284-104, tel: 528-5935.

Guatemala
Vallarie #1, 5th floor, tel: 546-4876.

Haiti
Taine #229, tel: 250-7918.

Honduras
Av. Juárez #64-911, tel: 585-3554.

Hungary
Av. de las Paimas #2005, tel: 296-0523.

Iceland
Arqultectos #55-A, tel: 516-7882.

India
Musset #325, tel: 531-1050.

Indonesia
Julio Verne #27, tel: 520-4167.

Iraq
Reforma #1875, tel: 596-0254.

Ireland
Av. Chapultepec #18, 2nd floor, tel: 510-3867.

Israel
Sierra Madre #215, tel: 540-6340.

Italy
Palmas #1994, tel: 596-3655.

Jamaica
Eucken #32, tel: 250-0011.

Japan
Reforma #395, tel: 525-4620

Korea
Homero #823, tel: 254-1499.

Lebanon
Julio Verne #8, tel: 540-3295.

Monaco
Reforma #156, 16th floor, tel: 566-7944.

Morocco
5 de Mayo #29-108, tel: 510-0961.

GUADALAJARA

1. Cathedral
2. Degollado Theater
3. Palacio de Gabierno
4. State Museum
5. Hospicio Cabanas
6. Mercado Libertad
7. San Juan de Dioś Church
8. Templo de San Francisco
9. Templo de Aranzazu
10. Templo de Santa Monica.
11. Templo de San Felipe Neri
12. University of Guddalajara
13. Templo Expiatorio
14. Plaza de la Liberacion
15. Plaza de los Laurels
16. Plaza de Armas
17. Parque Morelos
18. Parque Revolucion

Netherlands
Blvd. Manuel Avlla Camacho #1, 8th floor, tel: 557-9588.

Nicaragua
Durango #199-202, tel: 526-7688.

Norway
Virreyes #1460, tel: 540-3486.

Pakistan
Hegel #512, tel: 545-2129.

Panama
Campos Ellsesos #111-1, tel: 250-4229.

Paraguay
Ejercity Nacional #1112-1201, tel: 557-8140.

Peru
Lope de Vega #247, tel: 254-2736.

Philippines
Monte Antuco #505, tel: 540-0766.

Poland
Cracovia #40, San Angel, tel: 550-4700.

Portugal
Paimas #765-202, tel: 520-7091.

Senegal
Reforma #444-801, tel: 511-8965.

Spain
Edgar Allan Poe #91, tel: 250-9244.

Sweden
Blvd. Avlla Camacho #1, 6th floor.

Switzerland
Hamburgo #66, tel: 533-0735.

Tunisia
Manual Lopez Cotilla #934-935, tel: 559-9333.

Turkey
Paimas #1525, tel: 520-2344.

United Kingdom
Lerma #71, tel: 511-4880.

United States of America
Reforma #305, tel: 5533-3333.

Union of Soviet Socialists Republics
Calzada Tacubaya #204, tel: 516-0870.

Uruguay
Hegel #149, 1st floor, tel: 531-0880.

Venezuela
Landres #167, tel: 533-6950.

Yugoslavia
Montanas Rocallosas Ote. #515, tel: 520-2523.

The following diagrams are intended to provide visitors to ancient Mexican sites an insight into the religious architecture of Mexico's five most important pre-Columbian ritual centers – Chichén Itzá, Teotíhua-can, Palenque, Monte Alban and Uxmal. As the distances between some of these complexes are quite far apart, you should plan carefully to avoid becoming unnecessarily rushed and exhausted during your visit. More detailed information can be found throughout this book

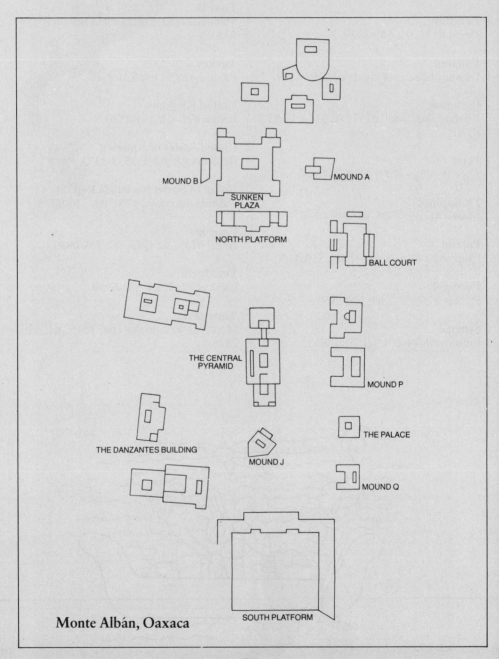

MOUND B

MOUND A

SUNKEN PLAZA

NORTH PLATFORM

BALL COURT

THE CENTRAL PYRAMID

MOUND P

THE PALACE

THE DANZANTES BUILDING

MOUND J

MOUND Q

SOUTH PLATFORM

Monte Albán, Oaxaca

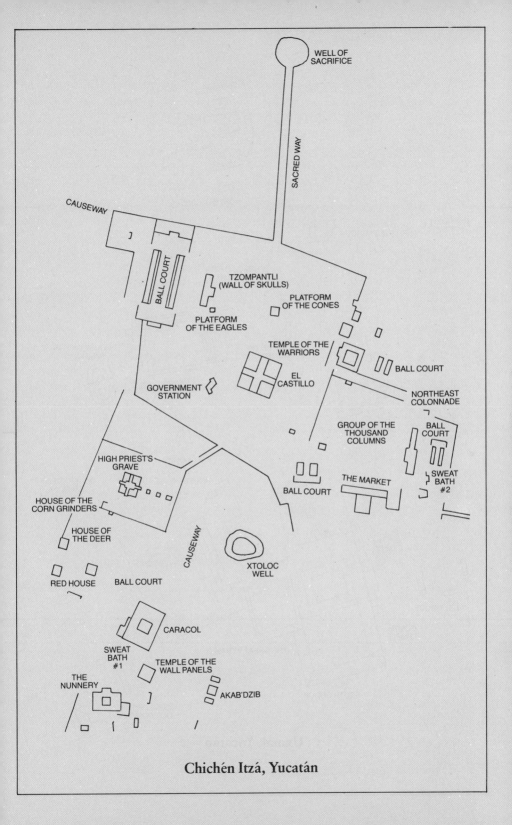

WELL OF
SACRIFICE

SACRED WAY

CAUSEWAY

BALL COURT

TZOMPANTLI
(WALL OF SKULLS)

PLATFORM
OF THE CONES

PLATFORM
OF THE EAGLES

TEMPLE OF THE
WARRIORS

EL
CASTILLO

BALL COURT

GOVERNMENT
STATION

NORTHEAST
COLONNADE

GROUP OF THE
THOUSAND
COLUMNS

BALL
COURT

HIGH PRIEST'S
GRAVE

THE MARKET

SWEAT
BATH
#2

HOUSE OF THE
CORN GRINDERS

BALL COURT

HOUSE OF
THE DEER

CAUSEWAY

RED HOUSE

BALL COURT

XTOLOC
WELL

CARACOL

SWEAT
BATH
#1

TEMPLE OF THE
WALL PANELS

THE
NUNNERY

AKAB'DZIB

Chichén Itzá, Yucatán

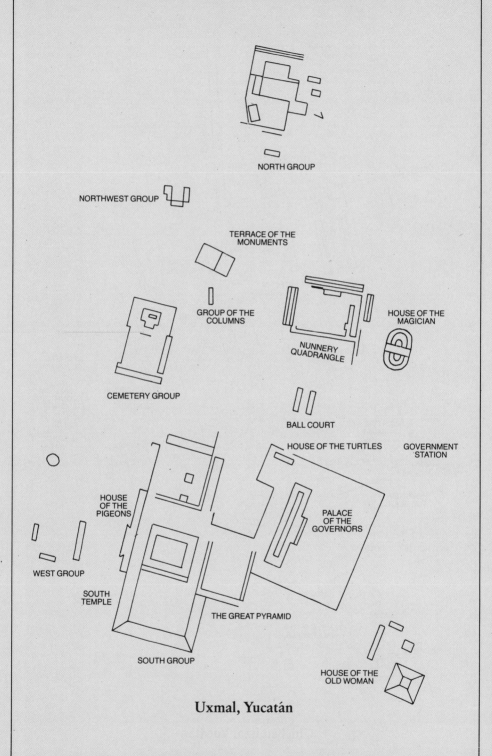

NORTH GROUP

NORTHWEST GROUP

TERRACE OF THE
MONUMENTS

GROUP OF THE
COLUMNS

HOUSE OF THE
MAGICIAN

NUNNERY
QUADRANGLE

CEMETERY GROUP

BALL COURT

HOUSE OF THE TURTLES

GOVERNMENT
STATION

HOUSE
OF THE
PIGEONS

PALACE
OF THE
GOVERNORS

WEST GROUP

SOUTH
TEMPLE

THE GREAT PYRAMID

SOUTH GROUP

HOUSE OF THE
OLD WOMAN

Uxmal, Yucatán

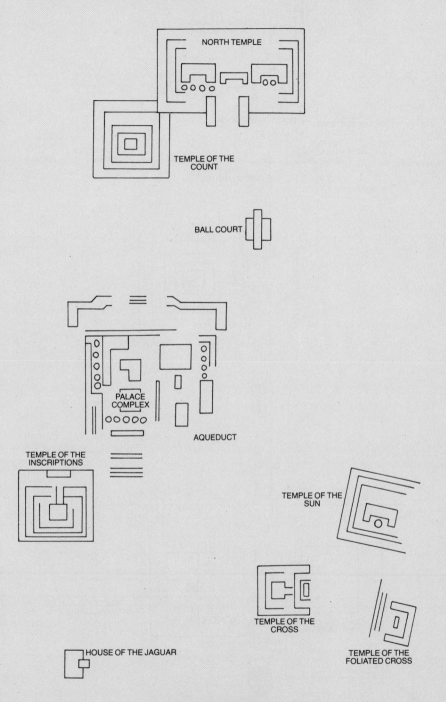

NORTH TEMPLE

TEMPLE OF THE
COUNT

BALL COURT

PALACE
COMPLEX

AQUEDUCT

TEMPLE OF THE
INSCRIPTIONS

TEMPLE OF THE
SUN

TEMPLE OF THE
CROSS

HOUSE OF THE JAGUAR

TEMPLE OF THE
FOLIATED CROSS

Palenque, Chiapas

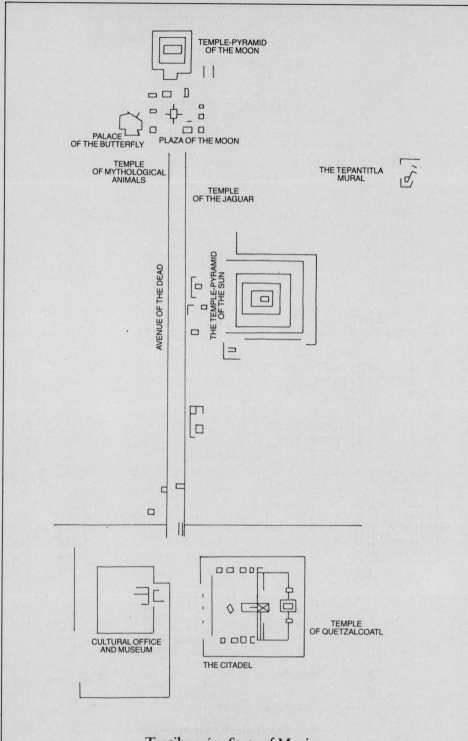

Teotihuacán, State of Mexico

ART/PHOTO CREDITS

INDEX

C

D

E

Encinas War, 95
encomienda (holder of a land grant), 52
Ensenada, 197, 200, 201-202
"Entremeses Cervantinos" (Play), 166
epidemics, 232
Escuela Nacional Preparatoria, *also* San
Ildelfonso, 125, 286
"esculptopintura" (combination of sculpture and
painting), 285
Escutia, Juan, 59
Espinosa Saucedo, Fermín, 311
Estadio Azteca, 135
Estadio Jalisco, 168
Estoril, 130
evangelistas (gospel writers), 124, 125
Expiatorio (cathedral, Guadalajara), 160

F

fajo (cup from which tequila is drunk), 161
Farallon island, *also* Animas Island, 213
fauna, 23, 29, 96
feathers
 in mosaic painting, 40, 99, 289
 as trade item, 44
featherwork
 Tarascan, 39
 Toltec, 40
Federal Palace (Querétaro), 171
Felipe Carrillo Puerto (town), 253
Ferdinand VII, King of Spain, 56
feria (bullfighting), *see* bullfighting.
Feria de San Marcos, 171, 173, 295
fiestas (festivals), 87, 92, 99, 102, 186 209, 294,
 295-299
 Carnaval, 227
 of the Dead, 173, 297, 288-299
 of Lunes del Cerro, 259
 in Oaxaca, 292
 of St. Francis of Assisi, 296
 of San Sebastion, 264, 267, 268-269, 292
 of the Virgin of Guadalupe, 127, 227, 294, 315-318,
  316, 317, 319
Fish Mercado (Ensenada), 202
fishes, 30, 197, 202, 216, 227
fishing, 185, 213
 in Acapulco, 225
 in Baja, 197
 in Cabo San Lucas, 205
 in Ciudad Victoria, 187
 in the Dead Sea, 264
 in Ensenada, 202
 in Monterrey, 186
 in Mulegé, 204
 in northeast Mexico, 185, 189
 along the Pacific coast, 209, 211, 211, 213, 214,
  215
 in Río Lagartos, 252
 in Tampico, 242
flamingos, 30, 32-33, 251
flatland, 25, 27
flora, 2-3
Flores de la Torre, Capt. Juan, 91
flower battles, 295
Fonart (museum, Acapulco), 224
Forgotten Peninsula, The (book), 197
Fort San Diego (Acapulco), 220, 226

Fortin de las Flores, 244
France, 60, 63, 100
Franciscans, 41, 91, 149, 159, 197, 231, 317
French
 army in Mexico, 145, 180, 182, 233, 292
 influence on the fiesta, 295
 investment in Mexico, 62
 operated copper mine, 198
 pirates, 232
Frey, Charles, 264
Frissell Museum (Mirla), 260-261
Frontera, 233, 245
Frontón Mexico (Mexico City), 129
Frontón Palacio (Tijuana), 199
Frutería Aguilar (restaurant, Tijuana), 200
Fuentes, Carlos, 14
futbol, see soccer

G

gachupine (Spanish-born Mexican), 55, 56, 318
Gadsden Purchase of 1853, 59
Gage, Friar Thomas, 54
 comment on Oaxaca, 257
Gallery (disco, Acapulco), 224
gambling, 179, 295, 296
Goana y Jimenez, Rodolfo, 311
García Cave, 184, 186
Gracía Payón, J., 242
Gardner, Erle Stanley, 197
Garrido Canabal, Governor Thomás, 236
Garza-Sada family, 186
Gaviño, Bernardo, 310
geography, 14, 19, 21, 23, 25, 29-30
Germans, 262
Geronimo, 179
Getty, J. Paul, 222
Gilg, Father, 94-95
 comment on the Seris, 94-95
gnats (jejenes), 214
gods, 14, 34, 295
 Aztec, 14, 40, 277, 316
 Cora, 91
 Huichol, 87-89
 Lacandone, 96-97
 Mayan, 41-42
 Nonoalca, 41
 Olmec, 35
 Tarascan, 39
 Toltec, 40, 41
 Tzeltal, 102, 103-104
 Tzotzil, 102, 103-104
 Zapotec, 37, 40
 See also pre-Columbian art.
Goeritz, Mathias, 139
gold, 19, 40, 48, 49, 50, 51, 62, 179, 197
 mine, 193, 258
 in Mixtec graves, 38
 in Olmec art, 275
 rush, 198, 202
golf courses
 in Acapulco, 225
 in Cancún, 252
Gonzalez Camarena, Jorge, 286
González, de León (architect), 132
Government Store (Tijuana), 199
Gran Teocalli, 200

Great Britain, 60, 63, 68, 71, 74, 232
"Great Tenochtitlan, The" (mural), 119, 123
Grey, Zane, 197
greyhound races, 189, 200. *See also* dog races.
Grijalva river, 245, 265, 266
"Gringo Gulch", 215
"Grito de Delores" ("Cry of Independence"), 56, 58, 168
Grutas de Cacahuamilpa, 151
Guadalajara, 56, 91, 156-161, 188, 290
"Guadalajara" (song), 161
Guadalupe Island, 30
"Guadalupes" (secret society), 57
Guanajuato, 56, 70, 165-169, 165, 291
Guatemala, 262, 263, 265, 268
guayabera (men's shirt), 250
Guaymas, 95, 180, 204, 212
Guelatao, 258
Guerrero, 57, 76, 81, 292
Guerrero, Gonzalo, 230, 231
Guerrero, Negro, 198, 203, 204
Guerrero, Vicente, 57
Guerrero, Xavier, 236
Guillermo, Don, 151
guitars, 98, 291, 292, 302
Gulf of California, *also* Sea of Cortés, 202, 205, 207, 211
Guzman, Nuño Beltran de (conquistadore), *see* de Guazmán, Nuno Beltran.

H

hacendado (henchmen and supporters), 62, 63
hacienda (large land-holding), 52, 68, 71
Hacienda de Qunita Carolina, 190
Hakluyt, Richard, comment on the cargo found on a captured ship, 220
hammocks, 292
handicrafts, 178, 187, 188, 199, 223, 224, 259
    Chiapa de Corzo, 266
    Huichol, 215
    Mazatlán, 213
    Michoacán, 173, 174
    Oaxaca, 257, 259, 260
    Saltillo, 186
    San Angel, 135
    San Juan del Río, 171
    San Miguel de Allende, 167-168
    Tarascan, 99
    See also shopping.
hats, panama, 250, 292
Healy, Giles, 264
Hearst, William Randolph, 62, 63, 189
Hemingway, Ernest, comment on spectators at a bullfight 309
hennequen (cactus fiber used to make rope), 29, 62, 182, 236, 299
Hemiciclo (sculpture, Mexico City), 127
herbal medicine, 213, 257
Hermosillo, 183, 195, 211
Hernández, Amalia, 226
Herradura (brand of tequila), 161
Herreriano (refined architectural style of the Spanish renaissance), 149
Hidalgo, 65, 139, 187
Hidalgo, Father Miguel, 56, 57, 57, 123, 157, 167, 168, 170, 173, 180

monument of, 190
mural of, 157, 287
Hidalgo dam (El Fuerte), 213
Hidalgo del Parral, 77, 193
Holiday Inn (Acapulco), 223
Honda beach, 226
Honduras (town), 305
horchata (a non-alcoholic drink), 250
Hornos beach, 226
horse racing, 178, 189, 200, 295
horseback riding, 190, 201, 226
horses, 43, 38, 305, 306, 307
    introduction of…to Mexico, 305
Horsetail Falls, 186
Hospicio Cabañas (Guadalajara), 158, 286
Hotel Caesar (Tijuana), 200
Hotel Cortés (Mexico City), 128
Hotel de Mexico (Mexico City), 135
Hotel del Prado (Mexico City), 123
Hotel Ixtapan, 153
Hotel Mission Santa Isabel (Ensenada), 202
Hotel Presidente (Oaxaca), 259
Hotel Victoria (Oaxaca), 259
House of Culture (San Luis Potosí), 175
House of the Eleven Patios (Pátzcuaro), 173
House of the Giant (Pátzcuaro), 173-174
House of Tiles, *see* La Casa de los Azulejos
Houston, Sam, 58
huachinango a la Veracruzana (red snapper in a thick tomato sauce), 244
Huajuapan de Leon, 258
Huapanecs, 292
Huasteca, 187
Huasteca Canyon, 186
Huatecs, 38, 81, 231, 277, 278
Huehueteotl, *see* Xiuhtecuhtli.
huehuetl (drum), 301
Huejotzingo, 149
Huerta, Victoriano, 67
Huichols, 85, 86, 87-89, 270-271, 291
huipiles (blouses), 292
Huitzilopochtli, 45, 46, 47, 275, 276
Huixtla, 265
human sacrifice, 39, 41, 43, 44, 46, 275, 315. *See also* fiestas.
Hunac Ceel Cauich, 44
hunting, 185, 189, 190, 202, 211, 242
    for deer, 87, 89, 212
    for ducks, 30, 212, 213
    for gamebirds, 213
    for geese, 213
    for monkeys, 97
    for sharks, 95
    for wild pigs, 97
    for wild turkeys, 97
Hunting of the Snark, The (book), 202
hurricanes, 204
Hussong's (Cantina, Ensenada), 200, 202
Huxley, Aldous, 273
Hz'k'al (a phantasm), 103

I

Icacos, 226
IIchcansiho, 231
Iglesias de la Compañia (church, Puebla), 145
Ihuatzio, 98, 291

Mercado Libertad (Guadalajaran), 158
Mérida, 44, 231, 232, 234, 235, 235, 248, 249-250, 292
meseta (plateau), 98
mestizos (Spanish-Indians), 53, 55, 57, 60, 81, 82, 83, 87, 298
metal-work, 226
metate (stone implement to ground corn), 34, 289
Metepec, 153, 292
Metro, Mexico City (subway), 130, 131
Mexicali, 178, 198, 201
Mexicas, *see* Aztecs.
Mexico, origin of the name, 45
Mexico City, 14, 19, 24-25, 34, 45, 57, 59, 67, 67, 75, 111-112, 114-115, 117-137
  day trips from, 139-153
  1968 student riot in, 76, 128
Mexcaltitán, 214
Mexican Underwater Explorer's Club, 253
Mexican War, *see* War of Intervention.
Mexitli, 45
mezcal (fiery, alcholic drink), 172, 257, 260
mezcal de pechuga, 260
Mezquital valley (Hidalgo), 211
Micaotli, *see* Avenue of the Dead.
Michoacán, 25, 30, 39, 57, 70, 98, 165, 173, 184, 291
Mil Cumbres, 173
Minatitlán, 245
minerals, 21, 23, 62, 151, 165, 175, 179, 180, 183, 192, 193, 198, 212
Ministry of Education, 284
Ministry of Foreign Affairs, 128
Ministry of Public Education, 125
Mirador Hotel (Acapulco), 223
Mismaloya beach, 215
missionaries, 44, 179-180, 181, 301
missions,
  Dominican, 197
  Franciscan, 91, 95, 197
  Jesuit, 181, 182, 197, 203
Mitla, 37, 257, 260-261, 279
Mixcoacalli, 301
Mixteco, 36-37, 38, 39, 257, 279
Moctezuma brewery, 243
Moctezuma Ilhuicamina, 46
Moctezuma II, 23, 46, 48-49, 50, 51, 124, 232
mole (sauce), 140
Molino, Evaristo, 233
Monte Albán (Oaxaca), 37, 44, 261, 261, 279
Tomb 7, 37, 259
Tomb 104, 261
Tomb 105, 261
Montebello Lakes, 262, 264, 268
Montejo, Francisco, 96, 250
Montejo House, *see* Casa Montejo.
Montenegro, Roberto, 286
Monterrey, 14, 29, 59, 179, 184, 185-186, 189
Monterrey Institute of Technology, 185
Monument to the Race, 134
Monument to the Revolution (Mexico City), 128, 129, 193
Monumento a la Patria (Mérida), 250
Morado, José Chávez, 166, 286
Morales, Ignacio Diaz, 157
Morales Villavicencio, Juan, 96
Morelia, 56, 171, 173, 291
Morelos, 37, 57, 67, 69, 139, 150, 151, 292

Morelos, Father José María, 57, 173, 220
Morgan, Henry, 252-253
Morley, Sylvanus, 42, 286
  comment on the Palace of the Governor (Uxmal), 249
Mormons, 189
Morrones, Luis, 70
Morro Rock, 227
Morrow, Dwight, 160
mosaic painting, feather, 40, 99, 289
moscos (liquor of Toluca), 153
"Mother Mission" (Loreto), 204
mountains, 19, 23, 25
  as symbolism in art, 275
movie-making, 187. *See also* cinemas.
mudejar (Moorish), 149
muertito (deceased loved one), 173, 297
Mulegé, 198, 204
murals, 14, 127, 131-132, 136, 149, 156, 158, 284-286, 284, 285, 287
Murillo, 140
Museo de Antropología (Mexico City), 34, 132-134, 275 277, 280
Museo de San Carlos, 129
museums
  Fonart (craft), 224
  Frida Kahlo, 136
  Frissell, 260, 261
  Jalisca State (Guadalajara), 157
  Monterrey, 185
  Morelia Regional, 173
  Oaxaca Regional, 259
  Querétaro State, 171
  Quinta Cameros State, 190, 191
  Rufino Tamayo (Oaxaca), 259
  Tuxtla, 265
Museum of Dan Guillermo Spratling (Taxco), 151
Museum of Mexican History (Mexico City), 131
Museum of Mexico City, 124
Museum of Modern Art (Mexico City), 132
Museum of the Viceroyalty (Tepotzotlan), 139, 140
Museum of Western Mexican Cultures, 216
mushrooms, hallucinogenic, 257
music, 300, 301-303
  folkloric, 303
  Indian, 259
  mariachi, 156, 158, 161, 295, 301, 302
  ranchero, 301
  See also fiestas.
musical instruments, music myths
  about the arrival of the Aztecs and mother
    Nahuatl-speakers, 45
  about the moon, 40
  about Quetzalcoatl, 40-41
  about the sun, 39, 40, 47
  about Topiltzin, 41

N

Nahuas, 80, 81, 142, 296, 298
Nahuatls, 40
Nakawe, 87
Nanahuatzin, 47
Napoleon, *see* Bonaparte, Napoleon
Napoleon III, 60
National Federation of Farmers, *see* Confederacion Nacional de Compensinos.

National Museum of Anthropology, *see* Museo de Antropologia.
National Palace, 52, 119, 122, 123, 284
national parks, 23, 30
National Preparator School, *see* Escuela Nacional Preparatoria.
National Revolutionary Party (PNR), 70
National University of Mexico (UNAM), 41, 75, 136
Navojoa, 212
Nayarit, 39, 90, 290
Nebel, Carl, 38
negrete, Jorge, 161
negros (blacks) 53, 81
Netzahualcóyotl, 45, 131, 144, 301
Netzahuacóytl Theater (Acapulco), 223
Nevado de Colima, 216
Nevado de Toluca, *also* Xinantécatl, 23
Nevado y Fuego (crater), 25
New Galicia, 156
New Mexico, 21, 53, 59, 179, 180
New National Lottery Building (Mexico City), 128
New Vizcaya, 179
New Volcanic Axis, 19
New York School for Social Research, 286
"Night of the Iguana" (movie), 215
Nine, The (disco, Acapulco), 224
Nino Perdido, *see* Eje Central Lázaro Cárdenas.
Niños Heroes, Los, 59, 131
Noche Triste, 128
Nuestra Senora de la Concepción (Alamos), 212
Nogales, 178, 211
Nonoalcas, 41
Nonoalco-Tlatelolco, 128, 134
Nuestra Señora de Fátima (church, Hidalgo del Parral), 193
Nuestra Señora de la Concepción (ship) 220
Nueva Alemania, 265
Nuevo Léon, 178
Nuevo Puerto (restaurant, Rosarito Beach), 201
Nunnery Quadrangle, *249*, 280

O

Oxaca, 37, 38, 57, 59, 81, 257-261, 292, 295
    pre-Columbian art in, 277, 279
Oaxtepec, 152
Obispado (Monterrey) 185
Obregón, President Alvaro, 27, 67, 68, 69, 181, 182, 183, 290
Ocosingo, 268
Ocotlán, 149
O'Donoju, Juan 57
O'Gorman, Juan, 57, 136, 173, 286
oil, 14, 23, 29, 62, 69, 76-77, 92, 236, 237, 242, 245, 263
    nationalization of, 71
    See also Pemex.
Ojinga, 190
Ojo de Liebre, *also* Scammon's lagoon, 203
Old National Lottery Building, 128
Olmecs, 34-35, 36-37, 38, 262.
    See also pre-Columbian art.
Ometéotl, 14, 47
Ometepec, 292
onyx, 291
Opatas, 181, 182

Operation Condor, 213
opium, 213
Orendain (brand of tequila), 161
Organization of American States, 76
Originales de Mexico (store, Ensenada), 202
Orizaba, 243-244
Oropeza, Vincente, 306
Orozco, José Clemente, 125, 127, 156, 157-158, 160, *282-283*, 284, 285-286, *287*, 290
Ortega, Father, comment on the Cora homeland, 90
Ortiz, Pepe, 311
Ortiz de Castro, José Damían, 122
Ortiz de Domínguez, Josefa Miguel, *see* Domínguez, Josefa Miguel
Otomi, 81
Otomis, 187, 221, 298
Otumba, 144
Our Lady of Guadalupe, *see* Virgin of Guadalupe.
Our Lady of Loreto, 140
Our Lady of Solitude (Oaxaca), 259
Owen, Albert K., 191
Oxchuc, 268

P

PNR, *see* National Revolutionary Party.
PRI, *see* Partido Revolucionario Institucional.
Pachuca, 187
Pacific coast, 209-216
painting
    colonial, 128, 140
    European, 129
    feather mosaic, 40, 99, 289
    Huapanec, 292
    Huichol, *270-271*, 290
    Mayan, 245, 264
    modern, 132
    19th Century Spanish, 129
Pajarito, 103
"Pajarito", *see* Perez, Jacinto.
Palace of Buenavista, *see* Museo de San Carlos.
Palace of Fine Arts, *see* Bellas Artes.
Palace of the Counts (San Miguel de Allende), 167
Palacio Clavijero (Morelia), 173
Palacio de Cortés (Cuernavaca), 150
Palacio de Gobierno (Guadalajara), 157, 286, *287*
Palacio de Gobierno (Tlaxcala), 149
Palacio de Iturbide, 135
Palacio de Mineria (Mexico City), 128
Palafox Library (Puebla), 145
Palancar reef, 253
palapa (bungalow), 215
Palenque (Chiapas), 245, 246, *246*, 247, 262, 264
pan de cazon (shark cornmeal), 248
pan de pulque (pulque bread), 186
Pancho Villa, 193
Panteón Taurina, 169
Pánuco river, 242
Papagayo park, 227
Papaloapan river, 244
Papalopan Valley project, 75
Papantla, 92, 242
Paracho, 96, 174, 291
Paraiso Marriott (Acapulco), 244
Parangaricutiro, 25
Paraninfo (Guadalajara), 286
para-sailing, 215, 215, 225

Q

R